CRITICAL PERSPECTIVES ON WORK AND EMPLOYM

Series editors
Irena Grugulis, Durham University Business School, UK
Caroline Lloyd, School of Social Sciences, Cardiff University, UK
Chris Smith, Royal Holloway University of London School of Management, UK
Chris Warhurst, University of Sydney Business School, Australia

Critical Perspectives on Work and Employment combines the best empirical research with leading edge, critical debate on key issues and developments in the field of work and employment. Extremely well regarded and popular, the series has links to the highly successful International Labour Process Conference.

Formerly edited by David Knights, Hugh Willmott, Chris Smith and Paul Thompson, each edited volume in the series includes contributions from a range of disciplines, including the sociology of work and employment, business and management studies, human resources management, industrial relations and organizational analysis.

Further details of the International Labour Process Conference can be found at www.ilpc.org.uk.

Published:

Marco Hauptmeier and Matt Vidal
COMPARATIVE POLITICAL ECONOMY OF WORK

Carol Wolkowitz, Rachel Lara Cohen, Teela Sanders and Kate Hardy
BODY/SEX/WORK

Chris Warhurst, Françoise Carré, Patricia Findlay and Chris Tilly
ARE BAD JOBS INEVITABLE?

Irena Grugulis and Ödül Bozkurt
RETAIL WORK

Paul Thompson and Chris Smith
WORKING LIFE

Alan McKinlay and Chris Smith
CREATIVE LABOUR

Maeve Houlihan and Sharon Bolton
WORK MATTERS

Chris Warhurst, Doris Ruth Eikhof and Axel Haunschild
WORK LESS, LIVE MORE?

Bill Harley, Jeff Hyman and Paul Thompson
PARTICIPATION AND DEMOCRACY AT WORK

Chris Warhurst, Irena Grugulis and Ewart Keep
THE SKILLS THAT MATTER

Andrew Sturdy, Irena Grugulis and Hugh Willmott
CUSTOMER SERVICE

Craig Prichard, Richard Hull, Mike Chumer and Hugh Willmott
MANAGING KNOWLEDGE

Alan Felstead and Nick Jewson
GLOBAL TRENDS IN FLEXIBLE LABOUR

Paul Thompson and Chris Warhurst
WORKPLACES OF THE FUTURE

More details of the publications in this series can be found at
www.palgrave.com/business/cpwe

Critical Perspectives on Work and Employment Series
Series Standing Order ISBN 978–0–230–23017–0 (pb); 978–0–23016–3 (hb)

You can receive future titles in this series as they are published by placing a standing order. Please contact your bookseller or, in the case of difficulty, write to us at the address below with your name and address, the title of the series and one of the ISBNs quoted above.

Customer Services Department, Macmillan Distribution Ltd, Houndmills, Basingstoke, Hampshire, RG21 6XS, UK

Comparative Political Economy of Work

Edited by

Marco Hauptmeier
Cardiff University, UK

and

Matt Vidal
King's College London, UK

First published 2014 by
PALGRAVE MACMILLAN

Palgrave Macmillan in the UK is an imprint of Macmillan Publishers Limited,
registered in England, company number 785998, of Houndmills, Basingstoke,
Hampshire RG21 6XS.

Palgrave Macmillan in the US is a division of St Martin's Press LLC,
175 Fifth Avenue, New York, NY 10010.

Palgrave Macmillan is the global academic imprint of the above companies
and has companies and representatives throughout the world.

Palgrave® and Macmillan® are registered trademarks in the United States,
the United Kingdom, Europe and other countries

ISBN 978–1–137–32946–2 hardback
ISBN 978–1–137–32227–2 paperback

This book is printed on paper suitable for recycling and made from fully
managed and sustained forest sources. Logging, pulping and manufacturing
processes are expected to conform to the environmental regulations of the
country of origin.

A catalogue record for this book is available from the British Library.

A catalog record for this book is available from the Library of Congress.

Typeset by Cambrian Typesetters, Camberley, Surrey

Printed and bound by CPI Group (UK) Ltd, Croydon, CR0 4YY

Contents

Part II National Institutions

Part III Within-Country Diversity

Part IV International Organizations and Liberalization

List of Illustrations

Tables

Figures

Notes on Contributors

Agnes Akkerman is Associate Professor at the Department of Political Science at the Radboud University Nijmegen, the Netherlands. Her research interests include the consequences of industrial conflict, in particular the contagion of industrial conflict and the impact of industrial conflict on work relations, public sector networks and public organizations' performances. Her publications appear in journals such as *Sociology*; *Industrial Relations*; *Social Psychology*; *Public Administration*; and *Political Science*.

Lisa Berntsen is a Doctoral Candidate in Sociology at the University of Jyväskylä in Finland and in Global Economics and Management at the University of Groningen, the Netherlands. Her research focuses on union representation of migrant workers and migrant workers' working lives in the Netherlands. Her research is part of the European Research Council funded project 'Transnational Work and the Evolution of Sovereignty'.

Jürgen Beyer is Professor in the Department of Social Sciences at the University of Hamburg, Germany. His main fields of research are: economic and organizational sociology, capitalist diversity, and path dependence. Recent publications include 'Path Departure: The Internationalization of German Corporate Governance and Financial Accounting', in *Research in Social Change*, and 'The Same or Not the Same: On the Variety of Mechanisms of Path Dependence', *International Journal of Social Sciences*.

John Buchanan is Professor and Director of the Workplace Research Centre, University of Sydney Business School, Australia. Until recently his major research interest has been the demise of the classical wage-earner model of employment and the role of the state in nurturing new forms of multi-employer coordination in the labour market. Building on this, he is now devoting special attention to the evolution of the labour contract, the dynamics of workforce development and the relationship between work and health. His most recently co-authored book is *Safety in Numbers: Nurse–Patient Ratios and the Future of Health Care*.

Ian Clark is Professor of Employment Relations in the School of Management at the University of Leicester, UK, where he is part of the Centre for Sustainable Work Futures. Ian has published widely on economic performance, HRM in American multinational firms, private equity, the emergence of financial capitalism and the financial crisis. Ian was a member of the Treasury Select Committee on Private Equity, (2007–9) and has produced applied research for the GMB trade union, the ETUC and the Union of Communication Workers. Ian's current research focuses on financial capitalism and firms in administration and distress.

Richard Croucher is Professor of Comparative Employment Relations and Director of Research, Middlesex University Business School, London, UK. He is Visiting Professor at the Cranfield School of Management. He is the author of *Engineers at War* (1982); *We Refuse to Starve in Silence* (1987); and (with Elizabeth Cotton) *Global Unions, Global Business: Global Union Federations and International Business* (2010; 2nd edition 2011). He has published over fifty articles in leading journals which include *Human Relations* and *Industrial Relations: A Journal of Economy and Society*.

Claire Evans is a Tutor at Cardiff Business School, Wales, UK. She has been employed on a number of research projects since completing her doctoral research. The latter examined the impact of employee involvement and participation initiatives within four British manufacturing plants, and assessed the extent to which 'meaningful' participation, and the ensuing creation of 'genuine' trust, is possible within the context of the capitalist employment relationship. In addition to employee participation, her other research interests include trade union organizing strategies, as well as the 'greening' of work and skills.

Jörg Flecker is Professor of Sociology at the University of Vienna in Austria and Chair of the board of the Working Life Research Centre (FORBA). Until February 2013 he was the Director of FORBA. His main research interests focus on economic internationalization and restructuring, labour process analysis, industrial relations, and work and employment in the public services. Most recent publications include *Privatization of Public Services* (Routledge) and *Arbeit in Ketten und Netzen* (Edition Sigma).

Matt Flynn is a former researcher at the PCS union. He was Reader in Human Resource Management at Middlesex University Business School, London, UK, before moving in 2013 to teach at Newcastle University, UK. He is the Director of the Centre for Research into the Older Workforce.

Julie Froud is Professor at Manchester Business School, University of Manchester, UK, and also an affiliated researcher at CRESC (Centre for Research in Socio-Cultural Change). Julie is currently working on several connected strands of research: first, the role of finance and the largely unreformed trajectory of the sector since 2008; second, the role of elites in the economy; and, third, the importance of the foundational economy in rethinking industrial policy and rebuilding local economies. Her most recent co-authored book is *After the Great Complacence: Financial Crisis and the Politics of Reform* (Oxford University Press, 2011).

Inger Marie Hagen has worked at Fafo Institute for Labour and Social Research in Oslo in Norway since 1995. She has her PhD in Sociology from the University of Oslo in 2010 on employee representatives at company boards. In 2010–12 she held a post-doc position at the Department of Private Law. She participated in the white paper committee on Co-determination and Participation in 2010 appointed by the government and has published a number of reports and articles on industrial democracy. Hagen is currently President of the Norwegian Sociological Association.

Bettina Haidinger is a Senior Researcher at the Working Life Research Centre (FORBA) in Vienna and an External Lecturer for Economic Policy and Sociology of Migration at the Universities of Vienna and Linz in Austria. Her research includes migration, work and gender relations, industrial relations and employment policy. Recently, she published a monograph on the *Reproduction of the Transnational Household* (Westfälisches Dampfboot).

Enda Hannon is Senior Lecturer in Employment Relations at Kingston University, London, UK. His research focuses on the comparative political economy of employment and skills, and the drivers of job quality in low-wage, low-skill sectors. He has a particular interest in 'varieties of capitalism' research and the impact of industrial policy on employment. He has undertaken comparative studies on the food manufacturing, pharmaceutical and software sectors in the UK and Ireland, funded by the Economic and Social Research Council.

Marco Hauptmeier is Senior Lecturer and Director of the Employment Research Unit at Cardiff Business School, Wales, UK. He holds a PhD from Cornell University and his research interests include comparative employment relations, comparative political economy and institutional theory. Marco's work has been published in *Industrial Relations: A Journal of Economy and Society*; *Human Relations*; *British Journal of Industrial Relations* and the *European Journal of Industrial Relations*. He won an ESRC Future Research Leaders grant for a project on collective action of employers in the UK.

Jason Heyes is Professor of Employment Relations at Sheffield University Management School in the UK and Director of the School's Work, Organisation and Employment Relation Research Centre. His research interests relate to the interface between employment relations, the labour market and public policy. His current research focus relates to changes in employment relations, labour market policy and labour administration since the start of the economic crisis and the implications for the European Commission's flexicurity and wider social policy agendas.

Ursula Holtgrewe is the Scientific Director of FORBA, an independent research institute in Vienna, Austria, specializing in studies of work and employment. Her research interests are service work and organization, restructuring of companies' value chains, job quality and gender.

Giedo Jansen is a Postdoctoral Researcher at the Department of Political Science at the Radboud University Nijmegen, the Netherlands. His research is on the intersection of sociology, political science and industrial relations. He previously published work on the effects of social class and religion on party choice in modern democracies in journals such as *Electoral Studies*; *West European Politics*; and *Social Science Research*. He has a forthcoming article in *Industrial and Labor Relations Review* on the effects of company-level union organization on strike incidence across different trade union systems in the EU.

Sukhdev Johal is Chair in Accounting and Strategy at Queen Mary University of London, UK. His current research interests include critical research on UK finance, and how to adapt social and economic statistics to understand employment and wealth changes in the UK. He is a long-time research collaborator with the Manchester-based CRESC research team of Julie Froud *et al*. Recent books include *After the Great Complacence* (2011) with Ewald Engelen *et al*.; *Financialization at Work* (2008) with Ismail Erturk *et al*.; and *Financialization and Strategy* (2006) with Julie Froud *et al*.

Stefan Kirchner is a Postdoctoral Researcher in the Department of Social Sciences at the University of Hamburg, Germany. His current research focuses on innovative capabilities of organizations and sustainable working conditions. More specifically he is interested in the transformations of the German model of capitalism and the respective firm-level models as well as the implications of these transformations for job quality. He has been a visiting researcher at the Institute for Employment Research in Nuremberg, at the Social Science Centre Berlin, at the Max Planck Institute for the Study of Societies in Cologne and at Stanford University.

Vassil Kirov is Senior Researcher at the Centre Pierre Naville, University of Evry (France), and Associate Professor in the Institute for the Study of Societies and Knowledge, Bulgarian Academy of Sciences (ISSK-BAS). After graduating in sociology and economics, he studied for his PhD at the Paris Institute for Political Science (2002). His research interests are in the sociology of enterprise, work and organization, industrial relations and Europeanization. Vassil Kirov has been a researcher in large EU-funded research projects and has worked as an external expert for the European Commission, the International Labour Organisation, the European Foundation for Working and Living Conditions, etc. He has published books and articles in European academic magazines.

Hyunji Kwon is Lecturer of Comparative Employment Relations and International Human Resource Management at King's College London, UK. Her research agenda consists of international comparative studies examining the influence managerial choices for achieving workplace flexibility have on workers' outcomes in the context of deregulated, decentralized and increasingly unequal labor markets. Her recent research on workforce flexibility incorporates the gender dimension and changing employment relations in East Asia. Her work has been published in journals such as *Industrial and Labor Relations Review*; *British Journal of Industrial Relations*; and *Human Relations*.

Paul Lewis is a Lecturer in Political Economy and Director of the full-time MBA Programme at Birmingham Business School, UK. His research focuses on the role of institutions in shaping patterns of income distribution in national economies. He has been published in the *Cambridge Journal of Economics*; *Journal of Social Policy*; *Industrial Relations Journal*; and *Economic and Industrial Democracy*. He currently holds a British Academy/Leverhulme Small Research Grant, 'Employment Protection, Job Quality and the Distribution of Earnings' along with Jason Heyes.

Nathan Lillie is a University Lecturer in Social Policy at the University of Jyväskylä, Finland. He received his PhD in Industrial and Labour

Relations from Cornell University in 2003. He has written extensively on trade union strategies, transnational unionism, the political economy of labour, and labour migration. He is current Principle Investigator on the European Research Council Starting Grant funded project (TWES #263782) 'Transnational Work and the Evolution of Sovereignty'.

Sanghoon Lim is Associate Professor at the School of Business, Hanyang University, Seoul, South Korea. His research focuses on the changes in industrial relations systems including changing collective bargaining systems and the emergence of tripartism in Korea from a comparative perspective. His expertise also stretches to regional studies looking at regional development of labor market institutions. Following the tradition of the Wisconsin School where he received his PhD, he has tried to find feasible and hands-on solutions to contemporary problems of industrial relations and has actively participated in NGO activities and public affairs.

Guglielmo Meardi is Professor of Industrial Relations and Director of the Industrial Relations Research Unit at the University of Warwick, UK. He has published *Social Failures of European Enlargement* (2012) and co-edited *Economy and Society in Europe: A Relationship in Crisis* (2012). He is completing a comparison of the Europeanization of industrial relations in the six largest EU countries.

Glenn Morgan is Professor of International Management at Cardiff Business School in Wales, UK, and Visiting Professor at the Department of Business and Politics, Copenhagen Business School in Denmark. Recent edited books include *New Spirits of Capitalism? Crises, Justifications and Dynamics* (ed. with P. DuGay, Oxford University Press 2013); *Capitalisms and Capitalism in the 21st Century* (co-edited with R. Whitley, Oxford University Press, 2012); and *The Oxford Handbook of Comparative Institutional Analysis* (co-edited with Campbell, Crouch, Pedersen and Whitley, Oxford University Press 2010). He was editor of the journal *Organization* from 2004–08 and serves on a number of editorial boards. Recent publications have appeared in *Industrial Relations: A Journal of Economy and Society*; *Socio-Economic Review*; *Economy and Society*; *Organization Studies*; and *Journal of European Public Policy*.

Monique Ramioul is the Director of the Work and Organisation Research Group at the Research Institute for Work and Society, HIVA – University of Leuven (Belgium). She is a sociologist and holds a PhD in Social Sciences. Her main research interests include: organization restructuring; changes in work; skills and qualifications; and quality of work. Her research experiences include the management and coordination of large-scale European projects; the management of a research team; and research on work and organization in both qualitative (case studies) and quantitative (surveys) research studies.

Annika Schönauer is Senior Researcher and member of the management board at the Working Life Research Centre (FORBA) in Vienna, Austria. She holds a PhD in Sociology from Vienna University. Her main research areas are service sector work and work organization, internationalization and flexibilization of work.

Dean Stroud is a Lecturer at Cardiff School of Social Sciences, Cardiff University, Wales, UK. He has published mostly on trade union strategies in the area of workplace learning, particularly within old industrial sectors, such as the steel industry. As a result of his work in this area he has worked closely with Industri*ALL*, formerly the European Metalworkers' Federation, on developing approaches to workforce development in the European steel industry. He has a parallel interest in the fortunes of old industrial (steel) communities and the role of trade unions in managing change. More recent work has focused on the 'greening' of work and employment, and in particular the development of green skills within highly polluting sectors and building understandings of skills-based transitions from a high- to a low-carbon economy.

Martin Upchurch is Professor of International Employment Relations at Middlesex University Business School, London, UK. He worked for more than a decade for the Civil and Public Services Association (a constituent forerunner of the PCS union) before becoming an academic. He is co-author of *New Unions, New Workplaces* (2003); *The Realities of Partnership at Work* (2006); and *The Crisis of Social Democratic Trade Unionism in Western Europe* (2009). A co-authored book (with Darko Marinković) on *Workers and Revolution in Serbia* is due for publication late in 2013.

Matt Vidal is Senior Lecturer in Work and Organizations in the Department of Management at King's College London, UK. Matt's work has been published in *Critical Sociology; Human Relations; Industrial Relations; New Political Economy; Socio-Economic Review; Sociology Compass;* and *Work, Employment & Society.* He is co-editor of the 'Organizations & Work' section of *Sociology Compass;* editorial board member of *Work, Employment & Society;* editor-in-chief of 'Work in Progress', the blog for the Organizations, Occupations and Work section of the American Sociological Association; and is currently guest editing a special issue on Marxist approaches to organizational analysis for *Organization Studies.*

Ines Wagner is a Doctoral Candidate in Political Sciences at the University of Jyväskylä in Finland and in Global Economics and

Management at the University of Groningen in the Netherlands. Her research focuses on the posting of workers and micro-level regulation in Germany. Her research is part of the European Research Council-funded project 'Transnational Work and the Evolution of Sovereignty'.

Karel Williams is Director of the Economic and Social Research Council (ESRC) funded Centre for Research in Socio-Cultural Change (CRESC) at the University of Manchester, and Professor at Manchester Business School, UK. Karel has long standing research interests in manufacturing and is now exploring how long, fragile (supply) chains are part of the current economic problems in both manufacturing and in finance. His current research focus is on rethinking an economy overly dependent on finance and where democratic politics fails to prevent agenda setting by elites. His most recent co-authored book is *After the Great Complacence: Financial Crisis and the Politics of Reform* (Oxford University Press, 2011).

Serena Yu is a Senior Research Analyst at the Workplace Research Centre, located at the University of Sydney, Australia. Her research interests include the links between education and work, and between work and well-being. Serena is currently undertaking doctoral studies in the School of Economics, where her thesis relates to the dimensions of well-being in retirement.

Comparative Political Economy and Labour Process Theory: Toward a Synthesis

Matt Vidal and Marco Hauptmeier[1]

Comparative political economy and labour process theory, which both emerged as distinct literatures in the late 1970s, share extensive common ground yet remain surprisingly isolated from each other. This relative insularity is somewhat perplexing, given that models of production and employment relations systems have featured prominently in both literatures. On the one side, an enduring theme in comparative political economy has linked national institutions to employee representation and workplace voice (Dore 1973; Streeck 1984; Thelen 1991; Turner 1991), seemingly of interest to both labour process scholars and comparativists. On the other, labour process theory is about how politics and culture shape the organization of work and as such is a form of political economy. Yet, comparative political economists have focused mainly on macro and meso institutions (for example training regimes, inter-firm relations, corporate governance, finance systems, the state), while labour process scholars have continued to focus largely on the workplace issues of control, consent, resistance and accommodation. While scholars in each tradition have occasionally engaged debates and theories from the other tradition – as discussed below – such attempts have been relatively rare.

It is tempting to speculate about reasons for a lack of engagement between these two traditions. Methodologically, for instance, labour process scholars tend to prefer in-depth case studies of individual workplaces, while comparative political economists have typically deduced firm behaviour from national institutional context. In terms of academic discipline, labour process analysis has been largely based in the sociology of work and labour economics, while comparative political economy has been developed from within political science and industrial relations. Perhaps most importantly, there appear to be diverging theoretical commitments among scholars within each tradition: labour process researchers maintain the analytical priority of social relations at the point of production; comparativists hold to the fundamental importance of national-level institutions. Our goal here, however, is not to dwell on the curious insularity of these traditions but to look backward only in service of moving forward, exploring common themes in order to advance our argument that while both traditions have critical strengths each also has key weaknesses that may be remedied by more sustained engagement with the other. We hope that our proposal, as well as the chapters that follow, will be equally interesting and engaging for scholars working in both traditions.

We begin with an overview of the comparative political economy literature, focusing on its roots in research on neo-corporatism in Europe, debates over national models of capitalism, and more recent engagement with the themes of institutional change and within-country variation. We then provide a similar overview of labour process research, focusing on the problem of managerial strategy and workforce reactions, the diversity of labour processes, and attempts to understand connections between the labour process and the wider competitive and institutional environment. Our overviews are followed by a more critical assessment of each literature in light of the other, suggesting further areas of potential synthesis for future research.

We argue that comparative political economy has focused on institutional difference to the neglect of systemic capitalist processes, and on macro- and meso-level institutions to the neglect of the micro level, including labour process dynamics. Labour process theory can contribute to comparative political economy, we contend, with its analyses of how managerial strategy regarding work organization is often inconsistent and incoherent, and must be implemented in the context of deeply entrenched workplace politics and culture. The struggles between managers and workers over the extraction of labour effort – and how to interpret and respond to competitive (and institutional) pressures in order to survive and make a profit – feed back into the wider political economy. Even if managers could form consistent, coherent strategies, within the politics of production they must negotiate outcomes with workers, generating a fundamental source of variation at the organizational level. For its part, labour process theory has developed a systematic understanding neither of how institutions may shape and alter competitive pressures and accumulation dynamics, nor of the institutional distinctiveness of national contexts. National institutions provide a basic source of variation in the structure of employment relations systems, the latter being the most immediate context within which workplace dynamics unfold. Formal national and regional institutions moderate and give distinctive flavour to systemic capitalist pressures. In addition, systemic capitalist pressures as such – the need to survive the competitive struggle between firms, negotiate outcomes in the workplace and make a profit – are understood by owners, managers and workers on the ground through formal and informal cultural institutions, including ideologies of shareholder value and antiunionism, as well as various logics of management such as taylorism and employee involvement.

Comparative Political Economy

Our review of the comparative political economy literature is necessarily selective, focusing on mainstream approaches that examine work and employment relations or are of theoretical relevance to these. Comparative political economy initially developed in the 1970s out of political science, with important contributions also being made in industrial relations and comparative sociology. It emerged as a response to theorizing in the social sciences following World War II, most importantly neoclassical economics and modernization theory, which proposed a growing convergence of social and economic processes across countries. Theoretical orientations in the comparative literature differed widely, but an important common denominator was the focus on national institutions and politics in structuring and shaping social and economic life (for reviews of the various institutional theories see Hall and Taylor 1996; Morgan and Hauptmeier 2014).

Building blocks of comparative political economy

Neo-corporatism was an early strand in the literature (Schmitter 1974). It built on the insight that class conflict was very differently institutionalized across countries (Dahrendorf 1959) with implications for the power of working-class organizations and their ability to shape social and economic outcomes (Korpi 1983). The focus was on how intermediary organizations – primarily labour unions and employer associations – took part in the governance of the economy (Katzenstein 1985). Historically oriented studies revealed how both unions and employers played an important role in the creation of welfare states and in the subsequent governance of labour markets and welfare institutions (Esping-Andersen 1990). Another empirical focus was the response of countries to the 1973 oil crisis. Unions, employers and the state engaged in tripartite concertation and Keynesian-inspired macroeconomic governance (Scharpf 1991). Interest in neo-corporatism waned in the second half of the 1980s, but later made a surprising comeback when governments, labour unions and employers engaged in social pacts to negotiate economic adjustments in various European countries (Hamann and Kelly 2007).

While the neo-corporatist literature examined the role of labour unions in the wider political economy, industrial relations research showed how an institutional perspective informed an understanding of workplace dynamics. A seminal study was Ronald Dore's (1973) comparison of British and Japanese workplaces, which highlighted persistent differences in industrial relations. His explanation for the observed pattern relied on institutional and cultural factors, although he also considered the possibility of some scope for mutual learning across countries. In a similar institutional vein, Wolfgang Streeck (1984; 1992) detailed how sectoral collective bargaining, works councils, employment protection and the co-governance of the national training regime created good working standards and social benefits for German workers. Institutional factors imposed 'beneficial constraints' on management (Streeck 1997), which foreclosed low-wage employer strategies and also facilitated competitiveness and the export strategies of German firms in high-end market niches. Similarly, Lowell Turner (1991) found that institutionally guaranteed rights gave worker representatives the possibility to influence change processes and outcomes in Sweden and Germany, which contrasted with the weaker and more conflict-based influence of unions in the UK and US. Bruce Western (1997) examined the effect of market competition and internationalization on labour unions, arguing that the varying fortunes of labour unions in different countries can be explained by the extent to which labour unions were institutionally insulated from market competition.

Another strand in the comparative political economy literature developed sectoral analysis (Campbell et al. 1991; Hollingsworth et al. 1994). Based on detailed case studies, they argued that sectors were governed through a number of mechanisms including markets, states, hierarchies and associations. The varying prevalence of these mechanisms generates distinct modes of governance and outcomes across sectors, including in work and employment relations. Chapter 12 by Enda Hannon in this volume connects to this theme with a comparison of the pharmaceutical and food manufacturing sectors in the UK. Owing to the greater strategic importance of the pharmaceutical industry for the UK economy the state provides a number of direct incentives and resources to the pharmaceutical sectors, while the emphasis in the food manufacturing sector is on the regulation of business activities. The final chapter in J. Rogers Hollingsworth and collaborators' 1994 volume discussed the question of whether sectoral or national factors played a more important role in influencing economic processes. While contemplating that economic internationalization might lead to a greater salience of sectoral characteristics in influencing economic processes, they concluded that national factors, including national institutions, continued to be more important. The subsequent comparative political economy literature seemed to accept this conclusion and took a national turn, as discussed in the next section.

National models of capitalism

Globalization theorists argued that countries which do not liberalize labour markets and retrench welfare states would be shunned by multinational companies. In contrast, the emerging literature on national models suggested that countries compete successfully in the international economy with different national institutions, including those with strong labour representation, social protection and developed welfare states (Garrett 1998). One of the first national-models frameworks was the societal effects approach, which examined how organizations are shaped by the 'social fabric' of the national context within which they operate, including 'the interconnections between different social spheres such as manufacturing, industrial relations, education, training' (Maurice *et al.* 1980:61; see also Maurice *et al.* 1986). Another early approach, known as social systems of production, elaborated the argument that national economies coalesce into complementary institutional configurations (Hollingsworth and Boyer 1997). In a similar vein Richard Whitley (1999) proposed eight institutional dimensions that combine into one of six types of national business systems: fragmented, coordinated industrial district, compartmentalized, state-organized, collaborative and highly coordinated.

Building on the foregoing contributions, Peter Hall and David Soskice (2001; see also Hancké *et al.* 2007) developed the influential varieties-of-capitalism approach, which differentiated between so-called liberal market economies (Anglo-Saxon countries) and coordinated market economies (continental and Scandinavian countries and Japan). This theory uses a rational choice model to argue that companies have to solve coordination problems in different spheres – employment relations, skills/training, corporate governance, finance and inter-company relations – but do so very differently in liberal and coordinated market economies. The institutions in each type of economy and the comple-mentarities between them provide comparative institutional advantage, which firms seek to exploit. For example, in Chapter 6, Claire Evans and Dean Stroud compare how steel companies in Germany and Britain comply with European Union environmental regulation. In Germany different elements of the institutional framework complement each other, including the built-in environmental agenda in vocational educa-tion and continuous training, the long tenure of employees and the participation of employees in management decisions. These beneficial constraints allow companies not just to follow environmental regulation, but instead to turn the environmental agenda into an advantage by using it to save resources and develop innovative and productive work prac-tices. In Britain different institutional features matter, including narrower task-focused training, the exclusion of environmental issues in vocational education and training, smaller investments in continuous training and human resources, and fewer channels for worker participation in change processes. Overall, environmental regulation in Britain focuses on legal compliance so that innovative work practices are not systematically developed. In contrast, in Chapter 9 Giedo Jansen and Agnes Akkerman present a quantitative analysis of the relationship between increased employment flexibility and union capacity across the European Union states. Specifically, they examine variation across countries in how use of temporary employment and performance-based pay affects union membership and strike incidence, finding that the outcomes are not in the direction hypothesized by varieties-of-capitalism theory.

Along with Whitley (1999), scholars have developed typologies of national models that are more complex than the liberal/coordinated binary, including many examining distinctive national institutional arrangements in Southern and Eastern Europe, Latin America and Asia (Iankova 2002; Amable 2003; Schneider 2013; Witt and Redding 2013). Colin Crouch (2005) has levelled a formidable critique against cross-national typologies, arguing that individual countries should be studied not to determine the type into which they fit, but which types are found within them. In Chapter 11, Hyunji Kwon and Sanghoon Lim demonstrate another problem with developing ostensibly general typologies of national models based on a few starkly contrasting Western countries. Focusing on the banking sector in Korea, they document the surprising recent central-ization of collective bargaining despite a weak institutional basis for sectoral bargaining, most importantly relatively weak unions and a virtual absence of employer associations at the sectoral level. Yet, in contrast to the received wisdom from the European case, centralization in Korea was not associated with increased rigidity for employers. In response to corporate restructuring following the 1997 Asian financial crisis, employers and unions in the banking sector forged sectoral frameworks to deal with common problems while allowing room for flexible adaptation at the local level, resulting in a system Kwon and Lim characterize as 'coordinated and flexible'. Chapter 3 by Buchanan and colleagues further contributes to the attempt to move beyond static and overly stylized national models by focusing on the role of the state in private sector job growth. Their analysis provides evidence of a shift in the UK and Australia from a social welfare state in the Keynesian years of the 1950s and 1960s to a 'business welfare state' in the neoliberal 1980s and 1990s, the latter characterized by direct state support for full employment as well as indirect yet substantial support for job growth through public funding for employment in social services such as health and education.

Institutional Change and Within-Country Variation

A central problem facing the national-models literature is explaining institutional change, which can in part be traced back to its roots in historical institutionalism (Steinmo *et al.* 1992; Thelen 1999). The default theory suggests path-dependent institutional continuities reinforced by institutional complementarities that create lock-in effects. Change tends to take place at historical junctures through external shocks such as economic depressions or war, which opens up space for actors to significantly change institutions or create new ones. Absent such external shocks, institutions shape and inform actors in a routine manner, contributing to stable patterns of work and management. However, this model did not square with detailed empirical studies at the workplace level that observed important changes in employment relations (for example Bosch *et al.* 2009). Cracks appeared in the edifice of the national-models approach.

The determinist link between institutions and behaviour loosened as researchers recognized that individuals are not only passive recipients of institutional effects but have the capacity to change institutions. The volume by Wolfgang Streeck and Kathleen Thelen (2005) identified several mechanisms of institutional change (displacement, layering, drift, conversion and exhaustion). For example, layering means the addition of new elements or rules to already existing institutions, which gradually change the functioning and meaning of institutions. An extension of this research differentiates between various types of agency in institutional change, for example insurrectionaries, symbionts, subversives and opportunists (Mahoney and Thelen 2010). Subversives, for instance, develop various types of institutional avoidance strategies; they bend institutional rules or circumvent them altogether. In this vein, Streeck (2009) described how 'unruly capitalists' in Germany sought to break free from the institutional shackles of the social market economy that hold them back in world markets. Similarly, Martin Upchurch and collaborators in Chapter 13 demonstrate how unions may use the institutional environment in a proactive manner. Revitalization of unions occurs when political congruence is achieved through shared political frames, socialization and mobilization. This model is used to explain union growth in the adverse institutional environments in the UK, focusing on the Amalgamated Engineering Union (1935–45) and the Public and Commercial Services Union (since 2000).

Another emphasis in studying institutional change has been the role of ideas (Blyth 2002; Hay 2006; Jackson 2010; Hauptmeier and Heery 2014 forthcoming). Institutional rules can be ambiguous and thus open to different interpretations (Herrigel 2010; Jackson 2010). This theme is taken up by Marco Hauptmeier and Glenn Morgan in Chapter 8 based on a comparison of company-level employment relations in the auto industry in Germany and Spain. Their argument on the co-constitution of ideas and institutions recognizes that institutions constitute actors; the rights, resources and character of labour organizations at the company level across countries are institutionalized in very different ways. While this constitution of actors matters, the ideologies of actors change through various mechanisms as they adapt to a changing socio-economic context, with new ideologies leading in turn to novel ways of enacting or constructing institutions and hence the evolution of employment relations. Thus, actor ideas and institutions co-evolve over time.

These and other theories of institutional change departed from coherent and unitary models of national capitalism and allowed for a greater recognition of within-country variation (Whitley 1999; Herrigel 2000; Katz and Darbishire 2000; Crouch 2005; Whitford 2005; Deeg and Jackson 2007; Morgan 2007; Schneiberg 2007; Streeck 2009; Hauptmeier 2012; Wood and Lane 2012). Labour market segmentation theories go back to the 1970s in the USA (Bluestone 1970) and segmentation had occasionally been acknowledged in comparative political economy (for example Locke 1992 on Italy). More recently comparativists have highlighted growing divergence between insiders and outsiders under rising inequality within OECD countries (Palier and Thelen 2010; Emmenegger et al. 2012). Insiders typically benefited from standard employment relations, associated social benefits and employment protection, while outsiders were either unemployed or in an employment relationships characterized by low levels of pay, benefits and protection. Neoliberalization arguments suggest that deregulation undermines the position of workers across the board, but the point by Patrick Emmedegger and collaborators (2012) is more differentiated: policy changes have affected insider and outsiders in different ways. An important emphasis in labour market reforms was on the low-wage sector, making the hiring and firing of atypical workers easier, while many insiders continued to have more significant employ- ment protection. Anke Hassel (2012) described how such dualization processes took place within Germany, as companies built their competi- tiveness by collaborating with a core workforce of skilled, protected work- ers while taking advantage of low-cost/high-flexibility outsiders. In a similar vein, in Chapter 10 Stefan Kirchner and Jürgen Beyer identify different skill and flexibility profiles across the German economy, which demonstrate how companies forge competitive strategies in distinct ways within the national context. They show widespread divergence from the classical model of diversified quality production, including a large share of establishments now using external forms of flexibility.

Despite some recent exceptions, comparative political economy tended to focus on national contexts, bracketing international factors or covering them under the broad label of globalization. The great recession begin- ning in the late 2000s vividly showed how international factors impinge on work and economic governance within national context. Moving beyond the national focus, the volume by Morgan and Whitley (2012) developed a comparative political economy perspective that accounts for changing international influences, including the role of multinational companies and the rise of new economic powerhouses such as Brazil, Russia, India and China. In Chapter 16, Guglielmo Meardi focuses on the key role of international organizations such as the International Monetary Fund, European Central Bank and European Commission in pushing through transformative labour market reforms during the great recession. Both Spain and Italy came under pressure in the financial markets and required the support of international organizations to keep bond rates down and avoid bankruptcy. In return, the so-called Troika asked for far- reaching employment relations reforms, which primarily focused on the decentralization of collective bargaining and the liberalization of labour markets. Similarly, in Chapter 15, Nathan Lillie and collaborators focus on the role of European Union legislation for employment relations in the member states. Posted workers are sent by their employers, often work agencies and subcontractors, to other European countries but are managed according to the lower wages and standards of their home coun- try or the registered location of their work agency. European-posted worker legislation creates 'spaces of exception', which employers use to circumvent national employment relations and working standards, undermining the regulatory capacity of nation states within the European Union.

The Capitalist Labour Process

In the 1950s and 1960s, prominent American scholars such as Daniel Bell, Seymour Martin Lipset and Clark Kerr observed declining strike activity in the US – following the institutionalization of industrial conflict via collective bargaining – and declared that capitalism had solved its major problems (Burawoy 1979a). Then in 1974 Harry Braverman published his *Labor and Monopoly Capital*, which introduced Marxist labour process analysis into organizational analysis, fundamentally altering the field. Marx ([1867] 1990, ch. 7:293) argued that capitalist production consists of two distinct processes. The labour process concerns how humans transform nature into use values, referring to the configuration of objects, instruments and the social organization of work. The valorization process concerns the production of exchange values for sale on the market, referring to the extraction of surplus effort from workers by managers and owners. Managerial efforts to secure the appropriation of surplus value in the context of antagonistic relations (the valorization process) mean they often pursue control strategies that have detrimental effects on cooperation in the labour process (for elaborations on this theme, see Adler 2007). In what came to be known simply as labour process theory, Braverman argued that a core tendency of capitalist management was to deskill workers, primarily through taylorism: the simplification and standardization of production processes by engineers and managers to ensure that workers produce sufficient output. After Braverman the labour process literature has observed and theorized a range of managerial strategies for ensuring sufficient output. Some scholars have developed labour process theory within the broader Marxist research programme, although there has been a current attempting to distance labour process theory from Marxism (Spencer 2000). It should also be noted when considering the following that some of these debates were overlapping while others were more disconnected.

Multiple, Often-Incoherent Managerial Strategies, Workforce Resistance and Workplace Negotiation

Economist Andrew Friedman (1977:4) has noted that, although Marx did not systematically theorize how class struggle may generate changes *within* capitalism, worker resistance has forced 'accommodating changes'.

Friedman argued that large, unionized firms in the core of the UK economy were able to pursue a managerial control strategy of 'responsible autonomy', whereas managers of smaller firms in the periphery continued to exercise direct control via close supervision and taylorism. Around the same time, American economist Richard Edwards (1979) developed a similar theory based on historical analysis of the US, arguing that in addition to simple control, managers could engage in technical control, embedded into physical technologies such as the assembly line, or bureaucratic control embedded in company policy (including internal labour markets to induce loyalty). Like Friedman, Edwards argued that the various control strategies reflect broader labour market segmentation: simple control in the non-union, low-wage secondary labour market; technical control and bureaucratic control in the primary labour market, offering security, decent wages and promotion opportunities. American-based sociologist Michael Burawoy (1979a) turned the focus from managers to workers, asking why employees work so hard for the company. Burawoy argued that the 'politics of production' are fundamentally ideological; in unionized and bureaucratic factories workers may not need to be coerced but may actively, if unwittingly, consent to working hard in the interests of the company.

After a number of early contributions in the decade following Braverman (1974), on both sides of the Atlantic (Nichols and Armstrong 1976; Friedman 1977; Burawoy 1979b; Zimbalist 1979; Nichols 1980; Edwards and Scullion 1982; Littler 1982), the most active development of the labour process as a distinctive theoretical research programme occurred in Britain. Craig Littler (1982) and Paul Thompson (1983:215) argued that various managerial strategies may coexist within the same company. Similarly, Paul Edwards and Hugh Scullion (1982) argued that firms may not have an articulated strategy for controlling labour, and the debate between John Storey and Andrew Friedman in the journal *Sociology* suggested that mechanisms for control are often used in inconsistent and incoherent ways (Storey 1985; Friedman 1987).

A landmark in the literature was *Labour Process Theory* edited by David Knights and Hugh Willmott (1990), which included influential interventions in two regards. First, Thompson (1990) and Paul Edwards (1990) distanced labour process theory from Marxist value theory and class analysis, although maintaining a materialist foundation. Second, Knights (1990) and Willmott (1990) adopted a poststructuralist approach, an early position leading to the formation of the critical management studies research programme (see for example Alvesson *et al.* 2011). Paul Edwards (1990) elaborated on the relative autonomy of the labour process, arguing that the capital–labour relation 'generates pressures which have to be interpreted and acted on by employers and workers' but that such workplace dynamics may take on a logic of their own. Thompson (1990:98) specified what he called the 'core theory' of the labour process based on the four implications following from the fact that capital faces an enduring problem in translating purchased labour power into actual labour: (1) the capital–labour relation is a privileged focus of analysis; (2) the capital–labour relation is inherently antagonistic, even if the labour process is relatively autonomous; (3) competition compels transformations in the labour process; (4) thus managers have a control imperative, even if there are a range of strategies.

North American scholars also contributed a number of important studies and concepts. Randy Hodson (1991a; 1991b) showed that workplaces are characterized by diffused conflict which can take a variety of forms and is not limited to resisting managerial control but motivated by pride in work as much as a desire for autonomy (see also Edwards and Scullion 1982; Ackroyd and Thompson 1999). The rise of self-directed teamwork was widely studied, variously labelled as normative control (Barley and Kunda 1992), concertive control (Barker 1993), hegemonic control (Graham 1995) or post-bureaucratic control (Smith 2001). Back in Britain, Fleming and Sturdy (2009) proposed the concept of neo-normative control, referring to workplaces that attempt to harness values from outside of work in a way that resonates with the objectives of the business.

On the question of management strategy, Ruth Milkman (1997) found that local managers in a General Motors factory were unwilling to fully commit to new forms of participatory work mandated by corporate headquarters. And Steven Vallas (2003; 2006) showed that teamwork can undermine managerial legitimacy where actual changes lag behind or deviate from managerial rhetoric. More generally, Chris Warhurst and Paul Thompson (1998:11) noted the 'muddied realities' that typically result when 'managerial schemes are filtered through employee attitudes and self-organizing'. On worker orientations, Matt Vidal (2007a) found that individual preferences regarding particular practices at work are not consistent but depend on local plant context and are subject to revaluation. Jacques Bélanger and Paul Edwards (2007) argued that workplace compromise is particularly unlikely under the structural conditions of competitive product markets and technologies that limit worker autonomy, but the establishment of cooperation takes effort from all sides even under more favourable conditions.

Beyond Manufacturing: The Diversity of Labour Processes

A foundational contribution to the sociology of service labour processes was Arlie Hochschild's (1983) concept of emotional labour, referring to the unremunerated skill demanded by managers in which workers who interact with customers must manage their internal feelings in order to present a particular appearance (for an extension to the concept of aesthetic labour, see Warhurst *et al.* 2000; Williams and Connell 2010). Robin Leidner (1993) introduced the term 'interactive service work' and showed that the presence of customers complicates labour process dynamics. Depending on how their interests align within different contexts, customers may join with managers against workers or with workers against management (see also Fuller and Smith 1991; Lopez 1996; Bolton and Houlihan 2010; Lopez 2010). On this, Vassil Kirov and Monique Ramioul in Chapter 14 compare working conditions and employment relations in the cleaning industry in Norway, Belgium and Austria, showing that the demands of clients and cost pressures negatively impact working conditions in this highly competitive industry.

Labour process theory has highlighted important contours of variation within the service sector. In a relatively early contribution, Chris Smith and collaborators (1991) presented a volume on white-collar work that covered labour processes in a range of professions, arguing that differences between blue-collar and white-collar labour processes have less to do with objective qualities of the job and more to do with cultural distinctions granting higher status and more autonomy to so-called non-manual workers. Cameron Lynne Macdonald and Carmen Sirianni (1996) distinguished professionals from the 'emotional proletariat', the latter constituted by frontline service workers whose emotional labour is imposed rather than self-regulated. In the introduction to a volume on customer service, Andrew Sturdy (2001) noted that because some employers seek to ensure that workers present a consistent appearance to customers, the former hire based on stereotyped characteristics such as gender, race, age and beauty, thus generating labour market segmentation – echoing earlier feminist studies of gendered and racialized divisions of labour inside the firm (Cockburn 1983; Pollert 1988). However, as Marek Korczynski (2009) noted, inherent to the service labour process are contradictory logics: rationalization to achieve quantitative efficiency versus a customer-orientation aimed at creating satisfied customers (for an empirical example in call centres, see Korczynski *et al.* 2000). How this contradiction gets managed in particular workplaces and sectors is a central source of variation within and across types of service sector labour process. While variation across industries and occupations has been a common theme, empirical studies have also documented common pressures, including strong tendencies toward taylorism across service sectors and rising low-wage work within front-line services. Phil Taylor and Peter Bain (1999) found extreme taylorization of call centre work in the UK, noting widespread resistance to managerial attempts to monitor and measure workers' speech and effort. Consistent with Chris Smith and collaborators' (1991) earlier argument regarding the similarities across labour processes, Martha Crowley and collaborators (2010) showed that neotaylorist work intensification has become widespread across professions. In her review, Vicki Smith (1997) found that although important differences remain across occupations and hierarchies, the 'central features of employment instability, decentred control, and work intensification run across the occupational spectrum' (see also Thompson 2003). In their introduction to a recent volume on low-wage work, Françoise Carré and collaborators (2012) argued that behind the growth of low-wage work are cost-cutting business strategies under intensified competition, which are spread within industries following the lead of major employers such as Wal-Mart in the US and Tesco in the UK.

Extending Out from the Labour Process: Production Models and National Institutions

Two traditions within economics have attempted to develop institutional theories of macro growth regimes based in labour process analysis. The American radical economics tradition (Gordon *et al.* 1982; Gordon *et al.* 1987) articulated a theoretical framework based on a historical analysis of the US, linking the labour process and labour market dynamics with the wider institutions that constitute 'social structures of accumulation'. The latter go through cycles of exploration, consolidation and decay, with the postwar structure being based in labour market segmentation (see also Kotz *et al.* 1994). A similar but more influential approach known as regulation theory was developed by French political economists. Michel Aglietta ([1979] 2000) argued that the fordist labour process of taylorist mass production was matched with institutions supporting effective demand, most importantly union-based class compromise and the welfare state. This model was subsequently developed and generalized for comparative political economy by Robert Boyer (Boyer 1988; Boyer and Saillard 2002) and others to distinguish between regimes of accumulation and their institutional modes of regulation. Regulation theory provided the inspiration and much of the conceptual basis for a rich vein of research on models of production and their relationship to the wider institutional context, in particular its concepts of fordism and postfordism.

Debates about the spread of lean production from Japan engaged issues of organizational-level variation and the relation of production models to the wider institutional context. On the latter, some argued that lean production was dependent on the larger Japanese institutional environment (Ackroyd *et al.* 1988; Streeck 1996) but others showed that it could be transferred to new institutional contexts (Elger and Smith 1994a; Smith and Meiksins 1995; Delbridge 1998; Nichols *et al.* 2002; McKay 2006). While the widespread diffusion of lean across countries demonstrated that core lean practices could be transferred, debates over the nature of lean itself continued. German scholars Ulrich Jürgens and collaborators (1985; see also Jürgens *et al.* 1993) argued that lean is a form of neotaylorist work intensification while Americans Martin Kenney and Richard Florida (1988; 1993) argued that it is a form of post-taylorist work enrichment. Meanwhile Swedish sociologist Christian Berggren (1992) agreed with critics that lean is a form of work intensification in contrast to the Swedish model of truly post-taylorist, self-directed teamwork. The debates over the nature of lean production raged in the 1990s (Adler and Cole 1993; Tetsuro and Steven 1993; Wood 1993; Berggren 1994) with a general lack of agreement by the contending parties. Seeking to understand variation in the implementation of lean, Vidal (2007b) showed in the US that lean is more easily implemented in a largely neotaylorist fashion but may also include substantive participation from workers, depending on the strategic orientations of management, workforce dispositions, and union power (with unions typically pushing management in a more participatory direction). However, as Vidal (2011) and Thompson (2013) argued, while specific labour process models (systems of skill, control and coordination) like lean may spread relatively easily across national contexts, employment regimes (employment security, wage setting and voice systems) are more embedded in national institutions. Finally, Paul Thompson and Steve Vincent (2010) recently suggested that global value chain/production network analysis may provide an alternative to comparative institutionalism as a way for labour process theory to extend out beyond the labour process, an approach that has recently been developed by Taylor (2010) and Jörg Flecker and collaborators (2013).

Toward a Synthesis

What Can Labour Process Theory Contribute to Comparative Political Economy?

Comparative political economy has developed a number of critical empirical insights and theoretical explanations regarding the constitutive role of national institutions in the operation of national economies. We highlight two basic problems common in the literature for which labour process research can make important contributions. First, mainstream approaches within comparative political economy have focused on institutions to the neglect of systemic capitalist processes. Second, the literature has focused on macro- and meso-level institutions to the neglect of the micro level, including workplace dynamics. We argue that both of these issues have limited theoretical understanding and development in comparative political economy.

Mainstream approaches have fundamentally failed to develop an understanding of capitalism as a system, including dynamics of capital accumulation and tendencies toward stagnation and crisis. Such neglect has been most glaring in the varieties-of-capitalism school (Pontusson 2005; Peck and Theodore 2007; Thompson and Vincent 2010; Heyes *et al.* 2012; Vidal and Peck 2012) but has also been evident in more sociological approaches (Whitley 1999; Crouch 2005). Although some comparativists have emphasized common capitalist pressures (Boyer and Saillard 2002; Coates 2005; Streeck 2009), in our view they have not paid close enough attention to how accumulation and valorization pressures are processed and negotiated at the workplace level. From a labour process perspective, capitalists face valorization pressures and problems in terms of extracting sufficient effort and output from workers everywhere – even in Sweden and Germany. Now it is certainly the case that accumulation and valorization pressures are typically refracted through and shaped by national institutions as well as more diffuse managerial ideologies, but such pressures and the need to maintain profits under market competition can be intense enough to strongly impact national institutions and potentially erode them. Thus, as Jason Heyes and collaborators show in Chapter 2, dynamics that have led to a weakening of labour and strengthening of capital, as indicated by declining wage shares of national income, declines in union density and rising inequality, were present across liberal and nonliberal economies. Similarly, in Chapter 4 Vidal shows strong stagnationist tendencies across economies since the 1970s: The USA has experienced a low corporate profit and moderate growth levels maintained only via skyrocketing household debt; the UK low profit rates and four decades of stagnant growth due to an underconsumptionist distribution of the national income; and Germany a low corporate profit rate along with three decades of stagnant growth. The corporate sector in all three countries has attempted to restore a declining profit rate by increasing the profit share of total output via deunionization, reducing employment security, and returning to market-determined wages.

The second issue, a focus on macro and meso institutions, has generated a strong tendency to see national models as institutionally coherent – particularly in the regulationist (Boyer and Saillard 2002), social structures of accumulation (Hollingsworth and Boyer 1997) and varieties-of-capitalism approaches (Hall and Sosckice 2001). While there has recently been substantial movement in this literature down from the national level toward recognizing variation and segmentation within countries (Whitley 1999; Crouch 2005; Deeg and Jackson 2007; Morgan 2007; Schneiberg 2007; Streeck 2009), with a few notable exceptions (Whitford 2005; Wood and Lane 2012) there remains a reticence to embrace internal organizational dynamics and to examine how these might feed back into wider institutional environments. Our review of findings from the labour process literature demonstrated that business firms are not monolithic organizations with unitary and rational utility maximizing management, but heterogeneous organizations with layers of management in which any policy or strategy regarding the labour process – which may be more or less coherent – must be implemented in a context of entrenched workplace politics and culture.

Labour process scholars have documented and theorized workplace dynamics in a wide variety of contexts, showing how competitive pressures have generated increasing prevalence of low-wage work and rising work intensification and insecurity, across a range of manufacturing and service contexts, including a growing sector of interactive services. As Bettina Haidinger and collaborators show in Chapter 5, subcontracting and outsourcing in the parcel delivery and software development sectors are key drivers of labour market segmentation. It has been argued that the extension of supply chains from countries or sectors with high levels of employment protection and good employment regimes to peripheral countries or sectors is used to stabilize a core workforce. However, Haidinger and collaborators find that such supply chain extension reverberates back into more protected areas, fragmenting employment relations and destabilizing national or sectoral regime distinctiveness.

At an even more micro level, labour process research has emphasized organizational diversity, focusing on how market pressures are interpreted by managers within organizational contexts in which change must be negotiated. Such a workplace focus can help comparative political economy in working through issues with which it has recently begun grappling: understanding change and within-country variation. Perhaps the core insight that labour process theory can contribute to comparative political economy is that if we want to fully understand the functioning, problems, strategic dilemmas, and opportunities of the macro economy, we must understand the internal dynamics of organizations and how managers and workers react to, struggle over and attempt to reshape the complex pressures they face – both valorization/market pressures and institutional pressures. There is overlap here between labour process theory and those veins of institutional theory that theorize how actors may deviate from institutional prescriptions and reconfigure them (for example Hancké and Casper 2000; Crouch 2005; Greer and Hauptmeier 2008; Herrigel 2010; Jackson 2010; Mahoney and Thelen 2010; Greer and Hauptmeier 2012).

What Can Comparative Political Economy Contribute to Labour Process Theory?

Labour process theory has produced rich case studies of workplace dynamics and employment relations, developing detailed insights about how the interaction between various management control strategies and forms of resistance among workers makes negotiation in the labour process a fundamental source of variation in outcomes at the workplace level. Yet labour process theory is limited in two ways. First, labour process theory has not advanced a systematic understanding of how institutions structure and affect workplace dynamics and employment relations. Second and closely related, labour process theory has not developed a systematic appreciation of national contexts and, as a result, cross-national comparisons remain underrepresented in the literature (for exceptions see Littler 1982; Burawoy 1987; Elger and Smith 1994a; Meiksins and Smith 1996; Nichols et al. 2004; Warhurst et al. 2012). We argue in this section that engagement with the literature on comparative political economy can help labour process theory overcome some of these limitations.

By focusing on the workplace level, labour process theory does not sufficiently appreciate how institutions structure and shape work and employment relations. National institutions provide a basic source of variation in employment relations systems and workplace dynamics. For instance, institutionally guaranteed rights such as worker representation on supervisory boards can make an important difference for working standards and labour processes, while they remain a socialist dream in many other countries. Thus as Inger Marie Hagen shows in Chapter 7, board-level employee representatives are legally mandated in the Scandinavian countries, but there are important differences in how this requirement is implemented, depending on the institutionally supported role of the representatives: the industrial relations role of representing the interests of the workforce or the corporate governance role of managing exclusively in the interests of shareholders. In Norway the two roles have been tightly integrated, with employee representatives being able to leverage their industrial relations role to empower them to represent the workforce on the board. In Sweden employee representatives are not able to leverage any power from their industrial relations role, instead being powerless on the board, subject to a hegemonic shareholder value ideology. Denmark occupies a sort of middle ground in which both roles continue to exist, but without effectively integrating them into a single role. These distinct ways in which a similar institutional requirement is implemented are likely to have important and variable effects for labour process issues such as skills, training and employee involvement.

In countries with deregulated labour markets and company-based training regimes, deskilling might be a more common management control strategy, but in countries with a national training regime co-governed by labour unions, deskilling is much less feasible. While our appreciation of the organizational-level variation produced by labour process dynamics leads us to reject determinist arguments about national institutions, we argue that national and subnational institutional contexts generate strong *tendencies* toward particular forms of management control strategies. Some researchers have argued that economic globalization has changed the functioning of institutions or lessened their importance. This may very well be the case, but globalization processes continue to be filtered through institutions and actors respond to the challenges based on the institutional resources and instruments they have at hand.

Now, we are far from the first to call for connecting labour process theory to the wider political economy. For Marx ([1867] 1990) the labour process was intimately connected with wider accumulation dynamics, and developing these connections was an important goal of early labour process theory (Friedman 1977; Edwards 1979; Elger 1979; Gordon *et al.* 1982; Kelly 1985; Burawoy 1987; Knights and Willmott 1990). Regulation theorists (Boyer and Saillard 2002) have focused explicitly on cross-national institutional analysis, but this research has largely been conducted by macroeconomists who have failed to appreciate the diversity of labour processes. With more attention to variation in work organization, Tony Elger and Chris Smith edited a volume (1994a) on the spread of Japanese work organization, arguing in their introduction (1994b) for a need to study the interconnections between management models and the wider institutional context, but without assuming anything about coherence, convergence or divergence. Responding to the convergence/divergence debate, Chris Smith and Peter Meiksins (1995:262) developed a synthetic approach distinguishing three effects: system effects of global capitalism, societal effects of national institutions, and dominance effects associated with the power of the dominant state(s) in the global system (see also Thompson and Smith 1998). They argue that the concept of best practice is encouraged by the global system but complicated by institutional and cultural dynamics associated with society and dominance effects, which interact as competing pressures within workplaces to generate further indeterminacy in complex organizations, as different actors 'within the firm are differentially exposed to these pressures'. In response to a regime of financialized capitalism, Thompson (2003) urged labour process scholars to make connections to wider accumulation dynamics, arguing that shareholder value pressures have generated rising employment insecurity, which in turn can help explain the limited spread of high-involvement work systems in the US and UK (see also Thompson and Newsome 2004; Thompson 2013). Finally, Vidal (2013a; 2013b) recently presented evidence that the transformation in the US from a manufacturing-based, nationally bound growth regime to a service-based, internationalized regime has included a shift from a logic of employment internalization (vertical integration with internal labour markets and administratively determined wages) to one of employment externalization (vertical disintegration, lean staffing, and a return to market-determined wages). These various interventions notwithstanding, labour process theory and research have yet to develop a sustained engagement with the institutionalist vein of political economy.

The relative neglect of institutional analysis is not surprising when we consider the historical origins of labour process theory, which began to flourish in the 1980s in the UK and US where the institutional environment was deeply liberal and the assumption of convergence toward the US model was widely held. In addition, labour process scholars explicitly focused on common capitalist pressures on the labour process, both as a matter of theoretical interest and also perhaps as a way of differentiating themselves from industrial relations scholars who assumed the importance of variation in national systems.[2] However, in a broader comparative perspective, labour process theory has lacked the analytical tools to fully grasp that working lives and managerial approaches differ fundamentally between countries because of a range of institutions. These go beyond employment relations institutions, which give workers power and voice in the labour process in distinct ways, to include other institutions in the wider political economy such as systems of finance, corporate governance and the welfare state. These sets of institutions shape, among others, the extent of economic inequality, the participation of women (and mothers) in the labour market and the wage share of total national income (vis-à-vis the profit share). This broader set-up of the political economy fundamentally matters for workers and can only be fully grasped through institutional analysis.

Comparative political economy with its focus on institutional theory highlights the importance of institutions in structuring work and employment and as factors in explaining outcomes (Morgan *et al.* 2010;

Morgan and Whitley 2012). This provides leverage for understanding changes in differences across work and employment relations, in particular through cross-national research. This does not have to come in the functional or deterministic fashion of varieties-of-capitalism theory. Recent institutional analysis has developed a finer-grained understanding of institutional change including an appreciation of segmentation and dualization processes within countries. Institutions remain of primary importance for shaping work and employment relations across and within countries; in many cases formal national and regional institutions still moderate and give distinctive flavour to systemic capitalist pressures (Almond 2011; Delbridge *et al.* 2011). Further, systemic capitalist pressures as such are understood by agents on the ground through informal cultural institutions, such as the ideology of shareholder value or, indeed, the ideology of neoliberalism.

There is a rich set of theoretical and empirical research questions regarding the foregoing issues. Specifically, at the centre of the overlapping area between comparative political economy and labour process theory lie a number of questions regarding how owners, managers and workers react to, conform with, deviate from or recreate institutions – including formal institutions such as legal frameworks and informal institutions such as managerial ideologies and logics of corporate governance, employment relations and valorization.

Conclusion

A central aim of this book is to encourage a debate between comparative political economy and labour process theory, two literatures which have previously had limited engagement with each other. We have offered suggestions for what each literature may learn from the other. Labour process theory delivers detailed insights into workplace dynamics and processes and an understanding of the operation of similar capitalist processes across countries, while comparative political economy provides an understanding of how institutions structure and shape work and employment relations within and across countries. There were significant differences between earlier strands of both literatures. A primary focus of earlier labour process theory literature was on struggle and negotiation over the organization of work at the point of production, largely overshadowing wider institutions in society. A primary focus of earlier comparative political economy literature was on national institutions and coherent national models of work and employment, often without paying close empirical attention to political and cultural dynamics at the workplace level. More recently both literatures have moved closer towards each other. Important strands of comparative political economy have shifted their analytical focus below the national level and became more attentive to within-country variation and institutional change, while labour process theory has widened its analytical focus beyond the workplace and linked processes at the workplace level to internationalization, the cross-national diffusion of production models, financialization and global value chains. These movements, along with the chapters in this book, show that research at the intersection of comparative political economy and labour process theory is insightful and promising. It is possible to appreciate how national institutions and other wider societal structures are impacting employment relations without losing sight of workplace dynamics – and how the latter feed back into the former.

There are further examples that show what research at the intersection between the labour process and comparative political economy might look like. A consummate example is Virginia Doellgast's (2012) comparison of call centres in Germany and the US, which provides in-depth qualitative and quantitative data on work organization, labour conditions and employment relations at the establishment level. She recognizes that call centres in both countries operate in highly competitive markets and face strong pressures to cut costs. These pressures have led to deteriorating working conditions in both countries. Yet, there are nuanced but important differences in terms of processes and outcomes. In Germany, institutional resources such as works councils give labour voice and influence in change processes, thereby being able to positively impact working conditions and protect workers from regressive management tendencies. In the US, institutions provide labour with less leverage and power. Market pressures are more directly translated by management into deteriorating working conditions, with fewer possibilities for labour to influence outcomes. Doellgast appreciates processes, dynamics and market pressure at the workplace, but she also realizes how the labour processes in different countries are shaped by national institutions. Similarly, Thompson's (2013) disconnected capitalism thesis is theoretically attentive to how workplace processes are linked to macro-structures. Employers are pursing contradictory objectives in the institutional domains of work organization and employment relations: they are demanding and getting high performance in the labour process, but they are not able to offer a supportive employment system because of pressure from financial markets, which are inhibiting investments in employment security and training.

The broader lesson of such studies at the intersection of labour process theory and comparative political economy might be a research strategy that Burawoy (2009) called the 'extended case method'. He suggests extending out from micro processes to macro structures. According to Burawoy, painting a fine-grained image of micro processes is not sufficient and it is important to understand the macro drivers of changes and dynamics at the micro level. Researchers should explore the links between micro processes and macro structures including regional and national institutions, internationalization, financialization, and neoliberalism. Such an approach can be used to develop a comparative political economy of work that seeks to more fully understand the capitalist and institutional forces shaping employment relations and workplace dynamics. All the chapters in this volume are comparative and explore how micro processes are linked to wider macro structures, which demonstrates the potential of research at the intersection of labour process theory and comparative political economy.

Notes

1 Both authors contributed equally to this chapter. We are grateful to Ellen Christensen, Rick Delbridge, Tony Edwards, Ian Greer, Irena Grugulis, Chris Smith, Andy Sturdy, Paul Thompson and Chris Warhurst for providing expert written comments on this chapter. Any remaining problems are our own.
2 This last point on differentiation was suggested to us by Andy Sturdy.

REFERENCES

Ackroyd, S., G. Burrell, M. Hughes and A. Whitaker (1988) 'The Japanisation of British Industry?', *Industrial Relations Journal* 19:11–23.

Ackroyd, Stephen and Paul Thompson (1999) *Organizational Misbehaviour*. London: Sage.

Adler, Paul S. (2007) 'The Future of Critical Management Studies: A Paleo-Marxist Critique of Labour Process Theory', *Organization Studies* 28:1313–45.

Adler, Paul S. and Robert E. Cole. (1993) 'Designed for Learning: A Tale of Two Auto Plants', *Sloan Management Review* Spring:85–94.

Aglietta, Michel ([1979] 2000) *A Theory of Capitalist Regulation: The US Experience*. London: Verso.

Almond, Phil (2011) 'The Sub-National Embeddedness of International HRM', *Human Relations* 64:531–51.

Alvesson, Mats, Todd Bridgman and Hugh Willmott (eds) (2011) *The Oxford Handbook of Critical Management Studies*. Oxford: Oxford University Press.

Amable, Bruno (2003) *The Diversity of Modern Capitalism*. Oxford: Oxford University Press.

Barker, James R. (1993) 'Tightening the Iron Cage: Concertive Control in Self-Managing Teams', *Administrative Science Quarterly* 38:408–37.

▶

Barley, S.R. and G. Kunda (1992) 'Design and Devotion: The Ebb and Flow of Rational and Normative Ideologies of Control in Managerial Discourse', *Administrative Science Quarterly* 37:1–30.

Bélanger, Jacques and Paul Edwards (2007) 'The Conditions Promoting Compromise in the Workplace', *British Journal of Industrial Relations* 45:713–34.

Berggren, Christian (1992) *Alternatives to Lean Production: Work Organization in the Swedish Auto Industry*. Ithaca, NY: Cornell University Press.

Berggren, Christian (1994) 'NUMMI vs. Uddevalla', *Sloan Management Review* Winter:37–45.

Bluestone, Barry (1970) 'The Tripartite Economy: Labor Markets and the Working Poor', *Poverty and Human Resources Abstracts* 5:15–35.

Blyth, Mark (2002) *Great Transformations: Economic Ideas and Institutional Change in the Twentieth Century*. Cambridge: Cambridge University Press.

Bolton, Sharon C. and Maeve Houlihan (2010) 'Bermuda Revisited?: Management Power and Powerlessness in the Worker–Manager–Customer Triangle', *Work and Occupations* 37:378–403.

Bosch, Gerhard, Steffen Lehndorff and Jill Rubery (2009) *European Employment Models in Flux*. Basingstoke: Palgrave Macmillan.

Boyer, Robert (1988) 'Technical Change and the Theory of "Régulation"', pp. 67–94 in *Technical Change and Economic Theory*, edited by G. Dosi *et al.* London: Pinter.

Boyer, Robert and Yves Saillard (eds) (2002) *Régulation Theory: The State of the Art*. London: Routledge.

Braverman, Harry (1974) *Labor and Monopoly Capital: The Degradation of Work in the Twentieth Century*. New York: Monthly Review Press.

Burawoy, Michael (1979a) *Manufacturing Consent: Changes in the Labor Process UNDER Monopoly Capitalism*. University of Chicago Press.

Burawoy, Michael (1979b) 'The Politics of Production and the Production of Politics: A Comparative Analysis of Piecework Machine Shops in the United States and Hungary', *Political Power and Social Theory* 1:261–99.

Burawoy, Michael (1987) *The Politics of Production*. New York: Verso.

Burawoy, Michael (2009) *The Extended Case Method : Four Countries, Four Decades, Four Great Transformations, and One Theoretical Tradition*. Berkeley: University of California Press.

Campbell, John L., J. Rogers Hollingsworth and Leon N. Lindberg (1991) *Governance of the American Economy*, vol. 5. Cambridge: Cambridge University Press.

Carrè, Françoise, Patricia Findlay, Chris Tilly and Chris Warhurst (2012) 'Job Quality: Scenarios, Analysis and Interventions', pp. 1–22 in *Are Bad Jobs Inevitable? Trends, Determinants and Responses to Job Quality in the Twenty-First Century*, edited by C. Warhurst, F. Carrè, P. Findlay and C. Tilly. Basingstoke: Palgrave Macmillan.

Coates, David (2005) 'Conclusion: Choosing Between Paradigms – A Personal View', pp. 265–71 in *Varieties of Capitalism, Varieties of Approaches*, edited by D. Coates. Basingstoke: Palgrave Macmillan.

Cockburn, Cynthia (1983) *Brothers: Male Dominance and Technological Change*. London: Pluto.

Crouch, Colin (2005) *Capitalist Diversity and Change: Recombinant Governance and Institutional Entrepreneurs*. Oxford: Oxford University Press.

Crowley, Martha, Daniel Tope, Lindsey Joyce Chamberlain and Randy Hodson (2010) 'Neo-Taylorism at Work: Occupational Change in the Post-Fordist Era', *Social Problems* 57:421–47.

Dahrendorf, R. (1959) *Class and Class Conflict in Industrial Society*. Stanford University Press.

Deeg, Richard and Gregory Jackson (2007) 'Towards a More Dynamic Theory of Capitalist Variety', *Socio-Economic Review* 5:149–79.

Delbridge, Rick (1998) *Life on the Line in Contemporary Manufacturing: The Workplace Experience of Lean Production and the 'Japanese' Model*. Oxford: Oxford University Press.

Delbridge, Rick, Marco Hauptmeier and Sukanya Sengupta (2011) 'Beyond the Enterprise: Broadening the Horizons of International HRM', *Human Relations* 64:483–505.

Doellgast, Virginia (2012) *Disintegrating Democracy at Work: Labor Unions and the Future of Good Jobs in the Service Economy*. Ithaca, NY: ILR Press.

Dohse, Knuth, Ulrich Jürgens and Thomas Malsch (1985) 'From "Fordism" to "Toyotism"? The Social Organization of the Labor Process in the Japanese Automobile Industry', *Politics and Society* 14:115–45.

Dore, Ronald (1973) *British Factory – Japanese Factory: The Origins of National Diversity in Industrial Relations*. Berkeley: University of California Press.

Edwards, P.K. (1990) 'Understanding Conflict in the Labour Process: The Logic and Autonomy of Struggle', pp. 125–51 in *Labour Process Theory*, edited by D. Knights and H. Willmott. London: Macmillan.

Edwards, Paul K. and Hugh Scullion (1982) *The Social Organization of Industrial Conflict: Control and Resistance in the Workplace*. Oxford: Blackwell.

Edwards, R. (1979) *Contested Terrain: The Transformation of the Workplace in the Twentieth Century*. London: Heinemann.

Elger, Tony (1979) 'Valorization and 'Deskilling': A Critique of Braverman', *Capital & Class* 3:58–99.

Elger, Tony and Chris Smith (eds) (1994a) *Global Japanization? The Transformation of the Labour Process*. London: Routledge.

Elger, Tony and Chris Smith (1994b) 'Introduction', pp. 1–24 in *Global Japanization? The Transnational Transformation of the Labour Process*, edited by T. Elger and C. Smith. London: Routledge.

Emmenegger, Patrick, Silja Häusermann, Bruno Palier and Martin Seeleib-Kaiser (2012) *The Age of Dualization: The Changing Face of Inequality in Deindustrializing Societies*. Oxford: Oxford University Press.

Esping-Andersen, Gøsta (1990) *The Three Worlds of Welfare Capitalism*. Princeton, NJ: Princeton University Press.

Flecker, Jörg, Bettina Haidinger and Annika Schönauer (2013) 'Divide and Serve: The Labour Process in Service Value Chains and Networks', *Competition & Change* 17:6–23.

Fleming, Peter and A.J. Sturdy (2009) 'Just Be Yourself!: Towards Neo-Normative Control in Organisations', *Employee Relations* 31:569–83.

▶

Friedman, Andrew L. (1977) *Industry and Labour: Class Struggle at Work and Monopoly Capitalism*. London: Macmillan.

Friedman, Andrew L. (1987) 'The Means of Management Control and Labour Process Theory: A Critical Note on Storey', *Sociology* 21:287–94.

Fuller, *Linda* and Vicki Smith (1991) 'Consumers' Reports: Management by Customers in a Changing Economy', *Work, Employment & Society* 5:1–16.

Garrett, Geoffrey (1998) *Partisan Politics in the Global Economy*. Cambridge: Cambridge University Press.

Gordon, David M., Richard Edwards and Michael Reich (1982) *Segmented Work, Divided Workers: The Historical Transformation of Labor in the United States*. Cambridge: Cambridge University Press.

Gordon, David M., Thomas E. Weisskopf and Samuel Bowles (1987) 'Power, Accumulation, and Crisis: The Rise and Demise of the Postwar Social Structure of Accumulation', in *The Imperiled Economy*, edited by R. Cherry *et al.* New York: URPE.

Graham, Laurie (1995) *On the Line at Subaru-Isuzu: The Japanese Model and the American Worker*. Ithaca, NY: Cornell University Press.

Greer, Ian and Marco Hauptmeier (2008) 'Political Entrepreneurs and Co-Managers: Labour Transnationalism at Four Multinational Auto Companies', *British Journal of Industrial Relations* 46:76–97.

Greer, Ian and Marco Hauptmeier (2012) 'Identity Work: Sustaining Transnational Worker Cooperation at GM Europe', *Industrial Relations* (Berkeley) 51:275–97.

Hall, Peter A. and David Soskice (2001) 'An Introduction to Varieties of Capitalism', pp. 1–68 in *Varieties of Capitalism: The Institutional Foundations of Comparative Advantage*, edited by P.A. Hall and D. Soskice. Oxford: Oxford University Press.

Hall, Peter A. and Rosemary C.R. Taylor. (1996) 'Political Science and the Three New Institutionalisms', *Political Studies* 44:936–57.

Hamann, K. and J. Kelly (2007) 'Party Politics and the Reemergence of Social Pacts in Western Europe', *Comparative Political Studies* 40:971–94.

Hancké, Bob and Steven Casper (2000) 'Reproducing Diversity: ISO 9000 and Work Organization in the French and German Car Industry', pp. 173–88 in *National Capitalisms, Global Competition, and Economic Performance*, edited by S. Quack, G. Morgan and R. Whitley. Amsterdam: John Benjamins.

Hancké, Bob, Martin Rhodes and Mark Thatcher (2007) *Beyond Varieties of Capitalism: Conflict, Contradictions, and Complementarities in the European Economy*. Oxford: Oxford University Press.

Hassel, Anke (2012) 'The Paradox of Liberalization – Understanding Dualism and the Recovery of the German Political Economy', *British Journal of Industrial Relations*, first published online 20.09.2012.

Hauptmeier, Marco (2012) 'Institutions Are What Actors Make of Them: The Changing Construction of Firm Level Employment Relations in Spain', *British Journal of Industrial Relations* 50:737–59.

Hauptmeier, Marco and Edmund Heery (2014 forthcoming) 'Ideas at Work', *International Journal of Human Resource Management*.

Hay, Colin (2006) 'Constructivist Institutionalism', pp. 56–74 in *The Oxford Handbook of Political Institutions*, edited by R.A.W. Rhodes, S.A. Binder and B.A. Rockman. Oxford: Oxford University Press.

▶

Herrigel, Gary (2000) *Industrial Constructions: The Sources of German Industrial Power.* Cambridge: Cambridge University Press.

Herrigel, Gary (2010) *Manufacturing Possibilities: Creative Action and Industrial Recomposition in the United States, Germany, and Japan.* Oxford: Oxford University Press.

Heyes, Jason, Paul Lewis and Ian Clark (2012) 'Varieties of Capitalism, Neoliberalism and the Economic Crisis of 2008–?', *Industrial Relations Journal* 43:222–41.

Hochschild, Arlie (1983) *The Managed Heart: Commercialization of Human Feeling.* Berkeley: University of California Press.

Hodson, Randy (1991a) 'The Active Worker: Compliance and Autonomy at the Workplace', *Journal of Contemporary Ethnography* 20:47–78.

Hodson, Randy (1991b) 'Workplace Behaviors: Good Soldiers, Smooth Operators, and Saboteurs', *Work and Occupations* 18:271–90.

Hollingsworth, J. Rogers and Robert Boyer (1997) 'Coordination of Economic Actors and Social Systems of Production', pp. 1–47 in *Contemporary Capitalism: The Embeddedness of Institutions*, edited by J.R. Hollingsworth and R. Boyer. Cambridge: Cambridge University Press.

Hollingsworth, J. Rogers, Philippe C. Schmitter and Wolfgang Streeck (1994) *Governing Capitalist Economies: Performance and Control of Economic Sectors.* Oxford: Oxford University Press.

Iankova, Elena A. (2002) *Eastern European Capitalism in the Making.* Cambridge: Cambridge University Press.

Jackson, Gregory (2010) 'Actors and Institutions', pp. 63–86 in *The Oxford Handbook of Comparative Institutional Analysis*, edited by G. Morgan *et al.* Oxford: Oxford University Press.

Jürgens, Ulrich, Thomas Malsch and Knuth Dohse (1993) *Breaking from Taylorism: Changing Forms of Work in the Automobile Industry.* Cambridge: Cambridge University Press.

Katz, Harry Charles and Owen Darbishire (2000) *Converging Divergences : Worldwide Changes in Employment Systems.* Ithaca, NY: Cornell University Press.

Katzenstein, Peter J. (1985) *Small States in World Markets: Industrial Policy in Europe.* Ithaca, NY: Cornell University Press.

Kelly, John (1985) 'Management's Redesign of Work: Labour Process, Labour Markets and Product Markets', pp. 30–51 in *Job Redesign: Critical Perspectives on the Labour Process*, edited by D. Knights, H. Willmott and D. Collinson. London: Gower.

Kenney, Martin and Richard Florida (1988) 'Beyond Mass Production: Production and the Labor Process in Japan', *Politics & Society* 16:121–58.

Kenney, Martin and Richard Florida (1993) *Beyond Mass Production: The Japanese System and Its Transfer to the US.* Oxford: Oxford University Press.

Knights, David (1990) 'Subjectivity, Power and the Labour Process', pp. 297–335 in *Labour Process Theory*, edited by D. Knights and H. Willmott. London: Macmillan.

Knights, David and Hugh Willmott (1990) *Labour Process Theory.* London: Macmillan.

Korczynski, Marek (2009) 'Understanding the Contradictory Lived Experience of Service Work: The Customer-Oriented Bureaucracy', pp. 73–90 in *Service Work:*

Critical Perspectives, edited by M. Korczynski and C.L. Macdonald. London: Routledge.

Korczynski, Marek, Karen Shire, Stephen Frenkel and May Tam (2000) 'Service Work in Consumer Capitalism: Customers, Control and Contradictions', *Work, Employment & Society* 14:669–87.

Korpi, Walter (1983) *The Democratic Class Struggle*: Routledge & Kegan Paul London.

Kotz, David M., Terrence McDonough and Michael Reich (1994) *Social Structures of Accumulation: The Political Economy of Growth and Crisis*. Cambridge: Cambridge University Press.

Leidner, Robin (1993) *Fast Food, Fast Talk: Service Work and the Routinization of Everyday Life*. Berkeley, CA: University of California Press.

Littler, Craig R. (1982) *The Development of the Labour Process in Capitalist Societies*. London: Heinemann.

Locke, Richard M. (1992) 'The Demise of the National Union in Italy: Lessons for Comparative Industrial Relations Theory', *Industrial and Labor Relations Review* 45:229–49.

Lopez, Steven H. (1996) 'The Politics of Service Production: Route Sales Work in the Potato-Chip Industry', pp. 50–73 in *Working in the Service Society*, edited by C.L. Macdonald and C. Sirianni. Philadelphia, PA: Temple University Press.

Lopez, Steven Henry (2010) 'Workers, Managers, and Customers: Triangles of Power in Work Communities', *Work and Occupations* 37:251–71.

Macdonald, Cameron Lynne and Carmen Sirianni (1996) 'The Service Society and the Changing Experience of Work', pp. 1–26 in *Working in the Service Society*, edited by C.L. Macdonald and C. Sirianni. Philadelphia, PA: Temple University Press.

Mahoney, James and Kathleen Ann Thelen (2010) *Explaining Institutional Change: Ambiguity, Agency, and Power*. Cambridge: Cambridge University Press.

Marx, Karl ([1867] 1990). *Capital, Vol. 1*, tr. B. Fowkes. Harmondsworth: Penguin.

Maurice, Marc, Arndt Sorge and Malcolm Warner (1980) 'Societal Differences in Organizing Manufacturing Units: A Comparison of France, West Germany, and Great Britain', *Organization Studies* 1:59–86.

Maurice, Marc, François Sellier and Jean-Jacques Silvestre (1986) *The Social Foundations of Industrial Power: A Comparison of France and Germany*. Cambridge, MA: MIT Press.

McKay, Steven C. (2006) *Satanic Mills or Silicon Islands? The Politics of High-Tech Production in the Philippines*. Ithaca, NY: ILR Press.

Meiksins, Peter and Chris Smith (1996) *Engineering Labour: Technical Workers in Comparative Perspective*. London: Verso.

Milkman, Ruth (1997) *Farewell to the Factory: Auto Workers in the Late Twentieth Century*. Berkeley, CA: University of California Press.

Morgan, Glenn (2007) 'The Theory of Comparative Capitalisms and the Possibilities for Local Variation', *European Review* 15:353–71.

Morgan, Glenn, and Marco Hauptmeier (2014) 'Varieties of Institutional Theory in Comparative Employment Relations', in *The Oxford Handbook in Comparative Employment Relations*, edited by A. Wilkinson, G. Wood and R. Deeg. Oxford: Oxford University Press.

Morgan, Glenn and Richard Whitley (2012) *Capitalisms and Capitalism in the Twenty-First Century*. Oxford: Oxford University Press.

Morgan, Glenn, John Campbell, Colin Crouch, Ove Kaj Pedersen and Richard Whitley (eds) (2010) *The Oxford Handbook of Comparative Institutional Analysis.* Oxford: Oxford University Press.

Nichols, Theo (ed.) (1980) *Capital and Labour: Studies in the Capitalist Labour Process.* Glasgow: Fontana.

Nichols, Theo and Peter Armstrong. 1976. *Workers Divided: A Study in Shopfloor Politics.* Glasgow: Fontana.

Nichols, Theo, Nadir Sugur and Erol Demir (2002) 'Globalised Management and Local Labour: The Case of the White-Goods Industry in Turkey', *Industrial Relations Journal* 33:68–85.

Nichols, Theo *et al.* (2004) 'Factory Regimes and the Dismantling of Established Labour in Asia: A Review of Cases from Large Manufacturing Plants in China, South Korea and Taiwan', *Work, Employment & Society* 18:663–85.

Palier, Bruno and Kathleen Thelen (2010) 'Institutionalizing Dualism: Complementarities and Change in France and Germany', *Politics & Society* 38:119–48.

Peck, Jamie and Nik Theodore (2007) 'Variegated Capitalism', *Progress in Human Geography* 31:731–72.

Pollert, Anna (1988) 'Dismantling Flexibility', *Capital & Class* 34:42–75.

Pontusson, Jonas (2005) 'Varieties and Commonalities of Capitalism', pp. 163–88 in *Varieties of Capitalism, Varieties of Approaches*, edited by D. Coates. Basingstoke: Palgrave Macmillan.

Scharpf, Fritz Wilhelm (1991) *Crisis and Choice in European Social Democracy.* Ithaca, NY: Cornell University Press.

Schmitter, Philippe C. (1974) 'Still the Century of Corporatism?', *The Review of Politics* 36:85–131.

Schneiberg, Marc (2007) 'What's On the Path? Path Dependence, Organizational Diversity and the Problem of Institutional Change in the US Economy, 1900–1950', *Socio-Economic Review* 5:47–80.

Schneider, Ben (2013) *Hierarchical Capitalism in Latin America. Business, Labor, and the Challenges of Equitable Development.* Cambridge: Cambridge University Press.

Smith, Chris and Peter Meiksins (1995) 'System, Society and Dominance Effects in Cross-National Organizational Analysis', *Work, Employment & Society* 9:241–67.

Smith, Chris, David Knights and Hugh Willmott (1991) *White-Collar Work: The Non-Manual Labour Process.* London: Macmillan.

Smith, Vicki (1997) 'New Forms of Work Organization', *Annual Review of Sociology* 23:315–39.

Smith, Vicki (2001) *Crossing the Great Divide: Worker Risk and Opportunity in the New Economy.* Ithaca, NY: Cornell University Press.

Spencer, David A. (2000) 'Braverman and the Contribution of Labour Process Analysis to the Critique of Capitalist Production – Twenty-Five Years On', *Work, Employment & Society* 14:223–43.

Steinmo, Sven, Kathleen Ann Thelen and Frank Longstreth (1992) *Structuring Politics: Historical Institutionalism in Comparative Analysis.* Cambridge: Cambridge University Press.

Storey, John (1985) 'The Means of Management Control', *Sociology* 19:193–211.

Streeck, Wolfgang (1984) *Industrial Relations in West Germany: A Case Study of the Car Industry*. New York: St Martin's Press.

Streeck, Wolfgang (1992) *Social Institutions and Economic Performance: Studies of Industrial Relations in Advanced Capitalist Economies*. London: Sage.

Streeck, Wolfgang (1996) 'Lean Production in the German Automobile Industry: A Test Case for Convergence Theory', pp. 138–70 in *National Diversity and Global Capitalism*, edited by S. Berger and R. Dore. Ithaca, NY: Cornell University Press.

Streeck, Wolfgang (1997) 'Beneficial Constraints: On the Economic Limits of Rational Voluntarism', pp. 197–219 in *Contemporary Capitalism: The Embeddedness of Institutions*, edited by J.R. Hollingsworth and R. Boyer. Cambridge: Cambridge University Press.

Streeck, Wolfgang (2009) *Re-Forming Capitalism: Institutional Change in the German Political Economy*. Oxford: Oxford University Press.

Streeck, Wolfgang and Kathleen Thelen (2005) *Beyond Continuity: Institutional Change in Advanced Political Economies*. Oxford: Oxford University Press.

Sturdy, Andrew (2001) 'Servicing Societies? Colonisation, Control, Contradiction and Contestation', pp. 1–17 in *Customer Service: Empowerment and Entrapment*, edited by A. Sturdy, I. Grugulis and H. Willmott. Basingstoke: Palgrave Macmillan.

Taylor, Phil (2010) 'The Globalization of Service Work: Analysing the Transnational Call Centre Value Chain', in *Working Life: Renewing Labour Process Analysis*, edited by P. Thompson and C. Smith. Basingstoke: Palgrave Macmillan.

Taylor, Phil and Peter Bain (1999) '"An Assembly Line in the Head": Work and Employee Relations in the Call Centre', *Industrial Relations Journal* 30:101–17.

Tetsuro, Kato and Rob Steven (1993) 'Is Japanese Capitalism Post-Fordist?', pp. 69–100 in *Is Japanese Management Post-Fordist?*, edited by K. Tetsuro and R. Steven. Tokyo: Mado-sha.

Thelen, Kathleen (1999) 'Historical Institutionalism in Comparative Politics', *Annual Review of Political Science* 2:369–404.

Thelen, Kathleen Ann (1991) *Union of Parts: Labor Politics in Postwar Germany*. Ithaca, NY: Cornell University Press.

Thompson, Paul (1983) *The Nature of Work: An Introduction to Debates on the Labour Process*. London: Macmillan.

Thompson, Paul (1990) 'Crawling from the Wreckage: The Labour Process and the Politics of Production', pp. 95–124 in *Labour Process Theory*, edited by D. Knights and H. Willmott. London: Macmillan.

Thompson, Paul (2003) 'Disconnected Capitalism: Or Why Employers Can't Keep Their Side of the Bargain', *Work, Employment & Society* 17:359–78.

Thompson, Paul (2013) 'Financialization and the Workplace: Extending and Applying the Disconnected Capitalism Thesis', *Work, Employment & Society* 27:472–88.

Thompson, Paul and Kirsty Newsome (2004) 'Labor Process Theory, Work, and the Employment Relation', pp. 133–62 in *Theoretical Perspectives on Work and the Employment Relationship*, edited by B.E. Kaufman. Champaign, IL: Industrial Relations Research Association.

Thompson, Paul and Chris Smith (1998) 'Beyond the Capitalist Labor Process Workplace Change, the State and Globalisation'', *Critical Sociology* 24:193–215.

▶

Thompson, Paul and Steve Vincent (2010) 'Labour Process Theory and Critical Realism', pp. 47–69 in *Working Life: Renewing Labour Process Analysis*, edited by P. Thompson and C. Smith. Basingstoke: Palgrave Macmillan.

Turner, Lowell (1991) *Democracy at Work: Changing World Markets and the Future of Labor Unions*. Ithaca, NY: Cornell University Press.

Vallas, Steven P (2003) 'Why Teamwork Fails: Obstacles to Workplace Change in Four Manufacturing Plants', *American Sociological Review* 68:223–50.

Vallas, Steven Peter (2006) 'Empowerment Redux: Structure, Agency, and the Remaking of Managerial Authority', *American Journal of Sociology* 111:1677–717.

Vidal, Matt (2007a) 'Lean Production, Worker Empowerment, and Job Satisfaction: A Qualitative Analysis and Critique', *Critical Sociology* 33:247–78.

Vidal, Matt (2007b) 'Manufacturing Empowerment? "Employee Involvement" in the Labour Process After Fordism', *Socio-Economic Review* 5:197–232.

Vidal, Matt (2011) 'Reworking Postfordism: Labor Process Versus Employment Relations', *Sociology Compass* 5:273–86.

Vidal, Matt (2013a) 'Low-Autonomy Work and Bad Jobs in Postfordist Capitalism', *Human Relations* 66:587–612.

Vidal, Matt (2013b) 'Postfordism as a Dysfunctional Accumulation Regime: A Comparative Analysis of the USA, the UK and Germany', *Work, Employment and Society* 27:451–71.

Vidal, Matt and Jamie Peck (2012) 'Sociological Institutionalism and the Socially Constructed Economy', pp. 594–611 in *The Wiley-Blackwell Companion to Economic Geography*, edited by T. Barnes, J. Peck and E. Sheppard. Oxford: Wiley-Blackwell.

Warhurst, Chris and Paul Thompson (1998) 'Hands, Hearts and Minds: Changing Work and Workers at the End of the Century', pp. 1–24 in *Workplaces of the Future*, edited by P. Thompson and C. Warhurst. London: Macmillan.

Warhurst, Chris, Dennis Nickson, Anne Witz and Anne Marie Cullen (2000) 'Aesthetic Labour in Interactive Service Work: Some Case Study Evidence from the "New" Glasgow', *The Service Industries Journal* 20:1–18.

Warhurst, Chris, Françoise Carré, Patricia Findlay and Chris Tilly (2012) *Are Bad Jobs Inevitable? Trends, Determinants and Responses to Job Quality in the Twenty-First Century*. Basingstoke: Palgrave Macmillan.

Western, Bruce (1997) *Between Class and Market: Postwar Unionization in the Capitalist Democracies*. Princeton, NJ: Princeton University Press.

Whitford, Josh (2005) *The New Old Economy: Networks, Institutions, and the Organizational Transformation of American Manufacturing*. Oxford: Oxford University Press.

Whitley, Richard (1999) *Divergent Capitalisms: The Social Structuring and Change of Business Systems*. Oxford: Oxford University Press.

Williams, Christine L. and Catherine Connell (2010) '"Looking Good and Sounding Right": Aesthetic Labor and Social Inequality in the Retail Industry', *Work and Occupations* 37:349–77.

Willmott, Hugh (1990) 'Subjectivity and the Dialectics of Praxis: Opening up the Core of Labour Process Analysis', pp. 336–78 in *Labour Process Theory*, edited by D. Knights and H. Willmott. London: Macmillan.

▶

Witt, Michael A. and Gordon Redding (2013) 'Asian Business Systems: Institutional Comparison, Clusters and Implications for Varieties of Capitalism and Business Systems Theory', *Socio-Economic Review* 11:265–300.

Wood, Geoffrey T. and Christel Lane (2012) 'Institutions, Change and Diversity', pp. 1–31 in *Capitalist Diversity and Diversity Within Capitalism*, edited by C. Lane and G.T. Wood. London: Routledge.

Wood, Stephen (1993) 'The Japanization of Fordism', *Economic and Industrial Democracy* 14:535–55.

Zimbalist, Andrew (ed.) (1979) *Case Studies on the Labor Process.* New York: Monthly Review Press.

Systemic Problems of Advanced Capitalism

Varieties of Capitalism Reconsidered: Learning from the Great Recession and Its Aftermath

Jason Heyes, Paul Lewis and Ian Clark

The word 'crisis' has been widely used to describe the circumstances experienced by developed economies in the wake of the collapse of Lehman Brothers in 2008. The *Oxford English Dictionary* provides three definitions of a crisis. A crisis may be a 'time of intense difficulty or danger'; a 'time when a difficult or important decision must be made'; or the 'turning point of a disease when an important change takes place, indicating either recovery or death'. All of these definitions have relevance for the post-2008 economic crisis. It has clearly been a situation of great difficulty and danger: while economic meltdown was avoided, economies experienced substantial reductions in GDP and employment and at the time of writing (almost five years after the initial shock) there are only tentative signs of an economic recovery. Important decisions have had to be made, for example the decision of governments to shore up their economies in the early stage of the crisis by taking some banks into public ownership and injecting massive fiscal stimuli. The ballooning public debts resulting from state action to prevent economic collapse have led governments to implement severe austerity measures, which have been met with public protest and industrial action. Other important decisions have been postponed or avoided, most notably in relation to the continuing instability in the Eurozone.

Whether the crisis represents a turning point is more difficult to judge. Commentators initially spoke of the exhaustion of neoliberalism, the discrediting of the approach to macroeconomic management that had dominated the previous three decades and the rehabilitation of Keynesianism. However, while efforts by the state to use fiscal and monetary policy to stimulate demand in the early stages of the crisis may have had a Keynesian hue, the subsequent turn to demand-sapping austerity measures indicated that the Keynesian moment had passed. Despite widespread condemnation of the investment practices of parts of the financial sector, awareness of the role of governments in creating a context in which such practices could thrive, and public policy debate relating to the future of the financial services sector, little has been done to create a stricter regulatory environment for finance.

Developments since 2008 have also represented a crisis for the social sciences and for the economics profession in particular. Intellectually committed to a belief in the intrinsic efficiency of financial markets, mainstream economists failed to spot the potential for a financial crisis.[1] Moreover, it was widely assumed that macroeconomic policies founded on the assumptions of New Classical economics had tamed the business cycle and delivered a 'Great Moderation'[2] or, in the words of Gordon Brown, the UK chancellor of the exchequer (finance minister) from 1997 until 2008, an end to 'boom and bust'. An emphasis on economic stability and neglect of underlying tensions was not only to be found in the economics mainstream. The comparative economic analyses offered by political economists during the period of the Great Moderation also focused on sources of stability in developed economies, highlighting the apparent robustness of different institutional arrangements and their consequences for the operation of national economies, while underemphasizing social relations, economic processes and pressures for change. The 'varieties-of-capitalism' analytical framework propounded by Hall and Soskice (2001) proved particularly influential and its organizing concepts have been taken up by researchers working in various social science fields, including employment relations and social policy. Studies conducted by researchers in the varieties-of-capitalism tradition have produced valuable insights and a considerable amount has been learned about the role that institutions play in shaping economic activities and outcomes. In this chapter, however, we argue that a preoccupation with institutions, and an associated neglect of social agency and the dynamics of the capitalist mode of production, have left the varieties-of-capitalism framework of analysis conceptually and theoretically ill-equipped to provide insights into the causes and consequences of the post-2008 crisis and the dynamics of change within and across economies. In particular, the varieties-of-capitalism framework has little analytical purchase on the growth of the finance sector as a distinctive fraction of capital, the role of the state in promoting specific accumulation paths and shifts in capital–labour relations, all of which have influenced the causes and specific characteristics of the crisis. We further argue that the varieties-of-capitalism framework provides an inadequate guide for understanding responses of national governments to the crisis and the implications for workers. In the spirit of not wasting a serious crisis,[3] we spell out the implications and suggest ways forward.

The first section below examines competing explanations of the causes of the crisis. The second examines responses to the crisis. We argue that the current search for a new basis for accumulation is resulting in the articulation and implementation of reforms designed to weaken the position of labour and that this tendency is observable in countries associated with different varieties of capitalism. While the content of policies and degree of change differ in important respects, employment and social protections are being eroded in both 'coordinated market economies' and 'liberal market economies' (to use Hall and Soskice's terms) as governments drive through reforms to deliver austerity and attempt to restart growth. In the third section we demonstrate that the tendency towards a weakening of labour's position was evident in both coordinated market and liberal market economies long before the crisis erupted. This tendency cannot be easily explained via the varieties-of-capitalism framework of analysis, which predicts that governments, employers and trade unions in coordinated economies have an incentive to preserve employment and social protections because of the competitive advantages they supposedly provide. In the conclusion, we argue that comparative political economy needs to move beyond a preoccupation with static institutions and pay greater attention to the dynamics of capitalism, class relations and the capitalist state within and across national boundaries.

From Moderation to Mayhem

The role of institutions in promoting or impeding economic growth has become a major area of enquiry for social science. The breakup of the Soviet Union, relative quiescence of labour and general crisis of confidence of the political left have discouraged interest in non-capitalist approaches to economic organization. The focus of attention over the past two decades has instead been on alternative ways of organizing capitalism through markets, hierarchies and networks and the implications of different approaches for the functioning and competitiveness of capitalist economies. The varieties-of-capitalism approach to comparative institutional analysis has become particularly influential in this regard. Hall and Soskice sought to distinguish differences in the way firms attempt to resolve 'coordination problems' in the spheres of industrial relations, vocational training, corporate governance, inter-firm relations, and the day-to-day management of the employment relationship. They distinguished between 'liberal market economies' in which coordination is achieved through formal contracting and market-mediated exchanges, and 'coordinated market economies' in which economic activity is coordinated through complementary institutions and networks that facilitate access to information, skills and other resources. According to Hall and Soskice (2001:57), the increased mobility of capital facilitated by international liberalization has enhanced the ability of firms in liberal market economies to pressure governments to deregulate markets and weaken trade unions. Weaker regulation is assumed to be of benefit 'since firms that coordinate their endeavours primarily through the market can improve their competencies by sharpening its edges' (ibid.). In coordinated market economies (such as Germany, Austria and the economies of Scandinavia), by contrast, 'governments should be less sympathetic to deregulation because it threatens the nation's comparative institutional advantages' (Hall and Soskice 2001:58). Hall and Soskice also argued that, since both employers and workers derive advantages from strong institutions, they are likely to take a common position in defence of regulation, preferring institutional reform to deregulation and liberalization. The implication is that rights and entitlements in respect of welfare provision and employment are likely to be maintained.

Several attempts have been made to extend and refine the varieties-of-capitalism typology. Amable (2003) substituted 'continental' (for example Germany) and 'social-democratic' (for example Denmark) models of capitalism for Hall and Soskice's coordinated market economy category, while also suggesting 'Asiatic' (for example Japan) and 'Mediterranean' (Spain Portugal, Greece and Italy) models. King (2007) has sought to incorporate the economies of Central and Eastern Europe into the varieties-of-capitalism framework, referring to them as 'liberal-dependent' economies, which resemble the liberal market economy type while typically having a greater reliance on foreign capital. The varieties-of-capitalism framework has thus offered researchers a variety of analytical categories with which to order their comparative data, theoretical tools with which to explain persistent national differences in the character and consequences of institutions, and a means of incorporating economic phenomena within their analyses (without having to engage with economics as an academic discipline). However, the varieties-of-capitalism framework has also met much criticism. Hall and Soskice have been accused of providing a static and functionalist analysis that neglects issues of power and conflict (Coates 2005; Streeck and Thelen 2005) and that is unable to move beyond the coordinated–liberal market economy bifurcation (Hay 2005). Their account has also been criticized for having a manufacturing bias (Blyth 2003), for having little to say about the service sector, and for focusing on national systems while neglecting international economic activity, spatial dynamics and uneven development (Peck and Theodore 2007).

Most pertinent for our discussion is the limited ability of the varieties-of-capitalism framework to explain significant departures from established policies and practices. Echoing neoclassical economists, Hall and Soskice's explanation for change in 'national systems' emphasizes the importance of 'external shocks' in technology and tastes, which 'unsettle the equilibria on which economic actors have been coordinating and challenge the existing practices of firms' (Hall and Soskice 2001:62.). In the absence of such external shocks, actors will behave in ways that reflect and serve to reproduce institutional structures. Governments will respond positively to pressures exerted by firms (and trade unions) anxious to maintain established sources of comparative advantage. More recent contributions to the literature have attempted to increase the dynamic content of the varieties-of-capitalism framework. Hancké et al. (2007), for example, have called for a more sophisticated understanding of interests in capitalist societies and greater recognition of the importance of the role of the state, which has typically received only a cursory examination in the varieties-of-capitalism literature. They have also questioned whether the cross-class coalitions that are said to underpin national institutions will crack under new economic pressures, such as increased competition from low-wage economies (Hancké et al. 2007:28–9). In keeping with Hall and Soskice, however, all sources of change are treated as exogenous. While some recent and influential theories of institutional evolution have sought to endogenize change by treating it as a constant feature of any economy (Mahoney and Thelen 2010), these accounts have retained an emphasis on the 'complementarity' of institutions and varietal stability in their attempts to demonstrate that inherited institutions are '"fitted" or adapted to new circumstances, new interests, and new power constellations' (Thelen 2005:291; see also Hall and Thelen 2009:255). National varieties and the interests of their key actors, primarily national producers and their employees, are analysed in relation to the reproduction of comparative advantages in production. Analyses have tended to neglect the underlying dynamics (and tensions) within capitalism that are common to all capitalist economies and have also failed to incorporate adequately the actions and interests of transnational financial capital and the state. The latter, as Appelbaum et al. (2013) argue, tend to be reduced to a political technology that manages different types of business systems. This approach fails to accommodate the emergence of new, globally focused financial intermediaries which are not necessarily embedded in, or constrained by, national business systems.

These theoretical omissions within mainstream economics and the varieties-of-capitalism approach help to explain why the growing sources of instability that ultimately produced the current economic crisis were missed. Advocates of the varieties-of-capitalism framework, alongside advocates of neoclassical approaches, externalized sources of tension and transformation from their models, but the conditions that led to the crisis were created by processes that were occurring within and across capitalist economies. Of particular importance were the progressive weakening of the position of labour (Nolan 2011) and the developing importance of finance capital to the process of capital accumulation. These developments were in large part a consequence of state action to resolve the crisis conditions of the 1970s. Governments of developed Western economies converged on a set of measures intended to restore conditions for healthy capital accumulation. The measures, commonly referred to collectively as 'neoliberalism', took the form of state policies designed to weaken the position of labour and deliver a decisive shift in the balance of social forces in favour of the capitalist class. Our interpretation of neoliberalism is in line with that of Harvey (2010:10) and Gamble (2009:78), who highlight states' deliberate strengthening of capitalist power and the privileging of finance over production. Understanding neoliberalism, and by extension the post-2008 crisis, therefore necessitates that attention be paid to the relationship between capital, labour and the state on the one hand, and to particular fractions of capital on the other.

'Financialization' and National Accumulation Strategies

The varieties-of-capitalism analytical approach has focused on the role of institutions in supporting distinct corporate strategies, with an implicit focus on different types of productive activity operating within relatively closed national economies. Two important and interlinked developments have been neglected as a consequence: the rise of finance as a distinctive, 'footloose' fraction of capital, and an increase in the importance of finance to the growth strategies of leading economies.

While 'financialization' has, like globalization, become a popular but largely obfuscating term, the financialization literature has nonetheless highlighted three important processes (Blackburn 2006; Callinicos 2010). First has been the growing importance of financial institutions, as measured by their size and profitability. In the US, financial sector debt rose from 22 per cent of GDP in 1981 to 117 per cent in late 2008 while the share of corporate profits increased from 10 per cent in the early 1980s to 40 per cent in 2006 (Crotty 2009:576). Feeding the beast of finance requires a base of traditional loans and credit from which more esoteric products may be derived. The result has been a second key process of financialization, which is the progressive encroachment of finance into everyday life (for example through increased mortgage lending and the provision of consumer credit). This has also increased the importance of financial transactions to the profitability of non-financial firms (Froud *et al.* 2006; O'Sullivan, 2000:192–3). These two processes are manifestations of what has been termed profit financialization (Nölke and Perry, 2007; Deeg, 2010). A third important process is that of control financialization (ibid.), whereby the maximization of shareholder value becomes the dominant influence on the corporate governance of listed companies.

The importance of finance capital to national growth trajectories has varied between countries. One group of countries, including the US, UK, Spain and Ireland, have developed strategies of accumulation that have attached great importance to finance capital. These we term finance-led growth strategies. The UK provides an instructive example. UK governments after 1979 allowed one of the most rapid deindustrializations of any Western economy while simultaneously strengthening the institutional foundation for finance-led accumulation. The withdrawal of state support from industry and severe monetary contraction in the early 1980s, and the inability of employer and trade union organizations to act as forces for modernization, exacerbated pre-existing structural weaknesses in the UK's manufacturing base, reinforcing a vicious circle of low wages, low investment and low productivity (Nolan 1989). By contrast, a coalition composed of Anglo-American institutional investors and senior figures within the Bank of England and the government was able to push successfully for the removal of controls on capital and a minimalist approach to regulation (Macartney 2011:32).

In other leading economies finance has played a lesser role. Countries such as Germany, Japan and China have pursued a second growth strategy, which we label export-led growth. It relies on competitiveness in international markets, primarily in goods, but increasingly in tradable services, and is characterized by countries running sustained large current account surpluses which are recycled into trading partners and accounted for as corresponding capital account deficits. Both export-led and finance-led growth strategies have, however, proved to be unstable. The UK, and other countries that pursued finance-led growth, became overly dependent upon their financial services sectors for tax revenues, balance of payments contributions and high remuneration employment in global hubs such as

London and New York. They also came to depend on finance to create demand in the economy through the provision of consumer credit, which gave rise to inflated asset prices that in turn enabled credit to be extended yet further. As a consequence, ratios of household debt to gross disposable income in these countries have become the highest among all developed countries (IMF 2008:18). Export-led growth has been associated with a different set of problems. Fundamentally, if consumer spending and domestic investment by government and companies, which generate imports, cannot keep up with the surplus generated by exports, the difference has to be recycled to the rest of the world through the purchase of foreign real and financial assets. The consequence has been global economic imbalances, of which the persistent current account deficit of the US, which is mirrored (and made possible) by the persistent current account surplus of China, is the most obvious example. A further example is provided by Germany, which has been able to dominate trade and capital flows within the EU while recycling its current account surpluses through lending to banks and foreign direct investment in other (typically economically weaker) EU member states (Lapavitsas 2012:28–31).

The Weakening of Labour

In both growth strategies we can identify logics that imply a weakening of the position of labour in relation to capital. Finance-led growth and control financialization imply a short-term emphasis on high returns on capital, potentially leading to downward pressure on wages, other terms and conditions, and less secure employment (Froud *et al.* 2006, O'Sullivan, 2000:192–3). The tendency towards control financialization has been exacerbated by the increased involvement of private equity funds in the ownership and management of 'portfolio' firms (Clark 2009, 2011). Export-led growth, by contrast, implies demands for unit cost reductions, which fall on labour directly through calls for more flexible labour markets and indirectly through reductions in non-wage costs such as the taxes that fund welfare state services.

The weakening of labour can be demonstrated by reference to the indicators shown in Table 2.1, which includes information for countries that Hall and Soskice labelled liberal market economies and those they identified as coordinated market economies, as well as Central and Eastern European and Mediterranean economies. Since the 1980s there has been a widespread tendency for labour's share of national income to diminish as productivity increases have outstripped growth in real wages (see also Vidal 2013). The total labour income share in most of the countries listed in the first part (a) of Table 2.1 was lower in 2007 than in 1985. The exceptions included the UK and the US; however, both countries were in the vanguard of neoliberalism and experienced a downward shift in labour income share at an earlier point (the late 1970s in the case of the US, and the early 1980s in the case of the UK). New Zealand and Australia also experienced a downward trend shift in the early 1980s, as did the Netherlands. While the data for Denmark suggest stability, the labour income share from the mid 1990s onwards was consistently lower than it had been during the preceding 20 years. Financial liberalization has contributed to the erosion of labour income shares by strengthening imperatives for firms to suppress growth in wages and salaries so as to increase returns for investors (that is profit financialization). A recent analysis by the ILO (2009:53) concluded that 'for the five most financialized countries, wage share declined by 3.6 per cent over the period 1989 to 2005, while for the five least financialized countries, wage share declined by 2 per cent'.

The decline in labour's share of income is an indication of the progressive weakening of trade unions and collective bargaining in many countries over the past three decades. Density rates have declined in almost all countries, regardless of the 'variety of capitalism' with which they have been associated. Among countries characterized by Hall and Soskice as 'liberal market economies', where collective bargaining is often enterprise-based, union membership losses have coincided with a reduction in the proportion of workers covered by collective bargaining. Falling density has also coincided with reduced coverage in Germany, although in most other coordinated market economies and Mediterranean economies coverage typically remains far more extensive than in liberal market economies. In general, inequality in countries with extensive collective bargaining coverage continues to be less pronounced than in countries with more restricted coverage. However, the degree of inequality in many Mediterranean economies – as measured by the Gini coefficient – is comparable to that found among liberal market economies, despite marked differences in collective bargaining coverage (see Table 2.1(b)). Moreover, the data for a number of coordinated market economies and Mediterranean economies, including Finland, Sweden, Austria and Italy, suggest that high (and in some cases increased) levels of bargaining coverage have not necessarily prevented increases in inequality among wage earners and lower labour income shares. Apparent institutional stability has therefore masked a weakening in the ability of labour to influence distributional outcomes in these countries, particularly given the increasing emphasis that is being placed on company-level pay-setting processes in most coordinated market economies.

Table 2.1(a) Indicators of the position of labour: trade union density, GINI coefficient, total labour income share

	Trade union density*			GINI coefficient**			Total labour income share***		
	1985	1995	2007	Mid-'80s	Mid-'90s	Mid-2000s	1985	1995	2007
Liberal market economies									
UK	44.3	33.1	27.9	0.32	0.35	0.34	0.69	0.69	0.7
USA	17.4	14.3	11.6	0.33	0.35	0.37	0.67	0.68	0.68
Ireland	51.5	45.1	32.4	0.32	0.32	0.32	0.67	0.58	0.53
Canada	35.3	33.7	27.3	0.29	0.29	0.32	0.63	0.65	0.62
Australia	45.9	32.4	18.5	(...)	0.30	0.31	0.67	0.66	0.61
New Zealand	56	27.1	21.5	0.26	0.33	0.33	0.54	0.52	0.53
Mean	41.7	31.0	23.2	0.30	0.32	0.33	0.65	0.63	0.61
Coordinated market economies									
Germany	34.7	29.2	19.9	0.25	0.27	0.30	0.72	0.74	0.68
Austria	45.9	32.4	18.5	0.23	0.23	0.27	0.69	0.68	0.62
Sweden	81.3	83.1	70.8	0.20	0.22	0.24	0.69	0.61	0.62
Japan	28.8	24	18.3	0.30	0.32	0.31	0.59	0.57	0.5
Neths.	28	25.7	19.3	0.26	0.28	0.27	0.67	0.7	0.66
Belgium	52.4	55.7	52.9	(...)	0.28	0.27	0.72	0.69	0.69
Denmark	78.2	77	69.1	0.21	0.21	0.23	0.71	0.68	0.7
Finland	69.1	80.4	70.3	0.20	0.23	0.27	0.68	0.63	0.6
Mean	52.3	50.9	42.4	0.23	0.25	0.27	0.68	0.66	0.63
Mediterranean market economies									
France	13.6	8.9	7.6	0.31	0.28	0.28	0.75	0.72	0.7
Greece	(...)	31.3	24.5	0.33	0.32	0.31	(...)	0.62	0.59
Italy	42.5	38.1	33.5	0.31	0.35	0.35	0.77	0.73	0.71
Spain	10.2	16.3	14.2	0.30	0.28	0.31	0.63	0.66	0.63
Portugal	44.6	25.4	20.8	(...)	0.34	0.38	0.59	0.58	0.58
Mean	27.7	24	20.1	0.31	0.31	0.33	0.68	0.66	0.64
Central and Eastern European economies									
Poland	(...)	45.2	15.2	(...)	(...)	0.38	(...)	0.54	0.47
Czech Rep	(...)	46.3	20.5	(...)	0.25	0.27	(...)	0.56	0.6
Slovakia	(...)	56.1	18.8	(...)	(...)	0.27	(...)	0.47	0.5
Hungary	(...)	49.1	16.9	(...)	0.27	0.30	(...)	0.66	0.61
Mean	(...)	49.2	17.8	(...)	0.26	0.30	(...)	0.56	0.55

Notes
* Trade union density corresponds to the ratio of wage and salary earners who are trade union members, divided by the total number of wage and salary earners: OECD *Labour Force Statistics*.
** Gini coefficient after transfers and taxes, working age population (18–65) only.
*** Figures relate to the business sector, minus agriculture.
Source: OECD statistics.
Where 2007 are unavailable, the 2006 figure is used.

Table 2.1(b) Indicators of the position of labour (continued): collective bargaining coverage, EPL score, gross replacement ratio

	Collective bargaining coverage*			EPL score**			Gross replacement ratio***		
	1985	1995	2007	1985	1995	2007	1985	1995	2007
Liberal market economies									
UK	64.0	36.0	34.6	0.6	0.6	0.75	21	18	15
USA	20.5	16.2	13.3	0.21	0.21	0.21	15	12	14
Ireland	60.2	60.0	44.0	0.93	0.93	1.11	28	26	37
Canada	37.0	36.7	31.5	0.75	0.75	0.75	19	19	12
Australia	85.0	70.0†	40.0	0.94	0.94	1.15	24	27	20
New Zealand	(…)	43.3	17.0	(…)	0.86	1.47	31	27	25
Mean	53.34	43.7	30.0	0.68	0.72	0.91	23	21.5	20.5
Coordinated market economies									
Germany	75.0	70.0	62.8	3.17	3.09	2.12	28	26	24
Austria	95.0	98†	99.0	2.21	2.21	1.93	29	33	32
Sweden	85.0	94.0	91.0	3.49	2.47	1.87	28	27	32
Japan	26.0	21.5	16.1	1.84	1.84	1.43	10	10	8
Neths.	85.0	87.0†	82.3†	2.73	2.73	2.04	55	52	34
Belgium	96.0	96.0†	96.0†	3.15	3.15	2.18	43	39	40
Denmark	83.0	84.0	80.0	2.40	1.50	1.50	53	65	48
Finland	77.0	82.2	90.0	2.33	2.16	2.02	34	36	34
Mean	77.6	79.1	77.2	2.67	2.39	1.89	35.5	36	31.5
Mediterranean market economies									
France	90.0	(…)	90.0†	2.79	2.98	3.05	34	37	39
Greece	70.0	65.0	65.0†	3.56	3.50	2.73	7	15	13
Italy	85.0	82.0	80.0	3.57	3.57	1.82	(NA)	19	32
Spain	82.0†	(…)	84.5†	3.82	3.01	2.98	34	39	36
Portugal	75.0	71.0†	65.0†	4.19	3.85	3.46	22	35	43
Mean	80.4	72.7	76.9	3.59	3.38	2.81	24.3	29	32.6
Central and Eastern European economies									
Poland	(…)	(…)	38.0	(…)	1.40	1.90	(…)	(…)	10
Czech Rep.	(…)	65.3	44.0	(…)	1.90	1.96	(…)	(…)	6
Slovakia	(…)	(…)	(…)	(…)	1.80	1.34	(…)	(…)	8
Hungary	(…)	(…)	37.0	(…)	1.27	1.65	(…)	(…)	13
Mean	(…)	(…)	39.7	(…)	1.59	1.71	(…)	(…)	9.3

Notes
*The collective bargaining coverage data are derived from the Amsterdam Institute for Advanced Labour Studies' Database on Institutional Characteristics of Trade Unions, Wage Setting, State Intervention and Social Pacts in 34 countries between 1960 and 2007, compiled by Jelle Visser (available at http://www.uva-aias.net/208). The figures indicate 'employees covered by wage bargaining agreements as a proportion of all wage and salary earners in employment with the right to bargaining, expressed as percentage, adjusted for the possibility that some sectors or occupations are excluded from the right to bargain'.
** EPL OECD Version 1.
*** Defined as the average of the gross unemployment benefit replacement rates for two earnings levels, three family situations and three durations of unemployment. *Source*: OECD Statistics.
†Indicates that the figure for that year is unavailable and that the figure for the preceding or following year has been used, according to availability.

Inequality has also been exacerbated by an erosion of social protections in some EU member states. The OECD and the European Commission have encouraged a shift towards work-first-oriented social policies involving reductions in the duration of social benefits, increased restrictions on benefit entitlements and steps to link entitlements to participation in the labour market (van Berkel 2010). Again, the process has been uneven and social protections within coordinated market economies typically remain superior to those in liberal market economies. Nevertheless, a tendency towards a weakening of social protection is apparent across both varieties of capitalism. The strength of employment protections, as measured by the OECD's Employment Protection Legislation index, has also weakened in many countries and governments have also relaxed restrictions on the creation of atypical jobs. This is not to say that there has been an untrammelled race to the bottom: employment rights have been strengthened for some groups within some countries while in some liberal market economies there has been a general improvement, albeit from a very low base.

Industrial Relations and Social Policy since 2008

Hall and Soskice's analysis of varieties of capitalism would have difficulty in explaining these common tendencies across liberal and coordinated market economies. The emphasis in their account is on how institutional differences come to be reinforced because of the competitive advantages that they bestow upon firms. Government policy is treated largely as a straightforward response to firms' (producers) perceived interest in maintaining established conditions. Thus, liberal social policies encourage the flexible labour markets and general skills that firms in liberal market economies, such as the UK and US, are said to demand. By contrast, stronger employment protections and superior unemployment benefits are said to encourage investments in higher-level, industry-specific skills that firms in coordinated market economies, such as Austria and Germany, are said to require (Hall and Soskice 2001:50–1). Hall and Soskice argue that since both employers and workers in coordinated market economies derive advantages from strong institutions they are likely to join together in lobbying governments to maintain them. Rights and entitlements in respect of welfare provision and employment are therefore likely to be maintained in coordinated market economies.

This prediction is not well supported by the evidence of the changes that had been taking place across both liberal and coordinated market economies prior to the 2008 economic crisis and that have accelerated in its wake. These developments are leading to a further weakening in the position of labour both in and out of work. A further weakening of employer support for centralized collective bargaining has been witnessed in some coordinated market economies, for example Sweden, where the principle of industry agreements has come under pressure from service sector employers, and Finland, where in 2011 employers initially refused to negotiate a new national framework agreement. Both liberal market economies (for example Ireland) and coordinated market economies (Germany and Sweden) have sought to increase 'work incentives' by weakening unemployment benefit entitlements and, in the Swedish case, entitlements to sick pay. Governments from across the different varieties of capitalism have also introduced reforms designed to encourage the greater use of atypical contracts. The maximum length of fixed-term contracts has been increased in a number of countries, including Portugal, the Czech Republic and Romania (Clauwaert and Schömann 2012:11). Some countries (for example the Netherlands and Poland) have increased the number of permitted renewals of fixed-term contracts while others, such as Spain and Greece, have introduced new types of atypical contracts for younger workers, which exempt employers from social security contributions (ibid.). Alongside these measures, several countries (including Slovakia, Spain and the UK) have weakened individual and collective rights in respect of 'standard' employment. Typical measures have included longer 'probationary periods' for newly recruited employees, cuts in severance pay and weaker negotiating and consultation rights for employee representatives (see Heyer and Lewis 2013).

Discussion and Conclusions

The inability of the varieties-of-capitalism framework to account either for the crisis or for the common tendencies that have emerged in relation to employment relations and social policies point to fundamental limitations in the analytical approach. Prime among these is the problem that the varieties-of-capitalism approach does not offer an analysis of capitalism as such. The main concerns of contributors to the varieties-of-capitalism literature have been to examine the various roles that markets, hierarchies and networks play in coordinating economic activity and to analyse the comparative advantages conferred by different institutional constellations. However, the concept of capital is not employed. There are no 'capitalists' in the varieties-of-capitalism framework, only 'firms'. By extension, Hall and Soskice, and those following in their wake, pay scant attention to the processes through which capital is accumulated and fail to distinguish between different fractions of capital. No distinction is made between, on the one hand, the properties of capitalism as a mode of production and its associated imperatives (in particular, pressure to extract, realize and accumulate surplus value and develop the forces of production) and, on the other hand, the institutions associated with national social formations and their supposed incentive structures. As a consequence, the possibility that the former might be analytically at least as important as the latter is not recognized. The former implies constant movement – economies and society are continually changing, even if such changes are not immediately apparent (Allen 1975). The latter, by contrast, implies that stable structures give rise to regular and predictable behaviour with no transformative implications for economies or societies.[4] Moreover, the varieties-of-capitalism framework focuses on the role of institutions as facilitators of, rather than obstacles to, competitiveness. Marx, by contrast, emphasized that accumulation of capital inevitably gives rise to obstacles to accumulation that must be overcome in order for accumulation to continue (Marx and Engels 1968:38). In contrast to varieties-of-capitalism-rooted analysis, which, in keeping with neoclassical economics, tends to regard the causes of crises as exogenous (for example Iversen 2007), Marx's analysis of capitalism emphasized the endogenous causes of disruptions to the circulation of capital and processes of accumulation (Marx 1971). Periods of apparent stability mask underlying contradictions. In this chapter we have argued that the deliberate promotion of the interests of finance capital coupled with the weakening of labour relative to capital explains the relative stability of the period 1980–2008,[5] yet we have also argued that these twin processes sowed the seeds of the current crisis.

Capitalism is founded on an essential social relation wherein workers sell their labour power to employers. Understanding the dynamics of production, distribution and exchange in particular time periods, however, requires that attention be given to relationships between capital, labour and the state. The crisis has raised a number of issues in this regard. Firstly, the highly contagious character of the financial crisis has highlighted the fact that capital circulates within and between countries. There is need to analyse the spatial dynamics (Peck and Theodore 2007) of financial and industrial capital, a task that the closed economy framework of varieties-of-capitalism analysis does not easily lend itself to. The increasing interest in global value chains (for example Newsome et al. 2012) is a welcome development in this regard.

Second, the crisis has demonstrated the continued value of analysing capitalism in class terms and the need to pay adequate attention to the role of the state. The conditions that gave rise to the financial crisis need to be understood in terms of the state privileging a particular fraction of the capitalist class – financial capital – while, in the UK at least, neglecting the interests of industrial capital. The state is therefore instrumental in forging the character of accumulation (Coates 1999, 2000). Equally, the developments that we have discussed in this chapter, such as the declining labour share, can only properly be comprehended in terms of shifts in the relative power of capital and labour and the role of state policy in contributing to these shifts. In many countries national governments are currently attempting to recreate the conditions for accumulation by exerting downward pressure on wages, eroding employment protections and weakening social protections.[6] While austerity measures have led to popular protests and industrial action, including mass strikes in some countries, they have not, as yet, resulted in outright 'legitimation crises' for nation states (Habermas 1988). It is likely that the weakening of labour, which itself has been brought about in large part by state actions, has increased the freedom of the state to attempt to restore accumulation through an immiseration of workers. Effective opposition requires powerful actors and 30 years of neoliberalism have substantially weakened Europe's trade unions. In the absence of an articulated alternative to malfunctioning strategies of accumulation, political opposition is instead manifesting itself through an alarming increase in support for far-right movements.

These developments point to a third issue that has (re)surfaced in the wake of the crisis, which is that of state autonomy. During the 1970s and 1980s, this issue was discussed in terms of how much autonomy the state had from capital (Miliband 1977; Poulantzas 1973, 1978). The relationship between capital and the state was central to subsequent debates concerning the extent to which the policy choices available to national governments were being constrained by 'globalization' (for example Cerny 1995). The crisis has raised a further question, of how much autonomy states have from other states. States exist in relation to each other and the austerity measures currently being enacted in the most financially distressed European countries are a consequence of the unequal distribution of economic and political power across the EU, reflected in the German–French-initiated intensification of the growth and stability pact. State autonomy is also limited by supranational institutions (in particular the IMF), credit rating agencies and financial interests, which are encouraging a return to pre-crisis orthodoxy and the re-establishment of 'sound finance' through debt reduction. This attempt to restructure economies from above through the use of external political and economic pressure is very far from the path-dependent and incremental changes that the varieties-of-capitalism approach seeks to account for and suggests a need for further research on the roles of international financial and political actors in influencing the scope for national governments to make choices in respect of social protection, employment and industrial relations policies. It also presents an example of how attempts to re-establish conditions for the accumulation of capital can impinge upon the apparent interests of national capitalists by, in the cases of Greece, Spain and Ireland, encouraging outward migration by young, well-educated workers, for example. Efforts to restart accumulation can have their own contradictions.

A final issue relates to the need for research which examines the consequences of 'financialization' for employment relations at the level of the firm. As argued in this chapter, capital markets and institutional investors, including private equity firms, have emerged as important actors influencing the timing and nature of the restructuring and reorganization of UK enterprises. There is a need for further research into the ways and extent to which the priorities of financial capitalism have come to dominate in firms' decision-making processes and the intended and unintended consequences of financialized business models for employment relations (on these issues, see Appelbaum *et al.* 2013). Given the variegated character of financialization (Macartney 2011), comparative research on these issues would be particularly beneficial.

While this chapter has provided a critical engagement with varieties of capitalism, we do not deny that studies conducted by researchers in the varieties-of-capitalism tradition have produced valuable insights: a considerable amount has been learned about the role that institutions play in shaping economic activities and outcomes. However, the varieties-of-capitalism framework is conceptually and theoretically underequipped to grasp the dynamics of change within and across economies. We need to ask a different set of questions about the nature and fundamental causes of changes in capitalist economies and relations between state forces, capital and labour within and across national boundaries. There is also a need to be aware that changes in underlying social relations do not necessarily lead to institutional change in the short run. Institutional analyses must therefore be accompanied by analyses of shifts in the distribution of power and associated processes of transformation.

Notes

1 In fact several economists had predicted a crisis (for example Brenner (2004), Harvey (2005), Keen (1995), but most were working outside the paradigm that dominated policy thinking.
2 The term was coined by Stock and Watson (2002) but entered public discourse after being popularized by Ben Bernanke, chairman of the US Federal Reserve.

3 During an interview at a *Wall Street Journal* event in November 2008 Rahm Emanuel, US President Barack Obama's chief of staff, said that 'you never want a serious crisis to go to waste. What I mean by that is it's an opportunity to do things that you could not do before'. The quotation was widely reported.

4 Note the earlier discussion regarding the political and dynamic nature of national institutional systems.

5 The 'dotcom' crisis at the beginning of the twenty-first century was considered serious by many commentators at the time, but in hindsight the speed with which the global economy and the value of financial assets recovered renders it relatively minor compared with the current crisis.

6 The ideational basis of states' economic policies and the extent to which they identify such policies within an overarching growth or accumulation strategy is an interesting area for further research.

REFERENCES

Allen, Vic L. (1975) *Social Analysis: A Marxist Critique and Alternative.* London: Longman.

Amable, Bruno (2003) The Diversity of Modern Capitalism. *Oxford University Press.*

Appelbaum, Eileen, Rosemary Batt and Ian Clark (2013) 'Implications of Financial Capitalism for Employment Relations Research: Evidence from Breach of Trust and Implicit Contracts in Private Equity Buyouts', *British Journal of Industrial Relations,* 51, 3:498–519.

Blackburn, R. (2006) 'Finance and the Fourth Dimension', *New Left Review* 39: 39–70.

Blyth, Mark (2003) 'Same As It Never Was: Temporality and Typology in the Varieties of Capitalism', *Comparative European Politics* 1, 2:215–25.

Bosch, Gerhard, Jill Rubery and Steffen Lehndorff (200) 'European Employment Models Under Pressure to Change', *International Labour Review* 146, 3/4:253–77.

Brenner, Robert (200) 'New Boom or New Bubble: The Trajectory of the US Economy', *New Left Review* 25, January–February 2004.

Callinicos, Alex (2010) *Bonfire of Illusions: The Twin Crises of the Liberal World.* Cambridge: Polity Press.

Cerny, Philip G. (1995) 'Globalization and the Changing Logic of Collective Action', *International Organization* 49, 4:595–625.

Clark, Ian (2009) 'Owners Not Managers: Disconnecting Managerial Capitalism? Understanding the Take Private Equity Business Model', *Work, Employment and Society* 2, 4:359–78.

Clark, Ian (2011) 'Private Equity, Union Recognition and Value Extraction at the AA', *Industrial Relations Journal* 42, 1:36–50.

Clauwaert, Stefan and Isabelle Schömann (2012) 'The Crisis and National Labour Law Reforms: A Mapping Exercise', European Trade Union Institute. Working Paper No. 2012.04. Brussels: ETUI.

▶

Coates, David (1999) 'Models of Capitalism in the New World Order: The UK Case', *Political Studies* 47, 4:643–60.

Coates, David (2000) *Models of Capitalism: Growth and Stagnation in the Modern Era.* London: Polity.

Coates, David (ed.) (2005) *Varieties of Capitalism, Varieties of Approaches.* Basingstoke: Palgrave Macmillan

Crotty, James (2009) 'Structural Causes of the Global Financial Crisis: A Critical Assessment of the 'New Financial Architecture', *Cambridge Journal of Economics* 33, 4:563–80.

Deeg, Richard (2010) 'Institutional Change in Financial Systems', pp. 309–34 in *The Oxford Handbook of Comparative Institutional Analysis*, edited by G. Morgan *et al.* Oxford: Oxford University Press.

Froud, Julie, Sukhdev Johal, Adam Leaver and Karel Williams (2006) *Financialization and Strategy: Narrative and Numbers.* London, Routledge.

Gamble, Andrew (2009) *The Spectre at the Feast: Capitalist Crisis and the Politics of Recession.* Basingstoke: Palgrave Macmillan.

Glyn, Andrew (2006) *Capitalism Unleashed: Finance, Globalization and Welfare.* Oxford: Oxford University Press.

Habermas, Jurgen (1988) *Legitimation Crisis.* Cambridge: Polity.

Hall, Peter A. and David Soskice (2001) 'An Introduction to Varieties of Capitalism', pp. 1–70 in *Varieties of Capitalism: The Institutional Foundations of Comparative Advantage*, edited by P.A. Hall and D. Soskice. Oxford: Oxford University Press.

Hall, Peter A. and Kathleen Thelen (200) 'Institutional Change in Varieties of Capitalism', pp. 251–72 in *Debating Varieties of Capitalism*, edited by B. Hancké. Oxford: Oxford University Press.

Hancké, Bob, Martin Rhodes and Mark Thatcher (2007) 'Introduction: Beyond Varieties of Capitalism', pp. 1–38 in *Beyond Varieties of Capitalism: Conflict, Contradictions and Complementarities in the European Economy*, edited by B. Hancké, M. Rhodes and M. Thatcher. Oxford: Oxford University Press.

Harvey, David (2010) 'The Enigma of Capital and the Crises of Capitalism. London: Profile Books.

Hay, Colin (2005) 'Two Can Play at That Game… Can They? Varieties of Capitalism, Varieties of Institutionalism', pp. 106–21 in *Varieties of Capitalism, Varieties of Approaches*, edited by D. Coates. Basingstoke: Palgrave.

Heyes, Jason and Paul Lewis (2013) 'Employment Protection Under Fire: Labour Market Deregulation and Employment in the European Union', *Economic & Industrial Democracy*, first published online 25.07.2013.

ILO (2008) *World of Work Report 2008: Income Inequalities in the Age of Financial Globalization.* Geneva: ILO.

ILO (2009) *World of Work Report 2009: The Global Jobs Crisis and Beyond.* Geneva: ILO.

IMF (2008) *Global Financial Stability Report – Financial Stress and Deleveraging, Macrofinancial Implications and Policy.* Washington, DC, October.

Iversen, Torben (2007) 'Economic Shocks and Varieties of Government Responses', pp. 278–306 in *Beyond Varieties of Capitalism: Conflict, Contradictions and Complementarities in the European Economy*, edited by B. Hanké, M. Rhodes and M. Thatcher. Oxford: Oxford University Press.

▶

King, L.P. (2007) 'Central European Capitalism in Comparative Perspective', pp. 307–27 in *Beyond Varieties of Capitalism: Conflict, Contradictions and Complementarities in the European Economy*, edited by B. Hanké, M. Rhodes and M. Thatcher. Oxford: Oxford University Press.

Lapavitsas, Costas (2012) *Crisis in the Eurozone*. London: Verso.

Macartney, Huw (2011) *Variegated Neoliberalism: EU Varieties of Capitalism and International Political Economy*. London: Routledge.

Mahoney, James and Thelen, Kathleen (eds) (2010) *Explaining Institutional Change: Ambiguity, Agency and Power*. Cambridge: Cambridge University Press.

Marx, Karl (1971) *Capital, Vol. 1*. London: George Allen & Unwin.

Marx, Karl and Friedrich Engels (1968) 'Manifesto of the Communist Party', in K. Marx and F. Engels, *Selected Works*. London: Lawrence & Wishart.

Miliband, Ralph (1977) *Marxism and Politics*. Oxford: Oxford University Press.

Newsome, Kirsty, Paul Thompson and Johanna Commander (2012) '"Good When They Want to Be": Migrant Workers in the Supermarket Supply Chain', *Human Resource Management Journal* 23, 2:129–43.

Nolan, Peter (1989) 'Walking on Water? Performance and Industrial Relations Under Thatcher', *Industrial Relations Journal* 20, 2:81–92.

Nolan, Peter (2011) 'Money, Markets, Meltdown: The 21st-Century Crisis of Labour', *Industrial Relations Journal* 42, 1: 2–17.

Nölke, Andreas and James Perry (2007) 'The Power of Transnational Private Governance: Financialization and the IASB', *Business and Politics* 9, 3:.

O'Sullivan, Mary A. (2000) *Contests for Corporate Control. Corporate Governance and Economic Performance in the United States and Germany*. Oxford: Oxford University Press.

Peck, Jamie and Nik Theodore (2007) 'Variegated Capitalism', *Progress in Human Geography* 31, 6:731–72.

Poulantzas, Nicos (1973) *Political Power and Social Classes*. London: New Left Books.

Poulantzas, Nicos (1978) *State, Power, Socialism*. London: Verso.

Rodrigues, Suzana and John Child (2010) 'Private Equity, the Minimalist Organization and the Quality of Employment Relations', *Human Relations* 63, 9:1321–42.

Streeck, Wolfgang and Kathleen Thelen (2005) 'Introduction: Institutional Change in Advanced Political Economies', pp. 1–39 in *Beyond Continuity: Institutional Change in Advanced Political Economies*, edited by W. Streeck and K. Thelen. Oxford: Oxford University Press.

Stock, James H. and Mark W. Watson (2002) 'Has the Business Cycle Changed and Why?', NBER Working Paper No. 9127. Cambridge, MA: National Bureau of Economic Research.

Van Berkel, Rik (2010) 'The Provision of Income Protection and Activation Services for the Unemployed in "Active" Welfare States. An International Comparison', *Journal of Social Policy* 39, 1: 17–34.

Vidal, Matt (2013) 'Postfordism as a Dysfunctional Accumulation Regime: A Comparative Study of the US, UK and Germany', *Work, Employment & Society*, 27, 3: 451–71.

Do the UK and Australia Have Sustainable Business Models?

3

John Buchanan, Julie Froud, Sukhdev Johal, Karel Williams and Serena Yu

Crises usually generate new understandings of how the world works. The economic upheavals and subsequent interventions of 2007–09 associated with the Global Financial Crisis of those years are no exception. After years of assuming they had found a way to beat the trade cycle, leaders of the finance sector were forced to eat humble pie. Blythe Masters, then chairperson of the Securities Industry and Financial Markets Association in the US, spoke for many when she addressed that organization's AGM on 28 October 2008. She noted the industry should accept its share of responsibility for the crisis. Most significantly she asserted it was also important 'to own the responsibility of rebuilding a more systematically sustainable business model'. (Tett 2009: 296)

This openness to new ideas is something quite novel among adherents and practitioners of the prevalent policy orthodoxy. Since the later 1970s, the narrative of increasing influence has been that the only way to create sustainable economic well-being is to reduce state claims on, and interference with, markets. Shrinking the public sector to enable private sector expansion has been assumed to be central to employment growth in particular. Events during the period 2007–09 have established that conducting affairs on the basis of this narrative cannot deliver sustainable economic well-being.

The key elements of a 'new model' are now emerging. Previously the dominant narrative assumed the state worked best when it operated like a 'night watchman' – securing the perimeters of social and economic life but letting markets work their wonders within this social space. Now it is widely accepted and expected that the state is akin to the emergency department of a large teaching hospital. That is, it is a highly sophisticated, very expensive agency that can mobilize life-sustaining interventions at a moment's notice, the instant life-threatening events occur.

But the necessity of an 'activist, interventionist' state, as opposed to the fantasy of the 'minimalist state', has been a longstanding reality of market societies. Recent decades are often referred to as the 'neoliberal' or 'free market' era. We believe it is more accurate to characterize them as the latest variant of 'state-dependent markets'. The recent crisis has merely made manifest what has been integral throughout. 'The market' is not an autonomous domain that needs to be liberated. Rather it is a social space that is politically constructed but which then develops its own dynamic. The challenge is to understand the actual business model at work in generating and distributing goods and services. Critical to this venture is not taking the rhetoric of the architects of the age at face value. Such rhetoric is useful for understanding public discourses guiding decision-making – it is not necessarily helpful for understanding what has really been going on.

How are we to make sense of the current situation?[1] Recent literature from the labour process tradition and the comparative political economy of work and employment relations provide promising leads. Within the labour process tradition, writers such as Thompson and Vincent (2010) and Vidal (2011, forthcoming) have argued for the importance of locating the restructuring of employment within the context of broader political economic developments. For authors such as these such 'context' is explicitly 'theorized', albeit on the basis of slightly different bases. Vidal, after careful reconsideration of debates in the 1980s and 1990s, calls for a critical reworking of Marxist regulation theory. Thompson and Vincent suggest a more eclectic approach based on a range of 'framings' settled at 'different levels of abstraction' that draws directly upon the critical realist tradition for understanding 'causal mechanisms'. While far more open than the Marxian-inspired analyses of the past, these approaches still give a high degree of analytical weight to conceptual priors. For us, the challenge is to allow empirical work to play a greater role in driving analysis and not merely filling it out. Similarly, the most influential approach in comparative political economy today, the varieties-of-capitalism literature, is also problematic. The most influential formulation of this approach by Hall and Soskice, for example, builds analysis around a purportedly conceptually parsimonious framework that assumes 'really existing capitalisms' take one of two general forms: 'coordinated' or 'liberal' market economies (for example Hall and Soskice 2001).

Thoughtful, searching critiques of this approach have identified the many limitations of working with such dichotomous categories. The most powerful note that this approach overlooks both the deep commonalities in contemporary capitalist social formations (for example Pontusson 2005) as well as failing to capture the many variegated forms it takes (for example Peck and Theodore 2007). One of the most powerful critiques of this school concerns its seemingly illuminating, but in fact highly limiting, notion of path dependence for understanding the evolution of contemporary capitalism. Colin Crouch argues that it is unhelpful to think of the trajectory of contemporary economic development as following one of the two distinct market paths – 'coordinated' or 'liberal'.

Our analysis is in the tradition of these more recent formulations with their very open categories and interest in allowing data as much power as possible in shaping analysis. As Crouch has argued,[2] the pathways of political–economic evolution are not so much like the neat networks of freeways and main roads of modern times and rather more like the pilgrim and transport routes of medieval Europe. He captures the nature of this different notion of pathway well when he observes that such medieval routes were not

> road[s] in the sense we understand today, but a series of alternatives. At one point a river might be in flood on the way the pilgrims were using, and local people would tell them that when that happened they had to take a different path through the hills. Or there might be wolves in the hills; in which case another way through was advised... the 'paths' used by social actors might often be far more like the pilgrims' route than the modern concept of fixed, sign-posted roads with clear boundaries. (Crouch 2005:1)

We call our approach 'a number and narratives' mode of analysis – or what can be described as a conceptually minimalist, empirically resourceful epistemology (Froud *et al.* 2006:4–6). Crouch's very open notion of pathway is an excellent example of conceptual minimalism – it allows data more than analytical priors to structure the analysis. In creating new knowledge of the current situation we pay special attention to prevailing narratives and ascertaining what is implicit within them. Identifying the 'undisclosed' provides real power in understanding the core generative mechanisms at work in contemporary capitalist societies. The analysis then deepens initial conceptually driven insights with a scrutiny of statistics. These too need to be carefully handled – not such so much in an econometric sense but in the sense of how at their most basic level of categorical framing and temporal presentation they often hide more than they reveal. Reconfiguring the categorical and temporal reference points for statistics can shed blinding new light on the dynamics actually at work in the past and in the current situation.

We begin our analysis by noting that the undisclosed business model in places like the UK and Australia today involve more than just the emergency department and nightwatchman roles for the state summarized above.

Even at the height of the allegedly 'new golden age' the state provided ongoing support for the private sector. If the 1950s and 1960s were marked by the emergence of the social welfare state, the 1980s and 1990s have witnessed the emergence of the business welfare state. Business welfare dependence has two dimensions. First, as has long been recognized in the Keynesian and Marxian traditions, without very direct government support the private sector cannot deliver ongoing full employment. Second, as we will show below, a key site of this support is in the provision of 'privately provided' publicly funded social services like health and education. In addition to its emergency department role the state has also been the crutch the private sector relies on to overcome it anaemic performance in creating jobs even in the 'good times'.

Our argument is simple. For decades now the dominant policy narrative has been that the market-liberal economies of English-speaking countries like UK and Australia have achieved enviable employment outcomes because of superior reliance on markets to order economic and social life. This narrative and the numbers commonly associated with it are summarized in the next section. A closer look at the numbers of job creation reveals a very different story. In the section after, we show that the UK's strong employment numbers were primarily a result of active state and para-state job creation. Without this support employment growth in that country would have been anaemic. We then compare this situation with that of Australia. In the 1990s Alan Greenspan described the great southern land as a 'miracle economy'. And from 2004 to the present it has experienced one of its strongest resources booms ever – driven primarily by demand from China. The improvement in the terms of trade alone boosted Australian GDP by 9 percentage points between 2004 and 2008 (Richardson, 2009). Yet even with this policy purity and exceptional 'gift from nature', private employment growth has merely kept pace with that in the public sector. Moreover, the aggregate employment growth has been anaemic in another sense – the jobs created have been increasingly degraded in terms of entitlements attached to them and the desirability in the hours worked. Australia has among the highest levels of underemployed part-timers and involuntary extended hours fulltime workers among the advanced industrialized nations (Buchanan *et al.* forthcoming 2013a). If Australia is as good as it gets then clearly the policy regime that has deified markets and endeavoured to rebuild the world in their image is not only unattainable – its cannot deliver on decent job creation.

This chapter is a modest contribution to the important project of identifying how to engage with and help improve a deeply flawed reality. Exposing the undisclosed and unsustainable nature of employment created under a growth regime of state-dependent markets that prevailed even before the crisis of 2007–9 is a critical first step. Establishing what needs to be explained and superseded is vital before analyses of causes and devising options for action can commence. Our final section draws out the broader analytical and policy significance of our empirical material. Our central finding is that there is a need to move beyond 'neoliberal' discourse as having anything useful to contribute in understanding where the jobs came from and where they will come from in the future. In short, the challenge is not to accept the legacy of the Thatcher–Regan era as something to build on. That legacy at the level of discourse and problem definition is real and needs to be challenged. Understanding the substantive legacy concerning the dynamics of job creation requires careful scrutiny of the active role of the state. In short, the substantive challenge is to move beyond the 'emergency department + business welfare dependence' business model. Instead we need to identify how the state can support sustainable jobs that are worth having and in sufficient numbers for all who want to work. Structuring life around the assumption that markets represent the masters of economic destiny is unhelpful. Instead we need to identify how the state, directly, and working with markets as servants, can ensure sustainable and desirable outcomes, especially in the realm of working life.

The Dominant Narrative: Leading Cases

In recent years the dominant narrative about economic and social development has been shaped by the notion that markets provide a superior way of ordering human affairs. For the last three decades policymaking in many of the English speaking OECD countries has been increasingly informed by the vision of the night watchman state. Public policy, it has been assumed, should liberate pre-given market forces from intrusions and imperfections. And in the alleged rare cases where markets 'fail', intervention should be designed along market lines.

In this chapter we explore the narrative and especially the numbers associated with the key indicator of economic performance: job creation.

Jobs are still the principal way contemporary advanced societies provide material well-being for the bulk of their populations. We examine job creation dynamics in two countries which are commonly accepted as leading examples of the 'free market' model – one providing a 'worst case' example, the other 'a best case'. The UK, since Margaret Thatcher was elected prime minister in 1979, has been widely accepted as the pioneer of the now dominant policy narrative concerning the superiority of markets in ordering human affairs. Tony Blair and his New Labour government prided themselves on embracing the Iron Lady's maxim that 'There is no alternative' to market modes of organizing an advanced capitalist society. Despite its reputation for policy innovation, the mass of literature on the UK's economic decline is without parallel in the English-speaking world. It is arguably the paradigmatic case of a country endeavouring to reposition itself – unsuccessfully – as a former imperial power in a rapidly changing world. We compare UK developments with those in Australia. While the shine has come off the 'Thatcherite miracle' with the widespread and widely supported intervention in the UK finance sector in 2008–9, Australia has – to date – avoided any major banking collapse during the Global Financial Crisis and has been one of the few countries to have avoided a technical recession. Thus we compare the nature of employment growth in the leading case of neoliberalism in a country in decline with that of the country where the model appears to have worked best and is associated with ongoing positive economic development. Do lessons from Australia offer insights into how a variant on the Thatcherite model can deliver superior employment outcomes?

Political Arithmetic I: The Accepted Figures

The ascendancy of the free market model was achieved because it appeared that countries embracing its precepts achieved superior economic performance. Above all, creating large numbers of jobs was taken as the prime indicator that the model directly benefited all – not just those threatened by inflation or the recipients of unearned income like profits. And, prima facie, the employment numbers have been impressive. The OECD Secretariat in Paris regularly compared the job performance of English-speaking countries like the USA, UK and Australia with those of the European Union. And for the three decades after 1979 the story seemed pretty clear. In this section we briefly recount some of the commonly cited numbers concerning our two cases of interest: the UK and Australia.

The United Kingdom

Until recent times, the UK has also had very low levels of unemployment. From highs of over 10 per cent during the recessions of the 1980s and early 1990s, unemployment had trended down to around 5 per cent before the Global Financial Crisis. On the continent, unemployment in the European Union averaged around 8 per cent over this period (Eurostat online database).

One of the key features of this employment growth has been the decline of that provided directly by the public sector and the concurrent increasing proportion attributable to private sector jobs. This is evident in Figure 3.1. As the figure shows, the proportion of jobs in public sector fell from 23 per cent to 19 per cent between 1992 and 2009 (Office for National Statistics).

In addition to the apparent private sector engine of employment growth, it is widely accepted that the leading economic sectors have been the most 'market'-based. That is, they are sectors that have flourished without the presence of an active industry policy. These sectors include the finance and creative industries in the UK. Indicators of this dynamism are provided by Figure 3.2. Between 2001 and 2006, for example, rates of profitability in the finance sector were very high. As a share of the UK's total gross operating surplus the sector's share rose from around 5 per cent to just under over 12 per cent.

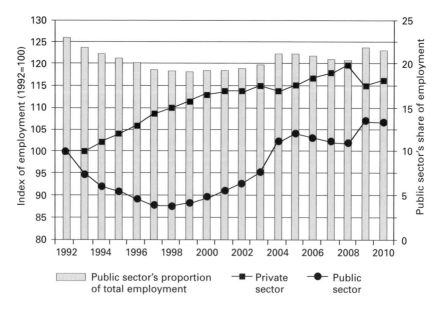

Figure 3.1 UK public and private sector employment growth, 1992–2009. Base index = 100.

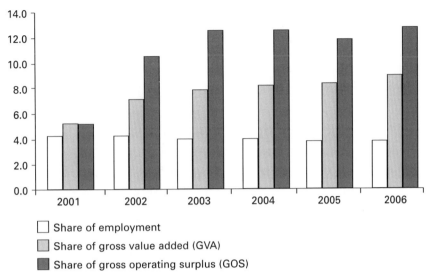

Share of employment

Share of gross value added (GVA)

Share of gross operating surplus (GOS)

Figure 3.2 Finance sector's share of UK employment, gross value added and gross operating surplus 2001–6.

Source: Buchanan *et al.* (2009).

Australia

Prima facie, the numbers for Australia provide even stronger support for the dominant narrative. Australian employment growth has been strong over the last two decades, averaging 1.7 per cent per annum, compared with a benchmark OECD index of 1.1 per cent growth. Over 10.8 million working Australians underpin a resilient ratio of employment to population of 61.5 per cent, a figure which, while cyclical, has trended up from around 55 per cent in the mid 1980s. This is illustrated in Figure 3.3.

Meanwhile, Australia's headline unemployment rate has weathered the latest economic crisis very well, rising only marginally above historical lows to around 5.5 per cent. The resilience of the Australian economy, and the labour market, has certainly been upheld as an economic triumph amid broad-based malaise in the US and Europe.

Moreover, the strength of the Australian labour market has been credited to private sector catalysts, with employment growth firmly concentrated in sectors such as professional and technical services, and administrative and support services. Figure 3.4 shows the relative strength of private sector employment between 1984 and 2009, as well as the contraction in the public sector over the 1990s. In addition, we illustrate the contributions of the public sector to the level of aggregate

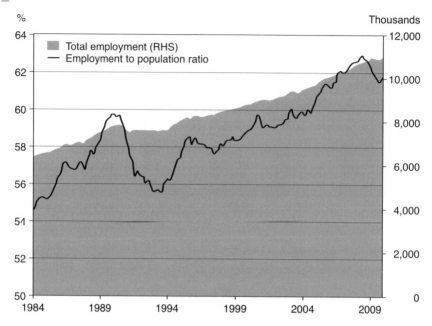

Figure 3.3 Aggregate Australian employment 1984–2009.
Source: ABS Cat. No. 6202.0 Labour Force Survey.

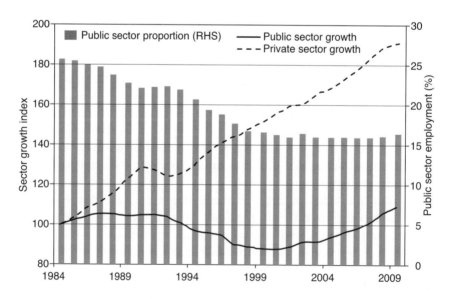

Figure 3.4 Australian public and private sector employment growth, 1984–2009.
Base index = 100.

Source: ABS cat. no. 6202.0 Labour Force Survey; ABS Cat. No. 6248.0.55.001 Wage and Salary Earners, Public Sector.

employment, which will be discussed at length later. Figure 3.4 shows that public employment has stabilized at around 17 per cent of total employment. This compares to an OECD average measure of total public employment, around 18 per cent in 2000, although the trend has been increasing over time and ranges from 8.4 per cent in Japan to 31.2 per cent in Norway (Algan *et al.* 2002)

In addition to a private sector engine of employment growth, as in the UK it is widely accepted that the leading economic sectors have been the most 'market'-based: the finance and mining industries in Australia. Certainly, the two sectors have experienced a significant period of great profitability since the early 1990s, despite the volatilities inherent to the mining sector and the financial crisis between 2007 and 2009. The scale of mining and finance sector profits each represent around 4 to 5 per cent of GDP, compared with total industry profits (including mining and finance), which add up to around 14 per cent overall. Distinctive trends since 2002 show the strong profitability growth in mining and finance, compared with flat performance for broader Australian industry.

Political Arithmetic II: The Numbers That Matter

The validity of the orthodox narrative and numbers story has been progressively diminishing as a result of periodic and increasingly severe financial upheavals. Iconic events associated with the Long-Term Capital Management crisis of the 1990s and 'the tech wreck' and Enron and Worldcom debacles in the early 2000s indicated that we may not actually be living in the best of all possible worlds. This became patent for all to see with the upheavals in 2008 associated with Bear Sterns, Lehman Bros and American Insurance Group in the USA and Northern Rock and the Royal Bank of Scotland in the UK. The response to crises in these and similar organizations revealed that massive state intervention is required to save the market from itself. Spectacular though such events have been, it is important to note that the now accepted role of the state as the emergency department does not mark limits to its role as a crutch for the private sector. A closer look at the jobs created during the so-called 'new golden age' reveals that the private sector has at best been a source of anaemic job growth. In the case of the UK's strong employment aggregate outcomes have only been achieved by direct government support for new job creation. In the case of Australia despite vigorous 'marketization' of all realms of public policy and the gift of an extraordinary resources boom, the private sector remains no more important a source of jobs today than it did when a hard-line neoconservative, neoliberal government took power 14 years ago. Moreover, much of the employment created during that time has been of significantly poorer quality in terms of entitlements like paid leave and the adequacy of hours worked by those holding both part-time and fulltime jobs.

The UK: Public Sector 'Filling In' Jobs, Not Crowding Them Out

A better grasp of where the jobs have come from is provided when we consider sources of employment growth by industry. Figure 3.5 summarizes these trends in the UK for the last two decades.

These data confirm the long-term trends of deindustrialization in Britain. Between 1991 and 2007 alone over 1.3 million manufacturing jobs disappeared. What is less well appreciated is the relative unimportance of banking and finance as a subset of the broader business services category in terms of employment growth. While significant for profits its contribution to the absolute number of jobs in the UK remained virtually unchanged over this period – up by only 35 730 (Buchanan *et al.* 2009). As a proportion of total employment it actually fell. The key sources of employment growth have been non-banking business services and social services, as employment in business services increased by over 2 million. This probably reflects increasing contracting out – especially of things like cleaning, administrative support, IT and the like. Such a development

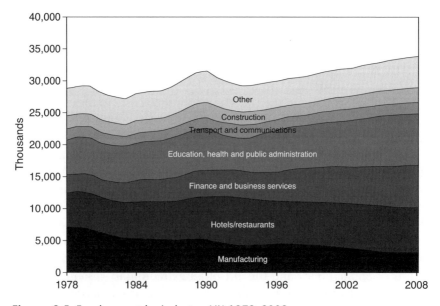

Figure 3.5 Employment by industry, UK 1979–2009.

could be consistent with the marketizing of services that were previously done in-house by organizations. The growth in social services, however, is harder to explain. Between 1980 and 2007 it grew by 2.5 million and as a proportion of employment grew from around 21 to 26 per cent of all employed persons in the UK. Given the small scale of the private sector in UK health and education this development highlights the need for closer examination of just what has been behind such a large swathe of employment growth.

A close scrutiny of employment statistics reveals that the traditional distinction between 'public' and 'private' employment is difficult to maintain. In the past the convention has been to allocate workers to sectors on the basis of the ownership status of the enterprise for which they work. This underestimates the degree to which public funds provide the source of employment for jobs in firms that are, as a matter of formality, defined as private enterprises. In work recently completed we have shown how, by considering data at the four-digit standard industry classification level, it is possible to get a more precise count of 'para-state' as well as direct state employment (see Buchanan *et al.* 2009, especially 16–24). On the basis of the calculations made there nationally, state and para-state employment make a major contribution to job creation. As Table 3.1 shows, between 1998 and 2007, state and para-state employment increased by nearly 1.3 million, from 6.2 to 7.5 million. This accounted for no less than 57 per cent of the total increase of 2.24 million in the number of employees from 24.2 to 26.6 million over this period. The pattern from 1998 to 2007 was one of sustained increase on a large base with a 21 per cent increase in state and para-state employment over the decade after 1998 so that state and para-state together employed nearly 7.5 million or 28 per cent of the workforce by 2007. The weight and force of state and para-state employment creation, as well as the huge base, is such that, if the UK has a 'leading sector', it is the state. And this requires us to re-evaluate what Mrs

Table 3.1 Private, state and para-state employment, UK, 1998 and 2007

Year	Private sector	State and para-state	Total
1998	18 166 357	6 188 681	24 355 038
2007	19 137 998	7 461 206	26 599 204
Difference	971 641 (5.3%)	1 272 525 (20.6%)	2 244 166 (9.2%)

Notes: State and para-state sector refers to traditional public sector activities plus activities classified where the State provides a share of the income. The underlying data reflect SIC classifications at the time of collection and exclude Northern Ireland and the self-employed.

Source: Buchanan *et al.* (2009).

Table 3.2 Change in UK female employment between 1998 and 2007, split by private and state and para-state sectors

	Private sector	State and para-state	Total
Change between 1998 and 2007 (per cent)	211 538 (19%)	903 767 (81%)	(100%)

Notes: State and para-state sector refers to traditional public sector activities plus activities classified where the state provides a share of the income. The underlying data reflect SIC classifications at the time of collection and exclude Northern Ireland and the self-employed.

Source: Buchanan et al. (2009).

Thatcher did and whether the 1980s represent a break. In our view, the employment outcome of the 1990s and 2000s is in line with pre-1979 trends. The difference is that back in the 1970s and 1980s it was argued that the expansion of state employment was 'crowding out' private activity but it now looks more like 'filling in the gaps' left by the private sector.

In terms of gender and contribution to the creation of female employment, state and para-state made a much larger contribution. Employment is heavily gendered because rank-and-file workers in health and education are disproportionately female. In both 1998 and 2007, just over 69 per cent of the state and para-state (S&PS) workforce is female and this female S&PS workforce always splits more or less equally into half fulltime and half part-time female workers whereas only 21 per cent of male S&PS workers are part-time. The end result is that the state and para-state sector is dominant in the creation of new fulltime and part-time jobs for women. As Table 3.2 shows, over the period 1998–2007, S&PS accounts for an extra 904 00 female jobs which split 60–40 between fulltime and part-time, and these 904 000 new jobs account for no less than 81 per cent of the total 1.1 million increase in female employment over these years. If high-income capitalist countries are changing because wage-earning households are increasingly dependent on two wage earners, in the UK case, the state and para-state sector more than any other puts the second wage-earner into the average household.

This development appears to be closely linked to increasing public expenditure in the UK under new Labour from 2000 to 2007: an increase of about 10 percentage points. During this period real expenditure increased sharply from £411 billion to £606 billion in a period of prosperity; and the largest increases in expenditure were discretionary increases in spending on health and education, which together accounted for some £80 billion of the total near £200 billion increase in public expenditure.

Australia: As Good As It Gets?

When we consider the numbers more carefully, challenges to this dominant narrative arise quickly in the case of Australia too. First, with regard to the financial services and mining sectors, their substantial contributions to national income are not reflected in their employment base. While financial services contributes around 10 per cent to Australian GDP, only 4 per cent of total employment resides in this sector, totalling 392 000 jobs. In the mining sector, a 7 per cent contribution to GDP compares with only 1.5 per cent of aggregate employment, despite the mining boom, comprising around 162 000 jobs.

By comparison, the sectors driving employment growth have been healthcare and community services, professional and technical services, and administrative services. For example, the public administration, education and health services sectors have grown their employment share from 20.9 per cent to 24.8 per cent since the mid 1980s. These sectors, along with retail and hospitality, remain the largest employers in Australia. These industry trends are illustrated in Figure 3.6.

Trends in public and para-state employment have been different in Australia. Australia has had, for much of the twentieth century, significant

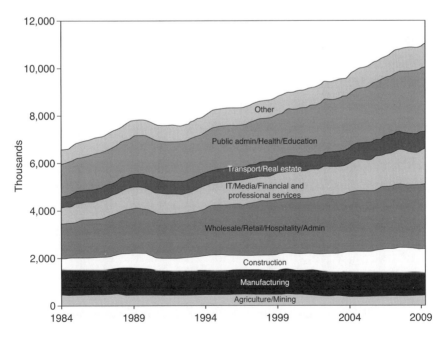

Figure 3.6 Employment growth by industry, Australia 1984–2009.

Source: ABS Cat. No. 6291.0.55.003 Detailed Labour Force Survey

private sectors in health and education. We endeavoured to replicate the methods used for the UK analysis and did not find a significant growth in para-state employment as was evident there. This is not surprising given that public expenditure in Australia has been more tightly controlled in recent decades – most stringently under federal Labor Party governments.[3] Australian trends in public employment are summarized in Figures 3.7 and 3.8. These reveal that public employment fell most rapidly under the federal Labor governments of the 1980s and early 1990s. The situation then stabilized under the neoliberal–neoconservative Howard government. Despite a vigorous programme of privatizations and marketization the private sector hardly increased in importance as a source of job creation since 1996. This is all the more remarkable given the resources boom triggered by surging demand from China, which boosted GDP by 9 per cent due to a strong terms of trade effect between 2004 and 2009 (Richardson, 2009).

It is important to note, however, that there has been a major deterioration in the quality of jobs created during this period. In 1984 less than 10 per cent of employment was casual; today this is over 20 per cent (Watson *et al.* 2003, ABS 2008), while there has been growth in part-time work – indeed Australia, with over 30 per cent of its workforce part-time, has very high levels of underemployment. The trend in part-timers wanting more hours is summarized in Figure 3.9. The part-time underemployed constitute

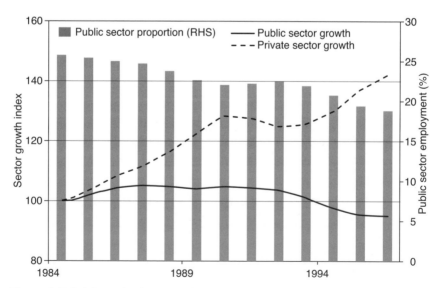

Figure 3.7 Public and private employment growth, Labor government years, Australia 1983–96.

Source: ABS Cat. No. 6202.0 Labour Force Survey; ABS Cat. No. 6248.0.55.001 Wage and Salary Earners, Public Sector.

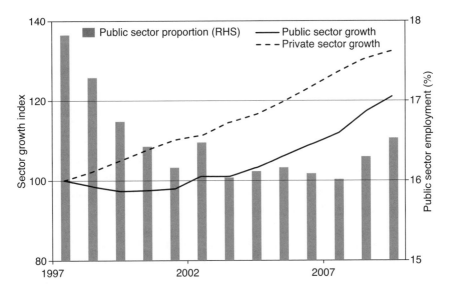

Figure 3.8 Public and private employment growth, Coalition government years, Australia 1997–2007.

Source: ABS Cat. No. 6202.0 Labour Force Survey; ABS Cat. No. 6248.0.55.001 Wage and Salary Earners, Public Sector.

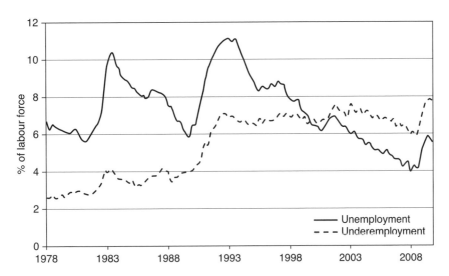

Figure 3.9 Rate of labour underutilization, 1978–2009.

Source: ABS 2008b, ABS 2008b. Labour Underutilisation, Cat. No. 6202.0

about almost 8 per cent of the labour force. The primary reason people desire more hours is to increase income (ABS, 2008). There is also a strong gender dimension to underemployment: of the 687 000 part-time under-employed workers in 2008, 447 000 were women. During the recent down-turn, however, the most rapid growth in underemployment has been among men.

While between a quarter and a third of Australia's part-timers desire more hours of work, those working full time put in among the longest hours in the advanced capitalist economies (OECD 2004). Those long work-ing hours appear even more intense for heads of households. In 2007, over half of all employed men were working more than 40 hours a week, while a third were working over 50 (Wooden and Drago 2007). Unsurprisingly, growing numbers of households now report major pressure on balancing work and care responsibilities, with over half fulltimers working more than 50 hours per week wanting shorter hours (Watson *et al.* 2003). This is not just a function of increased hours of work reported by individuals earlier. It is, rather, a function of the combined hours provided by dual earner house-hold. The dramatic shift here is evident in Figure 3.10.

The contrasting cases highlight two different forms of anaemia in the private sector. Without state support the UK model cannot deliver anything like full employment. And in the Australian case, even with the

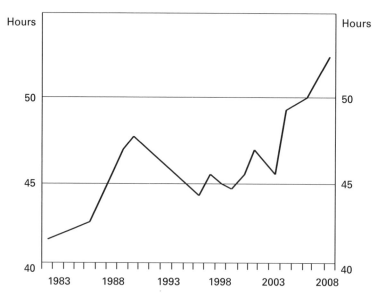

Figure 3.10 Australia: weekly hours worked by household, household head aged 25–39.

Source: ABS, cited in Richards (2009).

strong tail winds of a resources boom the private sector cannot do without the public sector to maintain high levels of employment. Worse still, if Australia is as good as it gets – should we really desire to replicate a policy regime that relies on chronic underemployment and involuntary extended hours to remain viable? Is this really as good as it gets?

Conclusions

A dark shadow similar to that which existed in the aftermath of World War I, described brilliantly by T.S. Eliot (1925), marks our own age. In moments of crisis, like that of 2007–9, the shadow is manifest for all to see. But as time passes the narrative adapts. For some adherents of the faith recent events represent nothing more than a minor aberration. According to a leading Australian employer representative, all we need to is 'reboot' the system and resume where we left off (BIS Shrapnel 2008).

The denial of immediate reality is breathtaking. A crisis that requires world governments to either spend or pledge 18 per cent of world GDP to stabilize (Rudd 2009) begs scrutiny. If former high priests of the faith like Alan Greenspan now acknowledge there are flaws in their models of how the world works (Tett 2009:297) it would only seem reasonable to expect others to follow suit. But narratives are resilient. And one of the key ingredients of the latest incarnation of economic liberalism is that its account of recent history remains, in the popular mind, unchallenged. Sure there may be the odd disturbance (aka asset bubble) in financial flows, but this is nothing the state acting as an economic emergency departmen cannot fix.

Our numbers pose a modest but corrosive set of findings. Not only do current political economic arrangements require massive intervention at key moments of potential catastrophe – even in boom times the state is needed to either 'fill in' or 'contribute equally' to employment growth. Markets may have worked wonders in making the rich richer, but they have only provided anaemic employment growth – quantitatively in the UK case, qualitatively in the best case possible – Australia in the 2000s. *In short, the market narrative makes a good story but cannot deliver sustainable employment in good times any more than it can in bad.*

For three decades it has been conventional wisdom that 'there is no alternative' to the market ordering of human affairs. Such teleological views of the past and the future – of both the left and the right – have never been helpful for grappling with reality and understanding the choices actually available at any particular moment. Our numbers provide a more telling criticism: other social arrangements were not only possible, they were in fact necessary to deliver the employment growth that so-called 'neoliberal' regimes 'delivered'.

More work needs to be done to explore what has driven the numbers summarized above. For the UK, how can public funding for para-state employment be maintained if government deficits continue to grow? If the official narrative about deficits prevails, there are limits to continued funding for para-state activity. Given the flaws in the official narrative and the limits of the substantive business model at work, is not now the time to seriously rethink the role of public finance as a positive force for economic renewal? Unless the deficit fetishism of the dominant narrative is discarded the prospects for anything like sustained employment growth in the UK are limited. The Australia case raises different but allied questions. What have been the transmission mechanisms, if any, between the resources boom and jobs growth? Could the windfall gains be managed better, possibly in the form of forced savings for social and economic renewal along the lines pursued by Norway, East Timor and New Guinea? Most importantly of all, if the current approach to labour standards remains unchanged, will 'economic success' along Australian lines merely coincide with a steady deterioration in the quality of life at work?

Answers to questions such as these will require moving out of the discursive shadows cast by the current policy narrative. Since the 1980s the leaderships of social-democratic parties have prided themselves on their 'realism' in embracing the 'market' vision of economic life; but it is now clear neoliberal categories are part of the problem if we are interested in devising enduring solutions to running contemporary capitalist societies. Any sustainable and enduring advance out of the current situation requires breaking with this narrative and its comforting fictions. Recognizing the positive and creative role the state and other non-market arrangements can and do play is vital. Far from being second-order options they are in fact central to economic and social renewal. Indeed, without the active role played by the state, the employment trends of the last 30 years would have been very different. New directions in both employment analysis and policy need to build on the old liberal collectivist insight that markets make good servants but poor masters (Buchanan *et al.* forthcoming 2013b).

Notes

1 This and the following paragraph draw heavily on very helpful substantive and editing suggestions provided by the editors of this collection.

2 The rest of this paragraph draws directly on reflections on Crouch's work in Buchanan *et al.* 2010.
3 Note this too was the case with the Rudd Labor government until the GFC. Like all other Western governments it broke with fiscal orthodoxy to prevent a financial crisis becoming a political and economic catastrophe. Indeed, it was one of the first governments to so act, and in per capita terms intervened on a bigger scale.

REFERENCES

Algan, Y., P. Cahuc and A. Zylerberg (2002) 'Public Employment – Does it Increase Unemployment?', *Economic Policy* 17:7–68.
Australian Bureau of Statistics (ABS) (2008) Cat. No. 6359.0 *Forms of Employment*, Canberra.
BIS Shrapnel (2008) *Economic Outlook Bulletin*, December (quoted http://www.man monthly.com.au/Article/Downturn-but-no-recession-for-Australia/433022. aspx).
Buchanan, J. *et al.* (2009) 'Undisclosed and Unsustainable: Problems of the UK National Business Model', University of Manchester Centre for Research on Socio-Cultural Change, Working Paper No. 75.
Buchanan, J. *et al.* (2010) *Impact Analysis of the Proposed Strengthen Australian Qualifications Framework*, Australian Qualifications Framework Council, Adelaide, July, available at: http://www.aqf.edu.au/Portals/0/Documents/AQFC%20-%20impact%20analysis%20-%20final%208Oct10%20(3).pdf.
Buchanan, J. *et al.* (2013a, forthcoming) 'Unsustainable Employment Portfolios', *Work, Employment and Society* 27:396–413.
Buchanan, J. *et al.* (2013b, forthcoming) 'Changing Employment Portfolios and Inclusive Growth in Australia: Redistributing Risks at Work', pp. 68–88 in *Inclusive Growth in Australia: Social Policy as Economic Investment*, edited by Paul Smythe and John Buchanan. Sydney: Allen & Unwin.
Coates, D. (ed.) (2005) *Varieties of Capitalism, Varieties of Approaches*. Basingstoke: Palgrave Macmillan.
Crouch, C. (2005) *Capitalist Diversity and Change: Recombinant Governance and Institutional Entrepreneurs*. Oxford: Oxford University Press.
Eliot, T.S. ([1925] 1975) 'The Hollow Men', *Collected Poems*, Faber & Faber, London.
Froud, J., S. Johal, A. Leaver and K. Williams. 2006. *Financialization and Strategy: Narratives and Numbers*, Routledge, London.
Hall, P. and D. Soskice (eds) (2001) *Varieties of Capitalism: The Institutional Foundations of Comparative Advantage*. Oxford: Oxford University Press.
OECD (2004) *Employment Outlook*. Paris.
Peck, Jamie and Nik Theodore (2007) 'Variegated Capitalism', *Progress in Human Geography* 31:731–72.
Pontusson, Jonas (2005) 'Varieties and Commonalities of Capitalism', pp. 163–88 in *Varieties of Capitalism, Varieties of Approaches*, edited by D. Coates. Basingstoke: Palgrave Macmillan.
Richards, T. (2009) *Housing Market Developments*, Reserve Bank of Australia, Sydney.
Richardson, D. (2009) 'The Benefits of the Mining Boom – Where Did They Go?', Technical Brief 3, Australia Institute. Canberra   ▶

Rudd, K. (2009) 'Pain on the Road to Recovery', *Sydney Morning Herald*, 25 July.

Tett, G. (2009) *Fool's Gold: How Unrestrained Greed Corrupted a Dream, Shattered Global Markets and Unleashed a Catastrophe*. London: Little-Brown.

Thompson, Paul and Steve Vincent (2010) 'Labour Process Theory and Critical Realism', pp. 47–69 in *Working Life: Renewing Labour Process Analysis*, edited by P. Thompson and C. Smith. Basingstoke: Palgrave Macmillan.

Vidal, Matt (2011) 'Reworking Postfordism: Labor Process Versus Employment Relations', *Sociology Compass* 5:273–86.

Vidal, Matt (2013) 'Post-Fordism as a Dysfunctional Accumulation Regime: A Comparative Analysis of the USA, the UK and Germany', *Work, Employment and Society* 27:451–71.

Watson, I., Buchanan, J., Campbell, I. and Briggs, C. (2003) *Fragmented Futures: New Challenges in Working life*, Sydney: Federation Press.

Wooden, M. and Drago R. (2007) 'The Changing Distribution of Working Hours in Australia', University of Mebourne, Melbourne Institute Working Paper No. 19/07.

Incoherence and Dysfunctionality in the Institutional Regulation of Capitalism

4

Matt Vidal[1]

A number of distinct theoretical approaches to comparative political economy have been developed since the late 1970s, but the field has been dominated for the past decade by Hall and Soskice's (2001) varieties-of-capitalism theory. Hall and Soskice must be commended for developing an exceptionally fruitful research programme. Their theory established a robust defence of European social capitalism, confronting the universalistic model of neoclassical economics largely on its own metatheoretical terms with a second, nonliberal type of capitalism (Coates 2005; Crouch 2005). By taking institutional variation seriously, varieties of capitalism is surely a vast improvement over neoclassical economics, and the efforts of Hancké *et al.* (2007) and others to refine the theory so that it may accommodate conflict and power are laudable. But to the extent that it is a rational choice, efficiency/equilibrium approach, varieties of capitalism theory maintains core deficiencies of mainstream economics – in particular a severely limited ability to theorize dynamics of capital accumulation and crisis (Pontusson 2005; Peck and Theodore 2007; Thompson and Vincent 2010; Heyes *et al.* 2012; Vidal and Peck 2012).

Why, then, did Hall and Soskice's approach arise from just one among many to lead the field? In their otherwise sophisticated and balanced response to a wide range of critiques levelled at varieties-of-capitalism theory, Hancké *et al.* (2007:36) argued that Hall and Soskice (2001) 'revolutionized the study of contemporary political economy' with their core concepts of 'comparative institutional advantage, and complementarities, the (soft) rationalist method that underpinned it, the attention to institutions as the building blocks for coordination', and the typology between coordinated and liberal market economies. While it is true that Hall and Soskice worked with these concepts for years (see for example Soskice 1990), they were in academic circulation for decades. Thus, analysis of comparative institutional advantage, broadly conceived, had been conducted by a range of scholars including Maurice and collaborators (1980), Zysman (1983), Lane (1987, 1995), Boyer (1988b), Jessop (1989), Whitley (1992), Hollingsworth and collaborators (1994), Berger and Dore (1996) and Crouch and Streeck (1997). The concepts of institutional coordination and complementarity were central to Hollingsworth and Boyer's (1997) theory of social systems of production. Finally, the distinction between liberal and nonliberal forms of capitalism goes back at least to Dore (1973), and an essentially identical typology – Anglo-American versus Rhine capitalism – was popularized by Albert (1993). Ultimately, the influence of varieties of capitalism theory derives from its combination of a simple binary typology which has prima facie empirical plausibility – owing to its empirical referent being the remarkable contrast between the US and Germany – with a parsimonious and ostensibly rigorous rational-choice framework, thus imbuing its theoretical types with apparent empirical realism and actual analytical utility, however crude its descriptive accuracy and limited its analytical reach.

In this chapter I contribute to the development of an alternative research programme for comparative political economy, one that is sociological rather than economistic, accords a central role to the dynamics of accumulation and class struggle instead of efficiency and equilibrium, and does not privilege institutional coherence and complementarity over incoherence and dysfunctionality. My approach can broadly be termed Marxist institutionalism. More specifically, I work within the tradition of regulation theory (Boyer 1979; Lipietz 1982; Boyer 1988a; Aglietta [1979] 2000). However, while my regulation theoretic approach (Vidal 2012, 2013a, 2013b) is deeply inspired by Aglietta, Boyer and Lipietz, I differ from their Parisian school in arguing that its core distinction between a regime of accumulation and mode of regulation is theoretically untenable.

I begin by building on comparativists such as Crouch (2005) and Streeck (2009), who have emphasized how economies are institutionalized in ways that are often incoherent, incongruent and dysfunctional. I then argue that the historical growth regime approach of regulation theory provides a sounder basis for comparative political economy than the cross-sectional typological approach. Specifically, I elaborate an argument against synchronic approaches such as varieties of capitalism, which are ahistorical despite their attempts to add historical content into their types (Streeck 2009), in favour of diachronic approaches, which are better able to accommodate structural commonality *and* institutional variation among capitalist political economies. From there I present an argument for rejecting regulation theory's concept of a coherent institutional mode of regulation before presenting a theoretical reconstruction of regulation theory based on a distinction between functional and dysfunctional accumulation regimes. The final section applies the framework to the US, the UK and Germany, arguing that all are generic postfordist regimes, but each is dysfunctional in a distinct way, reflecting the nationally specific historical development of its institutional configuration within the generic structural context of postfordism. The latter is briefly elaborated for the US case, emphasizing the growth of bad jobs driven by a shift from a dominant logic of employment internalization under fordism to one of externalization under postfordism.

The Institutional Regulation of Capitalism

The failure to theorize core capitalist dynamics has not been limited to the varieties-of-capitalism school of comparative political economy, as indicated by Streeck's (2009:1) recent plea that 'The time has come to think, again, about the *commonalities* of capitalism.' Now, I endorse Streeck's (2009:3, 12–13) argument that institutional change cannot 'be explained in terms of an institutional theory *as such* but only in terms of a theory *of capitalism* as a substantive, that is, historical social order'. I return later to draw on his powerful argument that much of comparative political economy tends to 'organize empirical observations in historically invariant and in this sense static property spaces', pursuing a form of 'pseudo-universalistic *variable sociology*' that does not truly appreciate historical change, bringing into analysis 'at best, chronological time'. Unfortunately, however, Streeck (2009:241) largely ignores the continuous body of Marxist political economy from Marx's day to the present (for a review of recent debates, see Vidal 2012, 2013b), instead developing his own theory of 'unruly capitalists', which is surprisingly universalistic and ahistorical given the central thrust of his book. Streeck discusses accumulation dynamics but his model of unruly capitalists is heavily abstracted from such dynamics, with the dispositions of otherwise asocialized capitalists shaped exclusively by their control of capital in an undifferentiated context of competition. My argument here is that it is better to begin with accumulation, commodity and class relations to understand how these are institutionalized in specific times and places, interacting with other institutions and giving rise to specific social contexts within which various individual and capitalist class fractions develop understandings of their interests.

Both Streeck (2009) and Hall and Thelen (2009:261) reference Sewell's (2008) article on the temporalities of capitalism, which reminds them that, in Hall and Thelen's words, 'tumult is a permanent feature of capitalism'. Neither acknowledges how much Sewell (2008:525) builds on Marx, accepting the latter's basic argument that, in Sewell's words, 'the goal of capital is to generate profit; the rule that dominates capitalist economic life is accumulation of capital for accumulation's sake'. Importantly for Sewell, this accumulation dynamic gives capitalism a sort of contradictory temporality: repetitive cycles in the midst of continuous transformative change. Sewell's argument is a compelling extension, but the transformative nature of capitalist social relations has never been more eloquently articulated than by Marx and Engels ([1848] 1948) themselves:

> The bourgeoisie cannot exist without constantly revolutionizing the instruments of production, and thereby the relations of production, and with them the whole relations of society... Constant revolutionizing of production, uninterrupted disturbance of all social conditions, everlasting uncertainty and agitation distinguish the bourgeois epoch from all earlier ones... All that is solid melts into air, all that is holy is profaned.

Institutional Incoherence and Incongruence

Although accumulation for accumulation's sake and class struggle make capitalist social relations intrinsically dynamic, the institutionalization of social relations is also a fundamental element of human societies, giving them mid-term stability. When political economists first began explicitly comparing different economies, the postwar period displayed a remarkable stability across the OECD for around two decades. And while the 1970s were tumultuous, the 1980s and 1990s appeared to be periods of relative stability in national institutions (although already in the 1990s certain European countries were liberalizing financial and labour markets). Comparisons of Germany, Japan and the US displayed striking contrasts between what appeared to be highly coherent national systems, with complementary institutions generating important synergies. Based on such observations, the best way to explain the divergence between liberal and nonliberal forms of capitalism seemed to be an emphasis on complementarity and allied concepts of path dependency, increasing returns and lock-in. Thus, Boyer and Hollingsworth (1997:53) argued that 'any economy consists of a combination of institutional arrangements, all of which complement one another and thus acquire some efficiency'. Hall and Soskice (2001) articulated similar ideas, adopting a rational choice framework and the metaphor of institutional equilibrium, suggesting that institutional complementarities increase productivity and comparative advantage, hence institutional coherence and complementarity will tend to be maximized and firms in these contexts will make decisions consistent with their institutional environment.

In the face of increasing liberalization pressures and a growing low-wage sector in Germany, Hall and Thelen (2009:266–8) have articulated a defence of the durability of nonliberal capitalism that highlights the limits of a strong coherence and complementarities approach. They argue that liberalization is a concept so 'crude' that it 'obscures more than it illuminates' – a curious plea for nuance coming from the same scholars who classify Japan, Germany and Sweden as a single type of capitalism (Pontusson 2005; Peck and Theodore 2007). But to argue that the two types of economy 'operate according to different logics', that 'the differences among them are in kind rather than degree' and that there is no single continuum between them is to assert by definition that coordinated market economies are unable to be liberalized. Surely there are forms of market coordination in nonliberal economies just as there are forms of strategic coordination in liberal economies, both socially constructed institutional settlements capable of being radically reconstructed in the image of the other (although with the construction of nonliberal institutions being much more difficult). To be fair to Thelen, elsewhere (Palier and Thelen 2010) she has argued that growing dualization in Germany and France, between protected workers in the core and vulnerable workers in the periphery, distinguishes them from the Nordic countries (but see Schnyder (2012) on the growing low-wage sector in Sweden).

Institutional coherence and complementarity have dominated the comparative literature to the neglect of alternative configurations and outcomes. My goal here is not taxonomic but, if, following Deeg (2007), coherence refers to where two institutions share common principles, and complementarity where the conjunction of two institutions results in superior performance for a given outcome (either via synergy or supplementarity), then incoherence is where two institutions may coexist despite being based on conflicting principles, and incongruence an actual discordance among outcomes. Short of 'paralysing juxtaposition', to use Herrigel's (2005) term, institutional settlements may be relatively stable yet be more or less severely incoherent and incongruent. And we must remember Jackson's (Crouch et al. 2005) keen observation that although complementarities may be found for specific outcomes, in the real world there are many outcomes for which two institutions may have effects, making it highly unlikely that two institutions have an overall complementarity.

A number of incoherent institutional settlements have been noted within the German political economy. Herrigel (2000) documented a 'decentralized industrial order' of small- and mid-sized firms operating according to principles different from the better-known 'autarkic industrial order' of large, vertically integrated firms. Jackson (2003) and Höpner (2005) examined the rise of shareholder value pressures and practices alongside the maintenance of employee voice mechanisms. Deeg (2005) argued that a group of large banks have adopted a market logic while others have continued operating according to a consensual, voice logic, generating institutional 'bifurcation' into two heterogeneous subsystems. Doellgast (2012) demonstrated that unions, works councils and training systems in the German service sectors are much less coherent than those in the manufacturing sectors. Finally, Hermann (2008) showed how biotech firms were able to pursue radical innovation strategies in the German economy, which was supposedly institutionally conducive only to incremental innovation strategies. If institutional incoherence refers to the coexistence of conflicting principles, institutional incongruence refers to discordant outcomes. Examples from Germany include the rise of a low-paid and insecure sector alongside a protected workforce (Hassel 2007) and within the low-wage sector the weakening of collective bargaining (Lillie and Greer 2007) and an increasing difficulty for unions to engage in strategic coordination (Doellgast 2009).

More broadly, the growth of bad jobs and rising inequality in the midst of continued growth – common to Germany as well as the US, the UK and other OECD countries – are manifestly discordant outcomes produced by various national institutional configurations that are arguably incongruent as such. Examples of institutional incoherence can also be readily compiled for the US case. Thus Whitford (2005) showed that in manufacturing many firms were developing collaborative production networks which, although experiencing many problems, were forging a strategic path not consistent with or supported by the wider institutional framework. Similarly, Schneiberg (2007:49) documented 'substantial "off path" organization' with the establishment of publicly owned firms and cooperatives – coordinated economies – in US infrastructure industries over the first half of the twentieth century.

Considering incoherence and incongruence in theoretical terms, Whitley (1999) argued that contradictions and conflicts between competing principles and institutional logics lead to variation in institutional coherence. Quack and Morgan (2000:36–7) distinguished the coherent version of path dependency from 'dialectical' and 'experimental' versions. Both of the latter two types thrive on organizational diversity and permit the endogenous creation of new paths within the old. Dialectical path dependency emphasizes contradictions and tensions within institutional systems, and experimental path dependency highlights endemic uncertainty. Streeck and Yamamura (2003:45) argued similarly that 'socioeconomic systems... often seem beset with "dialectical" contradictions and riddled with self-made dysfunctions that can be fixed only provisionally'. Crouch (2005:11) noted that rule-breaking behaviour is common and that 'in real life, reproduction is never perfect, and individuals nearly always bring some idiosyncrasy, some independence and novelty to how they perform their roles'. Morgan (2007) argued further that firms do not simply accept institutional constraints and that national economies are characterized by a range of institutional logics at various levels. Wood and Lane (2012:9) discussed competing institutional orders and social structures as 'multi-layered and polyvalent'. Streeck (2009:107, 122–5) argued that functions turn into dysfunctions, that national models are 'precarious and temporary', and that dialectical change occurs through the accumulation of destabilizing consequences that result from the routine operation of an institution. On the latter he discusses, among many other examples, industry-level bargaining in Germany forcing small firms to increase productivity to pay for high wages but ultimately leading them to defect when they reach the limits of their productive capacity.

Cross-Sectional Types Versus Historical Growth Regimes

In order to properly understand both difference and similarity, it is necessary to move beyond cross-sectional typologies to study capitalism as a historical social formation. As Streeck (2009:102, 13) argued, focusing on cross-sectional comparisons misses commonalities across cases, because it emphasizes static properties rather than dynamic processes. Cross-sectional typologies, further, are based on 'a very narrow universe of space and time' that is unable to fully appreciate 'the uniqueness of a country's institutional order'. As an example, consider Hall's (2007) chapter on the evolution of European varieties of capitalism. There he presents nice in-depth profiles of Germany, Sweden and France that emphasize historical uniqueness, but when discussing the latter two cases the coordinated/liberal typology recedes into the background and it is hard to see what the typology could add to the analysis, other than highlighting that all engage in *some form* of strategic coordination in the context of nonliberal yet *very different* institutions in three countries.

The most theoretically developed alternative to the cross-sectional typological approach is the historical growth regime approach of regulation theory. Now, Crouch (2005:25) argued that the regulation approach is not a theory 'of true diversity in the sense of a continuing multiplicity of forms' because it is an evolutionary theory that sees later forms as 'superior' to earlier forms they superseded. But as Stephen Jay Gould (1992) has argued, Darwinian evolution does not imply superiority, in the sense of progressivity, because the mechanisms of selection are contingent and fortuitous events. Similarly, as Boyer (2005) and others have insisted, institutional co-evolution is characterized by contingencies, trial and error, and political struggle. At the same time, as Marxists have emphasized, there are also common pressures and similar technological and developmental trajectories, including explicit attempts to adopt what are perceived as best practices, such as the exporting of American institutions to Europe (Djelic 1998). *Pace* Crouch, regulation theory provides a methodological and conceptual apparatus for developing truly historical growth models that balance the need to appreciate difference and similarity across capitalist political economies. Specifically, a growth regime such as fordism is not an ideal type, based on which actual national deviations can be measured and classified, but a generic historical model designating a basic set of technological and structural characteristics which are common to a set of countries. In the fordist case these characteristics are a manufacturing-based economy with oligopolistic competition, producer-driven national supply chains, a Keynesian welfare state and international trade and capital controls. Within this generic model, each country will have its own more or less distinct institutional configuration.

This historical accumulation regime approach can accommodate continuity and change in a way that is unburdened, as is a typology such as coordinated/liberal capitalism, by the need to maintain fundamental characteristics of the type over time. In moving beyond reifying cross-sectional typologies of institutional variety, this approach is consistent with Peck and Theodore's (2007:733) notion of variegated capitalism, which emphasizes the combined and uneven development of national regimes and their 'polymorphic interdependence' within the global capitalist economy.

Now, the danger of shoehorning real, complex political economies into a theoretical straightjacket always exists, but this is far more likely based on a cross-sectional rather than a historical typology. What is the difference between specifying a core theoretical basis for a cross-sectional typology (for example strategic coordination) versus a theoretical basis for a generic historical growth regime? The historical core specifies a commonality, the cross-sectional core a distinction. The cross-sectional typology will produce difference as a matter of theoretical principle (Peck and Theodore 2007), whether it exists or not, as we have seen with Hall and Thelen's (2009) argument that coordinated economies cannot be liberalized. The historical typology could also be in danger of seeing similarity where it does not exist, but if used judiciously, with openness to the possibility of deviations from the criteria of commonality to the extent that a distinctive generic regime may develop – something I ponder in the conclusion with regard to postfordism in Germany – then it provides a sounder basis for empirical research and theoretical development. The cross-sectional approach can accommodate hybridization and the endogenous development of new types, but this shifts the analysis from the cross-sectional to the historical, and any enduring emphasis on the priority of institutional variation will continue to obscure or miss fundamental, constitutive aspects of distinct capitalist economies.

Regulation Theory Without the Mode of Regulation

Aglietta's *A Theory of Capitalist Regulation* ([1979] 2000) is a magisterial work that elaborated an institutional political economy of capitalism based on the theoretical architecture of Marx's *Capital*, Volumes 1 and 2, remaining largely faithful to Marx's classical formulations while creatively developing them to analyse the US case. In its subsequent thirty-year trajectory, regulation theory has increasingly shed its Marxian analytical orientation in favour of an evolutionary micro-organizational framework and a post-Keynesian macroeconomic framework.

Neither the term 'mode of regulation' nor any similar concept appears in Aglietta's original 1979 text, where he used the concept of accumulation regime to refer to the entire social formation in a given period. In terms of English-language publications, Boyer (1979) introduced the concept in a seminal article where he distinguished a competitive *régulation* – used as a noun, like a *mode* of regulation – from a monopolistic *régulation*. In the former, wages do not follow productivity growth, so real wage growth has to occur through price reductions. In the latter, explicit wage indexation becomes standardized through collective bargaining. In the same paper, Boyer articulated what has become the standard growth model of regulation theory. The competitive mode of regulation was 'incompatible with the new mode of accumulation at the end of the First World War... Recovery from the crisis presupposes a return to the *coherent relationship* between economic and social structures *and* the type of *regulation*' (Boyer 1979:112, emphasis added).

While there are a range of approaches in the broad family of regulation theory (for an overview, see Jessop 1990), the growth model developed by Boyer, and subsequently applied in a range of interesting studies by Lipietz (1987; 1988; 2001), has been the most influential. When most scholars think of regulation theory it is likely the Parisian school's mode of regulation that comes to mind. While Boyer and Lipietz have done much to expand the space for evolutionary and institutional research within economics and made numerous empirical and theoretical contributions in the process, my careful reading of the literature leads me to conclude that the Parisian school's growth model is irreparably ambiguous and ultimately redundant. In my analysis, the best hope for revitalizing regulation theory is to reject the concept of a mode of regulation and reconstruct the theory around the concepts of functional and dysfunctional accumulation regimes.

An Unsound Distinction Between Redundant Concepts

Early in the discussion, de Vroey (1984) argued that the notions of accumulation regime and forms of regulation should be treated as synonymous and understood in their broadest sense, but this call apparently fell on deaf ears. In an influential formulation, Lipietz (1987:14, 15) defined an accumulation regime as 'a fairly long-term stabilization of the allocation of social production between consumption and accumulation', and a mode of regulation as 'a set of internalized rules and social procedures which incorporate social elements into individual behaviour' via norms, habits, rules and laws. Fourteen years later, Lipietz (2001) used identical definitions. Boyer (1988a: 71, 75–6, emphasis original) defined an accumulation regime as 'the whole set of regularities which allow a general and more or less consistent evolution for capital formation'. The mode of regulation, then, is 'any set of rules and individual and collective behaviours which... make possibly conflicting *decentralized decisions* compatible... control and regulate the prevailing *accumulation regime*... [and] reproduce *basic social relationships* through a system of historically-determined institutional forms'. The 'combination' of an accumulation regime and a mode of regulation constitutes a 'mode of development'. These concepts are defined in identical terms in Boyer and Saillard's *Régulation Theory: The State of the Art* (2002a).

It is hard to make sense of this core distinction. The mode of regulation boils down to the institutional forms. But how do these differ from 'the whole set of regularities' which constitute the accumulation regime? Table 4.1 lists three elements in Boyer's definition of the accumulation

Table 4.1 Defining characteristics of the Parisian mode of development

Accumulation regime	Mode of regulation
A pattern of productive organization	The technical and social division of labour
Income shares	The determinants of direct and social wages
The volume and composition of effective demand	The standard of living of wage-earners in terms of the volume and origin of the commodities they consume

Source: Boyer (1988a).

regime and mode of regulation that refer to effectively identical socio-economic objects. If there is a distinction to be made here it can only be between actual social organization (the mode of regulation), on the one hand, and the broad outcome of that, the patterns that result from it (the accumulation regime), on the other. But this defines an accumulation regime as an outcome of its institutional formation, and does not provide any analytical power over the simpler alternative of focusing exclusively on the institutional forms.

In places, Boyer (Boyer and Saillard 2002b:38) suggests that the two concepts are different 'levels of analysis', but there is no further comment on this other than that one is a 'pattern' and the other 'specific configurations'. The only regulationist I am aware of who has attempted to elaborate the distinction between levels of analysis is Jessop (1989), who argues that the accumulation regime is the abstract model and the mode of regulation refers to concrete national configurations. This seems like a reasonable distinction – indeed it is similar to what I propose below – but it is clearly a use of the framework different from how it is predominantly used by Boyer and Lipietz, namely, a mode of regulation stabilizes an accumulation regime resulting in a particular mode of development. And it does not provide a theory of growth and crisis based on the interaction between an accumulation regime and mode of regulation, as for instance where Boyer (Boyer and Saillard 2002a) distinguished crises of the accumulation regime from those of the mode of regulation, referring to distinct socioeconomic structures rather than different levels of abstraction of the same structure.

The more common interpretation of the cryptic formulations of the Parisian school is that an accumulation regime (referring to economic relations) and the mode of regulation (referring to social institutions) must come into a sort of fit, with strong growth occurring only when a coherent institutional mode of regulation has been consolidated to stabilize an underlying economic regime. Thus, in Peck and Tickell's (1994:284) interpretation, a postfordist mode of development would require a 'structural coupling' between the accumulation regime and a new, coherent mode of regulation. Similarly Jessop and Sum (2006:226) noted a 'growing interest in what one might call the 'co-constitution' of [accumulation regimes] and modes of regulation' – although they did not provide any citations to this vein of regulationist research.

The Social Construction of Accumulation Regimes

In short, regulationists working in the Parisian vein have systematically failed to specify the analytical basis for a rigorous distinction between the accumulation regime and its mode of regulation. Although it has been elaborated too vaguely to be certain, the accumulation regime/mode of regulation distinction would seem to be yet another manifestation of the enduring yet highly problematic distinction between the economic and the social – as if there is an asocial economic realm that exists independently of cultural and political institutions – an argument increasingly criticized as illegitimate by economic sociologists (Krippner 2001; Vidal and Peck 2012). In my reformulation, accumulation regimes are understood as being constituted by cultural and political institutions. Indeed, as Nicolaus (1968) demonstrated, Marx saw the material *forces* of production as a fundamentally social and historical product.[2] There is no accumulation regime apart from the institutions that constitute it. Accumulation regimes refer to the entire complex of cultural–cognitive, normative, regulative and organizational institutions in a national social formation, which may be more or less compatible in key respects but also multiscalar (Peck and Theodore 2007), multifaceted, incoherent and incongruous.

Functional and Dysfunctional Accumulation Regimes

The most central issue for regulation theory is how capitalism is able to achieve expanded reproduction (growth) despite conflictual relations of production and inherent tendencies toward crisis. The question of growth cannot be separated from the question of crisis. While Boyer (1990) has argued that crises may occur either in the mode of regulation or the regime of accumulation, my reformulation reserves the term *crisis* for protracted periods of negative or near-zero growth, typically associated with bubbles (due to speculation with surplus capital and/or disproportionate growth fuelled by loose credit), and always followed by large-scale devaluation of capital.[3] If we want to reserve the term 'crisis' to refer to extended recessions resulting in extensive bankruptcies, the destruction of capital value and widespread corporate restructuring, then it makes sense to refer to the other 'crisis tendencies' associated with Marxist crisis theory as something else. I use the term stagnationist tendencies, referring in particular to (1) the rising technical composition of capital (that is, a rising capital/labour ratio, which puts downward pressure on profits), (2) a profit squeeze, and (3) underconsumptionism (the restriction of consumption power). Each generates fragility, instability and stagnation, intensifying the contradiction between the dual tendencies toward overproduction (a glut of commodities or excess industrial capacity) and underconsumptionism. In addition to the Marxist stagnationist tendencies, I borrow from Kaleckian macroeconomics to argue that a fourth stagnationist tendency is (4) debt-led growth, in which consumer credit plays a significant role in sustaining consumer demand (in the context of a declining wage share of GDP).

Marx and subsequent Marxists have extensively discussed counter-tendencies to the stagnationist tendencies. From a regulation theoretic perspective, such countertendencies are established only under certain institutional conditions (elaborated in the following section). An accumulation regime is thus *functional* when all four stagnationist tendencies have been offset within a particular institutional settlement. In such a context the economy will grow at steady rate, likely well above the 3 per cent per annum that is commonly deemed normal growth. An accumulation regime is *dysfunctional* when there is evidence that one or more stagnation tendencies are no longer being offset, but the economy remains out of crisis for an extended period of time. Based on the manifestation of stagnationist tendencies, there are three forms of dysfunctional accumulation:

1. A *declining or historically low profit rate* along with an associated rise in the capital/labour ratio (technical composition of capital) or the wage share of national income (profit squeeze).
2. *Underconsumptionism*, as indicated by declining or historically slow growth (below 3 per cent p.a.) along with a decline in the wage share.
3. *Debt-led growth*, as indicated by moderate growth levels and a declining wage share offset by rising/high household debt levels.

Fordism and Postfordism in the US, the UK and Germany

Here I present a generic model of the fordist and postfordist accumulation regimes based on my macroeconomic analysis of the US, the UK and Germany (Vidal 2013b) and my in-depth institutional analysis of the US case (Vidal 2012). A generic accumulation regime specifies the systemic pressures facing each country but leaves open the distinct institutional settlement realized within the generic structural context. For instance, in the US case, owing to the leading role of the Walton family of Wal-Mart, the largest employer in the country, I have labelled the postfordist regime there 'Waltonism' (Vidal 2012). Specification of the particular institutionalization of postfordism in Germany and the UK will have to await future research. The contrast between a generic accumulation regime and its unique institutionalization in individual countries is similar to Jessop's (1989) method of articulation, distinguishing an abstract regime of accumulation from more concrete modes of regulation, but as argued above, it is necessary to move beyond the latter because of its association with the Parisian growth model in which a stable mode of development requires that an *economic* regime must come into a close fit with a coherent *institutional* mode of regulation.

The *fordist accumulation regime* is defined as a generic social formation in which (1) the core employment sector is mass production manufacturing with (2) oligopolistic competition, (3) producer-led national supply chains and (4) a financially autonomous Keynesian state under an international system of structured capital and trade controls. This structural context made it possible to take wages out of competition in the core of the economy and allow high profits and high wages simultaneously. In the US a class compromise between capital and labour was institutionalized through the Treaty of Detroit in 1950 between the Big Three auto companies and the United Auto Workers. West Germany and the UK developed a similar structural context, the former realizing class compromise rooted in family-oriented Christian Democracy, the latter largely failing to reach a sustained class compromise over production control and wages. Peck and Tickell (1994) thus distinguished classical fordism in the US from 'flex-fordism' in West Germany and 'blocked fordism' in the UK (in addition to classifying a number of other mostly OECD countries). But rather than argue that each country has a coherent mode of institutional regulation of its underlying 'macroeconomically coherent production–distribution–consumption relationship' – hence distinguishing the economic from the institutional – I am proposing a distinction between a generic structural context (a developmental phase) and the particular national settlements realized in each country as matters of historical conjuncture. My working hypothesis is that most OECD countries achieved functional settlements because of the structural context of fordism, while under postfordism they will mostly be dysfunctional.

The fordist regime in the US effectively offset the various crisis and stagnation tendencies for fifteen or so years from 1950 to the mid 1960s.

Downward pressure on the profit rate owing to a rising technical composition of capital (physical capital/labour) was offset by a continuous rise in productivity, the latter facilitated by taylorist mass production and a growing domestic mass consumption market. Underconsumptionism (and hence the need for debt-led growth) was offset by rising real wages, the latter achieved in a large core sector of mostly unionized, vertically integrated firms with well-defined career ladders, along with a Keynesian welfare state.

The extent to which other OECD economies had a similar experience must await future research, but Glyn and colleagues (2007) presented data showing a profit squeeze beginning in the late 1960s for the US, France, Germany, Italy, the UK and Japan. With a secular decline in profit rates across the OECD, national fordisms transitioned into a dysfunctional regimes over the 1970s. Again in the US case, the corporate response to the fordist crisis was widespread restructuring, which accelerated the changing division of labour through global outsourcing and diversification of large corporations into a range of service sectors, resulting in a shift in power from manufacturing firms toward large retailers controlling global supply chains (Vidal 2013a). This corporate restructuring (along with technical change) ushered in the *postfordist regime*, a generic social formation in which (1) the core employment sector is producer and consumer services with (2) intense competition, (3) buyer-led international supply chains, and (4) financially constrained neoliberal states under globalized finance and highly liberalized trade. The basic characteristics of the fordist and postfordist accumulation regimes are listed in Table 4.2.

In the remainder of this chapter, I provide an overview of the different ways in which the postfordist regime has become dysfunctional in the US, UK and Germany. The fact that the growth regime in each country is

Table 4.2 Defining characteristics of the fordist and postfordist accumulation regimes

Fordism	Postfordism
Core employment sector in mass production manufacturing	Core employment sector in professional and consumer services
Oligopolistic competition	Intense competition
Producer-led national supply chains	Buyer-led international supply chains
Financially autonomous Keynesian state under an international system of structured capital and trade controls	Financially constrained neoliberal state under globalized finance and highly liberalized trade

Table 4.3 Sources of dysfunctional accumulation in postfordism

Manifest stagnationist tendencies	US	UK	Germany
Declining profit rate	Yes	Yes	Yes
Underconsumptionism	–	Yes	–
Debt-led growth	Yes	Possibly	–

dysfunctional in a different way suggests that each has a more or less distinct institutional configuration. Following this I briefly elaborate further on the institutional configuration in the US case. Given length constraints, this discussion will necessarily be highly schematic and incomplete. The discussion is not meant to resolve all of the problems raised above, but to illustrate how the theory provides a framework for the analysis of common capitalist pressures (here the stagnationist tendencies) and distinctive national institutional configurations.

Elsewhere (Vidal 2013b) I have presented macroeconomic data showing that the model of postfordism as an inherently dysfunctional regime fits the US, UK and Germany. Table 4.3 presents a summary of the findings. In terms of the average private sector profit rate, there is no rate that is normal across time and space; rather, what is considered a satisfactory profit rate depends on historical and comparative levels, with an unsatisfactory profit rate being indicated mainly by widespread corporate restructuring and/or disinvestment and reinvestment of capital. The postfordist regime in the US has been and continues to be dysfunctional because it has not experienced a sustained recovery in its profit rate (which averaged 21 per cent between 1945 and 1965, declined to a trough of 9 per cent in 1982, and averaged just 13 per cent between 1983 and 2006) and because it maintained moderate growth levels (3.2 per cent over the 1970s, 1980s and 1990s) via debt-led growth, and experienced dismal growth of 1.8 per cent in the 2000s. Debt-led growth was indicated by a decline in labour's share of national income (from 60 per cent in 1970 to 51 per cent in 2005) and a dramatic rise in household debt to income ratios (from 58 per cent 1960 to 137 per cent in 2007).

The postfordist regime in the UK has been and continues to be dysfunctional because it has not experienced a sustained recovery in the profit rate (from a high of 44 per cent in 1950, falling more or less continuously until hitting a low of just 8 per cent in 1975, remaining at or below 10 per cent until 1981, after which it began a slight recovery with peaks of 15 per cent in 1997 and 16 per cent in 2007) and it has experienced four decades of stagnant growth (below 3 per cent in each of the decades since the 1960s with just 2.0 per cent in the 2000s). Stagnation began in the 1970s but the decline in labour's share (from 74 per cent in

1975 to 60 per cent in 2008) and the profit rate recovery both began in 1980, suggesting a shift in the cause of stagnation from the profit rate decline under fordism to underconsumptionism in the postfordist regime. Household debt-to-income ratios rose dramatically (from 106 per cent in 1995 to 176 per cent in 2007) but not enough to boost growth out of stagnation, suggesting it may not be a debt-led regime, although it is likely that growth would be even more dismal without credit-driven consumption.

Finally, the postfordist regime in Germany has been and continues to be dysfunctional because it has not experienced a sustained profit-rate recovery (from a peak of 16 per cent in 1963 and again at 16 per cent in 1968, dropping steadily to a trough of 8 per cent in 1981, thereafter recovering slightly to a peak of 10 per cent in 1994 and rising only to 11 per cent in 2007) and because it has experienced three decades of stag-nant growth (around 2 per cent in the 1980s and 90s, dropping to just 1.2 per cent in the 2000s). Its wage share did not begin a sustained decline until 1993 (from 66 per cent to 57 per cent in 2007), suggesting that the stagnant growth is not driven by underconsumptionism but largely by a consistently low profit rate, likely in combination with global overpro-duction in manufacturing.

In terms of understanding distinct institutional settlements in each country, regulation theory has emphasized the changing articulation among institutional domains (Boyer 2000). The so-called standard model of employment – fulltime, long-term employment with a single employer, including security and opportunities for training and promo-tion – is actually a fordist creation. This model was made possible because competition and finance were subordinated to work and employment relations, the former through oligopolistic competition in the core manu-facturing sector and the prevalence of a logic of growth – as opposed to shareholder value – within business, the latter because fordism still provided opportunities for intensive growth and profit based on mass consumption. Additionally, as Morgan and Goyer (2012) argued, the Bretton Woods system of international exchange rate stability, capital controls and national monetary policy autonomy allowed finance to be subordinated to national growth, permitting different social settlements to be forged among the OECD economies.

Classical fordism in the US was characterized by logics of growth and *internalized employment relations*, meaning that best business practice was understood to include vertically integrated firms with internal markets, including detailed job ladders with well-defined training and promotion opportunities, and administratively determined wages associated with positions rather than individuals. The pressure of declining profits provided the context within which intensified competition and financialization began to dominate employment relations. In particular, the internationalization of production and the rise of a logic of shareholder value combined to generate a new predominant logic of *externalized employment relations*, namely outsourcing and deunionization, reducing employment security, training and promotion opportunities, and returning to market-determined wages (Vidal 2013a). The ascendance of the logic of shareholder value ensured that the externalization logic took hold even in core service sectors like retail sales, leisure and hospitality that are ostensibly more shielded from international wage competition than jobs subject to offshoring. Along with the broader transition to a service economy (driven by global outsourcing and corporate restructuring), employment externalization in the US has generated a rise in entry-level jobs with low wages and no training or promotion opportunities, and a decline in mid-level jobs, leading to polarized job growth. There is also evidence of polarized job growth in the UK and Germany (Fernández-Macías 2012). The extent to which a logic of employment externalization has driven job polarization in the UK and Germany, as well as examination of the broader institutional settlements, will have to await future research.

Conclusion

This chapter has covered a lot of ground in a limited space, and as a result there will no doubt be objections to various arguments that have been made but not fully defended. While I do not expect critical readers to accept all of my sometimes broad-brush arguments as such, my hope is that the arguments made here will be plausible and provocative enough to achieve two objectives. First, I hope to have raised serious concerns about the validity of cross-sectional typologies for comparative political economy. However much scholars attempt to add historical content to cross-sectional typologies of capitalism, such typologies are fundamentally ahistorical in so far as they are encumbered by the need to maintain core characteristics of the individual types. When the starting premise is the existence of two or more distinctive types of capitalism, it is hard to avoid reifying one's types. In the dynamic, restless world of global capitalism, national institutional settlements are subject to a range of transformative internal and external pressures. A sounder approach to comparative political economy is to appreciate that global capitalism is a variegated system of combined and uneven development in which groups of countries experience common developmental phases, common structural contexts within which each individual country realizes a more or less distinct conjunctural social formation.

Second, I hope to have convinced readers that a Marxist regulationist approach offers a theoretical framework for comparative political economy that is able to illuminate and explain both systemic commonalities as well as institutional differences across countries. The basic research programme of regulation theory is to understand how capitalism, with its inherent tendencies toward class conflict and crisis, is able to realize expanded reproduction. However, if regulation theory is to be viable it must move beyond the Parisian school's distinction between an underlying accumulation regime and a coherent national mode of regulation, which, with its functionalist and mechanistic undertones, has made many scholars who might otherwise be sympathetic to regulation theory shy away from it. Theoretically, it is based on an untenable distinction between the economic and the social. Empirically, national institutional settlements typically contain a range of incoherent principles, conflicting logics and macroeconomic dysfunctions that are simply inconsistent with the notion of a coherent institutional mode of regulation.

I proposed a constructionist theory of accumulation regimes, in which the latter are functional if the national institutional configuration is able to offset various stagnationist tendencies – a declining or low profit rate, underconsumptionism or debt-led growth – and dysfunctional if one or more of these tendencies becomes manifest. During the fordist period in the US case, from 1950 to the mid 1960s, various crisis and stagnation tendencies were offset and the country experienced a historically unprecedented combination of high profits and rising real wages. The tendency toward a declining rate of profit was offset by a continuous rise in productivity associated with mass production for an expanding domestic mass consumption market, including institutional supports for mass consumption such as strong unions and a Keynesian welfare state. Underconsumptionism and excessive household debt were offset by rising real wages associated with core employment in a manufacturing sector characterized by oligopolistic competition. Within this structural context, the institutional settlement included the internalization of employment into vertically integrated corporations with well-developed internal labour markets. As the fordist regime entered into terminal crisis in the late 1960s under the weight of declining profit rates, the corporate sector engaged in widespread restructuring (aided by a liberalizing state and international trade regime), leading to a structural transformation of the economy to one characterized by core employment in services, intense and internationalized competition, and buyer-led international supply chains. The emerging institutional settlement in this context included employment externalization via outsourcing, subcontracting and lean staffing strategies, anti-unionism and a return to market-determined wages associated with performance.

My argument is that Germany and the UK developed along very similar structural trajectories, experiencing structural conditions close to the US under the fordist and postfordist period. I presented evidence that at a macroeconomic level each of the three countries is experiencing dysfunctional growth, although each in a different way, likely reflecting distinctive institutional configurations within broadly similar structural conditions. There is also evidence that each country is experiencing a rising proportion of bad jobs in overall job growth, which is polarized in all three countries. The fact that both of these outcomes – dysfunctional macro growth and discordant job growth – are common across the three countries gives a high level of plausibility to the theoretical framework presented here. However, there remain of course a number of unresolved issues and open questions. Most importantly for my argument here is the question of how closely the generic regimes of fordism and postfordism fit Germany and the UK. For example, how far does the generic postfordist regime fit Germany in terms of buyer-driven commodity chains? Germany also differs from the US and the UK in terms of distinctive institutions supporting demand, including less household debt, a more equal distribution of wages and better social provision. And future research will have to determine the extent to which a dominant logic of employment externalization is shaping employment outcomes in Germany and the UK, as it is in the US. The point of the research programme is not to shoehorn distinctive national configurations into theoretical types, but to grasp and understand the complex interconnections between generic historical accumulation regimes and the distinctive ways they become institutionalized in particular countries, in particular by examining connections between macroeconomic dynamics and meso- and micro-organizational trends.

Notes

1 I would like to thank Ellen Christensen, Ian Greer, Marco Hauptmeier, Jamie Peck and Gerhard Schnyder for providing detailed and very helpful comments on this chapter.
2 For an elaboration of Marx as a (realist) social constructionist, see Vidal and Peck (2012) and for other formulations of constructionist institutionalism, in which even the most liberal economies are seen as deeply

institutionalized, see Whitley (1999), Quack and Morgan (2000), Crouch (2005) and Hay (2005).

3 This section draws heavily from Vidal (2013b), which provides an in-depth discussion of Marxist crisis theory.

REFERENCES

Aglietta, Michel ([1979] 2000) *A Theory of Capitalist Regulation: The US Experience.* London: Verso.

Albert, Michel (1993) *Capitalism Against Capitalism.* London: Whurr.

Berger, Suzanne and Ronald Dore (eds) (1996) *National Diversity and Global Capitalism.* Ithaca, NY: Cornell University Press.

Boyer, Robert (1979) 'Wage Formation in Historical Perspective: The French Experience', *Cambridge Journal of Economics* 3:99–118.

Boyer, Robert (1988a) 'Technical Change and the Theory of "Régulation"', pp. 67–94 in *Technical Change and Economic Theory*, edited by G. Dosi *et al.* London: Pinter.

Boyer, Robert (1988b) 'Wage/Labour Relations, Growth, and Crisis: A Hidden Dialectic', pp. 3–25 in *The Search for Labour Market Flexibility: The European Economies in Transition*, edited by R. Boyer. Oxford: Clarendon Press.

Boyer, Robert (1990) *The Regulation School: A Critical Introduction.* New York: Columbia University Press.

Boyer, Robert (2000) 'Is a Finance-Led Growth Regime a Viable Alternative to Fordism? A Preliminary Analysis', *Economy and Society* 29:111–45.

Boyer, Robert (2005) 'Coherence, Diversity, and the Evolution of Capitalisms – The Institutional Complementarity Hypothesis', *Evolutionary and Institutional Economic Review* 2:43–80.

Boyer, Robert and J. Rogers Hollingsworth (1997) 'The Variety of Institutional Arrangements and Their Complementarity in Modern Economies', pp. 49–54 in *Contemporary Capitalism: The Embeddedness of Institutions*, edited by J.R. Hollingsworth and R. Boyer. Cambridge: Cambridge University Press.

Boyer, Robert and Yves Saillard (eds) (2002a) *Régulation Theory: The State of the Art* London: Routledge.

Boyer, Robert and Yves Saillard (2002b) 'A Summary of *Régulation* Theory', pp. 36–44 in *Régulation Theory: The State of the Art*, edited by R. Boyer and Y. Saillard. London: Routledge.

Coates, David (2005) 'Paradigms of Explanation', pp. 1–25 in *Varieties of Capitalism, Varieties of Approaches*, edited by D. Coates. Basingstoke: Palgrave Macmillan.

Crouch, Colin (2005) *Capitalist Diversity and Change: Recombinant Governance and Institutional Entrepreneurs.* Oxford: Oxford University Press.

Crouch, Colin and Wolfgang Streeck (ed.) (1997) *Political Economy of Modern Capitalism: Mapping Convergence and Diversity.* London: Sage.

Crouch, Colin *et al.* (2005) 'Dialogue on "Institutional Complementarity and Political Economy"', *Socio-Economic Review* 3:359–82.

de Vroey, Michel (1984) 'A Regulation Approach Interpretation of Contemporary Crisis', *Capital & Class* 23:45–66.

▶

Deeg, Richard (2005) 'Change from Within: German and Italian Finance in the 1990s', pp. 169–202 in *Beyond Continuity: Institutional Change in Advanced Political Economies*, edited by W. Streeck and K. Thelen. Oxford: Oxford University Press.

Deeg, Richard (2007) 'Complementarity and Institutional Change in Capitalist Systems', *Journal of European Public Policy* 14:611–30.

Djelic, Marie-Laure (1998) *Exporting the American Model: The Postwar Transformation of European Business*. Oxford: Oxford University Press.

Doellgast, Virginia (2009) 'Still a Coordinated Model? Market Liberalization and the Transformation of Employment Relations in the German Telecommunications Industry', *Industrial and Labor Relations Review* 63:3–23.

Doellgast, Virginia (2012) *Disintegrating Democracy at Work: Labor Unions and the Future of Good Jobs in the Service Economy*. Ithaca, NY: ILR Press.

Dore, Ronald (1973) *British Factory – Japanese Factory: The Origins of National Diversity in Industrial Relations*. Berkeley, CA: University of California Press.

Fernández-Macías, Enrique (2012) 'Job Polarization in Europe? Changes in the Employment Structure and Job Quality, 1995–2007', *Work and Occupations* 39:157–82.

Glyn, Andrew, Alan Hughes, Alain Lipietz and Ajit Singh (2007) 'The Rise and Fall of the Golden Age', pp. 39–125 in *The Golden Age of Capitalism: Reinterpreting the Postwar Experience*, edited by S.A. Marglin and J.B. Schor. Oxford: Oxford University Press.

Gould, Stephen Jay (1992) *Ever Since Darwin: Reflections in Natural History*. New York: Norton.

Hall, Peter (2007) 'The Evolution of Varieties of Capitalism in Europe', pp. 39–85 in *Beyond Varieties of Capitalism: Conflict, Contradictions, and Complementarities in the European Economy*, edited by B. Hancké, M. Rhodes and M. Thatcher. Oxford: Oxford University Press.

Hall, Peter A. and David Soskice (2001) 'An Introduction to Varieties of Capitalism', pp. 1–68 in *Varieties of Capitalism: The Institutional Foundations of Comparative Advantage*, edited by P.A. Hall and D. Soskice. Oxford: Oxford University Press.

Hall, Peter and Kathleen Thelen (2009) 'Institutional Change in Varieties of Capitalism', pp. 251–72 in *Debating Varieties of Capitalism: A Reader*, edited by B. Hancké. Oxford: Oxford University Press.

Hancké, Bob, Martin Rhodes and Mark Thatcher (2007) 'Introduction: Beyond Varieties of Capitalism', pp. 3–38 in *Beyond Varieties of Capitalism: Conflict, Contradictions, and Complementarities in the European Economy*, edited by B. Hancké, M. Rhodes and M. Thatcher. Oxford: Oxford University Press.

Hassel, Anke (2007) 'What Does Business Want? Labour Market Reforms in CMEs and Its Problems', pp. 253–77 in *Beyond Varieties of Capitalism: Conflict, Contradictions, and Complementarities in the European Economy*, edited by B. Hancké, M. Rhodes and M. Thatcher. Oxford: Oxford University Press.

Hay, Colin (2005) 'Two Can Play at That Game... or Can They? Varieties of Capitalism, Varieties of Institutionalism', pp. 106–21 in *Varieties of Capitalism, Varieties of Approaches*, edited by D. Coates. Basingstoke: Palgrave Macmillan.

▶

Herrigel, Gary (2000) *Industrial Constructions: The Sources of German Industrial Power* Cambridge: Cambridge University Press.

Herrigel, Gary (2005) 'Institutionalists at the Limits of Institutionalism: A Constructivist Critique of Two Edited Volumes from Wolfgang Streeck and Kozo Yamamura ', *Socio-Economic Review* 3:559–67.

Herrmann, Andrea M (2008) 'Rethinking the Link Between Labour Market Flexibility and Corporate Competitiveness: A Critique of the Institutionalist Literature', *Socio-Economic Review* 6:637–69.

Heyes, Jason, Paul Lewis and Ian Clark (2012) 'Varieties of Capitalism, Neoliberalism and the Economic Crisis of 2008–?', *Industrial Relations Journal* 43:222–41.

Hollingsworth, J. Rogers and Robert Boyer (1997) 'Coordination of Economic Actors and Social Systems of Production', pp. 1–47 in *Contemporary Capitalism: The Embeddedness of Institutions*, edited by J.R. Hollingsworth and R. Boyer. Cambridge: Cambridge University Press.

Hollingsworth, J. Rogers, Philippe C. Schmitter and Wolfgang Streeck (1994) *Governing Capitalist Economies: Performance and Control of Economic Sectors.* Oxford: Oxford University Press.

Höpner, Martin (2005) 'What Connects Industrial Relations and Corporate Governance? Explaining Institutional Complementarity', *Socio-Economic Review* 3:331–58.

Jackson, Gregory (2003) 'Corporate Governance in Germany and Japan: Liberalization Pressures and Responses During the 1990s', pp. 261–305 in *The End of Diversity? Prospects for German and Japanese Capitalism*, edited by K. Yamamura and W. Streeck. Ithaca, NY: Cornell University Press.

Jessop, Bob (1989) 'Conservative Regimes and the Transition to Post-Fordism: The Cases of Great Britain and West Germany', pp. 261–99 in *Capitalist Development and Crisis Theory: Accumulation, Regulation and Spatial Restructuring*, edited by M. Gottdiener and N. Komninos. New York: St Martin's Press.

Jessop, Bob (1990) 'Regulation Theories in Retrospect and Prospect', *Economy and Society* 19:153–215.

Jessop, Bob and Ngai-Ling Sum (2006) *Beyond the Regulation Approach: Putting Capitalist Economies in Their Place.* Cheltenham: Edward Elgar.

Krippner, Greta R. (2001) 'The Elusive Market: Embeddedness and the Paradigm of Economic Sociology', *Theory and Society* 30:775–810.

Lane, Christel (1987) 'Capitalism or Culture? A Comparative Analysis of the Position in the Labour Process and Labour Market of Lower White-Collar Workers in the Financial Services Sector of Britain and the Federal Republic of Germany', *Work, Employment & Society* 1:57–83.

Lane, Christel (1995) *Industry and Society in Europe: Stability and Change in Britain, Germany and France.* Aldershot: Edward Elgar.

Lillie, Nathan and Ian Greer (2007) 'Industrial Relations, Migration, and Neoliberal Politics: The Case of the European Construction Sector', *Politics & Society* 35:551–81.

Lipietz, Alain (1982) 'Towards Global Fordism?', *New Left Review* I/132:31–47.

Lipietz, Alain (1987) *Mirages and Miracles: Crisis in Global Fordism.* London: Verso.

▶

Lipietz, Alain (1988) 'Accumulation, Crises, and Ways Out', *International Journal of Political Economy* 18:10–43.

Lipietz, Alain (2001) 'The Fortunes and Misfortunes of Post-Fordism', pp. 17–36 in *Phases of Capitalist Development: Booms, Crises and Globalizations*, edited by R. Albritton, M. Itoh, R. Westra and A. Zuege. Basingstoke: Palgrave Macmillan.

Marx, Karl and Frederick Engels ([1848] 1948) *The Communist Manifesto*. New York: International Publishers.

Maurice, Marc, Arndt Sorge and Malcolm Warner (1980) 'Societal Differences in Organizing Manufacturing Units: A Comparison of France, West Germany, and Great Britain', *Organization Studies* 1:59–86.

Morgan, Glenn (2007) 'The Theory of Comparative Capitalisms and the Possibilities for Local Variation', *European Review* 15:353–71.

Morgan, Glenn and Michel Goyer (2012) 'Is There a Global Financial System? The Locational Antecedents and Institutionally Bounded Consequences of the Financial Crisis', pp. 119–45 in *Capitalisms and Capitalism in the Twenty-First Century*, edited by G. Morgan and R. Whitley. Oxford: Oxford University Press.

Nicolaus, Martin (1968) 'The Unkown Marx', *New Left Review* I/48:41–61.

Palier, Bruno and Kathleen Thelen (2010) 'Institutionalizing Dualism: Complementarities and Change in France and Germany', *Politics & Society* 38:119–48.

Peck, Jamie and Nik Theodore (2007) 'Variegated Capitalism', *Progress in Human Geography* 31:731–72.

Peck, Jamie and Adam Tickell (1994) 'Searching for a New Institutional Fix: The After-Fordist Crisis and the Global-Local Disorder', pp. 280–316 in *Post-Fordism: A Reader*, edited by A. Amin. Oxford: Blackwell.

Pontusson, Jonas (2005) 'Varieties and Commonalities of Capitalism', pp. 163–88 in *Varieties of Capitalism, Varieties of Approaches*, edited by D. Coates. Basingstoke: Palgrave Macmillan.

Quack, Sigrid and Glenn Morgan (2000) 'Institutions, Sector Specialisation and Economic Performance Outcomes', pp. 27–52 in *National Capitalisms, Global Competition, and Economic Performance*, edited by S. Quack, G. Morgan and R. Whitley. Amsterdam: John Benjamins.

Schneiberg, Marc (2007) 'What's on the Path? Path Dependence, Organizational Diversity and the Problem of Institutional Change in the US Economy, 1900–1950', *Socio-Economic Review* 5:47–80.

Schnyder, Gerhard (2012) 'Like A Phoenix from the Ashes? Reassessing the Transformation of the Swedish Political Economy Since the 1970s', *Journal of European Public Policy* 19:1126–45.

Sewell, William H. (2008) 'The Temporalities of Capitalism', *Socio-Economic Review* 6:517–37.

Soskice, David (1990) 'Reinterpreting Corporatism and Explaining Unemployment: Coordinated and Non-Coordinated Market Economies', pp. 170–211 in *Labour Relations and Economic Performance*, edited by R. Brunetta and C. Dell'Agringa. London: Macmillan.

Streeck, Wolfgang (2009) *Re-Forming Capitalism: Institutional Change in the Germany Political Economy*. Oxford: Oxford University Press.

▶

Streeck, Wolfgang and Kozo Yamamura (2003) 'Introduction: Convergence or Diversity? Stability and Change in German and Japanese Capitalism', pp. 1–50 in *The End of Diversity? Prospects for German and Japanese Capitalism*, edited by K. Yamamura and W. Streeck. Ithaca, NY: Cornell University Press.

Thompson, Paul and Steve Vincent (2010) 'Labour Process Theory and Critical Realism', pp. 47–69 in *Working Life: Renewing Labour Process Analysis*, edited by P. Thompson and C. Smith. Basingstoke: Palgrave Macmillan.

Vidal, Matt (2012) 'On the Persistence of Labor Market Insecurity and Slow Growth in the US: Reckoning with the Waltonist Growth Regime', *New Political Economy* 17:543–64.

Vidal, Matt (2013a) 'Low-Autonomy Work and Bad Jobs in Postfordist Capitalism', *Human Relations* 66:587–612.

Vidal, Matt (2013b) 'Postfordism as a Dysfunctional Accumulation Regime: A Comparative Analysis of the USA, the UK and Germany', *Work, Employment and Society* 27:451–71.

Vidal, Matt and Jamie Peck (2012) 'Sociological Institutionalism and the Socially Constructed Economy', pp. 594–611 in *The Wiley-Blackwell Companion to Economic Geography*, edited by T. Barnes, J. Peck and E. Sheppard. Oxford: Wiley-Blackwell.

Whitford, Josh (2005) *The New Old Economy: Networks, Institutions, and the Organizational Transformation of American Manufacturing*. Oxford: Oxford University Press.

Whitley, Richard (1999) *Divergent Capitalisms: The Social Structuring and Change of Business Systems*. Oxford: Oxford University Press.

Whitley, Richard (ed.) (1992) *European Business Systems: Firms and Markets in Their National Contexts*. London: Sage.

Wood, Geoffrey T. and Christel Lane (2012) 'Institutions, Change, and Diversity', pp. 1–31 in *Capitalist Diversity and Diversity within Capitalism*, edited by C. Lane and G.T. Wood. London: Routledge.

Zysman, John (1983) *Governments, Markets, and Growth: Financial Systems and the Politics of Industrial Change*. Ithaca, NY: Cornell University Press.

National Institutions

Value Chains and Networks in Services: Crossing Borders, Crossing Sectors, Crossing Regimes?

Bettina Haidinger, Annika Schönauer, Jörg Flecker and Ursula Holtgrewe

The relocation of work across regional and national borders has attracted research interest since the debate on the 'new international division of labour' in the 1970s. This also goes for the lengthening of value chains caused by the increasing vertical disintegration of transnational companies. While research on global value chains has focused on inter-firm power relations and related questions of economic development for a long time, more recently the analysis of issues related to work and employment in this context has regained currency. Obviously, the quality of work and employment is directly related to the restructuring of value chains and production networks: wage differentials between countries are the main driver of work relocation in labour-intensive sectors, and differences in working hours and health and safety regulations also influence decisions on business locations. A comparative perspective taking into account the institutional embeddedness of capitalist modes of production is thus essential for understanding the functioning of value chains and networks. However, although both approaches share a reference point in world system theory (Bair 2005; Bair and Werner 2011), so far the debates in comparative political economy have hardly been incorporated into global value chain research – and vice versa (Lane 2008).

This chapter discusses current developments of value chains and networks from a comparative perspective. In doing so it makes explicit some of the links between the rather separated debates of global value chain and production network analysis on the one hand, and the comparative discourse on varieties of capitalism and national employment regimes on the other. In this context, subcontracting and outsourcing are part and parcel of segmented labour markets. It has been argued that tapping a less protected peripheral labour market (within a country or abroad) may stabilize the core segment which is often equated with a 'national regime' or particular variety of capitalism, but more recent evidence shows how the lengthening of value chains may also lead to a fragmentation of employment systems and thus undermine an overall 'regime', weakening the distinctiveness of a variety of capitalism (Flecker and Meil 2010). In addition, cross-border networks and value chains allow companies' 'regime shopping' and 'institutional arbitrage', and the threat of this already may weaken labour and undermine its capacity to defend particular characteristics of a national regime (Doellgast and Greer 2007). Vice versa, patterns of value chain restructuring have also been found to vary in the context of various employment regimes (Holtgrewe *et al.* 2009).

The empirical focus of this chapter is on the service sector, which has only recently gained attention in value chain and network research. Looking at two highly diverse industries, namely parcel delivery on the one hand and software development on the other, different types of value chains are analysed from a comparative perspective. Both of the sectors in focus – as our empirical evidence shows – are increasingly subject to value chain restructuring, though in different modes and with different focus.

The chapter is structured as follows. First, we synthesize theoretical considerations on the functioning of (global) service value chains and networks with debates about the role of institutions and governance for production and employment regimes. For this, we draw on both bodies of literature: on studies of the emergence and restructuring of (global) value chains and outsourcing processes on the one hand and on those studies of varieties of capitalism and national employment regimes that take the sectoral logic of production and employment regimes explicitly into account. This exercise will pave the way for analysing findings from two empirical studies in the logistics and information technology sector.

Service Value Chains: Vertical Disintegration, Sectoral Governance and Segmented Employment Regimes in a Flexible Service Economy

The concept of the value chain is usually used to denote organizationally or spatially separated stages of an entire production chain, for example from research and development to the distribution of products (Gereffi *et al.* 2005) Recent research has started to acknowledge the increasing externalization and outsourcing of service functions and has shifted attention to the service sector (Flecker and Meil 2010; Thompson *et al.* 2013; Flecker *et al.* 2013). In various industries and the public sector, complete generic business functions such as specialized accounting, research and development, human resources and information technology service provision, including call centres (Huws *et al.* 2004; Marchington *et al.* 2005; Batt *et al.* 2009; Taylor 2010), have been reshaped into value chains and networks of service provision that cross organizational and national boundaries. Another important externalized business function is distribution, for example transport services and logistics, where so-called third-party firms take over the linking of the production with the retailing and distribution sphere (Newsome 2010).

Vertical Disintegration in a Flexible Service Economy

The lengthening of value chains – including service value chains – has been reflected as 'the *emergence of a flexible service economy* [that] could be regarded at least in part as a manifestation of organizations' outsourcing strategies' (Rubery 2006:6, emphasis added). Wills (2009:444) even speaks of a 'capitalism where subcontracted employment relations are becoming paradigmatic'. An increasing number of workers are no longer directly employed by the organization where and/or for whom they work but by third-party firms subcontracted by the lead firm, resulting in fragmented employment relations and working conditions (Meil 2009; Flecker 2010). By way of subcontracting, companies may tap the lower end of a segmented labour market and get access to low-waged or less-protected workers or may stretch activities across borders by offshoring (Sass and Fifekova 2011).

Some forms of outsourcing, such as software development and information technology services, affect the higher-skilled end of the labour market. Regarding the impact on work organization, optimistic views claim that networked organizations offer opportunities for new ways of working, less hierarchy and more opportunities for self-development or gaining access to new or complementary knowledge. Information technology is classified as a sector where external sourcing of technologically complex products requires more collaborative forms of network governance, in particular when services are offshored (Lane 2008).

Focusing on negative consequences, Frade and Darmon (2005) describe value chains in general as 'risk-and-flexibility transfer chains' in which the main reasons for externalization strategies are cost-cutting and risk-spreading and result in the extension of precarious employment. As we shall see, value chains in logistics for example are comprised of a real cascade of subcontracting entities. Relations among them are characterized by short-term contracts and increased competition (Wills 2009:445). Service providers pass on time and cost pressure at the expense of their employees' pay and standards of work. Here, the distinction between market transactions and employment relationships becomes blurred, with 'extended hierarchies' in inter-firm networks (Thompson 1993) and labour processes under the control of both the employer and the employer's client organization (Marchington *et al.* 2005; Rubery 2006). Indeed, 'business to business contracting may act to place very strict constraints on the subcontracting organizations in terms of wage levels, work organization and even working time arrangements'. (Rubery 2006:10). These strategies of interorganizational contracting lead to a segmentation of production processes with consequences for the organization of industrial relations: jobs may be moved from a well-organized core to a more poorly organized periphery of firms that have no or less-favourable collective agreements negotiated by different unions (Doellgast and Greer 2007; Meil 2009; Batt *et al.* 2009). The bypassing of employment protection by offshoring or making recourse to labour not covered by the 'original' sectoral employment regulations contributes to increased variation and uneven distribution of wages and working conditions within a sector.

Value Chain Governance: Blurring Sector Specificities

Value chains and production networks however are not driven purely by economies of cost but are shaped by their institutional environments. Critics have argued that global value chain research scholars 'focus narrowly on the governance of inter-firm transactions' (Coe *et al.* 2008:272). Expanding the notion of governance, Global Production Network scholars conversely 'attempt to encompass all relevant sets of actors and relationships' including states and multiscalar regulatory systems as well as labour agency. The relationship of institutional environments and company strategies to extend value chains or production networks thus requires further investigation.

The well-known varieties-of-capitalism approach argues that national institutions steer the actions of companies towards the path prescribed by the encompassing national model of capitalism (liberal or coordinated) (Hall and Soskice 2001), which generates specific strengths (comparative advantages) and weaknesses. The theory thus predicts a sectoral specialization of entire national economies, resulting in a comparative institutional 'home' advantage against other national contexts (Hall and Soskice 2001:56; Crouch 2009). Gallie (2007:16–19) argues that this approach lacks a concept of power and, following Korpi (2006), emphasizes the relative power resources of capital and labour including workers' mobilization and welfare state development as crucial determinants for the emergence of certain regime types.

Lane (2008) was the first to integrate the role of national institutions along the lines of varieties of capitalism into global value chain research and to explore the 'circumstances in which global firms either reinforce and even export national institutionalized practices or corrode national patterns of firms' co-ordination with other actors' (p. 234). Lane concentrates her analysis on national (and international) institutions' influence on *firms' strategies* to succeed in a globally competitive environment and, vice versa, on the ways in which globally operative firms impact on developments in institutions by exercising strategic choices for or against a particular institutional context, a practice also known as 'regime shopping'.

While this approach regards institutional environments as fairly stable, other scholars put more emphasis on the strategic or emergent impact of such strategies on institutional change. National business actors do challenge institutional arrangements that they see as inadequate for their business activities or utilize gaps in coordination processes to redesign institutional arrangements with either adapting or disruptive effects (for example Oliver 1991; Streeck and Thelen 2005; Whitford 2005).

While 'outsourcing' in Lane's (2008) interpretation of regime types is only referred to as 'gaining access to new or complementary knowledge in industries' and as a cost-cutting strategy, for Gallie (2007:13,19) outsourcing and subcontracting exacerbate the dualization of labour markets in those regime types that have established a secondary labour market that used to support the high wages and job security in the core segment. Threats of exit to cheaper production sites across countries or of outsourcing certain business tasks function as a means to (de)regulate workplace conditions. In coordinated institutional contexts, there have been attempts by social actors to negotiate concessions to retain jobs; the workers taking pay cuts, or reductions or unpaid increases in working time in exchange for job security guarantees (Meil 2009; Flecker and Meil 2010). Therefore, core workforces, in spite of the stability of institutions such as sector-level agreements, may still be weakened by the movement of some jobs to another sector or another country.

For Crouch et al. (2009) and Thelen (2012:145) *sector specificities* are crucial for institutional or companies' adaptive strategies or deviation from the established (national) governance system. When companies discover a viable alternative to the national corset by accessing resources or rules in the global system, sectoral or corporate arrangements may become decoupled from the national production system. This sector specificity translates also into variation within industrial relations models. According to Bechter *et al.* (2012:199), 'some countries that are often considered as "models" of industrial relations types emerge as particularly differentiated by sector, to the point where the cogency of the concept of model has to be questioned'.

For the sectors investigated in this chapter it is also necessary to consider the influence of international regulatory bodies, such as the European Union and its liberalization and deregulation policies in formerly nationally controlled or monopolized sectors (Doellgast and Greer 2007:59; Hermann and Flecker 2012). Consequently, incumbent companies faced politically initiated price competition and new industry segments providing outsourced services at lower costs – such as information technology, call centres, cleaning, logistics and temporary agency services – expanded and diversified. The effect was a self-nourishing boom in business process outsourcing. Indeed, not only the European Union as a single market but also the General Agreement on Trade in Services (GATS) allows for an easier configuration and strategic expansion of transnational production networks through labour mobility and free capital flows. We shall see that these strategies are mostly accomplished by making use of regional, historical ties, as in the case of Austria and the Central and Eastern European countries.

To sum up, with regard to the interrelationship between (service) value chains and national institutional settings, the following three scenarios can be distilled from the literature on comparative political economy and global value chains:

First, subcontracting and outsourcing need to be seen in the context of segmented labour markets in so far as tapping the less-protected peripheral labour market may support the conditions in the core labour market of a sector which, in turn, is often equated with a national regime or variety of capitalism.

Second, subcontracting and outsourcing may lead to a fragmentation of sectoral employment systems and thus undermine an overall national or sectoral regime, weakening the distinctiveness of a variety of capitalism.

Third, cross-border networks and value chains open up opportunities for regime shopping and institutional arbitrage. The threat already may weaken labour and undermine its capacity to defend particular characteristics of a national regime.

Methodology

The empirical foundation of this chapter rests on two sectoral studies – one on the information technology sector, in particular software development, the other one on parcel delivery as part of the logistics sector. Our approach in contrasting service value chains in the two sectors is entirely comparative, examining employment relations in different industry environments and from varying national origins. Firms in the two industries shape the value chain in different ways: logistics firms externalize a delivery chain consisting of various chain links and software companies outsource and offshore for knowledge generation and innovation processes as well as cost reasons.

The sector study on information technology presents two empirical company cases carried out between 2007 and 2011.[1] Data analysed have been derived from qualitative research, including semi-structured interviews with employees, works councils and management staff and relevant sector experts, as well as fieldwork including visits to company sites. In the following a short overview on the three company cases is given: TraditionIT is an Austrian software company employing some 3000 engineers, half of them in Central and Eastern Europe. This case describes software development within a global corporation and the upgrading of the Hungarian subsidiary. A central aspect is the competition along the value chain. HealthIT is an Austrian start-up company specializing in on the development of smartphone applications. The company's staff consists of the two founders, two employees and some freelancers. An interesting dynamic in this case is that the company is turning back from an attempt at international relocation of programming, and nevertheless retains a cost-saving and innovation strategy at the same time.

The second sector study was carried out as part of the joint project SODIPER between researchers and trade union representatives on global delivery chains in Austria, Germany, the Czech Republic and Hungary.[2] Various kinds of empirical sources were approached, collected and used: All in all, 31 semi-structured interviews with couriers – including self-employed drivers and workers employed by subcontractors – were conducted. Additionally, the Austrian team used fieldnotes from informal conversations with more than thirty drivers during two union organizing activities. Furthermore, interviews with human resource managers of parcel delivery firms and with other relevant experts and stakeholders were carried out in all four countries involved in the project. Finally, findings and points of discussion compiled within country-specific and international workshops were also part of the empirical material used for the project reports (Haidinger 2012).

Two Sectors in Focus

The two empirical examples will elaborate on the theoretical considerations laid down above in the section on service value chains and exemplify (1) the emergence or persistence of segmented labour markets and fragmented employment relations in service value chains; (2) differences in production, industrial relations or employment regimes for shaping the global or cross-border integration of service value chains; (3) the role of national and transnational institutions for influencing processes and outcomes of outsourcing and restructuring in service value chains.

Before drawing on the theoretical considerations we will briefly describe the service value chains at stake for each of the sectors, differentiating between countries and company cases covered by the two case studies.

Parcel Delivery

In each of the countries covered by the SODIPER research (Austria, Germany, the Czech Republic and Hungary) a dozen global competitors are competing for market shares in the parcel delivery sector. They are the ones providing the international transport backbone and logistics. But the operational business as such – the picking up and delivery of parcels from and to customers as well as sorting processes – is increasingly carried out by formally independent small and medium-sized enterprises.

The delivery chain is made up of up to four chain links resulting from the creation of new intermediate markets in a previously integrated production process. First, at the top end of the delivery chain, transnational corporations including former incumbents of postal services can be found. Few of them are still employing couriers. Instead, they award contracts to 'service partners'. As the second link in the chain, these service partners are small or medium-scale firms that directly negotiate contracts stipulating areas, prices, fines, appearance of vehicles and drivers for delivery and collection. While they are formally independent actors, in fact they remain heavily dependent on the original service provider and hardly enter negotiations on an equal footing with transnational corporations. The third link in the delivery chain is either the self-employed driver, the employed driver, or, again, a smaller subcontracting entity hiring a few (self-) employed drivers (in that case the fourth chain link) for the delivery of the parcels.

Along two dimensions (segmented labour markets and fragmentation and the role of national and transnational institutions) indicated in the introduction of this chapter, we will lay down the sector's specific entanglements of service chain organization and institutional embeddedness.

Labor Relations: From Global Players with Incumbent History to Self-Employed Couriers

The parcel delivery sector is characterized by a scattered and multilayered structure involving several actors: A number of trades – haulage, postal service providers, light lorry transport – with diverging enterprise sizes operate in the sector. 'Global players' acting as general contractors employ – depending on the country-specific history of the firms – a relatively large number of workers in storage, logistics and back offices. Besides this more or less stable core workforce, labour is outsourced mainly in two ways: in storage and sorting, temporary agency workers gain importance; in delivery and collection subcontracting is the rule. These global players stand in stark contrast to a huge number of small enterprises – the service providers – that employ less than nine persons and are subject to high fluctuations with respect to market entry and insolvencies.

Not only are business structures vertically fragmented; working conditions and employment relations for every single chain link differ substantially. Thus the *first* segment identified in the parcel delivery chain benefits from highly standardized work and employment covered by collective agreements, protected by labour law and supported by works councils or other forms of labour representation. Former national incumbents (Österreichische Post AG, Deutsche Post DHL, Česká pošta, Magyar Posta) still hold a privileged position in terms of business-to-business and business-to-customer market coverage and in terms of employment conditions for deliverers. However, the stability and formality of contracts are at risk: the Austrian Post – but also Deutsche Post DHL, though not Magyar Posta – increasingly outsource employment and act as both contractor and employer for parcel deliverers. The Austrian Post has also introduced new employment contracts at the company itself. A new collective agreement offering worse employment conditions for new entrants compared with those for employees subject to the 'old contract' was a cornerstone in regaining terrain in the market segment of parcel delivery.

The *second* group – couriers directly employed by a competing service provider – is relevant only in Germany where multinationals providing parcel deliveries have a longer tradition of market participation. Instead, couriers that have formerly been employed by the contractor itself fall in all other countries into the *third* group: couriers employed by subcontractors may be covered by collective agreements. Thus, sector-level collective agreements are hardly ever applied to this group apart from in Austria where coverage by sector collective agreement is obligatory. In all four countries, regulations covering these employment relations are very often bypassed or breached. *Fourth*, self-employed or otherwise precariously employed couriers are least protected by collective agreements, by labour law and by health and safety provisions. What is more, the diminishing regulative coverage of workplaces along the vertically structured delivery chain goes hand in hand with thinning workplace representation. In the case of self-employed couriers no proper representation was found at all – provided neither by unions nor by employers' organizations. For the Austrian case segmentation is clearly shaped by workers' migrant backgrounds. Owing to the restricted labour market access of third-country nationals and their subsequent difficulty in integrating into the Austrian labour market a substantial number of drivers with migrant backgrounds work either as self-employed or in (precarious) employment for small service providers.

Workers in each of these four groups are integrated into the institutions of work regulation to varying extents. According to Gallie (2007:12) this segmentation of formerly internal labour markets is 'driven by ever greater international competition and more volatile product markets' and initiated by employers seeking to maximize their flexibility. The peripheral workforce down the delivery chain bears the main burden of adjustment; however the segmentation of the labour market in parcel delivery and the fragmentation of working conditions does not lead to a 'protected core of skilled workers... complemented by an increasingly vulnerable periphery of lower skilled' (Gallie 2007:12). Instead, outsourcing is weakening employment protection and even threatens the entire workforce while it indicates to workers and their representatives that one of the groups hitherto perceived as core and stable may be the next to be outsourced.

Liberalization Processes, Sectoral Fragmentation and Union Decline

Our research showed that from country to country business logics in parcel delivery are relatively coherent: multinational logistics firms including former national monopolists dominate as contractors and subcontract orders to small and medium-sized firms and self-employed drivers. Thus, labour standards deteriorate with the increasing length of the chain cascade. This section will take into account two aspects, that indicate rather a convergence of the national institutional settings and regulations within which parcel delivery is embedded. The first aspect encompasses deregulation processes of postal services on the European level. The second aspect, and a consequence of the first, is the particular challenges that sector fragmentation poses for the national systems of industrial relations.

In accordance with the European Directives on the liberalization of the postal market, the European postal market has been gradually opened to competing providers of postal services including parcel delivery. The entry of alternative competitors into a former (at least partly) monopolized market and liberalization processes changed both the logic of service production and the mode of industry governance in postal services (Hermann *et al.* 2008). These changes impacted on the institutional variety of sectoral collective agreements, on employment forms and on the quality of work and employment. To different degrees, all employers resort to temporary, part-time work and minor employment, on-call work and temporary agency work, and to outsourcing services like for example parcel delivery to bypass provisions such as employment protection, holiday remuneration or sick leave. The rendering precarious of employment conditions and the fragmentation of employment contracts in the parcel delivery industry during the past 25 years must be related to this de-standardization of labour relations and the decline of unions' and works councils' standing in this sector:

On the *company level* the outsourcing of operational activities to smaller entities laid the ground for weak labour representation in the sector. Small and medium-sized companies often are not inclined to allow works councils or unions in their companies. In order to stay competitive, the management of contractor companies exerted pressure on unions and works councils who attempted to preserve wage levels and jobs. Though under constant pressure, works councils and unions in former monopolies retained greater influence on work organization and employment models than in the new competitor companies, where workers' representatives are either non-existent or weak (Artus *et al.* 2009).[3] On the *sectoral level*, a diversity of collective agreements (as in Austria) or the employers' unwillingness to engage in collective bargaining (as in Germany, the Czech Republic and Hungary) made it impossible for labour organizations to keep uniform wage levels and working conditions for the entire sector.

Industrial relations legacies in the four countries studied differ substantially (Bechter *et al.* 2012), with Austria being almost entirely covered by sector-level collective agreements, Hungary and the Czech Republic classified as 'mixed' or 'transitional' model and Germany with a declining importance of sector level bargaining in some sectors including logistics and parcel delivery. Nevertheless, the four countries follow a rather similar sectoral model of industrial relations. Hence, differences on the formal level among the four countries are blurred in practice. While in the Czech Republic and Hungary only the former monopolies are covered by strong industrial relations regulations (and these are lacking for new competitors in parcel delivery), a comprehensive industrial relations system is evaded in the case of Austria by the use of bogus self-employment and in the case of Germany by non-adherence to collective agreements and by hiring staff in minor and therefore less protected employment. The national institutional setting of industrial relations does – for this sector – not make much of a difference for the better or worse protection of working conditions and the level of fragmentation encountered; factual differences in the configuration of employment relations among the four countries in this sector are smaller than might be expected. Here, on the one hand, sector logics and dynamics play an important role in the country-specific deviation from national industrial relations regimes – as was also pointed out by Bechter *et al.* (2012). On the other hand, liberalization and privatization processes strengthened via the supra-national level as part of a neoliberal world order have constraining effects on national institutions and politics (Brenner *et al.* 2010:186).

Software Development

The second case study in focus encompasses business and labour relations in the Austrian information technology (IT) industry and in software development in particular. Looking at the involvement of Austrian IT companies in international networks, there are on the one hand large IT companies or corporations with headquarters or subsidiaries in Austria. On the other hand IT companies including start-ups and long-established companies specialize in (niche) products or services mainly for the Austrian market but also partly for an international one (Flecker and Schönauer 2012). Still, Austria is – compared with other countries – a rather small IT location and by no means a key player in the international division of labour in the IT sector. Yet it is an interesting case when it comes to looking at developments in inconspicuous countries in order to analyse general tendencies in the IT industry. Global value chain research in an Anglo-Saxon context often, more or less implicitly, assumes a global convergence of restructuring patterns. Recent studies include more variety, and it has been shown how value chains are strongly structured along global historical connections (Batt *et al.* 2009; Holtgrewe *et al.* 2009). The

Austrian IT sector is a good example to show that even if the division of labour in value chains follows (among others) a cost-saving strategy, it does not necessarily lead to global sourcing. Nevertheless historical legacies are important for the internationalization of Austria's IT sector, as they facilitate 'near-shoring' to Central and Eastern European countries.

Varieties of Service Value Chains and Consequences of Regime Shopping

Austrian IT companies are involved in (inter)national service value chains and networks in diverse forms. On the one hand access to new markets is a driver of the international expansion of Austrian firms. On the other hand foreign direct investment simultaneously following a logic of cost-saving and skill-seeking lengthens the service value chains (Sass and Fifekova 2011:1598). The Austrian IT sector shows that companies use service value chains for different forms of the division of labour simultaneously. Most of them are found below the surface of company borders and are often invisible from outside: cooperation for product development across national and company borders takes place; virtual teams work on the same subjects; subprojects are relocated along the value chain. In addition, there is also some offshoring of standardized tasks (such as low-level support or programming), but this does not occur on a grand scale. In the 1990s the transition to market economies in Central and Eastern Europe brought important changes also for the Austrian IT sector. Many Austrian companies seized the opportunity to relocate parts of their production to the low-cost countries on the doorstep. People often refer to the cultural proximity between Austria and its neighbouring countries where German is quite often spoken, as well as, increasingly, English. Beyond that, these countries have not only lower labour costs but also liberalized labour markets, all of which invites companies to 'regime shop'.

An example for an intense connection to Eastern Europe is the company TraditionIT.[4] In the 1990s, the Austrian software company strongly expanded to several Central and Eastern European countries to benefit from both low wage levels and the supply of highly skilled workers. The relocation of work hardly met any opposition during that boom period of the IT industry. Management's main argument was that a mixed calculation of labour costs would render the company's projects cheaper and thus the company more competitive and the jobs securer. However, for several years now projects have been assigned on a cost basis within the corporation the Austrian software firm is part of. As labour costs have risen considerably in Hungary the subsidiary there has also come under competitive pressure from locations with lower labour costs. Building upon the high skill levels of the workforce it attempted to upgrade its activities and to take over high-value tasks. Another competitive advantage of the Hungarian subsidiary facilitated by the lax regulatory environment lies in the opportunities to deploy workers flexibly. Owing to Austria's tight regulation of labour immigration, body leasing to the Austrian company was becoming more and more difficult, which resulted in additional pressures to actually relocate work.[5] However, as managers explained, relocation is more cost-effective if larger chunks of work are moved. And the assignment of whole projects or comprehensive subprojects implied an upgrading of the Hungarian subsidiary. In addition, the Hungarian management relocated tasks to low-cost locations in Romania in order to cope with cost competition.

While it was first argued that investment in neighbouring countries with lower wage levels would help to increase competitiveness and thus save jobs in Austria, after some years downsizing was put on the agenda, with mass layoffs unprecedented in the Austrian company. Reduced company turnover resulted in redundancy measures at the Austrian location while the subsidiaries with lower labour costs partly expanded further. The layoffs first were achieved through voluntary redundancy and golden handshakes. Only recently did the company use forced redundancies. The change in business conditions and corporate strategies together with the upgrading of foreign subsidiaries made a threat of what originally had had the effect of securing high-wage jobs in Austria. Further, such developments in the IT industry also show that the periphery's dependent position also fails to cushion the core workforce in another way: working conditions of peripheral workers may serve as a benchmark for core workers who are increasingly pressured to accept an intensification of work, a greater demand for temporal flexibility and in addition some formalization and standardization of tasks (Flecker *et al.* 2013).

Segmented Labour Markets: Internationalization Not the One Best Way

The example of the Austrian IT sector shows that companies not only benefit from other countries' lower labour standards; they also know how to use loopholes in national regulations for their interests. In Austria, freelancers play an important role, especially for the group of small and medium-sized (start-up) companies. They allow firms to keep fixed costs low and predictable and still get access to highly skilled, innovative and flexible experts. In software development freelancers may even work from abroad, so that companies are not limited to the regional or national labour market. The following example of HealthIT, however, shows how difficulties in cross-border collaboration with IT freelancers led to a painful retreat from international relocation in a small start-up company.

HealthIT is an Austrian start-up company founded in 2010 around an innovative and promising product idea: a specialized health application for smartphones. At the beginning of the product development HealthIT cooperated with a set of freelancing and highly specialized programmers all over the world. The experts' task was to execute work orders coming from the product development team in Austria. Although the company drew on a successful and experienced cooperation, the global decentralization of programming to freelancers soon had to be cancelled. Management did not succeed in organizing the complex and dynamic phase of early product development within a decentralized team. The lesson learned was that 'outsourcing is possible, if you have a separate module, if you know what you want and what the output should be; then it is great, then it works'. As a consequence they returned to spatially centralized working, actually using physical pinboards for project management. The company kept some cooperation with freelancers as long as they worked from the company's office for at least three days a week.

The case of HealthIT shows that in the case of outsourcing to highly qualified experts, standardization of procedures or codification of information does not appear to be necessary, as long as modules and interfaces are adequately defined. During a phase of innovation and conceptualization, in this case networked collaboration did not work. The case also shows that in the IT sector outsourcing of work to freelancers does not automatically mean a process of precarization. The experts' work is well paid and their scope for autonomy within and control over the work process is wide. Highly skilled workers in the IT industry can be in a comparatively strong bargaining position and therefore able to influence their working conditions even if they are positioned further down the value chain (Flecker *et al.* 2013). While the spatial consolidation in combination with functional aspects for organizing and controlling software development proved crucial in this case, paradoxically the ensuing very integrated work processes are not reflected in the employment relations. Local workers are still hired as freelancers even though Austrian labour law requires standard employment relationships for this type of work organization.

Discussion and Conclusion

Recent interpretations of the varieties-of-capitalism approach (Brenner *et al.* 2010; Lane 2010; Thelen 2012) put different explanatory factors into the forefront of discussing differences in national regimes. On the one hand the sector dynamics play a role (Bechter *et al.* 2012, Crouch et al. 2009) and may challenge (or even undermine) a national employment or production regime in particular if sector specificities converge across different regimes. On the other hand, supranational processes of liberalization such as the common market regime under the European Union leadership (Thelen 2012) have to be implemented on the national level and decisively influence the emergence of new market structures and new sectoral employment regimes. However, national regulatory arrangements and institutional forms may prove durable, 'albeit within the broad parameters of a market-orientated, commodifying rule-regime' (Brenner *et al.* 2010).

This chapter has taken up these considerations and tried to link them with the debate on (global) value chains and global production networks in the globalizing service sector. By drawing on two contrasting examples of service sector industries, namely parcel delivery as part of the logistics sector and software development in the IT sector, the chapter has highlighted three types of entanglement between (service) value chains and 'variegated' (Brenner *et al.* 2010) national institutional settings.

First, subcontracting along value chains, outsourcing and offshoring need indeed to be interpreted in the context of segmented labour markets (Rubery 2006). Our empirical evidence showed that tapping a less protected peripheral labour market through subcontracting and outsourcing does not necessarily support the conditions in the core labour market (Gallie 2007) but leads to a fragmentation of the entire employment system within a sector. Thus, a national or at least sectoral regime with (or with the threat of) insecure and unstable forms of employment not only at the periphery of the labour market is at risk of being undermined. In addition, outsourcing cannot merely be interpreted as a cost-saving strategy. Though outsourcing of high-skill work such as software development may enhance flexibility and shift the risks of off-peak times to external partners, it is also pursued to tap external expertise. Fragmentation here is harnessed to innovating work processes and ideas but has its limitations in unstructured development processes. In contrast to these business practices, outsourcing and subcontracting in the parcel delivery industry follow a pure logic of 'risk-and-flexibility transfer chains' (Frade and Darmon 2005) in which the main reason for externalization strategies is cost-cutting and risk-spreading and results in the extension of precarious employment. Both sectors show a high level of fragmentation in two aspects: On the one hand employment relations recur on employment regulations from different sectors as in the parcel delivery. On the other hand inter-firm networks displace employment contracts (Thompson 1993, Marchington *et al.* 2005). Interestingly, despite the importance of market-based relations in the production processes of both sectors, the governance of the labour process is highly integrated and centralized through technological means. In case of software development, knowledge, as an essential part of the means of production, must not get lost; in parcel delivery the couriers' performance as the last link of the chain of the outsourced delivery process is surveilled in detail in order to streamline the delivery process even more.

Second, subcontracting and outsourcing lead to a fragmentation of employment systems and undermine national regimes rather than stabilizing them. The example of parcel delivery has shown that business dynamics within a sector play an important role in the country-specific deviation from national industrial relations regimes. The parcel delivery industry is characterized by a 'chain logic' of organizing the entire delivery process, of establishing market relations within the production process of the commodity 'delivery' and of devolving business risks to the bottom end. These business organization strategies lead to, or indeed pursue, fragmentation of employment and working conditions. In addition, liberalization and privatization policies strengthened by supranational (GATS) and EU-level impositions to liberalize further the trade in services have fostered these fragmentation tendencies and have weakened national institutions. In parcel delivery the liberalization of postal services and the growing importance of new global competitors decisively shaped the market structure for postal and delivery services, the way delivery services are provided and the constitution of this particular labour market segment. Therefore, despite different employment regimes and systems of industrial relations between countries, the sector's organization is very similar across regime types. Regimes do not 'converge', and path dependencies in regime types might follow different strategies and trajectories; however, outcomes with respect to prevailing working conditions in a sector can still be strikingly similar.

Third, cross-border networks and value chains allow for regime shopping and institutional arbitrage. The case of information technology in Austria has revealed the main drivers of regime shopping: differentials in labour costs between old and new EU member states; different levels of flexibility due to diverse labour regulations or workforce characteristics; and the possibility of tapping labour markets offering highly skilled graduates. Our empirical example also showed the importance of historical legacies and cultural proximity for the spatial relocation of business services. The country-specific background and language skills of employees themselves may foster the expansion to a specific country. Therefore, we can conclude also that the expansion of value chains is multidimensionally embedded, as

Lane (2008) suggests: not only does management's strategic regime shopping to save labour and other costs play a role, but so also do components such as migration regulations existing between two countries, the possibilities of upgrading relocated tasks within the value chain and the effectiveness of transnational communication and control structures. When these components are weighed, relocation and offshoring in the IT sector need not always emerge as the best option for making production processes more efficient. Nevertheless, regime shopping may have cushioned the core workers in the home country and thereby maintained typical forms of employment for some time. With growing competition and companies' growing restructuring experience, however, regime shopping is more likely to result in benchmarking across countries and companies, concession bargaining and redundancies – making it difficult for trade unions to defend jobs and traditional employment relationships.

Notes

1 TraditionIT and HealthIT: 'Dynamic of transnational value chains in Austria's IT industry', funded by Austrian National Bank's Anniversary Fund (project number: 13609).
2 'Social Dialogue and Participation Strategies in the Global Delivery Industry: Challenging Precarious Employment Relations' (SODIPER), funded by the European Commission, DG Employment and Social Affairs (VP/2010/001/0226).
3 Union density at Magyar Posta: 55 per cent; union density at Deutsche Post DHL: 70 per cent; union density at Österreichische Post AG: 85 per cent; union density at Česká pošta: 45 per cent
4 For reasons of anonymity pseudonyms are used for company names.
5 This was before the labour market transition regulations for the new European Union member states were suspended in 2011.

REFERENCES

Artus, Ingrid, Sabine Böhm, Stefan Lücking and Rainer Trinczek (2009) 'Arbeitsbeziehungen in Betrieben ohne Betriebsrat', *Industrielle Beziehungen* 16, 2:180–81.
Bair, Jennifer (2005) 'Global Capitalism and Commodity Chains: Looking Back, Going Forward', *Competition & Change* 9, 2:153–80.
Bair, Jennifer and Marion Werner (2011) 'Commodity Chains and the Uneven Geographies of Global Capitalism: A Disarticulations Perspective', *Environment and Planning A* 43, 5:988–97.

▶

Batt, Rosemary, David Holman and Ursula Holtgrewe (2009) 'The Globalization of Service Work: Comparative Institutional Perspectives on Call Centers', *Industrial & Labor Relations Review* 62, 4:453–88.

Bechter, Barbara, Bernd Brandl and Guglielmo Meardi (2012) 'Sectors or Countries? Typologies and Levels of Analysis in Comparative Industrial Relations', *European Journal of Industrial Relations* 18, 3:185–202.

Brenner, Neil, Jamie Peck and Nik Theodore (2010) 'Variegated Neoliberalization: Geographies, Modalities, Pathways', *Global Networks* 10, 2:182–222.

Coe, Neil M., Peter Dicken and Martin Hess (2008) 'Global Production Networks: Realizing the Potential', *Journal of Economic Geography* 8, 3:271–95.

Crouch, Colin, Martin Schröder and Helmut Voelzkow (2009) 'Regional and Sectoral Varieties of Capitalism', *Economy and Society* 38, 4:654–78.

Doellgast, Virginia and Ian Greer (2007) 'Vertical Disintegration and the Disorganization of German Marchington, Mick, Damian Grimshaw, Jill Rubery and Hugh Willmott (2005) *Fragmenting Work. Blurring Organizational Boundaries and Disordering Hierarchies.* Oxford: Oxford University Press.

Flecker, Jörg (2010) 'Fragmenting Labor: Organisational Restructuring, Employment Relations and the Dynamics of National Regulatory Frameworks', *Work Organisation, Labour and Globalisation* 4, 1:8–23.

Flecker, Jörg and Pamela Meil (2010) 'Organisational Restructuring and Emerging Service Value Chains – Implications for Work and Employment', *Work, Employment & Society* 24, 4:1–19.

Flecker, Jörg and Annika Schönauer (2012) 'Die Internationalisierung österreichis-cher IT-Unternehmen – zur Dynamik von Wertschöpfungsketten und Arbeit', *Wirtschaft und Gesellschaft* 38 3:567–99.

Flecker, Jörg, Bettina Haidinger and Annika Schönauer (2013) 'Divide and Serve: The Labor Process in Service Value Chains and Networks', *Competition and Change* 17, 1:6–23.

Frade, Carlos and Isabelle Darmon (2005) 'New Modes of Business Organization and Precarious Employment: Towards the Recommodification of Labor?', *Journal of European Social Policy* 15, 2:107–21.

Gallie, Duncan (2007) *Employment Regimes and the Quality of Work.* Oxford: Oxford University Press.

Gereffi, Gary, John Humphrey and Timothy J. Sturgeon (2005) 'The Governance of Global Value Chains', *Review of International Political Economy* 12, 1:78–104.

Haidinger, Bettina (2012) 'On the Move in Global Delivery Chains: Labor Relations and Working Conditions in the Parcel Delivery Industries of Austria, Germany, the Czech Republic and Hungary', *SODIPER Synthesis Report.* Vienna: FORBA.

Hall, Peter A. and David Soskice (2001) *Varieties of Capitalism: The Institutional Foundations of Comparative Advantage.* Oxford: Oxford University Press.

Hermann, Christoph and Jörg Flecker. (eds) (2012) *Privatization of Public Services. Impacts for Employment, Working Conditions, and Service Quality in Europe.* Routledge: New York.

Hermann, Christoph, Thorsten Brandt and Thorsten Schulten (2008) 'Commodification, Casualisation and Intensification of Work in Liberalised European Postal Markets', *Work Organisation, Labour & Globalisation* 2, 2:40–55.

▶

▶

Holtgrewe, Ursula, Jessica Longen, Hannelore Mottweiler and Annika Schönauer (2009) 'Global or Embedded Service Work: The (Limited) Transnationalisation of the Call-Centre Industry', *Work, Organisation, Labor and Globalisation* 3, 1:9–25.

Huws, Ursula, Sabine Dahlmann and Jörg Flecker (2004) 'Outsourcing of ICT and Related Services in the EU. A Status Report', Report for the European Foundation for the Improvement of Living and Working Conditions. Luxembourg: Office for Official Publications of the European Communities.

Korpi, Walter (2006) 'Power Resources and Employer-Centered Approaches in Explanations of Welfare States and Varieties of Capitalism: Protagonists, Consenters and Antagonists', *World Politics* 58, 2:167–206.

Lane, Christel (2008) 'National Capitalism and Global Production Networks: An Analysis of Their Interaction in Two Global Industries', *Socio-Economic Review* 6, 2:227–60.

Meil, Pamela (009) 'Value Chain Restructuring and Its Effects on the Employment Relationship and Working Conditions', pp.11–27 in *Challenges for Europe Under Value Chain Restructuring*, edited by P. Meil. Leuven: HIVA.

Newsome, Kristy (2010) 'Work and Employment in Distribution and Exchange: Moments in the Circuit of Capital', *Industrial Relations Journal* 41, 3:190–205.

Oliver, Christine (1991) 'Strategic Responses to Institutional Processes', *Academy of Management Review* 16, 1:145–79.

Rubery, Jill (2006) 'Segmentation Theory Thirty Years On', paper presented to the 27th Conference of the International Working Party on Labour Market Segmentation (IWPLMS), Copenhagen, September 2006.

Sass, Magdolna and Martina Fifekova (2011) 'Offshoring and Outsourcing Business Services to Central and Eastern Europe. Some Empirical and Conceptual Considerations', *European Planning Studies* 19, 9:1593–609.

Streeck, Wolfgang and Kathleen Thelen. (eds) (2005) *Beyond Continuity: Institutional Change in Advanced Political Economies*. Oxford: Oxford University Press.

Taylor, Phil (2010) 'The Globalization of Service Work: Analysing the Transnational Call Centre Value Chain', pp. 244–68 in *Working Life: Renewing Labor Process Analysis*, edited by P. Thompson and C. Smith. Basingstoke: Palgrave Macmillan.

Thelen, Kathleen (2012) 'Varieties of Capitalism: Trajectories of Liberalization and the New Politics of Social Solidarity', *Annual Review of Political Science* 15:137–59.

Thompson, Paul (1993) 'Postmodernism: Fatal Distraction', pp. 183–203 in *Postmodernism and Organisations*, edited by J. Hassard and M. Parker. London: Sage.

Thompson, Paul, Kristie Newsome and Joanna Commander (2013) 'Good When They Want to Be: Migrant Workers in the Supermarket Supply Chain', *Human Resource Management Journal* 23, 2:129–43.

Whitford, Josh (2005) *The Old New Economy*. Oxford: Oxford University Press.

Wills, Jane (2009) 'Subcontracted Employment and Its Challenge to Labor', *Labor Studies Journal* 34, 4:441–60.

Greening Steel Work: Varieties of Capitalism, the Environmental Agenda and Innovating for the Greening of the Labour Process

6

Claire Evans and Dean Stroud

Sustainable development and the regulation of environmental issues is a relatively recent policy direction for the European Union (EU), but it is growing in importance and scope (for example, the Amsterdam and Lisbon Treaties). Conventional free-market thinking equates compliance with environmental legislation as raising costs for firms, thereby reducing the market share of domestic companies on global markets. Porter and van der Linde (1995) propose, however, that environmental regulation induces innovation by raising industry's awareness of otherwise missed opportunities. Whether regulation, and the need to improve environmental performance, is viewed as an economic opportunity to innovate or as a threat that must be complied with can be attributed in part to company 'mind-set' (Porter and van der Linde 1995). With regard to institutional factors, Porter and van der Linde focus on the form that legislation should take, and how such regulation prompts change at firm level. While both company mind-set and legislative frameworks are no doubt important, the authors are silent on the subject of the wider institutional complementarities that might be necessary for the emergence of such perspectives within firms. Here, we argue that the institutional context in which a company is embedded (gives shape to managerial philosophy and) is the principal determining factor in the way companies perceive and act upon environmental regulation as an opportunity for innovation. Thus, we extend Porter and van der Linde's analysis by focusing on the centrality of institutional factors to the emergence of 'environmental innovation' at the company level.

Drawing on case study evidence from a project conducted on the European steel industry, we examine how, and to what extent, institutional contexts – specifically those in Germany and the UK – impact upon company-level approaches to environmental innovation and the greening of jobs, work, training and skills. The industry constitutes an interesting focus for analysis: it is carbon/resource-intensive and, in significant ways, is subject to environmental regulation. In particular, the industry argues that carbon emissions policy and the implementation of the Emission Trading Scheme is jeopardizing European steel production (EEF 2010). To meet these challenges and corporate social responsibilities, the sector has pledged its commitment to sustainable steel production and meeting environmental/economic challenges, as well as 'greening' (or upskilling) the workforce in line with such processes (ESTEP 2010). The greening of skills and occupations across the industry is required, not only to secure competent and environmentally safe performance of specific job roles, but also because such knowledge and skills can facilitate worker involvement in proposing (and implementing) suggestions for further green improvements (see Dierdorff *et al.* 2009).

Data were collected on German and UK systems of vocational education and training – which need to respond to employer demands for green skills – as well as on environmental policy, practice and innovation at the EU and member state level. In addition, data were sought on supporting organizational mechanisms within case study firms in Germany and the UK – for example, training strategies and programmes, environment policy and practice. The German case study was conducted at the ThyssenKrupp Steel Europe AG in Duisburg. It is an integrated plant employing approximately 13 000 people, which produces both hot-rolled and cold-rolled products. The UK research sites were the Tata Steel Europe plants in Port Talbot and Llanwern in South Wales. The Port Talbot site is an integrated steelworks, which produces hot-rolled, cold-rolled and metallic-plated strip products. Approximately 6000 direct employees and subcontractors work at the plant. The Llanwern site has a finishing capacity only (that is, production of completed steel products only, but no steel-producing capacity) and employs around 1200 people. A number of group and individual interviews were conducted with key personnel at each plant, including environmental managers, health and safety coordinators, section managers, engineers, apprentices and training staff. The research was guided by two principal research questions, which focused on exploring: (1) the industry's 'green' training and skill needs, and (2) current industry/company strategies on green skills training and environment policy and practice.

While labour process scholars (for example, Thompson and Smith 2010) have examined the dynamics of workplace control, resistance and organization in great detail, here we focus on the question of divergent managerial strategies for workforce skills and autonomy in two firms from the same industry. Our analysis centres on company environmental strategies of *compliance* and *innovation* and the ways in which each intersects with the green skills agenda, training programmes and, ultimately, the greening of work and skills in the steel industry. It is evident that industry-driven requirements on environmental regulation (and training to meet regulations) exist where such directives penetrate operations and that policy on the environment is – in this respect – focused on compliance. Innovation, on the other hand, focuses investment (of and in resources), but the parameters for such activity differ from place to place – dependent, we argue, on the institutional context within which companies operate and within which managerial philosophies are shaped. The environmental agenda provides an opportunity for innovation and, as such, the potential for enhanced training provision and workforce involvement in the securing of environmental improvements. This path (and the pace of change) to a greener labour process in the steel industry is determined in significant ways by institutional contexts and frameworks – particularly those concerned with vocational education and training and the broader developmental mechanisms within which companies work – and it is these that frame innovative behaviour at the workplace (Lundvall 2004; Newell *et al.* 2009).

ThyssenKrupp demonstrates a more developmental orientation with clear evidence of an environmental innovation approach. This is supported by robust institutional frameworks that incorporate changes in skill needs into education and training responses, thus serving necessary innovations in occupations, workplace practices and processes. Change at the Tata plants is guided however by short-term economic priorities. The focus is on compliance with regulations and innovation is concerned with immediate cost reductions, rather than longer-term strategies such as those focused on investment in workforce development (to support innovation). The latter is further undermined by institutional frameworks that disincentivize such development. In this context, the green agenda is not perceived as an avenue of innovation, instead being viewed as a restriction on business, or at least as a secondary consideration to economic matters. Thus, while 'pathway determinacy' within national economies is subject to complex and nuanced readings (see Crouch 2001), the implementation of change is argued to be much more dynamic in the context of coordinated market economies, such as Germany, than in liberal market economies, such as the UK, where there are significant barriers to the vision for, and investments in, both the technology and the skills necessary for green innovation (Kemp and Loorbach 2006).

Institutional Context: Innovation, Green Skills and the Environment

Hall and Soskice's (2001:38–44) distinction between liberal market economies and coordinated market economies identifies significant variations in the institutional, ideological and cultural patterns specific to these two types of capitalism – particularly with regard to innovation. The different production, labour market, industrial relations and status systems associated with these types mean that the basis of competitive advantage therein differs significantly, particularly with regard to the strategies pursued by companies on innovation and – closely aligned with this – workforce development. The following subsection discusses the intersection of green skills development with the environmental agenda and patterns of innovation in differing institutional contexts.

Coordinated Market Economies

Although markets and hierarchies are important in coordinated market economies like Germany, such economies are characterized by strong networks of social institutions that regulate economic action within markets. Here, markets are 'deeply embedded in an array of co-operative, redistributive and regulatory institutions' (Streeck 1992:6). In Germany, these institutions include powerful employer associations, strong trade unions, and networks of cross-shareholding, as well as legal or regulatory systems that encourage information-sharing and collaboration (Hall and Soskice 2001). The financial system is less market-based and firms raise capital on a long-term basis through regionally based banks as opposed to the stock market (Tylecote and Conesa 1999). This provision of 'patient capital' has meant that firms are able to adopt longer-term, developmental orientations, which in turn facilitates technological innovation (Streeck 1995). Indeed, Germany ranks second in the EU in terms of its innovation performance, just behind Sweden, another coordinated market economy (European Commission, 2012).

Innovation and capital investments in technology are facilitated by this institutional framework, as is the cultivation of stable, collaborative employment relations in German firms. Hall and Soskice (2001:39) suggest, moreover, that coordinated market economies – like Germany – are more suited to *incremental innovation* and 'small-scale improvements to existing product lines and production processes'. The latter are supported and reinforced by other institutions, including regulations that protect job security and worker autonomy, and ensure enhanced worker participation in organizational decision-making, for example works councils (Streeck 1992; Lane and Bachmann 1997). Such legislation acts as a 'beneficial constraint' – that is, an institution not originally created to further economic efficiency, but which manifests as a source of superior performance (Streeck 2004). The features that typify German firms (that is, high levels of industry-specific technical skills among the workforce, worker autonomy and extensive information and knowledge sharing) originate from long-term, secure employment relationships. The latter are organized around a dominant production paradigm of diversified quality production and essential for the generation and implementation of incremental innovations (Lane 1995). It is these practices that are a principal source of competitive advantage for German process and engineering firms (Hall and Soskice 2001).

Such approaches are mirrored in the support of skills development. Workers perceive proposals for improvement to be an integral part of their job and innovation in this way is supported by high training levels. The German system is renowned for high levels of industry-specific engineering and technical skills, cultivated both within firms and in the wider vocational education and training system (Culpepper 1999). Indeed, vocational education and training programmes are perceived as principal contributors to industrial competitiveness, with high-quality teaching and learning and responsiveness within the vocational education and training system to industrial innovations and changing employer demands (Bosch and Charest 2008). The system contains robust frameworks for incorporating changes in industry/occupational skills needs into training/qualificational responses, namely the institutions that support sectoral dialogue between social partners (CEDEFOP 2010). The Federal Institute for Vocational Education and Training works closely with the partners so as to update the training regulations that govern the curricula of formally designated occupations.

There is no overarching state-driven green skills policy, but occupational competences, and the training regulations/vocational-education-and-training curricula that accompany them, have been greened. Environmental protection has been at the centre of German public policy development for decades, in part a reflection of the strong environmental movement, the ensuing political success of German Green Party and the subsequent integration of environmental issues into the other parties' policies (Blühdorn 2009). Further, environmental policies have long been perceived as a mechanism to develop market opportunities for domestic firms. Subsequently, environmental protection issues have been integrated into all initial and continuing vocational education and training regulations through collaboration between the Federal Institute for Vocational Education and Training and the social partners (CEDEFOP 2010). This process of organic collaboration stands in sharp contrast to the top-down attempts to drive such agendas in the UK.

Liberal Market Economies

Within liberal market economies, such as the UK, the market is the dominant coordinator of economic action (Korczynski 2000). State policy and regulation ensures that market forces prevail and this encourages short-term, low-trust relations between economic actors (Hall and Soskice 2001). Moreover, liberal market economies are organized around a stock-market-based financial system, which makes them averse to particular types of risk-taking (Gospel and Pendleton 2003). Financial institutions in the UK offer capital to industry on the basis of high returns and short payback targets. The dominance of shareholder values means that profits are generally not reinvested and go disproportionately into dividend payments (Heery and Wood 2003). Such demands, in conjunction with other institutional factors (such as the predominance of low-wage, low-skill labour), combine to produce an extant development paradigm that is 'locked in' to trajectories driven by short-term benefits (Kemp and Loorbach 2006).

The consequence is significant implications for both technological investment and workforce development (a long-term project with uncertain return on investment) at the firm level (Lloyd and Payne 2002). Voluntarist market-based training systems mean that there is little legal compulsion for employers to risk engaging in skill enhancement and the weak regulation of employment protection contributes to high levels of staff turnover (Burchell *et al.* 2002). The UK vocational education and training system has, more generally, been criticized for the poor quality of its processes and outcomes, and is seen as being of low status (Bosch and Charest 2008). These problems have contributed to a widespread deficiency in intermediate-level and technical skills. The pattern of skills distribution in the UK labour market is one of bifurcation, with significant numbers of the workforce having low skills, alongside comparatively high numbers of graduates. This is reflected and reinforced within work organizations – those at the bottom of the organizational hierarchy without formal qualifications are less likely to receive training than are their better-qualified, managerial and professional colleagues (Hoque 2008). This organizational divide is symptomatic of, and perpetuates, a managerial predilection for centralized modes of control and unilateral decision-making (Hall and Soskice 2001).

Such factors, in combination with other typical conditions of UK organizations – low trade union density and collective bargaining coverage, deficient employee involvement, low-trust employment relations, authoritarian management styles and job insecurity – are inimical to worker-driven incremental innovations (Hall and Soskice 2001). In combination, these factors result in the taylorist mass production paradigm that prevails, characterized by strict division of labour, narrow tasks and management hierarchy (Lane 1995; Boreham 2002). At the same time, this model is seen as conducive to high-risk processes of *radical innovation*. Particularly suited to 'substantial shifts in product lines... or major changes to the production process', radical innovation is reliant on institutional frameworks that posses few restrictions on labour mobility (Hall and Soskice 2001:39). The focus here is on a fluid labour market, a reliance on general skills and the production of goods requiring lesser-skilled but lower-cost labour (ibid.)

In terms of environmental innovation, the cumulative effect might be significant barriers at firm level to the vision for, and investments in, the skills necessary for green innovation. This is compounded by prevailing social norms in the UK, which have meant that green issues have tended not to be seen as offering credible potential for innovation, and have frequently been viewed as an unnecessary restriction on business, or at least as a secondary consideration (European Commission 2009). Nonetheless, from 2008 the need to cultivate green economic growth had started to permeate the wider UK skills agenda. The then government identified a 'green skills' base as vital to any transition to a low-carbon economy (BERR 2009). Moreover, there was recognition that there was a distinct lack of such skills provision within the vocational education and training system, largely due to the exclusive reliance on employer demand to stimulate this. However, the previous government's intention to implement a remedial green skills strategy has ostensibly been abandoned by the current government, and wider environmental policies are increasingly being attacked (Harvey 2011). A recent study has identified that the UK has the largest green skills deficit across nine EU countries, and that apposite vocational education and training provision has still not been developed (IES 2012).

Greening Steel Work

As part of the restructuring of the European steel industry, there is a pressure on employers to advance current workforce skill profiles. These development strategies have however been implemented in uneven and different ways by steel companies across Europe (Stroud 2012). Another pressure on the sector is the need to meet environmental regulations, driven by the threat of sanctions for non-compliance, the need to reduce costs through maximizing efficiency and optimizing resource use, in addition to being seen to act responsibly (EUROFER 2010). We now provide an account of the efforts of both companies to green operations, highlighting where such imperatives overlap with processes of innovation and workforce development.

Environmental Policy and Practice

Both Tata and ThyssenKrupp include environmental protection as central elements in their corporate social responsibility policies. At ThyssenKrupp, policy is influenced by the parent company, ThyssenKrupp AG. ThyssenKrupp AG explicitly commits to 'continuous improvement' as regards environmental protection, resource conservation and sustainability, with a designated person with overall responsibility for environmental matters across all plants on the group board. The board also drives an environmental and climate management system across its companies. This defines uniform requirements and targets to be met by all plants. The parent company runs regular internal training programmes, in order to facilitate plant conformance to these targets.

At ThyssenKrupp, environmental policy is said to be of central importance, with a 'long tradition'. It describes its environmental performance as far superior to that of competitor companies (confirmed by interviewees at Tata Steel, who described ThyssenKrupp as having implemented pioneering environmental technology). The policy comprises ten basic guidelines, with the stated aim of achieving long-term sustainable development (ThyssenKrupp 2011). This is supported by a sustainability management system, the appointment of a sustainability management officer and the creation of an interdisciplinary sustainability team, which emphasizes the company view that 'sustainability' is an avenue for 'seizing future opportunities', a 'key driver for innovation' and leads to 'continuous improvement of the economic, environmental and social performance of the company' (ThyssenKrupp 2009).

These goals are seen as consistent with each other, rather than oppositional, and foster 'outstanding technological competency' and the 'promotion of innovation'. Technological innovation extends to environmental protection – for example the recycling of process gases to produce electricity. At ThyssenKrupp this system has been in place for many years and produces practically all required electricity. Tata, however, only implemented such a system at Port Talbot in 2010, which meets just 10 per cent of the facility's electricity needs. In light of such practices, various ThyssenKrupp reports describe legislative compliance as a given, detailing therein all the numerous voluntary measures that go beyond such prescriptions. Tata, however, states that 'its first priority is to remain compliant and meet legislative requirements' (Tata Steel 2011). This compliance-driven approach was confirmed by a number of interviewees:

> In terms of the environment, the company is driven by compliance... we're doing it because it has to be done. Things are maybe just starting to change...we're seeing some projects for improvement, not just compliance. (Senior Engineer, Llanwern, 2011)

Moreover, interviewees revealed (declining to provide specific examples) that compliance is not always attained:

> Port Talbot has struggled to meet compliance targets. (Environmental Compliance Manager, Port Talbot, 2011)

Tata's environmental policy states that it will 'encourage' employees, contractors and suppliers to act in an environmentally responsible manner, but this falls somewhat short of ThyssenKrupp's pursuit of 'active contribution' from the workforce.

To support engagement with environmental issues at Port Talbot, there is a 'small' Environmental Department, established in 1998. The head of department reports directly to the plant director. This is a relatively recent development which has resulted from a 'greater priority now being placed on environmental aspects' (Interview Notes, Port Talbot, 2011). The Environmental Department operates two strategies. The focus of one dedicated team is on attaining compliance with legislation. The second strategy, implemented by a dedicated team of five environmental engineers working with the R&D department, is one of 'innovation' through capital expenditure projects. There is a 'pot' of £5 million allocated for such expenditure. The innovation section monitors data from a variety of sources gathered across the plant and develops schemes to improve compliance or enhance the efficiency of processes, projects described as involving 'step changes'. The innovation strategy is improvement-led and a number of interviewees from both the Environment and Health & Safety departments perceived this as indicating that:

> Environment is moving up the company agenda, in the same way that health and safety has. (Environmental Innovation Manager, Port Talbot, 2011)

However, outside these departments, cynicism was expressed:

> The emphasis is on yield, rather than the environment... it's about cost savings to be had, getting the most out of the hot mill for example. (Port Talbot, Technical Manager 1)

> Efficiency and cash are inextricably linked. It's cost that's important within the business, the environmental stuff is a 'green corporate social responsibility spin' for customers, because it's what they want to hear. (Technical Manager 2, Port Talbot, 2011)

Economic goals then take precedence over environmental aspects:

> It all comes down to cost, particularly the cost of energy at the moment. There are loads of initiatives to reduce energy consumption at the moment but they're clear that these are cost-driven rather than for environmental reasons. The business is not in a particularly healthy state at the moment. (Technical Officer, Port Talbot, 2011)

At ThyssenKrupp, however, alongside the Sustainability Team, there is a dedicated and longstanding Environment and Climate Change Department (ECCD). Moreover, there is a team of section-based environmental representatives, who act as 'contact partners for the parent company' and conduct daily environmental inspections (Interview Notes, Duisburg, 2011). These representatives also run environmental training for the workforce, and administer internal audits of green skills. The representatives are accountable to local management in the respective areas, but have independence from the line with regard to the undertaking of environmental inspections, reporting directly to the parent group – a system that has 'proved to be highly effective' (ECCD, Interview Notes, Duisburg, 2011).

Further, at ThyssenKrupp, regulations and objectives pertaining to environmental protection are documented in the centrally accessible Environmental Management Handbook, described as a 'key instrument' for communication of environmental matters. All environmental protection aspects are contained therein – as well as within work instructions/operating procedures – and presented in a format of comprehensible, practical guidelines. 'Info-Points' are available within each work area and provide employees/trainees with information on relevant environmental protection issues, health and safety, as well as other subjects: '[T]he company is constantly in contact with the plant operators to discuss environment-related decisions' (ECCD, Interview Notes, Duisburg, 2011).

This differs from practice at Tata, where environmental protection issues are not explicitly identified in a dedicated resource, but are implicit within work protocols/standard operating procedures and related risk assessments – for example, procedures for preventing gas emissions. Protocols are stored in a central database, accessible to all employees, but after initial instruction (usually task-based and centred on 'learning by doing'), reliance is placed on employees retrieving data and/or the efficacy of external supervision. A number of interviewees complained that procedures might be updated, but practice did not always keep pace, and that novel environmental issues that emerge from evolving work practices are not always recognized and incorporated into procedure or practice (as innovations). This 'system' is supported by three-times-a-month health and safety/environmental 'lead safe audits' conducted by section leaders and a system of spot check 'walkovers', which involve environmental staff questioning randomly selected workers on environmental/safety aspects. There is no planned programme and limited environment staff availability means that such checks are infrequently conducted. This is in contrast to practice at ThyssenKrupp, where the *independent* environmental representatives conduct daily inspections.

Innovation and Greening Steel Work

There are clear distinctions outlined above in approaches to environmental policy and practice at the company level. It is equally the case that there are different approaches to skills development (including green skills) at the case study companies. In keeping with other large German corporations, employee development is a high priority at ThyssenKrupp, with an inclusive approach adopted. On average, each employee receives three days of formal training per year (ThyssenKrupp 2009). Moreover, *all* employees participate in a developmental performance management system, with a mandatory interview conducted annually.

With regard to environmental training specifically, there is compulsory annual retraining for all managers and if employees desire/need training in a particular environmental topic, they contact the HR department:

> One of the main instruments to keep the employees up to date is an occupational qualification plan assessing systematically what issues are relevant and which qualifications are needed in the various work areas... The plan covers, for example, legal mandatory qualifications and

requirements that arise in the context of commissions… Therefore regular votes are taking place in the enterprise [involving the department managers and employees] in order to organize additional training. (Environmental Protection Officer, Duisburg, 2011)

For further specialized training over a wide range of environmental topics, the company commissions the relevant professional association. Moreover, regular environmental training updates are provided by the prevention officer for environmental protection and disseminated across the plant at all levels. Employees are involved in processes of environmental improvement and seminars are offered to the entire workforce, so as to inform and to encourage participation.

At Tata, there is an emphasis on task-based learning for the workforce in general. Protocols and standard operating procedures, which specify correct and safe ways of working for all tasks, are in place and accessible so as to direct behaviour and work performance. Operators are shown by experienced workers how to work in accordance with protocols. Environmental aspects are thus implicit within the procedures, rather than explicitly articulated. In terms of more formal training, there is a two-day induction for all new employees and this incorporates a rudimentary introduction to environmental issues, with emphasis on the costs of non-compliance incurred by the company. Thereafter, environmental issues *might* be covered on 'Journey Days' (a UK-wide, cross-plant culture change initiative), which are held approximately every 6 months. Where environmental issues have been included, cost of waste, cost of legislative breaches and the need to save money are the principal emphases. Furthermore, section managers – at their discretion – might refer to environmental aspects as part of their 'Toolbox Talks', which are designed to inform, instruct and train operatives about the issues that arise in their specific work area. In sum, there is no dedicated environmental training programme. Indeed, given the acknowledgement that operations management do not always 'buy in' to environmental concerns, such issues might not constitute a high priority when agendas are being formulated.

Managers at Tata receive limited but more systematic training on environmental matters and opportunities to pursue professional qualifications (via, for example, the Institute of Environmental Management and Assessment foundation course). In this respect, there is a 'training divide' between managers and managed, which occurs despite environmental staff explicitly acknowledging that it is operators who require rigorous training input within the subject area. Despite recognizing that such training might help the Environmental Department move away from its current approach of 'reactive firefighting', an environmental manager stated:

> If I had a guaranteed sum of money, I wouldn't spend it on training. It just wouldn't be a priority. (Environmental Manager, Port Talbot, 2011)

There are also distinct differences on how apprenticeship training is delivered at the two companies. Tata apprentices stated that there had been no specific, formal, off-the-job training on environmental issues, aside from the induction and one Journey Day. Heavy emphasis is placed on personal safety and the need to carry out risk assessments, but connections with environmental protection are not made explicit. For apprentices, as well as operators, there is also a heavy emphasis on task-based, experiential learning:

> It depends on who's showing you what to do, how organized the department is and how much time they've got for you. (Year 3 Apprentice, Port Talbot, 2011)

All of the Tata apprentices interviewed were unanimous that environmental legislation and topics were covered in the most cursory of fashions in the accompanying education they received off-the-job in college.

Such practice can be compared with that at ThyssenKrupp. The off-the-job educational provision received at vocational school places heavy emphasis on green aspects of the occupations. There are formally assessed environmental projects and environmental questions feature in the final examinations. In the work placement phase of their programme of study, the content of the training provision is governed by an in-company training plan, which must correspond to the occupational training regulations. The latter contain strong emphasis on environmental aspects. ThyssenKrupp's apprentices also attend the company's well-resourced, technical training centre. Apprentices receive tuition on relevant environmental topics and are given work-related environmental projects to complete. The company aims to develop apprentices who are:

> capable of thinking and acting independently [and who can] participate and think in terms of the real processes at work, [and] apply their technical knowledge to solve problems. (Trainer, Duisburg, 2011)

Training staff stated that they aim to impart a level of understanding, to the extent that trainees are able to:

analyse the working process, be aware of and understand the possible impacts of their actions... to ultimately increase their autonomy. (Trainer, Duisburg, 2011)

These goals of autonomy and adaptability contrast with the more static and narrow conception of competence at Tata. ThyssenKrupp clearly has a more comprehensive and systematic approach to development, while Tata's efforts focus on formal development of managers and those in professional occupations. These approaches to development – inclusive as opposed to bifurcated respectively – are reflected in (and reinforced by) the approach to innovation adopted.

Thus, at Tata, environmental improvements at the plant are driven in a top-down fashion, by the Innovation Section of the centralized Environmental Department in conjunction with the R&D department, both of which are staffed by highly qualified employees. Characteristically for liberal market economy organizations, the identification of projects is decided centrally and involvement of employees in processes of technical and organizational change is limited or non-existent. Shopfloor workers lack appropriate training and the rigid and proceduralized work organization discourages engagement with such agendas (Lundvall 2004). Moreover, information, communication and awareness-raising are still at a somewhat rudimentary phase:

Our resources to communicate with the workforce are extremely limited. (Environmental Innovation Manager, Port Talbot, 2011)

ThyssenKrupp, however, promotes involvement of the workforce across the board in continuous improvement, both generally and specifically, on environmental improvement projects. There is, of course, a specialist R&D function with responsibility for a large number of sophisticated process and product innovations. ThyssenKrupp spent around €240 million on R&D in fiscal year 2007–8 and has 1,580 employees working in this function across the segment as a whole. In addition, all employees are comprehensively involved in working on efficiency improvements – the 'Best' programme, the 'Ideas' scheme and the compulsory plant-wide efficiency programmes. The 'Ideas' programme is ThyssenKrupp's highly successful suggestions scheme. The participation rate was 617 suggestions per 1,000 employees in 2008. The number of suggestions for improving processes and optimizing efficiency that warranted reward was 9,430 in 2007–8, up from 7,824 in 2005–6. These employee-generated suggestions create annual savings of around €15.5 million (ThyssenKrupp 2009).

Discussion and Conclusions

Tata and ThyssenKrupp approach environmental matters in different ways. Both companies exhort corporate social responsibility regarding the environment, but the evidence suggests a distinctive variation of approach towards green innovation and skills across the two cases. Our argument is that these differences are attributable principally to the institutional contexts in which the companies are located, rather than generated as part of managerial philosophy independent of political and economic context.

In the German context, institutions such as the structure of the financial system and provision and availability of capital, social partnership and high skill levels have, in general, facilitated a more developmental, longer-term perspective and high innovation performance (European Commission 2012). Moreover, the long-established political strength of the green party, extensive environmental legislation, and high levels of environmental awareness in the wider society provide support for environmental protection. Being situated within this environment facilitates ThyssenKrupp's high-value-added strategy, which is based on technological innovation and a highly skilled workforce who are involved in continuous improvement activity. It is, moreover, equally applicable to the firm's environmental agenda. Environmental regulation, and the consequent need to improve environmental performance, is viewed as an economic opportunity to innovate through further investment in new technology and complementary skills. Environmental regulation in this context constitutes a 'beneficial constraint' (Streeck 2004).

This contrasts with the situation at Tata where a short-term financial perspective dominates that company's decision-making processes, characteristic of liberal market economy contexts (Kemp and Loorbach 2006). The focus here is on compliance with regulation and innovation focuses on immediate cost reductions, rather than longer-term strategies such as those focused on investment in workforce development. The latter is further undermined by institutional frameworks that disincentivize such developments. The green agenda is perceived as a restriction on business, reflecting the extant value orientation of the wider polity. Economic goals take precedence over environmental aspects at Tata and although there are benefits to be gained from such efficiency drives, without embedded recognition that pursuing long-term environmental goals can only be beneficial, any behavioural changes are likely to be externally imposed and therefore short-lived, as signified by the Environmental Department's description of their approach as one of reactive fire-fighting or trying to comply with regulations.

Across the two plants there are evident synergies with Porter and van der Linde's (1995) dichotomy of environmental innovation approaches. The latter can be divided into (1) those that focus on using technology to minimize the cost of dealing with pollution once it has occurred, and (2) those that focus on improving resource productivity in the first place. On both aspects, ThyssenKrupp performance is superior. The first approach focuses on taking the resources embodied in pollution and converting them into something of value through capital-intensive, technological innovations (for example, recycling of process gases). The long-term vision and level of capital investment necessary for such pioneering innovations suggests an incremental approach typical of coordinated market economy contexts. However, at the same time, it represents a substantial and relatively rapid shift in operations and is in some ways more typical of radical innovation, which runs counter to the predictions of the Hall and Soskice model. Indeed, a small number of studies have argued that coordinated market economy institutions are conducive to radical innovation and this example adds further support to such contentions (see Allen and Funk 2008).

The second approach, of resource productivity, includes more efficient utilization of particular inputs, waste reduction and better product yields. Such improvements are analogous to incremental innovations, which are customarily secured through the mechanism of involvement of the entire workforce in continuous improvement programmes (Hall and Soskice 2001). The innovations derived from such programmes have been widely recognized as constituting a significant contribution to long-run advantage for object-oriented producers, such as steel firms, which operate in highly competitive, globalized markets with tight profit margins (Tylecote and Conesa 1999). The institutions associated with coordinated market economies are argued to be far more conducive to the effectiveness of such programmes. For success, extensive input from knowledgeable, autonomous, loyal employees who feel secure in their jobs is required (Hall and Soskice, 2001). The data suggest that ThyssenKrupp comprehensively involves employees in efficiency improvement schemes and that these are highly effective. In contrast, Tata's approach to managing the employment relationship and structuring of the labour process, both of which are typical of liberal market economy contexts, can be perceived as inimical to the effectiveness of such programmes – merely focusing, as it does, on compliance.

Training strategies are also, of course, closely aligned to innovative behaviour at company level, with effective training and high skill levels associated with the cultivation of innovative behaviour and the ability to propose suggestions for improvement (Hall and Soskice 2001). The inclusive approach to employee development evident at ThyssenKrupp encompasses the environmental aspects of workers' jobs, with high-quality training comprehensively provided as to the use of novel green technological innovations as well as process improvement techniques. Such training aims to develop knowledge and attitudes that enable workers to use their autonomy and apply their problem-solving abilities, thereby securing continuous improvements. At ThyssenKrupp, company training is complemented by high-quality vocational education and training systems – the relationship between company training and the vocational education and training system is governed by the training regulations that exist for each designated occupation (Jensen *et al.* 2004). Companies must have training plans, which are structured by these training regulations, and the latter have been modified and updated to include environmental aspects, across all occupations. This greening has been driven by organic collaboration between the social partners (CEDEFOP 2010), meaning that the German vocational education and training system both shapes and responds to employers' training needs.

In contrast, the UK vocational education and training system has long been criticized for its deficiencies, including a failure to green extant provision and incorporate apposite environmental content (IES 2012). This lack of focus in public educational provision was identified by all the Tata apprentices. Moreover, the lack of formal training received at the plant, given the heavy emphasis on task-based learning, also extends to environmental protection. Less-formal development methods, such as 'learning by doing', can facilitate the passing on of 'bad practice', with clear scope for the establishment of erroneous ways of working (Gibb 2011). This work-based practice reflects inherent flaws within the qualification system (based on National Vocational Qualifications), which gives shape to the central form of training, learning and assessment within the wider vocational education and training/apprenticeship system. Assessment is based on learners being able to demonstrate narrow competence in completing a task, rather than evidencing their understanding of the broader, underpinning knowledge required for deeper comprehension (Boreham 2002).

These deficiencies in both company and vocational education and training system provision reflect the institutional context – there are systematic disincentives for workforce development. Endemic short-termism and a heavy emphasis on assured, definitive financial payback undermine long-term human-capital development projects. The case study data also indicate the existence of a 'bifurcated approach' to training at Tata Steel, with a clear 'training apartheid' between managers and managed as regards environmental training. There is a distinct lack of formal training for non-managerial staff and, moreover, the heavy emphasis on rigid adherence to standard operating procedures, in which environmental aspects are implicitly incorporated, can curtail not only workers' problem-solving ability but also their ability to adapt to novel situations as well as inhibiting the proposal of suggestions as to how improvements might be made. Of course, steel-making is a potentially hazardous occupation and safe working procedures must be specified and should be adhered to, but rigid adherence to 'one best way' of working can stifle innovative behaviour (Lundvall 2004). Such conditions are antithetical to workforce involvement in both continuous improvement generally and environmental improvement specifically.

This is further reinforced by the 'limited resources available' for formal communication with the workforce, reflecting the general lack of legal obligation for consultation and information in the wider context. Reliance is placed on line managers to informally communicate with their sections as to environmental aspects, despite the identification of a lack of line management 'buy-in'. Improvements are driven centrally, again reflecting the propensity for control structures and highly centralized decision-making in companies in liberal market economies. The Tata data reveal that, in liberal market economies such as the UK, there are significant barriers to the vision for, and investments in, both the technology and skills necessary for green innovation, with an extant development paradigm that is driven by short-term benefits (Kemp and Loorbach 2006). The ThyssenKrupp plant however demonstrates a more developmental orientation with clear evidence of an environmental innovation approach, which is supported by robust institutional frameworks. In sum, our analysis extends the prescriptions of Porter and van der Linde by identifying supporting institutional factors essential for the emergence of an 'environmental innovation' mindset at company level.

One final observation concerns the durability of coordinated market economy arrangements. Some commentators have pointed to their breakdown and others have put forward 'convergence/liberalization' arguments (see Streeck and Hassel 2004; Howell 2003). Indeed, there is a growing body of evidence which suggests that such changes are taking place (Hassel 2012). However, the high levels of in-firm training, the supportive vocational education and training system and the reliance on the participative efforts of the workforce within ThyssenKrupp, in conjunction with strong (environmental) legislation operating as a beneficial constraint, seem to suggest continuity of coordinated market economy arrangements, rather than transformation to a liberal labour market model. We believe that what our data suggest is not only the importance of institutional frameworks for shaping company strategies, but also some support for 'duality' arguments. The suggestion here is that the steel industry in Germany, as part of a manufacturing segment, has greater resistance to 'liberalization' than others parts of the economy (see Hassel (2012) on services), precisely because it is organized around a body of skilled, high-productivity core workers who have employment security.

REFERENCES

Allen, Matthew and Lothar Funk (2008) 'Institutions and Innovation: The Role of German Works Councils in Supporting Radical Change', paper presented at the *25th Celebration Conference on Entrepreneurship and Innovation – Organizations, Institutions, Systems and Regions*, Copenhagen, 17–20 June 2008.

BERR (2009) *Skills for Growth: The National Skills Strategy*. London: HM Government.

Blühdorn, Ingolfur (2009) 'Reinventing Green Politics: On the Strategic Repositioning of the German Green Party', *German Politics* 18:36–54.

Boreham, Nicholas (2002) 'Work Process Knowledge, Curriculum Control and the Work-Based Route to Occupational Qualifications', *British Journal of Educational Studies* 50:225–37.

Bosch, Gerhard and Jean Charest (2008) 'Vocational Training and the Labour Market in Liberal and Co-Ordinated Economies', *Industrial Relations Journal* 39:428–47.

Burchell, Brendon, David Lapido and Frank Wilkinson (2002) *Job Insecurity and Work Intensification*. London: Routledge.

CEDEFOP (2010) *Skills for Green Jobs: A European Synthesis Report*. Luxembourg: Publications Office of the European Union.

Crouch, Colin (2001) 'Heterogeneities of Practice and Interest: Feature Review of D. Coates, *Models of Capitalism*, 2000', *New Political Economy* 6:131–35.

Culpepper, Pepper D. (1999) 'The Future of the High Skill Equilibrium in Germany', *Oxford Review of Economic Policy* 15:43–59.

Dierdorff, Erich *et al.* (2009) *Greening of the World of Work: Implications for O*NET®-SOC and New and Emerging Occupations*. A Report for US Department of Labor Employment and Training Administration. Washington, DC: National Center for O*NET Development.

EEF (2010) *Changing the Climate for Manufacturing*. London: EEF.

ESTEP (2010) *A Bridge to the Future:2010 Activity Report*. Brussels: European Commission.

EUROFER (2010) *Manifesto of the European Steel Industry for the European Commission 2010–2014*. Brussels: Eurofer.

European Commission (2009) *Attitudes of European Citizens Towards the Environment*. Luxembourg: Publications Office.

European Commission (2012) *Regional Innovation Scoreboard 2012*. Brussels: DG Enterprise and Industry.

Gibb, Stephen (2011) *Human Resource Development*. 3rd edn. Basingstoke: Palgrave Macmillan.

Gospel, Howard. and Andrew Pendleton (2003) 'Finance, Corporate Governance and the Management of Labour: A Conceptual and Comparative Analysis', *British Journal of Industrial Relations* 41:557–82.

▶

Hall, Peter and David Soskice (2001) 'An Introduction to Varieties of Capitalism', pp. 1–70 in *Varieties of Capitalism: The Institutional Foundations of Comparative Advantage,* edited by P. Hall and D. Soskice. Oxford: Oxford University Press.

Harvey, Fiona (201) 'Autumn Statement: George Osborne Slams "Costly" Green Policies', *The Guardian* 29 November 2011.

Hassel, Anke (2012) 'The Paradox of Liberalization – Understanding Dualism and the Recovery of the German Political Economy', *British Journal of Industrial Relations,* first published online 20.09.2012.

Heery, Edmund and Stephen Wood (2003) 'Employee Relations and Corporate Governance', *British Journal of Industrial Relations* 41:477–9.

Hoque, Kim (2008) 'The Impact of Investors in People on Employer-Provided Training, the Equality of Training Provision and the "Training Apartheid" Phenomenon', *Industrial Relations Journal* 39:43–62.

Howell, Chris (2003) 'Varieties of Capitalism: And Then There Was One?', *Comparative Politics* 36:103–24.

IES (2012) 'Green Skills and Environmental Awareness in Vocational Education and Training – Synthesis Report', Research Paper 24, European Centre for the Development of Vocational Training. Brighton, June.

Jensen, B. Morten, Björn Johnson, Lorenz, Edward and Bengt Å. Lundvell (2004) 'Absorptive Capacity, Forms of Knowledge and Economic Development', Working Paper, Centre National de la Recherche Scientifique: Université de Nice – Sophia Antipolis.

Kemp, René and Loorbach, Derk (2006) 'Transition Management: A Reflexive Governance Approach', pp.103–30 in *Reflexive Governance for Sustainable Development,* edited by J. Voss, R. Kemp and D. Bauknecht. Northampton, MA: Edward Elgar.

Korczynski, Marek (2000) 'The Political Economy of Trust', *Journal of Management Studies* 37:1–21.

Lane, Christel (1995) *Industry and Society in Europe: Stability and Change in Britain, Germany and France.* Aldershot: Edward Elgar.

Lane, Christel and Bachmann, Reinhard (1997) 'Co-Operation In Inter-Firm Relations in Britain and Germany: The Role of Social Institutions', *British Journal of Sociology* 48:226–54.

Lloyd, Caroline and Jonathan Payne (2002) 'Developing a Political Economy of Skill', *Journal of Education and Work* 15:365–90.

Lundvall, Bengt Å (2004) 'National Innovation Systems – Analytical Concept and Development Tool', paper presented at the DRUID Tenth Anniversary Summer Conference 2005 on Dynamics of Industry and Innovation: Organizations, Networks and Systems, Copenhagen, 27–29 June 2004.

Newell, Sue, Maxine Robertson, Harry Scarborough and Jacky Swann (2009) *Managing Knowledge Work and Innovation* Basingstoke: Palgrave Macmillan.

Porter, Michael E. and Class van der Linde (1995) 'Towards a New Conception of the Environment-Competitiveness Relationship', *Journal of Economic Perspectives* 9:97–118.

Streeck, Wolfgang (1992) *Social Institutions and Economic Performance: Studies of Industrial Relations in Advanced Capitalist Economies,* London: Sage.

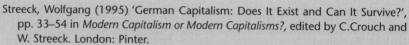

Streeck, Wolfgang (1995) 'German Capitalism: Does It Exist and Can It Survive?', pp. 33–54 in *Modern Capitalism or Modern Capitalisms?*, edited by C.Crouch and W. Streeck. London: Pinter.

Streeck, Wolfgang (2004) 'Educating Capitalists: A Rejoinder to Wright and Tsakalotos', *Socio-Economic Review* 2:425–37.

Streeck, Wolfgang and Anke Hassel (2004) 'The Crumbling Pillars of Social Partnership', *West European Politics* 26:103–24.

Stroud, Dean (201) 'Organising Training for Union Renewal: A Case Study Analysis of the European Union Steel Industry', *Economic and Industrial Democracy* 33:225–44.

Tata Steel (various) *Corporate Citizenship Reports*, available at http://www.tatas-teeleurope.com/en/news/publications/, retrieved 11 May 2011.

Thompson, Paul and Chris Smith (eds) (2010) *Working Life. Renewing Labour Process Analysis*. Basingstoke: Palgrave Macmillan.

ThyssenKrupp (various) *Annual Sustainability Reports*, available at http//www.thyssenkrupp-steel-europe.com/en/portraet/nachhaltigkeit/, retrieved 11 May 2011.

Tylecote, Andrew and Emanuelle Conesa (1999) 'Corporate Governance, Innovation Systems and Industral Performance', *Industry & Innovation* 6:25–50.

Board-Level Employee Representatives in Norway, Sweden and Denmark: Differently Powerless or Equally Important?

7

Inger Marie Hagen

The Nordic and labour market model has gained a lot of attention since the financial crises hit Europe and the US in 2008. These small Nordic economies seem to have found the solution to growth, peaceful labour relations and a stable environment for investors and shareholders. Or to rephrase – they have found a productive mixture of industrial relations and corporate governance.

The Scandinavian countries may very well illustrate Höpner's finding that 'countries with organized labour market institutions tend to have a high degree of organization of corporate governance and vice versa' (Höpner 2005:334). The countries serve as a core example of coordinated market economies (see Hall and Soskice 2001). However, while there are many macro and comparative studies on complementarity, institutional change, path dependency, and convergence, finding micro studies is a far more challenging task. Where do the institutions actually meet?

Our 'interaction point' is employee-elected members – employee representatives (ERs)[1] – on company boards. The arrangement might serve as an indicator of the mechanism operating when two institutional arrangements interact: the employees have the right to be represented in order to bring their opinions and interests to the board, but nevertheless the representatives have the same responsibilities as any other director and are subject to the same legal obligations found in company law and, more recently, ideals rooted in corporate governance codes in order to increase the value of the company and shareholder control. *Employee representatives* are part of the industrial relations system while *directors* in private companies relate to the way companies are regulated and governed based on the interpretation and importance of property rights.

Tripartism and social dialogue on different levels have been important part of the industrial relations system in all three Scandinavian countries and 'democratic capitalism' (Iversen and Thue 2008) has been used to label the business system. But important changes have taken place in both the industrial relations and the corporate governance regulatory regime. The aim is to identify how the two different institutions have affected the role of the ERs and to look for traces of dominance of the one or the other. My findings do indicate that both in Sweden and in Denmark the two positions (trade union representative and employee representative) coexist as distinct roles. However, the coexistence takes different forms. The Swedish representatives seem to be on the defensive, while the Danish simply point to different rules in the two positions. In Norway our findings indicate a real integration between the two roles. In short, the Swedish employee representatives are not able to use the industrial relations position to empower their role on the board, and corporate governance 'rules and ideology' dominate; in Denmark such empowerment seems irrelevant; in Norway it is very important, the employee representatives seemingly being able to forge a powerful mixture between the two positions based on the strength of the trade unions and the labour market institutions.

This chapter is constructed as follows. First the legal framework is presented. Next I examine the use of the arrangement and the level of influence among the employee representatives. I then return to the employee representatives as an interaction point of two institutional arrangements, while the final section is dedicated to using the different features of the national institutional arrangements for understanding the different positions of the employee representatives in the seemingly nearly identical Nordic economies. The data in this chapter are taken from two different sources: my previous work on employee representatives (summarized in Hagen 2010) and an ongoing project on 'sustainable companies'.[2]

Legal Framework

In different shapes and to different degrees, the right to elect employee representatives to the main governing body in companies is found in 18 countries in the EU/EEA area. Historically the arrangement has been highly contested among trade unions, and as Carly (2005) points out, this resistance postponed the establishment of a common European company form for more than 30 years.

Opponents of the arrangement emphasized the risk of employee representatives ending up as hostages of the capital side of the board by taking responsibly for board decisions made by the shareholder-elected majority. Accepting board positions was pictured as a betrayal of the working class and incompatible with the participation system based on collective agreements and the underlying labour–versus–capital conflict (Grønlie 1977). Supporters of the arrangement maintained the need for employee participation at the board level as a part of increasing democracy in all areas of society (Christensen and Westenholz 1999). The debate took place in the 1970s and the arrangement was introduced in a number of countries, among them Norway and Sweden in 1972 and Denmark in 1973. At the time the 'European company' (*Societas Europaea*) was finally established in 2001 most of the resistance among unions had faded and the possibility of extending the arrangement was welcomed by the European trade union federations. An important trigger has been the increased focus on corporate governance and the importance of the board as the most important tool for shareholders to regain corporate control.

Company law in the three countries is very similar. The 'Nordic board' has both controlling and executive competence, but 'day-to-day' running of the company is delegated to the CEO. In contrast for example to the German two-tier system where the employee representatives serve on the supervisory board, the Nordic employee representatives take part in both executive decisions and the supervision of the company. Table 7.1 gives an overview of the legal requirements. Both the election procedures and the threshold differ among the three countries even if – in a comparative setting – it makes sense to talk about a Nordic arrangement.

Similarities aside, important differences are found. First, while the Danish and Norwegian company acts contain provisions on employee representatives, in Sweden the provisions are found in a separate act (the 1987 Board Representation Act). Thus, the arrangement is undoubtedly a part of company law in Norway and Denmark while in Swedish legal literature this act has been considered a part of both company law and labour law (Hagen and Mulder 2012). In all three countries there is a dual objective – that having employees on the board should increase both productivity and employee influence (see NOU 2010:1). The legal placement might however tilt the expectations of the employee representatives in different directions and thus raise the question of their legitimacy when promoting employee interests on the board. Labour law is aimed at employee participation in matters on managerial prerogatives issues but also at conflict-solving procedures. Conflict resolution in company law is mainly a question of the rights of displeased shareholders and minority shareholder protection.

When we move on to the next important distinction we find that in the Swedish arrangement the labour law element is strengthened. All three countries are single-channel systems; the local trade unions are the

Table 7.1 Legal requirements on employee representatives in Norway, Sweden and Denmark

	Norway	Sweden	Denmark
Legal foundation	Norwegian Company Acts (and precept)	Act 1987 on board representation	Danish Company Act (and precept)
Threshold – company and group	30 employees (both)	25 employees in Sweden (both), but never in majority	35 employees (both)
Size matters?	30–49 empl: 1 rep 50+ empl: 1/3 of board 200: compulsory 1/3	25+: 2 reps 1000+ and more than one industry: 3 reps, but never in majority	35+ 1/3 (by at least 2 in company and 3 in group)
Depends on demand from company level	More than 50 per cent of the employees or by trade unions covering 2/3 of the employees	Local trade union with a collective agreement with the company	More that 50 per cent of the employees (a vote is needed unless agreement between employee–employer)
Parent level	More than 50 per cent of the employees in the group or trade unions with more than 2/3 of the employees may ask the industrial democracy tribunal (see below) to decide on a 'group arrangement'	Local trade union with a collective agreement with one of the companies in the group. The concerned unions shall agree upon appointment of employees' representatives; otherwise, the act provides a system for appointment	More than 50 per cent of the employees in the group (a vote is needed unless by agreement between employee–employer).
If disagreement – settled by the	'Industrial democracy tribunal' – a joint committee under the government's Ministry of Labour	The concerned unions shall agree upon appointment of employees' representatives; otherwise, the act provides a system for appointment. The Board Representation Tribunal – a joint (but a majority of employers) committee under the government's Ministry of Employment may decide exemption from the application of the act.	Any dispute are to be settled by the ordinary dispute settlement procedures

Eligible for office – company level	Employees in company	'Should be' employees	Employees in company
Eligible for office – group level	Employees in any company in the group	'Should be' employees in any company in the group	Employees in any company in the group
Electoral system	Either majority (direct) vote or by proportional representation or by agreement (only one list of candidates)	Appointment by trade union(s) bound by collective agreement	Majority vote (company) / Majority or indirect voting (group) / The choice is made by the electoral body.
Organized by	'Electoral board' in company/group	Trade union(s) – following a certain 'key' if disagreement between different trade unions	'Electoral board' in company/group
ER in board committees	No legal right	Legal right for one seat in the committee	No legal right
Restrictions of participation	None (same legal status as the shareholder elected directors)	Same legal status, except: Employees' representatives may not participate in dealing with issues related to the collective agreement or other issues in which the union has a material interest that may conflict with the interests of the company.	None (same legal status as the shareholder elected directors)
Transnational representation (group arrangements covering some or all foreign subsidiaries) in the group	Same procedures as 'ordinary group arrangements'	Unclear – possible if part of the company statutes (e.g. resolution at the general assembly is needed), or according to unions' agreements, or whom the act's system of appointment	More than 50 per cent of the employees in the group (or by agreement between employee–employer) AND By resolution at the general assembly The employees in Danish subsidiaries have the right to elect at least one director and if these employees exceed 1/10 of total number in the group, at least two directors.

representatives of the workers at company level. The Swedish provisions are in line with this principle: the legal act gives the rights to the trade unions in the same way as we find in the 1976 Codetermination Act. The employee representatives are appointed by the local trade union(s), and a collective agreement is needed. In Norway and Denmark company law does not follow the single-channel principle and the employee representatives are elected 'by and among all the employees'.

In Sweden there is no question of whether the employee representatives represent the unions or not. In Norway and Denmark we also often find trade union representatives serving as an employee representative, but this happens by 'planned coincidence'. In Norway the provisions governing election procedures make it a bit less incidental. In Norway and Denmark the legitimacy of the arrangement is closely linked (both historically and at present) to the fact that the employee representatives represent *all employees*. This implies that the arrangement is vulnerable to the criticism that it does not represent all workers in the company or in the corporate group. It is not uncommon for shareholder-elected members to remind the employee representatives that they are not representing the trade unions (Hagen 2010). In Sweden this argument does not apply.

When more and more companies are part of *international* corporate groups, the question of transnational representation becomes important for maintaining the legitimacy of the arrangement. There are important distinctions at this point (see Hagen and Mulder 2013 forthcoming for a full presentation). In short: in Norway the question of foreign representation does not in principle differ from the rule concerning national groups, while in Denmark and Sweden the issue is decided by the shareholders' annual or special general meeting, which could be conceived as an alien element – why should the shareholders have any role or impact on the way the employees elect their representatives?

Use and Importance: An Empirical Snapshot

The amount of research into the role and influence of the employee representatives is sparse in Scandinavia[3] and we have only a few surveys to rely on when presenting this snapshot. Representation has to be demanded by the employees/trade unions; it is not compulsory in any of the three countries – with the exception of Norwegian companies having more than 200 employees. Based on the figures available, the highest coverage is found in Norway: 67 per cent of all employees (in companies which are covered by the legislation) have elected representatives

(Falkum *et al.* 2009), while the corresponding figure in Denmark is 55 per cent (all figures on Denmark are from CO Industri). In both countries, company size is very important and in both countries the coverage seems fairly stable (all figures are from Hagen 2010). Turning to companies as the unit of measurement we find that 55 per cent of all Norwegian companies above the legal requirement threshold have representatives on their board (37 per cent in companies with 30–49 employees, 59 per cent in those with 50–199 employees and 74 per cent in those with more than 200 employees). In Denmark the figures are considerably smaller; all in all 24 per cent of all companies have boards with employee representatives (in 13 per cent of companies with 35–99 employees, in 32 per cent of those with 100–199 employees, in 54 per cent of those with 200–499 and in 35 per cent of those with above 500 employees).

We have not been able to identify figures from Sweden that allow us to go into particulars. Among all companies in manufacturing industry with more than 25 employees, employee representatives are found in 75 per cent of all of the companies. Company size is important in Sweden as well, owing to (1) the probability of finding a collective agreement needed for demanding representation but also because (2) the larger the company the more in line with regulations as such it will be, and the employee representatives arrangement will follow in accordance with these (Hagen 2010).

ER Influence and Power

How powerful are the employee representatives? How much influence do they have? Are they able to make a difference on behalf of the employees? The surveys and review of available statistics concludes that the employee representatives' influence at the board seems to be somewhere in 'the middle' when the respondents are asked to rank it from 'substantial' to 'none'. It is important to add that large individual differences are found. In Denmark, based on responses from employee representatives, 1 out of 5 answered that their influence amounted to none at all, while approximately the same number chose the opposite reply that it was very great. Rose (2008:231) concludes thus:

> This article presents some evidence that suggests that Danish share-holder elected board members share their influence with employee representatives, especially in listed firms...the results show that employee representatives are not trying to steer the firm in a particular direction. Instead it is reasonable to believe that they act as sparring partners, contributing to the supervisory board's decision-making

process with their knowledge and background information about the firm.

In 2005 we questioned both CEOs and employee representatives in a sample of the 1000 largest companies in Norway and in 2007 we got answers from 1000 CEOs in a representative sample of Norwegian limited or publicly quoted companies. The results indicate that two-thirds of the employee representatives picture their influence as somewhere in the middle (3 and 4 on a scale of 1 to 6), 22 per cent place themselves at the top level (5 and 6) and a few less, 17 per cent, at the bottom (1 and 2). Among the CEOs the assessment is very similar, which is very interesting and may be interpreted as a token of a common understanding and trust among the partners (all figures from Hagen 2010). Turning to the Swedish employee representatives, based on the study of Wallenberg and Levinson (2012), the findings indicate that the Swedish ERs enjoy less influence than the Norwegians and the Danes. Another important difference is that we do not find the same common assessment between the CEOs and the employee representatives in Sweden.

In all three countries the CEOs seem to support the arrangement. In Norway, only 7 per cent of the CEOs in companies with employee representatives answered that the number of employee representatives should be reduced (Hagen 2010). In Sweden only 7 per cent of CEOs expressed a 'rather negative' (no one chose to answer 'very negative') experience of employee board representation, 60 per cent being rather or very positive (Wallenberg and Levinson 2012). CEOs see employee representatives as a resource that contributes to positive relations, makes board decisions better rooted among employees, and facilitates the implementation of difficult decisions. No substantial employer resistance was found in Denmark, either (Rose 2008).

Turning to the qualitative results based on our interviews, important similarities were found between the three countries. None of our interviewees viewed themselves as inferior board members. Increased emphasis on shareholders' value was, however, easily recognized; the interests of the company are aligned with shareholders' interests. The board and its agenda have become more important and in particular the role of the board chair is emphasized. The struggle to prevent downsizing and the relocation of workplaces abroad is at the top of their agenda. One of the most important means is to collaborate on technological changes and improvements.

It is not possible to reach any conclusions based on our qualitative data; however, some hypotheses on the different paths of the three countries may be presented. Apart from the findings mentioned above, in Norway 'business as usual' seems to be a reasonable hypothesis:

> When I make a suggestion, the response is positive, I do feel that the rest of the board have respect for the things I say. (Employee representative, 2011 – all quotes translated by the author.)

> Yes, we're mixing positions, that's what the management wants and it's working really well. (Employee representative, 2011)

I also interviewed employee representatives in 2000 and 2003 (Hagen 2010) and the answers to my questions on the work and role of an employee representative were not very different 10 years later. Informal collaboration in the best interests of the company is emphasized. The employee representatives picture themselves as employee *representatives* and whether or not the issue at hand is solved by board discussions, informal meetings with the CEO or in more formalized social dialogue is not important (see also Falkum *et al.* 2009).

In Denmark, mixed positions were clearly preferred, but the different roles were emphasized and none of the respondents used issues belonging to the collective agreement area as examples of conflict issues. They placed great emphasis on common interests but also said that they expected the management and the majority of the board to uphold their part of the bargain and ensure the survival of the company in Denmark. In other words, we clearly found indications of the 'Danish compromise', for example:

> Yes, issues are solved, we're collaborating, and the management supports the 'Danish model'. (Employee representative, 2011)

In Sweden traces of a much harsher climate were found and the 'old days' were often mentioned:

> Earlier we had a lot of collaboration with the top management, but now – they have terminated the agreement on participation and do not really want to continue the social dialogue. Things have really changed. (Employee representative, 2011)

> In the board position, I do get information, but I have no influence. (Employee representative, 2011)

Less informal contact with the CEO was also mentioned and in contrast to the Danes and the Norwegians, assertions that 'this is the way we do it here' (in implicit reference to the collaboration model in Norway and Denmark) were not made. 'Defensive' might be a suitable keyword.

Based on the qualitative material, the Norwegian representatives seem to be the most influential – or to be more precise, based on their own expectations they appear that way. Our data are far from extensive enough to make firm conclusions, but it might nevertheless be worth pointing out some of the features mentioned by the Norwegian representatives. Even if the latter do recognize the role of the employee representative, the boundaries between the employee representative and the trade union representative are more blurred. They seem to have more informal contact with the management and whether this contact is based on the employee representative role or the trade union role is not important. Broadly speaking, the Swedish employee representatives seem to be in either a non-important or a conflict position face to face with management and the board majority, the Danes seem to reserve conflict (if any) for social dialogue and the 'Danish compromise' (Due and Madsen 2011) is easily recognized, while the Norwegians are less formal and more pragmatic, regarding the rules and regulations as not that important as long as they feel respected by the CEO and the board chair.

Employee Representatives and Their Institutional Framework

The distinction between the owners of the company (the shareholders) and the managerial prerogative is crucial for understanding the logic of the system of industrial relations. The managers act on behalf of the owners within their given authority. At company level the management and trade union representatives will (according to the relevant laws and collective agreements) negotiate, collaborate, argue and fight within these limits.

However, after more than 20 years of 'shareholder revolution' and widespread new corporate governance ideologies (see for example Clarke 2004; Aglietta and Rèberioux 2005) important changes are taking place and a different point of departure emerges. In the new ideologies, and with a strong basis in agency theory (Jensen and Meckling 1976), the *governing relation* or the central point in companies is found between the owners and the management, or – as emphasized in the different codes – between the board of directors and the top management. The conflict between managerial prerogative and organized labour is either simply overlooked or pictured as severely outdated.

A comparison between employee representatives enables us to look into how the interaction point between industrial relations and corporate governance varies across economies with a number of common institutional features, often referred to as 'the Nordic model'; social-democratic welfare regimes with generous universalistic arrangements (Esping-Andersen 1990). The political history has important common features (class compromises in the 1930s, strong trade unions, strong social-democratic parties, tripartism and neo-corporatism). Dølvik (2007) emphasizes a particular combination of centralization and decentralization based on the relationship between the different trade union levels. The trade union representatives in the companies have a significant role in implementing the central agreements and negotiation results at the firm level, all under the peace clause and with extensive participation rights. We might also add compressed wage structures, equal levels of income and a persistent Weberian work ethic (Hagen 2012).

Recent developments have brought about changes in the national systems. EU regulations have made substantial changes and particularly in Norway labour migration after 2004 has challenged the model. It is important to distinguish between changes concerning participation/codetermination and changes concerning collective bargaining and levels of wage negotiations.

All three countries are of course covered by the EU directive on information and consultation (2004/14/EC), but the national frameworks of legal acts/collective agreements offer far more extensive rights to worker participation. The Basic Agreements are the foundation of the social dialogue (for example mutual recognition; the right to organize and bargain and to take industrial action; the social partners' self-regulation; and the state's non-intervention) and the foundation for the Nordic single-channel system. The Norwegian Basic Agreement provides the actual rules and regulations and the agreement is negotiated every fourth year, while these rules are found in, respectively, the Swedish 1976 Co-Determination Act (MBL[4]) and the different sectoral collective agreements in Denmark. In all the relevant agreements we find three important features: first, the collaboration is based on a *mutual duty* towards the company, with increased productivity a typically common goal; second, based on the managerial prerogative, the *employer* has the right to *make the final decision* even if the trade unions disagree; but, third, the employer must inform and invite the trade union representatives to consultation and collaboration *prior to important decisions*, and failure to do so is a violation of the agreements (or, in Sweden, the MBL).

The regulatory framework on participation and codetermination has not changed. But, as already mentioned, an issue at hand is subject to managerial prerogative and we might also add that the employee representatives will always be in a minority position on the board. This implies that the strength and standing of the local trade union is crucial.

As regards collective bargaining, several changes have taken place, but (as stated by Berge *et al.* 2009), the right-wing governments in Sweden and Denmark have not challenged the trade union movement by changing the fundamental labour market model or labour law as such. The institutional framework is retained, but attempts to weaken the mechanism which supports recruitment into the trade unions (tax deduction and changes in the Ghent-system) have taken place in Sweden and Denmark. Second, attempts to weaken the position and the significance of the trade unions at macro level have been noticed. Trade union density in both countries has declined, but is still very high in comparative terms. The density in Norway has been remarkably stable. In all three countries, but most noticeably in Sweden and Denmark, decentralization has taken place, but still in the coordinated Nordic style, with sector agreements as default mechanisms. And again, as the number of issues at the local bargaining table has increased, local strength and density have become more and more important. The economic crises have had less effect in Norway, with the unemployment rate in 2013 still below 4 per cent, compared with figures for Sweden and Denmark of 8 per cent and 6 per cent, figures that in a 'Nordic model' are considerable.

Nordic Corporate Governance

Iversen and Thue (2008:6) emphasize that Nordic capitalism 'mirrored a high degree of equality and participation within the decisions making sphere, in the private, the economic and the political sphere'. Embedded in this capitalism was, as Sejerstad (2002) pictures Norway in the post-1945 period, a managerial capitalism subject to a regulatory regime where the social partner and the state sidelined the shareholders.

Important changes have taken place in this area in the Nordic countries as well as in the rest of the industrialized world, in line with neoliberalism and new ideologies. Yet, important distinctions are found in the Nordic countries even if the company laws are more or less identical with their strong minority shareholder protection (compared with the common legal system; see Bøhren and Ødegård 2000). The ownership structures in Sweden have historically been marked by large industrialists like the Wallenberg family while private foundations (for example Carlsberg or Edmond) have been important in Denmark. In Norway lack of private capital has been a significant factor. Looking at the ownership structure of listed companies today[5] we find that 40 per cent of all shares are owned by the state in Norway compared with only 1 per cent in Denmark and 8 per cent in Sweden. Only 7 per cent are owned by financial institutions in Norway (and this includes the 3 per cent to 4 per cent controlled by the state national pension fund) while the figure is 20 in Denmark and 27 in Sweden. Individual ownership is also very low in Norway – 4 per cent – compared with 17 per cent in Denmark and 16 per cent in Sweden.

The shareholder revolution also influenced the Nordic countries and ownership as a production factor is on the agenda (Bøhren 2010). Höpner (2005:348–9) points to the German example of increased shareholder orientation and maintained co-determination (through board representation) and participation (through works councils and trade unions):

> So far, co-determination seems to have opened the door for significant steps towards increased investor orientation, making possible relatively silent restructuring of the largest German companies that would have caused enormous conflicts with employees if co-determination were absent.

Many of the changes in German corporate governance fit well with the development in the Nordic countries: there has been increased competition due to European integration, Anglo-American company strategies have come into fashion, a corporate governance code has been established and has very rapidly achieved a law-like status even if any Nordic voice or foundation is hard to trace.

To put it rather bluntly, the shareholders have been on the offensive. The question is of course whether or not the Nordic labour market model has been strong enough to resist; or, to rephrase: based on the idea of hierarchies among complementary institutions from the regulation school (Boyer 2000), do we find that the hierarchy has changed and that the finance regime now commands a central position in the production regime in Nordic working life, even at local level? Vidal (2012:553), also from within the framework of the regulation school, argues that

> postfordist settlements are reactions to a dual institutional shift, as production has been subordinated to finance (hence shareholder value) while employment relations have been subordinated to new forms of competition (hence externalized employment).

From a Nordic viewpoint (as opposed to Vidal's Anglo-American one) we might argue that the Nordic model has prevented this externalization of employment, or at least limited it to the outskirts of the labour market.

Two Systems of Participation?

How then do the rights and obligations of the board, on the one hand, and the employee representatives and social dialogue based on labour law and collective agreements, on the other hand, relate to each other? Does – and if so how – employee representation constitute an interaction point between different institutional features taken from industrial relations and corporate governance? Are the two systems complementarity? Do changes in institutional framework influence the employee representatives in a particular direction?

We need to look for both formal and informal linkages between the two different areas of regulation. There are no provisions in the law or collective agreements where the different positions relate to one another. The actors themselves underline that these are two different positions. Consultations between the trade union and the employer will never take place on the board. Information given to the employee representatives there may not replace the information imparted by the employer according to the MBL or collective agreements. It is interesting to note the similarities between the Swedish and the Norwegian/Danish system here: the different electoral procedure in Sweden does not constitute a different understanding of the role of the ERs.

In all three countries there is a sharp legal distinction between serving as a trade union representative and an employee representative, a distinction that is recognized by all parties. But in all three countries we find different ways of combining the two positions. My earlier research from Norway (Hagen 2010) clearly indicated that the combination is crucial to the role of the employee representatives. The ability to bring exclusive information to the board is the most important resource in support of power and influence. This information is twofold: first, knowledge of everyday company matters (insight into the production process, suggestions for improvements/savings, need for new qualifications and also management behaviour at different levels of the organization); second, information on how the employees will react and respond to the decisions made by the board (for example will the employees comply with the new plans for restructuring?). This information is only available to the employee representative if they also hold the position of a trade union representative. Additionally, without the legitimacy of the trade union they can hardly speak on behalf of the employees. Or, in the words of a CEO in a large Norwegian company:

> I have no use for an employee representative who is not a leading shop steward. (CEO, 2008)

The CEOs want to relate to employee representatives who possess strong legitimacy among their co-workers; they need to be able to trust them if the employee representatives claim that the employees will react in a negative or positive way. Additionally, the CEOs emphasis time-saving and confidentiality issues as important arguments for mixing positions. Both issues relate to the obligation of informing and consulting the trade unions, as elaborated below. Neither Danish, Swedish nor Norwegian company law mentions the duty of confidentiality directly, but it is a part of the duty of all the directors to act in the best interests of the company. Public statements that might harm the company or have an impact on share prices should be kept confidential. It is not uncommon for the board to place an overall duty of confidentiality on everything that takes place at the board. This is however not a legal requirement.

Conflicts of Interests – Or Collaboration in the Best Interests of the Company?

As mentioned, in order to fulfil the obligations in the collective agreement/MBL, management has to consult and inform the trade union representatives prior to important decisions. In Figure 7.1 I have tried to sketch the decision-making process at board level in a situation where the company faces surplus capacity in the market and production has to decrease. Two different processes involving employee participation are

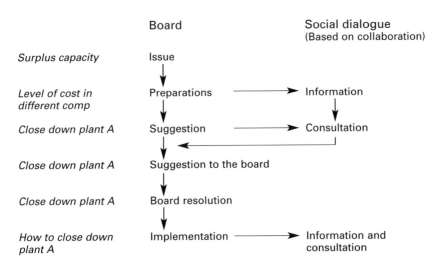

Figure 7.1 Codetermination at the board and participation based on the collective agreements.

illustrated, one at board level where the employee representative might or might not be able to influence the decision taken and the other based on the collective agreement (or MBL).

A difficult market situation encourages management to map the level of costs in different parts of the company (or different companies in the case of a group). Then a proposal is put to the board: plant (company) A has to close down. The decision will then be implemented by the management. On the right side of Figure 7.1 is shown the collaboration system. In an ideal company the issue at hand could possibly be a result of the social dialogue: what are the present challenges in our industry? Then the CEO would inform the trade union representatives that preparation for board consideration had started and would ask for their input. The next step would be to prepare a suggestion and start consultations with the trade unions. These consultation should then be either rejected or else used to moderate or alter the original suggestion. After the board makes their decision the social dialogue would start over again, this time with the aim of closing down plant A in the best possible way.

Using my interviews I have been able to construct schematically four different types of participation, as shown in Figure 7.2. The horizontal axis on Figure 7.2 makes a distinction between no social dialogue at all (board issues are not discussed with trade union representatives) and 'going by the book' (acting not only in line with the regulations but also in the spirit of the collaboration system, for example consultation before

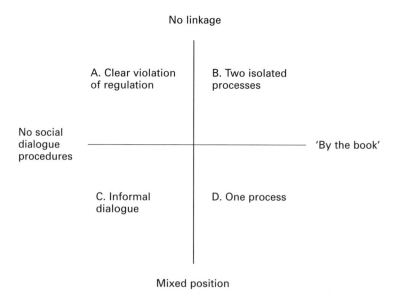

Figure 7.2 Four different ideal types of participation

a decision is made, collaboration in the best interest of the company as well as the employees). The vertical axis indicates the two different types of employee representative that might be elected: no linkage (an ordinary employee is elected), or a mixed position (a trade unionist is elected). Position A indicates the situation where we can assert that there has been a violation of the collective agreement. Position B indicates the situation in Figure 7.1. The relevant (depending on regulations in different jurisdictions and sectors) committees meet and collaborate. In the lower part of the figure two different paths are illustrated. Here we assume that the employee representative is chosen among the trade union reps, preferably the chair of the local trade union, or if on group level, the group shop stewards. Two possible situations might occur. In position C the collaboration takes place in an informal way, the CEO informs and consults the employee representative in order to obtain employee and trade union views and opinions, but the formal procedures are not important. In position D the two processes are merged together, the formal requirements are met, and the employee representatives participate in their role as a trade union representatives, wearing as the phrase goes, one of (at least) two hats.

In our interviews we have come across all four practices. However, the choice between the four ways needs to be analysed in line with the ways the different actors perceive the duty of confidentiality. In the example in Figure 7.1, strategies for coping with surplus capacity might be considered under this duty, as closing down one of the plants may affect share price. In position A, management may defend the non-inclusion of the trade unions by reference to confidentiality. To avoid a situation where a violation of rights based on collective agreements or law (MBL), the board may concentrate solely on issues with no impact on work and working conditions. It is hard to see such a board as actually in charge of the company or as in compliance with the responsibilities stated in the company acts. In one way or the other the trade unions representatives must get access to confidential information if the intention of the system of participation is to be fulfilled.

In situation B, where the management goes by the book but the employee representatives and the trade union representatives are not the same individuals, the issues at hand are presented to the trade unions. In some companies the management will include the trade union representatives (informally or in writing) under the confidentiality clause. The issues for the board will be discussed in line with the right side of Figure 7.1. 'Time-consuming' and 'impractical double treatment' are some of the statements I have heard concerning this procedure. In the last two positions in Figure 7.2 the employees have elected some of the trade union representatives to serve on the board. This way the issue of confidentiality is less of a problem and, as the figure illustrates, two different procedures are possible: either full treatment by the book (D) or informal dialogue between the employee representatives and the management (C).

In my earlier work (see Hagen 2010) the most powerful employee representatives were found in position C. The informal dialogue (often prior to the board meeting and even as employee representatives participated in drawing up the case documents) was an important source of influence. Because of the trade union position the CEO may trust the employee representative's statements concerning employee opinions and employee reaction to important changes. Without this connection, this dialogue might deteriorate to union careerists and end up far from the intentions of the collective agreements.

Based on my findings, Sweden would occupy position A and B, Denmark position B, and Norway position C. These findings are by no means representative, but enable us to draw up some Weberian ideal types based on our empirical findings and the different institutional frameworks in the three countries.

Employee Representatives: Part of Industrial Relations or Corporate Governance?

> Members of the board must not operate as individual representatives for specific shareholders, shareholder groups or other stakeholders... The composition of the board of directors should ensure that the board can attend to the common interests of all shareholders. (Norwegian Code of Corporate Governance 2012:33)

Similar passages can be found also in the Swedish and Danish. Taken literally, the possibilities of ensuring employee interests are limited. The duty of the employee representatives are towards the company, while the corporate governance norms have priority over the conflict-oriented dialogue between the social partners. The stronger the board, the more in line with corporate governance recommendations and the more managerial capitalism is a governance principle of the past, the more important are the arrangements as a possible area for employee influence.

All of my findings point to the importance of trade union connections when the employee representatives picture their role as influential members of the board. The strength of the industrial relations system at different levels is crucial and we need to look for the possibility of include and utilize this possibility. This leaves us with two important questions. (1) Are the trade unions, nationally as well as at company level, able to support the employee representatives with the necessary strength? (2) Are the employee representatives able to bring this strength to bear on the board's deliberations?

At national level the Norwegian trade unions do probably have an easier task to uphold their legitimacy than their Nordic colleagues. In a comparative perspective, concessions on government cutbacks, wages and social security have not been necessary in Norway, and the trade unions have not been challenged by the (social-democratic) government. Tripartite agreements on the 'big issues' (pensions, sick leave) are still the normal procedure. The Norwegian trade unions are still 'on the offensive' and new areas of regulation, particularly aimed at social dumping, are high on the political agenda. The Swedish and the Danish trade unions have experienced a harsher climate and the economic crisis seems to have weakened their position when entering into local social dialogue at company level.

My part of departure was to look upon the arrangement as a meeting point between to different institutional frameworks. The key seems to be the particular mixture of social dialogue and employee representatives' role locally. The legitimacy of the social dialogue is needed in order to bring employee interests into the decisions of the board and empower the employee representative.

The Norwegian ideal type was placed in position C in the model in Figure 7.2, namely informal collaboration across the agenda of the social dialogue (based on the agreements) and the agenda of the board and the corresponding employee representative role. By close and informal contact with the CEO the ERs take part in important decisions. The role as a trade union representative is the starting point; it is the strength of the trade union that makes the employee representative an interesting partner for the management and a director worth listening to for the shareholder-elected directors. Norwegian managers maintain that a two-channel system (employee participation by employee representatives and by trade union reps) are impractical and time-consuming; they want the employees to mix positions in order to reduce the number of people to inform and to cooperate with. To comply with this strategy may seem wise when the trade union representatives might lean on high-density, strong trade unions and – maybe the most important premise – a management rooted in the Nordic tradition of collaboration who display a sincere interest in social dialogue. During our interviews the shareholder-elected board members/chairs expressed the fact that employee participation is a self-evident part of the organization of the company; a productive social dialogue is a part of the CEO's responsibility.

However, the C-role depends on close contact with the CEO and is thus threatened if the latter rejects collaboration and emphasizes his or her role as the agent of the shareholders.

The Danish system, aka the Danish compromise, is described as informal. Nevertheless, we chose to construct the Danish ideal type by using position B as our point of departure. Despite the merging of positions (trade union representative serving as employee representative), the distinction between the two roles seems more noticeable than in Norway. The employee representatives expect the majority to stick to the rules, to keep Danish workplaces in Denmark and avoid the export of jobs, but do not cite trade union strength as a factor. The willingness to enter into compromises seems more risky because the employee representatives are less able to utilize the strength of the trade unions; it seems more like a compromise where the shareholder majority is in control of the agenda as illustrated by Lukes' third dimension of power (Lukes 2005). While the Norwegian employee representatives talked about 'company interests' as a goal where employee interests were included, the Danish employee representatives were more inclined to emphasize that shareholder interests were the foundation and that this was not to be questioned. In this sense the Danish willingness to compromise, often described as 'productive', might, unlike the industrial relations system, be a dangerous strategy, since the employee representative has no sanctions to apply when conflict occurs.

In Sweden the employee representatives give a picture of a situation with a far harsher climate of collaboration and with shareholders/CEOs less inclined to collaboration; thus we are inclined to use a mixture of positions A and B to characterize the typical Swedish pattern. Informal contact seems less frequent. The requirements in the MBL imply that most of the issues on the board agenda need to have a place in the information and consultation procedures, realized by collective agreements. The employee representatives gave several examples of clear violations of these rules, but were unable to prevent them from happening. The Swedish system seems to be twofold; either a violation as in A or a formalized position as in B. In neither of them the fact that employee representatives are appointed by the trade union seemed to empower the employee representative. To 'go by the book' seems more important than in Denmark and Norway. The arrangement in Sweden is closer to the industrial-relations system because of the legal position, and a conflict situation seems to be more expected by the actors.

The strength of the Norwegian employee representatives seems to be that they are able to use the merging of positions as a ground for the merging of issues; issues are to be solved and just *where* this happens seems less important. The trade union position reinforces the employee representative position and vice versa. This mutual empowerment was not expressed by the Norwegians' Danish and Swedish colleagues. Thus, the main differences were not found in the election procedures or trade union strength as such, but in the way the employee representatives were able to utilize the different positions and the degree of formalism. When looking at the employee representative arrangement as an indicator of the mixture of two different institutional frameworks we would emphasize, on an ideal type basis only, that the Norwegian employee representatives are important because of their industrial relations role, whereas in Denmark the industrial relations role seems more or less irrelevant and in Sweden the role is far more defensive and conflict-oriented. Thus the Norwegians seem more able to meet the shareholder revolution with the institutional strength of the labour market model.

As Mahoney and Thelen (2010:9) point out: 'Actors disadvantaged by one institution may be able to use their advantaged status vis-à-vis other institutions to enact change.' Or, more precisely in our context, the Norwegian employee representatives are able to use the legitimacy and the strength of the labour market model to prevent themselves from ending up in a marginalized position on a board increasingly inclined to interpret the interests of the company as the interests of the shareholders. The Swedes' ability to do this seems to be decreasing, while the Danes seem to be becoming less interested.

Notes

1 Or 'board-level employee representatives', which is an often used term; see for example Conchon (2011). In this chapter I use 'employee representatives'.

2 Interviews with employee representatives in Sweden, Denmark and in Norway were a part of this project. The interviews were mainly conducted in 2011 and the employee representatives were asked a number of questions concerning board competence, role expectations and regulatory tools concerning sustainable decisions. More information on the project can be found at http://www.jus.uio.no/ifp/english/research/projects/sustainable-companies

3 With a possible exception for Germany, this covers the rest of the countries with employee representatives as well. See Conchon (2011) for an overview.

4 It is important to note that the Act gives the right to join a trade union and that local agreements are anticipated.
5 Figures from 2009; source: NOU (2010:1).

REFERENCES

Aglietta, M. and A. Rebèrioux (2005) *Corporate Governance Adrift: A Critique of Shareholder Value.* Cheltenham: Edward Elgar.

Berge, Ø. et al. (2009) *De nordiske modellene etter 2000 – en sammenliknende oppsummering.* Fafo-notat 2009:11. Oslo: Fafo.

Bøhren, Ø. (2010) *Eierne, styret og ledelsen: corporate governance i Norge.* Bergen: Fagbokforlaget.

Bøhren, Ø. and B.A. Ødegaard (2000) *The Ownership Structure of Norwegian Firms: Characteristics of an Outlier.* Oslo: BI.

Boyer, Robert (2000) 'The Political in the Era of Globalization and Finance: Focus on Some Régulation School Research', *International Journal of Urban and Regional Research,* 24, 2:274–332.

Carly, M. (2005) 'Board-Level Employee Representatives in Nine Countries: A Snapshot', *Transfer* 11, 2/2005:231–43..

Christensen, S. and A. Westenholz (eds) (1999) *Medarbejdervalgte i danske virksomheder: fra lønarbejder til borger i virksomhedssamfundet.* Copenhagen: Handelshøjskolens.

Clarke, T. (ed.) (2004) *Theories of Corporate Governance.* London: Routledge.

Conchon, A. (2011) *Employee Representation in Corporate Governance: Part of the Economic or the Social Sphere?* Brussels: ETUI.

Due J. and J.S. Madsen (2011) *LO og fremtiden for den danske model.* Copenhagen: Faos.

Dølvik, J.E. (2007) 'The Nordic Regimes of Labour Market Governance: From Crisis to Success-Story?', Fafo-paper 2007:07. Oslo: Fafo.

Esping-Andersen, G. (1990) *The Three Worlds of Welfare Capitalism.* Cambridge: Polity Press.

Falkum, E., I.M. Hagen and S.C. Trygstad (2009) *Bedriftsdemokratiets tilstand.* Fafo-rapport 2009:35. Oslo: Fafo.

Grønlie, T. (1977) 'Norsk industripolitikk 1945–65', in *Vekst og velstand,* edited by Trond Bergh. Oslo: Universitetsforlaget.

Hall, P.A. and D. Soskice (eds) (2001) *Varieties of Capitalism: The Institutional Foundations of Comparative Advantage.* Oxford: Oxford University Press.

Hagen, I.M. (2010) *Det mektige mindretallet. Ansatterepresentasjon i styret mellom Corporate Governance og industrial relations.* Fafo-rapport 2010:02. Oslo: Fafo.

Hagen, I.M. (2012) 'The Sociology of Work', in *Introduction to Sociolog: Scandinavian Sensibilities,* edited by Gunnar Aakvaag, Michael Hviid Jacobsen and Thomas Johansson. London: Pearson.

Hagen, I.M and B.J. Mulder (2013 forthcoming) *Transnational Employee Representation at Company Boards? The Scandinavian Model.* Marco Biagi Foundation book series. Modena.

Hagen, I.M and B.J. Mulder (2012) 'Why Stakeholders?', in *European Company law and the Sustainable Company: A Stakeholder Approach,* vol. II, edited by Sigurt Vitols and Johannes Heuschmid. Brussels: ETUI.

▶

▶

Höpner, M. (2005) 'What Connects Industrial Relations and Corporate Governance? Explaining Institutional Complementarity', *Socio-Economic Review* 3, 2:331–58.

Iversen, M.J. and L. Thue (2008) ' Creating Nordic Capitalism: The Business History of a Competitive Periphery', in *Creating Nordic Capitalism*, edited by Susanna Fellman. Basingstoke: Palgrave Macmillan.

Jensen, M.C. and W. H. Meckling (1976) 'Theory of the Firm: Manerial Behaviour, Agency Costs and Ownership Structure', *Journal of Financial Economics*, repr. in *Theories of Corporate Governance*, edited by T. Clarke (2004). London: Routledge.

Lukes, S. (2005) *Power: A Radical View*, 2nd edn. Basingstoke: Palgrave Macmillan.

Mahoney, J. and K. Thelen(2010) *Explaining Institutional Change: Ambiguity, Agency, and Power*. Cambridge: Cambridge University Press.

Norwegian code of Corporate Governance 2012: http://www.nues.no/filestore/Dokumenter/2012–10–23CodeofPracticeforCorporateGovernance.pdf.

NOU (2010:1) *Medvirkning og medbestemmelse i arbeidslivet*. Oslo: Arbeidsdepartementet.

Rose, K. (2008) 'The Challenge of Employee Appointed Board Members for Corporate Governance, the Danish Evidence'. *European Business Organization Law Review* 2/2008:215–5.

Sejerstad, F. (2002) *Demokratisk kapitalisme*. Oslo: Pax.

Vidal, M. (2012) 'On the Persistence of Labour Market. Insecurity and Slow Growth in the US: Reckoning with the Waldonist Growth Regime', *New Political Economy* 2012/5:543–64.

Wallenberg, J and K. Levinson (2012) Anställdas styrelserepresentation i svenskt näringsliv – vad har hänt mellan 1999 och 2009?, *I Arbetsmarknad & Arbetsliv* 3/2012:67–80.

Ideas and Institutions: The Evolution of Employment Relations in the Spanish and German Auto Industry

8

Marco Hauptmeier and Glenn Morgan

Introduction

Cross-national differences of employment relations, HRM and working standards are an important empirical focus for the comparative literature in employment relations and political economy (see the contributions in Bamber *et al.* 2011). The primary explanatory approach puts societal institutions at the centre of analysis and links these to patterns of employment relations at the firm and plant levels. Institutionalist analysis rejects the idea that employment relations can be explained by efficiency considerations, technological determinants or the characteristics of markets and sectors. Instead it argues that actors see the challenges of efficiency, markets and technologies through the lens of a particular institutional logic or framework. Therefore, it is important to identify the institutional logic in particular national contexts. Hall and Soskice's (2001) distinction between liberal market economies and coordinated market economies represents one of the best-known and most used typologies of institutional logics in the analysis of employment systems. Institutional logics provide positive benefits to those who follow them by reducing uncertainties and coordination costs since the actors learn to apply a common set of rules. Failure to follow the rules leads to increased costs and sanctioning. For most actors, most of the time, it makes sense to conform with the institutional logic. The result is a virtuous circle of institutional reproduction. As actors commit more to the institutional logic, path dependency deepens and it becomes more and more difficult to move off track or change. Actors' preferences are shaped and determined by institutions which exhibit 'stickiness' in the face of external change processes.

It is immediately obvious, however, that the most interesting aspects of employment relations lie with the question of change. Where does change come from, who are the key actors in change processes and how are new institutional patterns established? Over the last decade, it is these sorts of questions which have most preoccupied researchers within the institutionalist framework (Campbell 2004; Crouch 2005; Hancké; Rhodes and Thatcher 2007; Kristensen and Lilja 2011; Morgan *et al.* 2005; Morgan et al. 2010; Morgan and Whitley 2012; Sorge 2005; Streeck and Thelen 2005; Streeck 2009). This involves moving the agenda beyond the initial formulations of authors such as Hall and Soskice (2001), Whitley (1999), Boyer and Hollingsworth (1997), and Amable (2003), where the focus was on discerning institutional complementarities and patterns that were presented as stable and determinant. Central to the institutionalist analysis of change has been the issue of agency; how do actors develop the capacity and capability for changing institutions? This chapter explores this question by examining employment relations in the auto industry in Germany and Spain.

Our analysis draws on the emerging interest in institutionalist analysis with the role of ideas and ideologies in the enactment, reproduction and transformation of institutions (Blyth 2002; Hauptmeier 2012; Hay 2006; Schmidt 2008). We are particularly concerned with two types of ideas in institutional contexts, normative beliefs and causal ideas (Goldstein and Keohane 1993; Hauptmeier and Heery forthcoming). Normative ideas are part of the actors' value and moral system and they inform actors which behaviour is legitimate and appropriate (March and Olsen 1989). Causal ideas refer to the actors' understandings of means–end relationships. They help actors to interpret and understand the social and economic world, in particular in situations of economic uncertainty, but causal ideas are also action-oriented and they provide actors with roadmaps on how to pursue their interests and preferences. Our goal is to provide a framework which allows us to discuss ideas and ideologies in the way we have defined them as not simply constitutive and reproductive of institutions but as capable of being analytically separable and 'causal' in their impact on how institutions work, a process which we perceive as enabling us to discuss ideas and institutions as co-constitutive without giving one primacy over the other. At a general level, therefore, we are advancing a constitutive argument, which has been become more common in the social sciences (e.g. Wendt 1998).

In order to achieve this, we follow other authors who have stressed that what we identify as institutions do not contain detailed scripts of how they are to be enacted. Actors have to interpret and implement institutional rules; they have to bring their own ideas and beliefs into the situation in order to make institutions work. While the process of interpretation and development of new ideas is constrained and shaped by the institutional framework, it is not determined. So the issue arises as to how much flexibility of interpretation exists, and, following from this, we can ask what the impact of one sort of interpretation of the rules versus another sort might be. Implicit in this is that different interpretations are going to have different impacts on both institutional reproduction and on the relations between actors enacting the institution. Therefore, we need to know what sorts of interpretations and ideas are brought to bear on institutions over time and with what effect. In particular we can ask both what sorts of ideas do actors bring into new institutional frameworks from previous contexts, that is what might be termed a form of 'ideational path dependency' (Hay 2006). In addition, we can ask what sorts of ideas may emerge during periods of institutional reproduction which may attract the adherence of actors and lead them to engage in new interpretations of the role and significance of existing institutional arrangements. This is clear once we consider how institutions operate in practice. So if we see the defining characteristic of institutions as consisting of a set of rules and expectations about behaviour in certain contexts, there are immediate questions which arise. How are those rules articulated and by whom? How is failure to follow the rules defined, by whom and with what sanctions? Where institutions are formalized – in law or codes of practice – then there is still debate over their meaning and implementation which requires resolving through prescribed institutional channels. We may anticipate that room for interpretation is always largest when new institutions are established; after an initial stage, this room for interpretation may close but it is unlikely to close completely, not least because, over time, environmental challenges may lead to cases that do not fit the existing rules, causing a secondary phase of interpretive openness and the development of new ideas.

We develop this argument in a number of steps. Based on a review of previous institutional literature in the next section, we spell out the different elements of the argument on the co-constitution of ideas and institutions in more detail. In the following empirical section, we develop the argument with two country case studies. The conclusion summarizes the argument and discusses the contribution of the chapter to the literature.

Agency and Institutions

The question of how institutions shape agency has always been at the heart of the institutional project. Early versions of institutionalism within the social sciences emerged to combat the notion that actors were rational decision-makers searching for the most efficient and effective way of achieving their own self-interests. Institutionalists tend to argue variations on the common line that the preferences of actors are prestructured by their embeddedness within existing systems of institutions that shape cognitive frames, normative orientations, and appropriate behaviours by sanctioning, formally or informally, deviance and rewarding conformity (for a review of institutional theories see Morgan and Hauptmeier 2014).

More recent developments, however, have emphasized that while there are institutional path dependencies that are difficult to break because of the complementarities and reinforcement effects between particular actors, institutions do evolve and change. Key to this is how actors engage with institutions and reshape them (Streeck and Thelen 2005). Therefore while the predominant orientation is that institutions determine actor behaviours, it is increasingly recognized that this has to be an interactive relationship in which actors are also determining how institutions work in practice (Mahoney and Thelen 2010a). What mechanisms enable actors to have this relative autonomy from the determining effect of institutions that allows them actually to reshape institutions?

Here an important starting point as already indicated is that institutional rules (no matter how formalized they are) can never be complete. Institutions leave room for interpretation and argument; they have to be enacted and this means worked on in various ways as external circumstances change setting new challenges for the actors about how to respond. This involves actors drawing on their stock of beliefs and ideas about what the institution means and how it works in order to understand the new circumstances and behave in an appropriate way. Where the institution is relatively new and therefore how it works in practice requires a lot of interpretive work, actors are likely to draw on ideas from before the new institutional formation. Just because a new institution has emerged does not mean that the ideas and ideologies of the actors from the previous period have simultaneously disappeared. Depending on the circumstances of the institutional transformation, they may linger on and influence the process of interpretation and implementation, a form of ideational path dependency (Hay 2006) that may have a different timescale from that involved in institutional transformation. Similarly, given a relative diversity of institutions in a societal and a global context, ideas may travel from one set of established institutions to another set, carried either directly through the movement of influential actors or indirectly through processes of imitation, copying and coercion (DiMaggio and Powell 1983). Such ideas can then be taken on by actors as a new way of seeing the institution and its functioning, and cause an incremental change that over the long term may be consequential. As meanings, ideas and beliefs change in these sorts of ways so do the ways in which institutions are enacted, even if in structural terms they appear to stay the same. The result may be incremental change over the medium term which is nonetheless consequential in the way the institution works and also in how it connects to and reproduces broader social processes.

Thelen's (2004) comparison of training regimes shows how an existing pattern of institutions comes to mean very different things as circumstances and actors change and new meanings and structures are created within the same old institutional shell. Essential to this type of argument is that institutions are not the outcome of any particular actors' set of ideas, no matter what their power. Institutions are perceived as temporary political compromises between competing social groups that represent not a normative commitment but a pragmatic adjustment to the politics of a particular context.

How the institution is enacted is therefore an outcome of the formal structures, the competing powers involved in enactment and the ideas which those actors bring into the implementation process. Changes in the balance of power within these different coalitional groups can lead to the possibility of institutional change. Such changes can be induced by a mixture of outside and inside forces that strengthen some groups and weaken others, thus making the old institutional compromises open to challenge and enabling actors to draw on either new or old ideas to make sense of the changes. As new outcomes emerge from the changed institutional structure, this can encourage actors to consider new ideas, for example moderating their opposition and instead working to support the institution once they begin to perceive that they are making gains under the new system.

In this analysis, therefore, we wish to put more weight specifically on ideas and beliefs in a number of respects. As a general point, if institutions do not have scripts, then the ideas and ideologies that actors bring to working them is crucial. This is in part because of the lack of synchronicity between ideational change and institutional change. Institutional change is a political process of power and compromise. The ideas and

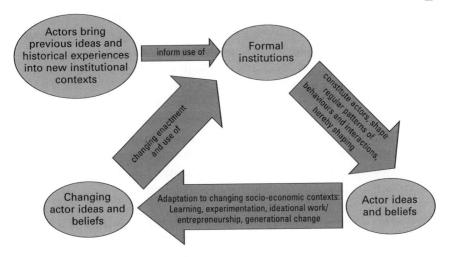

Figure 8.1 The co-constitution of ideas and institutions.

ideologies which different actors bring into that political process do not necessarily change the moment new institutions are established. One set of actors may pragmatically participate in an institution which they ideologically reject because they have little choice due to power differences. The question then arises as to whether this pragmatic adjustment eventually becomes more committed and they abandon their oppositional beliefs and take on new ideas that are supportive of the institution – or, alternatively, whether they continue to retain their original ideas and use the institutions as a way of refighting and reviving old battles. This suggests that we should consider the following stages in the co-constitution of actor ideas and institutions (see Figure 8.1).

First, actors have sets of ideas that pre-date any particular new set of institutions. These ideas and ideologies are taken into the new institutional contexts and actors initially interpret these institutions in part based on their previous ideas and in part based on the debates and arguments that have emerged in the course of the institutional change itself.

Second, however, institutions themselves do have a certain weight and impact on ideas; they constitute and reconstitute actors by defining resources, rights and instruments. As the case studies show, labour and employers are very differently institutionally defined across countries, with implications for their roles and identities in the employment relationship. Institutions tie actors down so that day after day actors interact in certain ways. This creates a continuous stream of experiences and regularized patterns of behaviour, which inform ideas of how things work within the firm and produce an image of the other side in the employment relations

(Guillén 2000). Thus, institutionalized patterns of employment relations develop on the company level, which shape actor ideas and ideologies.

Third, however, changing socio-economic contexts are a continuous impetus for changes of ideas and ideologies. As Bendix (1956) reminds us, ideologies are shaped not only by past experiences but also by current contingencies. Changing contexts change the resources and power of actors and thereby create new constraints, challenges and opportunities. Actors adapt to these changes through various mechanisms, including learning (Hall 1993), experimentation (Herrigel 2010; Kristensen and Morgan 2012), and various types of ideational work or entrepreneurship (e.g. brokerage, identity work, framing, bricolage, translation) (Campbell 2004; Hauptmeier and Heery forthcoming). Ideas are also brought in from other institutional contexts such as the whipsawing practices that diffused from US multinational companies to their European subsidiaries and are discussed in more detail later. Generational change also alters belief systems as the ideas and ideologies of groups of people develop in a time specific socio-economic context. For example, in the Spanish case the older generation of union leaders had been brought up under Franco and experienced high levels of repression and violence against trade unions; the younger generation of leaders may have heard about those times but their actual experience was embedded in a democracy.

Changes in contexts may also include direct economic challenges to the system where the current pattern of employment makes firms uncompetitive relative to firms from other contexts. This forces a more intensive distributional battle on actors where institutional rules and the accommodations which they facilitate are pushed to the limit or even transgressed by employers seeking to restore their competitiveness and maintain their profits or employees trying to retain or improve their standard of living. Contexts may also change because of new entrants into an institutional context such as the arrival of multinational firms. These might create new competitive pressures and challenges for incumbent companies in both product markets and labour markets. This in turn may trigger local firms to adaptation and develop new ideas and practices in part influenced by or emulating the models brought in by the new entrants.

Fourth, based on these changing ideas and ideologies the actors may make different use of institution that may not have formally changed; instead, the institutions are enacted in different ways. In this sense, the formal institutions remain the same but the meanings that actors bring into the institution have changed and so therefore have the way it operates, the practices associated with it, and its outcomes.

Our argument therefore is that what emerges is a continuous circular relationship between ideas and institutions. Ideas and institutions co-evolve over time as actors adapt through various mechanisms to a changing socio-economic world. As the following case studies show, once we give ideas and ideologies an analytical independence from institutions, we can start to compare over time how the process of co-constitution evolves in different contexts.

Changing Employment Relations: Case Studies

To accomplish this task, it is necessary to recognize that changing ideas and beliefs can often only be discerned over longer periods of time. Thus the research in Spain and Germany focused on the period between the 1970s and 2000s. Previous important reference points in the historical development of employment relations in each country are included in the narratives based on previous literature. Field research was carried out in the auto industry and focused on the company cases of General Motors (GM), Ford and Volkswagen (VW). Research methods included interviews, archival research and document analysis.

Spain

The transition from dictatorship to democracy was a watershed moment for employment relations. Unions were illegal and operated as clandestine organizations during the Franco regime (1939–75). In democratic Spain, unions became a legitimate social and economic actor. In 1978 the new Spanish constitution enshrined important union rights such as the right to strike. Subsequent labour laws, for example the Workers' Statute, set up the institutional framework of employment relations (Hamann 2011).

The auto company cases represent a specific institutional segment in Spanish employment relations. This institutional segment includes works council representation, company-level collective bargaining, established union organizations and the right to strike for unions at the company level. Only companies with at least 50 employees have works council representation. Spain has a multilevel collective bargaining system and it includes negotiations at the regional, sectoral and national level, but only about 10 per cent of the workforce is covered by company level collective bargaining agreements (Sanz de Miguel 2013) as in the examined company cases of GM, Ford and VW's subsidiary Sociedad Española de Automóviles de Turismo (SEAT).

The works council (comité de empresa) is the most important worker representation body on the company level (Martinez Lucio 1998). Works councils and unions formally represent different channels of interest representation, but in practice they are closely interrelated. The largest unions in Spain are the social democratic Unión General de Trabajadores (UGT) and the communist Comisiones Obreras (CCOO). In addition, in many auto companies the third largest union is the anarchist Confederación General del Trabajo (CGT). Different unions compile candidate lists for the union elections every four years, which determine the composition of the works council. The election system is representative and the different unions receive seats on the works council according to the election result (if they receive at least 5 per cent of the vote). The most important function of works councils is to negotiate collective bargaining agreements; works councils also have information and consultation rights on a wide range of employment relations issues, including labour contracts, company restructuring, absenteeism and disciplinary procedures. The primary leverage in the relationship with employers is provided through the right to strike, which is far-reaching and even includes even political strikes and participation in general strikes (Ortiz 1998, 1999, 2002).

Employment protection tends to be high for core workers and there are several constraints on the rights of managers to dismiss workers. Managers need to consult the works council on dismissals. If both parties do not reach an agreement, labour courts get involved and take the ultimate decision. Another factor related to the long tenures of auto workers is the tradition of members of families working for a specific company. Thus, it regularly happens that children of auto workers subsequently work in the same company. There exist a significant number of temporary workers, who do not enjoy the same institutional protection and they are used as a buffer to cope with market fluctuation.

The foregoing institutions constitute the collective actors and shape their orientation and beliefs. In other countries, such as the German example discussed later, institutional mechanisms exist to marginalize or integrate smaller union groups into the works council. In Spain, by contrast, various unions are represented in the works council. The continued presence of these different unions emphasizes the ideological contrasts between them and helps to maintain such differences over time. The different ideological positions are worked out through regular, separate union meetings on the company level, but are also reinforced by being integrated into different national union structures. The differences between the unions are mostly clearly pronounced in works council elections, in which unions articulate different sets of ideas aiming to attract worker votes. Ideological differences also come out during the collective bargaining rounds. The different unions articulate a list of demands for upcoming collective bargaining rounds and the involvement of several different unions tends to increase worker demands and the likelihood of conflict with management. The competition between unions and the resulting potential for conflict also affects the ideological orientation of management. If unions overburden the collective bargaining with demands or engage in frequent strike action, then this is likely to shape management's image of unions and see them as essentially in conflict rather than as potentially cooperative social partners.

A central influence here are the ideas and ideologies that existed before the introduction of the new institutional framework in democratic Spain. Union ideologies were crucially shaped through their clandestine work under dictatorship and their struggle for democracy. Unionists faced suppression by the Franco regime. For example, during a labour protest at SEAT in 1971 a worker got shot by the secret police and other workers were imprisoned for union work (Miguélez Lobo 1977). The ideological orientation of management was also shaped by the experiences under the Franco regime. Managers and employers were not exposed to free unions in the daily running of companies. This bred paternalistic ideologies at best and repressive management ideologies at worst (Guillén 1994). Managers of the former orientation believed that they knew what was best for workers, which could also include taking care of the social concerns of workers. These managers saw unions as unnecessary or as a disturbance. Other managers collaborated with the Franco regime. This led to direct suppression of workers and troublemakers were denounced to the state authorities.

Management and labour carried these ideas and ideologies with them into the new institutional environment in democratic Spain (Hauptmeier 2012). While the broader political purpose of the institutions was to create democratic relationships in the workplace and assist in the modernization and development of Spanish industry, the actors interpreted them in different ways and infused the new institutions with meanings based on their respective pre-existing ideologies. While there were important differences in the ideologies of the different unions, they were united in their opposition to management and they had learnt that fighting for social change made a difference. The unions, therefore, used the new institutional structure to push successfully for social and material improvements and this was regularly backed up through robust strike action. Management, on the other hand, saw itself as in ideological opposition to the labour unions. Managers had been used to unilateral decision-making within firms and had not yet fully embraced new employment relations ideas, around lean production, team work and employee involvement, that helped to transform employment relations in other countries. The result was a pattern of contentious and strike-prone employment relations in the 1980s. In formal terms, the institutions had changed but ideas and ideologies had not. In spite of the intentions of the shapers of the legislation, the new Spanish employment relations institutions did not immediately help to overcome the pre-existing ideological opposition between labour and management.

This pattern of contention continued and came to a head in different episodes in the 1990s. The economic environment became more competitive in the 1990s as the auto plants in Spain had to compete with other producers in the European single market, including growing competition from new plants in Eastern Europe. In this changing economic environment management regarded the pattern of the 1980s as no longer sustainable and thought that they could not any longer afford to give in to rising wage demands. Higher levels of management from the European and global headquarters got increasingly involved in managing employment relations at the Spanish subsidiaries and brought new ideas and practices into the Spanish institutional environment, aiming to adapt employment relations to the more competitive economic context.

GM sought to make its European subsidiaries, including the Zaragoza plant, more competitive through whipsawing, a management practice that was initially developed in the US context and then subsequently transferred and introduced in Europe in the 1990s. GM managers began to offer the production of new car models to different plants within Europe and the different plants could submit a tender for the allocation of production. Plants that won such a tender would receive a larger share or, in some cases, the entire production volume of new car models. Successful bids generally included concessions on the part of labour in terms of agreeing to more flexible work organization and/or a reduction or flattening off of increased in wages and benefits. In tight product markets whipsawing became a powerful management strategy vis-à-vis labour as only sufficient allocation of production would secure jobs and previous labour gains. Whipsawing was conducted at a higher management level, the European headquarters, but it proved highly disruptive to local employment relations and the Spanish unions were pressurized into labour concessions several times in the 1990s and 2000s (Greer and Hauptmeier 2008).

At VW's subsidiary SEAT the situation escalated in 1993. VW announced a loss of 1.5 billion German marks of which about 1 billion were attributed to SEAT. Subsequently, VW announced a major restructuring programme and sought to reduce SEAT's workforce by 12 000 employees. The unions organized strike action and large-scale demonstrations in Barcelona. However, the unions fought a losing battle. At some point during the conflict, the Catalan government began to support the restructuring plan after the multinational promised further investments. The regional labour relations board approved the temporary and permanent dismissals. The relationship between management and labour had reached a low point (Hauptmeier 2012).

At Ford the situation escalated in 1998. Ford management and the unions became embroiled in a bitter 11-month collective bargaining conflict during which the unions regularly went on strike. Management threatened to withdraw production from the Valencia plant and to transfer it to the Saarlouis plant in Germany, which however refused to do scab labour. The world headquarters got directly involved in the conflict and the CEO joined a negotiation round via teleconference from Detroit. He called the unions 'pirates' and threatened to close down the Valencia plant. Ultimately, after a long and protracted battle, the collective bargaining round ended with a compromise similar to previous collective bargaining rounds in the 1990s.

Both Ford and VW made it a priority to change labour relations following the respective conflicts but their approaches differed. VW brought in cooperative labour relations instruments and practices from Germany and also used the transnational labour institutions the European Works Council and the World Works Council. First, VW introduced so-called annual planning rounds, in which management and labour representatives jointly planned production for the following year. Management aimed to give labour more voice in management and planning processes. Second, VW released a greater number of works councillors from factory work than is required by Spanish labour law. VW had learnt in their plants in Germany that works councillors can play a meaningful role in governing the shop floor and they envisaged a similar role for the works councillors in Spain. Third, SEAT representatives took part in the meeting of the European and World Works Councils, which management used as an instrument to nurture cooperative employment relations. In contrast to other EWCs and WWCs, top management of VW, including the CEO, took part in the meeting with the aim of explaining the constraints faced by management in tight auto markets in the hope that this would help develop shared understandings and orientations. Despite these efforts by management to influence the ideological orientations of the unions, they were only successful to a limited extent. This can be seen most clearly in the issue of working time flexibility. VW had made progress in implementing far-reaching working time flexibility measures in its European plants since the mid1990s. However, the labour representatives at SEAT firmly stalled such initiatives several times. Employment relations at SEAT only changed after a leadership change within the two largest union groups, which also meant a generational change. Previous union leaders, who had been unionists under the Franco regime, stepped down. A new generation of union leaders came into office. They had only experienced union work under democracy and developed a very different ideological orientation, being more willing to cooperate with management. At about the same time, a leadership change in the HR function took place. A new manager with co-management experience from Germany was brought in. The relationship between labour and management changed qualitatively and a greater cooperation developed in the 2000s. Both parties jointly sought to keep the company competitive, while protecting worker gains as good as market conditions would allow.

At Ford management used a different set of tactics to influence the ideological orientations of the unions. Management pursued a 'divide and conquer' strategy. On the one hand, management systematically nurtured the more cooperative union the UGT, providing it with additional resources and releasing their works councillors from factory work. In addition, workers would be more likely to be hired if they were already a member of the UGT or had UGT family relatives in the factory. Being a UGT member also helped in getting promoted. On the other hand, management sought to suppress the more radical unions, giving their members and representatives more difficult work assignments and shifts. In addition, management twice dismissed works councillors from the anarchist union, the CGT, despite the legal protection of labour representatives in Spain. Workers at Ford increasingly realized that being a member of the UGT was advantageous and the ranks of the union swelled. This led to the paradoxical situation in 1999, when a majority of the workforce were already a member of the UGT, but this was not confirmed in the union election when a sizeable number of UGT members expressed a different ideological position and voted for the more radical unions. In 2003 the situation changed in favour of the UGT. Some of the more radical unions had problems organizing new union members and the UGT became the dominant union within Ford, which was also confirmed in the 2003 and 2007 union elections. Henceforth, management and UGT could regulate employment relations without the other unions and a social partnership approach emerged.

At GM, the Spanish unions sought to counter the forceful whipsawing through transnational worker cooperation in the European Works Council. For the Spanish unions it did not seem possible to counter transnational whipsawing within the context of national institutions and thus they developed new transnational ideas and practices in collaboration with other European unions within the European Works Council. In the 2000s the European Works Council organized several European work stoppages with the aim of bringing to an end transnational whipsawing and plant closures in Europe. The Spanish plant was one of the potential targets. As a response to this the European Works Council developed the idea that plants should 'share the pain', which meant that all GM plants in Europe agreed to labour concessions with the aim of avoiding letting GM management single out any single plant for closure. The Spanish unions did not doubt that GM was in a serious economic situation and this is why they organized concessions in collaboration with other unions in the European Works Council.

In summary, in the Spanish case the establishment of new institutions in the post-dictatorship period took place in a context where the actors took their old ideas and ideologies into the new context. As a result, the institutions never created the forms of cooperation which were envisioned; instead conflict remained and old ideas about the essential struggle between management and labour survived and were reinforced. The transition from a contentious, conflict-prone pattern in the 1980s to more cooperative, market-oriented relationship between management and labour in the 2000s took place with no major change in the formal institutions. It emerged because both sides began to see their future differently in the context of a more competitive auto market and began to develop new practices, meanings and ideas. At Ford and VW, both sides of the employment relationship increasingly shared an interest in keeping the plants competitive with the aim of securing profits and jobs. This was aided on the union side by generational and leadership change and on the employers' side by similar processes in the context of a broader internationalization of the management process. For VW, this involved bringing more German practices into Spain, partly through using the new European Works Council legislation, and thereby establishing stronger conditions for cooperation and helping employees' representatives see this possibility and start to enact the institutions in ways which reinforced this. For Ford, this involved breaking the coalitions between unions and collaborating with the more moderate union. Both VW and Ford then facilitated a change in how the same formal institutions worked by changing the ideas of managers and employees. At GM employment relations developed an important transnational dimension. Management forcefully engaged in transnational whipsawing in Europe, which the Spanish unions sought to counter through collaboration in the European Works Council, organizing European work stoppages and jointly organizing concessions. The Spanish unions at GM gradually developed a transnational ideology with the aim of preventing plant closure and whipsawing at GM in Europe (Greer and Hauptmeier 2012).

Germany

The auto cases are part of a specific institutional segment of German employment relations. It includes works council representation, sectoral collective bargaining, labour co-determination on the supervisory board, high employment protection and well-established training institutions. Only companies with over 500 employees, including the examined companies VW, GM and Ford, have labour representation on the supervisory board (Keller and Kirsch 2011). These various institutions constitute actors in the following ways.

Works councillors represent workers on the shop floor and they are voted for in workforce election every four years. They have co-determination rights in a number of important areas including work organization, working time, hiring and deployment of personnel, and dismissals. In effect management needs to negotiate changes in these areas with the works councils and reach an agreement. Co-determination rights increase the power of labour, for example in times of conflict works councillors can reject overtime or extra shifts, but they do not have the right to call a strike. Co-determination limits management's prerogative at the workplace and forces employers and works councillors to cooperate and compromise (Turner 1991).

Half of the supervisory board members are labour representatives, who are usually works councillors (including the head of the works council) and labour union representatives. The representatives of the shareholders have the right to nominate the chair of the supervisory board. The chair has a casting vote in the case of a tie; thus shareholder representatives have a voting majority. The supervisory board appoints all top managers, including the CEO and HR manager. In addition, the supervisory board agrees the budget and new investment decisions. Labour representatives have access to all company data, and thus labour can independently evaluate management strategies and the economic situation of the company.

In the metal sector, the labour union IG Metall and the employer association Gesamtmetall negotiate wages and other major working standards such as working time and job classifications. For the collective actors at the company level this means that a potentially contentious issue, the negotiation of wages, has been mostly removed from the company level. However, workers in auto companies tend to be unionized and thus they might take part in the generally short, ritualistic 'warning strikes' in the context of sectoral collective bargaining, which however do not lead to longer production stops. Works councils at the company level and unions at the sectoral level are legally independent, but in practice these are closely intertwined, as for example in the auto industry, where the large majority of works councillors as well as workers are members of the union IG Metall.

In addition, employment protection is established through different institutional mechanisms. German labour law stipulates compensation for dismissed workers, which increases with higher seniority. In addition, labour has co-determination rights in case of dismissal and can request retraining or social compensation for workers. The different institutional rules add up to long tenures of workers. As workers are a permanent asset, companies tend to invest continuously in the skills of workers. The vast majority of workers have gone through the training system, including the apprenticeship systems, and there tends to be an oversupply of skilled workers, which allows production to be flexible to new demands and challenges in the production process (Streeck 1992).

The new institutional framework for employment relations was introduced in democratic Germany in the early 1950s, including laws that regulated collective bargaining and worker representation. Important reforms of the works council legislation took place in 1972 and 1976, and by the end of the 1970s all key elements of the institutional framework had been established. It should be noted that both labour representatives and employers in the auto industry initially rejected important elements of the institutional framework. The institutions represented a compromise and did not immediately lead to a change in ideas. Employers at first continued to seek greater autonomy and discretion from works council interventions, unsuccessfully challenging the works council legislation in a string of legal battles in the 1970s. Works councillors in the big auto companies continued to envision a powerful auto workers' union modelled on the American union United Automobile Workers (UAW), in the hope that they be able to take full advantage of productivity gains in auto industry (without being dragged back by the lower average productivity in the metal sector as a whole). However, a compromise was eventually found and works councils began to negotiate higher wages at the company level (officially these negotiations were not called collective bargaining, but 'an adaptation of the sectoral agreement to the specific situation of the company'). Institutional constraints did not allow labour representatives and employers to fully realize their respective preferences, and both had to learn to live within the institutional constraints and were gradually socialized within these structures.

How do German institutions shape actors' ideas? An important point to emphasize here is what Streeck (1997) describes as 'beneficial constraints'. Employees and trade unions started with a view of wider solidarity than the firm or the plant but key institutions emerged at this level and this lived experience gradually reshaped the ideas and beliefs that were driving employees, drawing them into a more cooperative and managerial mind-set. First, through the integration of works councillors into the daily running of the company, works councillors primarily develop solidarity, preferences and interests at the company level. The representation of worker interests and the competitiveness of the company are seen as interrelated goals. The identification of workers and works councils with the company is facilitated through long-term tenures protected through job security. Second, the works councils' integration into management decisions breeds responsible union orientations. Unions not only learn about the constraints management is facing in highly competitive markets, but they also learn and realize that the decisions works councillors take on the shop-floor and on the supervisory board directly affect the productivity of the company, with implications for job security and pay. Third, works councils have full access to all company information and data. This 'open-book approach' allows them to independently verify and assess the situation of the company. Lack of information can be a source of mistrust in employment relationship in other countries. Equal access to information and data on the company level helps the growth of trust between the collective actors. Thus employees' ideas and ideologies, particularly those most closely engaged with running works councils, have evolved into this cooperative view and away from their original beliefs which were more embedded in visions of industrial conflict between workers and employers. This was an unexpected result of the establishment of the institutional complex but it reinforced that institutional logic.

Similar changes happened on the management side. Following management's opposition to the works council legislation in the 1970s, managers learnt to live with the works council. Managers gradually realized that works councils can be an asset in organizing production and dealing with conflict on the company level. Negotiations with the works council take longer than unilateral management decisions, but once both sides agree, works councillors help to implement new policies and streamline processes of change. In the following decades, managers remained critical of the union IG Metall, but increasingly appreciated the positive role of works councils on the company level. In an institutional context with co-determination rights on the shop floor and supervisory board, radical ideologies did not prosper and management tended to develop cooperative orientations and beliefs in the employment relationship. It is not so much that there are no conflicts of interests between management and labour, but instead there are institutional channels to work through them and negotiate continuously, which, repeated sufficiently, facilitates trust and a belief amongst management and works council that both parties can overcome differences.

In the 1980s, lean production helped to transform the relationships between works councils and management. The idea diffused from the US where companies and researchers alike sought to analyse the competitive advantages of the Japanese way of production and to transfer these lessons to their own companies. The model that emerged was generally known as 'lean production' and this became a powerful framing for organizational reform across the developed world. In Germany, both sides engaged actively in shaping both the understanding of the concept and the way in which it could be implemented without undermining the position of the workers in the German system. Management and works councils negotiated the changes and jointly implemented them. Management learnt that collaboration with the works councils allowed flexible deployment and redeployment of labour and smooth implementation of new types of work organization, achieving many of the advantages of 'lean production' without prompting the sort of resistance and conflict experienced elsewhere in Europe and the US in response to these changes. Wages at the auto companies continued to rise above the level of the collective bargaining agreement negotiated for the metal sector as a whole. Works councils negotiated a top-up with management at the company level. As a result, the wage level at the auto companies was between 20 and 25 per cent above the level of the sectoral collective bargaining agreement in the early 1990s.

The competitive environment markedly changed during the recession of the auto market in 1992–93. In the European single auto market competition became stiffer and German plants faced competition from lower-labour-cost plants in Southern and Eastern Europe. In addition, companies increasingly faced the problem of overcapacity in the European auto market, which made it difficult to run plants productively. As a response to the more difficult market environment, employers and works councils began in the 1990s and 2000s to negotiate so-called pacts for competitiveness and employment at the company level (Rehder 2003). Labour agreed to various measures to increase productivity and reduce costs in part by reducing the workforce through early retirements and natural wastage. In exchange the employees who were left were given guarantees of job security. An important new idea became working time flexibility. The works councils regarded the far-reaching collaboration in the area of working time flexibility as a mean to defend the continuing higher wage levels in Germany in comparison with other countries.

The negotiation and the exchange changed qualitatively in the 2000s in the face of increasingly difficult market conditions. Works councillors faced large-scale reductions of workforces following company losses. GM management planned to reduce the German workforce by 10 000 in 2004. Ford planned a reduction of 1300 employees in 2006. In both cases, the works councillors negotiated a socially responsible workforce adjustment; measures included voluntary compensation packages, early retirement and the retraining of workers. The relatively smooth adjustment negotiations were related to the point that works councillors had full access to company data, which clearly demonstrated to the labour representatives that the companies were in a dire economic situation. Negotiating a reduction of the workforce was also done with the intention of securing jobs for the existing workforce.

It is important however to note that two developments might undermine this continued cooperation by producing challenges to the existing ideas and ideologies of cooperation and partnership. First, management at different auto companies have introduced whipsawing practices, playing off different plants against each other in the context of new production assignments. The goal of this management-induced competition was to extract labour concessions, in exchange for the assignment of new production allocations. Management initially developed such whipsawing ideas and practices in the US; GM was the first auto company to introduce them forcefully in Europe, but they later diffused to other car makers. Management whipsawing practices affected the previous collaborative and cooperative patterns in different ways. At GM it undermined previous collaborations and labour began to organize previously unseen European work stoppages in collaboration with the European Works Council. In effect, one side of the relationship sought to introduce new ideas and practices into the environment. In doing so, it caused the other side, the employees, to reconsider their own practices and start to develop a new more active form of European-level solidarity. At VW, on the other hand, whipsawing did not affect the relationship strongly. Surprisingly, management was able to convince the works councils that a competitive production allocation was necessary to keep all the plants 'on their toes', which would enable them to survive in a competitive auto market and in this way sustain and secure jobs.

Second, works councils struggled to maintain solidarity between workers at the company level. Under strong economic pressure, works councils agreed to lower standards or wages for the periphery of the workforce.

This took different forms. Works councils, in the context of opening clauses in sectoral collective bargaining, agreed to lower second-tier wages for newly employed workers, employees in specific projects or service workers. In addition, works councils agreed to the use of temporary workers to help companies to deal with peak production. Collaborating in lowering wages and working standards for the periphery of the workforce was often done with the aim of defending the core workforce. In previous decades, a criticism of the functioning of works councils was that they nurtured company egoism that delivered for the community within the company, but inhibited broader union solidarities on the sectoral level. If the works council now can only ensure solidarity with the core of the company's workforce but not with a growing pool of temporary, low-paid, insecure and part-time workers within the firm or in the same plant, this might undermine the legitimacy of the works council and limit its regulatory capacity as co-manager. As the key actors in the works councils acquiesce in these management strategies, what is the consequence for the rest of the workforce who are left out of this social partnership? How will the resulting dualism (Emmenegger *et al.* 2012; Palier and Thelen 2010) impact on the ideas and ideologies of those inside the system as well as those outside?

In summary, in Germany, as in other countries, the employment relationship was initially rooted in industrial conflict and in opposing worldviews during the postwar decades. However, the institutional logic of the German institutions had a certain weight and gradually changed the ideas and ideologies of the collective actors. On the one hand, the institutionally guaranteed integration of works councillors in management decision-making processes gradually bred cooperative, responsible labour ideologies on the company level. On the other, given the far-reaching rights of works councillors, radical employer ideologies did not prosper and instead employers gradually learnt that works councils were an asset in the flexible organization of the production process. A cooperative employment relationship developed, which adapted through various measures to a changing economic context between the 1980s and 2000s. More recently, in the face of increased competition in the auto market, however, multinational companies brought new ideas and practices into the German institutional context such as intensifying whipsawing practices and the dualization of the workforce between core and precarious workers. These developments might undermine the actors' ideological commitment to the institutionalized patterns of employment relations, which might change the functioning and meaning of the German institutions yet again.

Conclusion

Institutional theory has been used as a primary approach to explain cross-national differences of employment relations. The national-models approach such as in the varieties-of-capitalism literature tends to link formal institutions to national patterns of employment relations. This institutional approach has been criticized for creating unitary and stable images of national employment relations that is not sensitive to within-country variation and change. Recent research has sought to address some of the weaknesses by putting a greater emphasis on agency and identifying new mechanisms of institutional change (Mahoney and Thelen 2010b; Streeck and Thelen 2005). This literature has questioned the tight link between institutions and agency by highlighting institutional ambiguity, gaps between rules and enactment and institutional avoidance strategies (Doellgast *et al.* 2009, Jackson 2005), while other authors have considered the role of ideas in institutional change and reproduction (Blyth 2002, Schmidt 2008). This chapter contributes to this literature by advancing an argument on the co-constitution of ideas and institutions. Institutions structure employment relations and routine patterns of interaction, which shape a continuous stream of experiences. This influences and shapes the ideologies and beliefs of actors over time. Actors develop an image of the opposite actor and an understanding of how the employment relationship works. However, as the actors adapt to new challenges and changing socio-economic contexts, their ideologies and beliefs change through various mechanisms such as learning, experimentation, various types of ideational work and the diffusion of ideas within multinational companies (Hauptmeier and Heery forthcoming). Actors with changing ideologies and beliefs enact and construct institutions in different ways, which changes their meaning and functioning. However, actors can never fully break free from institutional contexts and pressures; instead ideas and institutions co-evolve as the actors defend themselves by adapting to a continuously changing world.

REFERENCES

Amable, Bruno (2003) *The Diversity of Modern Capitalism*. Oxford: Oxford University Press.
Bamber, Greg, Russell D. Lansbury and Nick Wailes (2011) *International and Comparative Employment Relations: Globalization and Change*. Los Angeles: Sage.

▶

Bendix, Reinhard (1956) *Work and Authority in Industry; Ideologies of Management in the Course of Industrialization*. New York: Wiley.

Blyth, Mark (2002) *Great Transformations: Economic Ideas and Institutional Change in the Twentieth Century*. Cambridge: Cambridge University Press.

Campbell, John L. (2004) *Institutional Change and Globalization*. Princeton, NJ: Princeton University Press.

Crouch, Colin (2005) *Capitalist Diversity and Change: Recombinant Governance and Institutional Entrepreneurs*. Oxford: Oxford University Press.

DiMaggio, Paul J. and Walter W. Powell (1983) 'The Iron Cage Revisited: Institutional Isomorphism and Collective Rationality in Organizational Fields', *American Sociological Review* 48, 2:147–60.

Doellgast, Virginia, Rosemary Batt and Ole H. Sørensen (2009) 'Introduction: Institutional Change and Labour Market Segmentation in European Call Centres', *European Journal of Industrial Relations* 15, 4:349–71. doi: 10.1177/0959680109344366.

Emmenegger, Patrick, Silja Hausermann, Bruno Palier and Martin Seeleib-Kaiser (2012) *The Age of Dualization: The Changing Face of Inequality in Deindustrializing Societies*. Oxford: Oxford University Press.

Goldstein, Judith and Robert O. Keohane (1993) *Ideas and Foreign Policy: Beliefs, Institutions, and Political Change*. Ithaca, NY: Cornell University Press.

Greer, Ian and Marco Hauptmeier (2008) 'Political Entrepreneurs and Co-Managers: Labour Transnationalism at Four Multinational Auto Companies', *British Journal of Industrial Relations* 46, 1:76–97.

Greer, Ian and Marco Hauptmeier (2012) 'Identity Work: Sustaining Transnational Worker Cooperation at GM Europe', *Industrial Relations: A Journal of Economy and Society* 51, 2:275–97.

Guillén, Mauro F. (1994) *Models of Management: Work, Authority, and Organization in a Comparative Perspective*. Chicago: University of Chicago Press.

Guillén, Mauro F. (2000) 'Organized Labor's Images of Multinational Enterprise: Divergent Foreign Investment Ideologies in Argentina, South Korea, and Spain', *Industrial & Labor Relations Review* 53, 3:419–42.

Hall, Peter A. (1993) 'Policy Paradigms, Social Learning, and the State: The Case of Economic Policymaking in Britain', *Comparative Politics* 25, 3:275–96.

Hall, Peter A. and David Soskice (2001) 'An Introduction to Varieties of Capitalism', pp. 1–71 in *Varieties of Capitalism: The Institutional Advantages of Comparative Advantage*, edited by P.A. Hall and D.W. Soskice. Oxford: Oxford University Press.

Hamann, Kerstin (2011) *The Politics of Industrial Relations: Labour Unions in Spain*. London and New York: Routledge.

Hancké, Bob, Martin Rhodes and Mark Thatcher (2007) *Beyond Varieties of Capitalism: Conflict, Contradiction, and Complementarities in the European Economy*. Oxford: Oxford University Press.

Hauptmeier, Marco (2012) 'Institutions Are What Actors Make of Them – the Changing Construction of Firm Level Employment Relations in Spain', *British Journal of Industrial Relations* 50, 4:737–59.

Hauptmeier, Marco and Edmund Heery (forthcoming) 'Ideas at Work', *International Journal of Human Resource Management*.

▶

Hay, Colin (2006) 'Constructivist Institutionalism', pp. 56–74 in *The Oxford Handbook of Political Institutions*, edited by R.A.W. Rhodes, S.A. Binder and B.A. Rockman. Oxford: Oxford University Press.

Herrigel, Gary (2010) *Manufacturing Possibilities: Creative Action and Industrial Recomposition in the United States, Germany, and Japan*. Oxford: Oxford University Press.

Hollingsworth, J. Rogers and Robert Boyer (1997) *Contemporary Capitalism: The Embeddedness of Institutions*. Cambridge: Cambridge University Press.

Jackson, Gregory (2005) 'Contested Boundaries: Ambiguity and Creativity in the Evolution of German Co-Determination', pp. 229–54 in *Beyond Continuity: Institutional Change in Advanced Political Economies*, edited by W. Streeck and K. Thelen. Oxford: Oxford University Press.

Keller, Berndt and Anja Kirsch (2011) 'Employment Relations in Germany', pp. 196–223 in *International and Comparative Employment Relations: Globalisation and Change*, edited by G. Bamber, R.D. Lansbury and N. Wailes. Los Angeles: Sage.

Kristensen, Peer Hull and Kari Lilja (2011) *Nordic Capitalisms and Globalization: New Forms of Economic Organization and Welfare Institutions*. Oxford: Oxford University Press.

Kristensen, Peer Hull and Glenn Morgan (2012) 'From Institutional Change to Experimentalist Institutions', *Industrial Relations: A Journal of Economy and Society* 51:413–37.

Mahoney, James and Kathleen Ann Thelen (2010a) 'A Theory of Gradual Institutional Change', pp. 1–7 in *Explaining Institutional Change: Ambiguity, Agency, and Power*, edited by J. Mahoney and K. Thelen. Cambridge: Cambridge University Press.

Mahoney, James and Kathleen Ann Thelen (eds) (2010b) *Explaining Institutional Change: Ambiguity, Agency, and Power*. Cambridge: Cambridge University Press.

March, James G. and Johan P. Olsen (1989) *Rediscovering Institutions: The Organizational Basis of Politics*. New York: Free Press.

Martinez Lucio, Miguel (1998) 'Spain: Regulating Employment and Social Fragmentation', pp. 426–58 in *Changing Industrial Relations in Europe*, vol. 2, edited by A. Ferner and R. Hyman. Malden, MA: Blackwell.

Miguélez Lobo, Faustino (1977) *Seat, La Empresa Modelo Del Regimen*. Barcelona: DOPESA.

Morgan, Glenn, Richard Whitley and Eli Moen (2005) *Changing Capitalisms? Internationalization, Institutional Change, and Systems of Economic Organization*. Oxford: Oxford University Press.

Morgan, Glenn, John Campbell, Colin Crouch, Ove Kaj Pedersen and Richard Whieley (eds) (2010) *The Oxford Handbook of Comparative Institutional Analysis*. Oxford: Oxford University Press.

Morgan, Glenn and Richard Whitley (2012) *Capitalisms and Capitalism in the Twenty-First Century*. Oxford: Oxford University Press.

Morgan, Glenn and Marco Hauptmeier (2014) 'Varieties of Institutional Theory in Comparative Employment Relations', in *Oxford Handbook in Comparative Employment Relations*, edited by A. Wilkinson, G. Wood and R. Deeg. Oxford: Oxford University Press.

▶

▶

Ortiz, Luis (1998) 'Union Response to Teamwork: The Case of Opel Spain', *Industrial Relations Journal* 29, 1:42.

Ortiz, Luis (1999) 'Unions' Responses to Teamwork: Differences at National and Workplace Levels', *European Journal of Industrial Relations* 5, 1:49–69: 10.1177/095968019951004.

Ortiz, Luis (2002) 'The Resilience of a Company-Level System of Industrial Relations: Union Responses to Teamwork in Renault's Spanish Subsidiary', *European Journal of Industrial Relations* 8, 3:277–99.

Palier, Bruno and Kathleen Thelen (2010) 'Institutionalizing Dualism: Complementarities and Change in France and Germany', *Politics & Society* 38, 1:119–48.

Rehder, Britta (2003) *Betriebliche Bündnisse Für Arbeit in Deutschland: Mitbestimmung Und Flächentarif Im Wandel*, vol. 48. Frankfurt am Main: Campus.

Sanz de Miguel, Pablo (2013) 'Spain: Industrial Relations Profile': EIRO. Retrieved 18.8.2013, from http://www.eurofound.europa.eu/eiro/country/spain_4.htm.

Schmidt, Vivien A. (2008) 'Discursive Institutionalism: The Explanatory Power of Ideas and Discourse', *Annual Review of Political Science* 11:303–26.

Sorge, Arndt (2005) *The Global and the Local: Understanding the Dialectics of Business Systems*. Oxford: Oxford University Press.

Streeck, Wolfgang (1992) *Social Institutions and Economic Performance: Studies of Industrial Relations in Advanced Capitalist Economies*. London: Sage Publications.

Streeck, Wolfgang (1997) 'Beneficial Constraints: On the Economic Limits of Rational Voluntarism', pp. 197–219 in *Contemporary Capitalism: The Embeddedness of Institutions*, edited by J.R. Hollingsworth and R. Boyer. Cambridge: Cambridge University Press.

Streeck, Wolfgang and Kathleen Ann Thelen (2005) *Beyond Continuity: Institutional Change in Advanced Political Economies*. Oxford: Oxford University Press.

Streeck, Wolfgang (2009) *Re-Forming Capitalism: Institutional Change in the German Political Economy*. Oxford: Oxford University Press.

Thelen, Kathleen Ann (2004) *How Institutions Evolve: The Political Economy of Skills in Germany, Britain, the United States, and Japan*. Cambridge: Cambridge University Press.

Turner, Lowell (1991) *Democracy at Work: Changing World Markets and the Future of Labor Unions*. Ithaca, NY: Cornell University Press.

Wendt, Alexander (1998) 'On Constitution and Causation in International Relations', *Review of International Studies* 24, 5:101–8.

Whitley, Richard (1999) *Divergent Capitalisms: The Social Structuring and Change of Business Systems*. Oxford: Oxford University Press.

The Collapse of Collective Action? Employment Flexibility, Union Membership and Strikes in European Companies

9

Giedo Jansen and Agnes Akkerman[1]

Since the 1980s, collective bargaining has decentralized in many European countries, and labour markets have become more flexible. Collective arrangements have increasingly been replaced with flexible and individual employment relationships. This transition has been brought about by the desire of employers and policymakers to cope with the challenges of advanced globalized economies (Kalleberg 2009). In order to maintain their competitiveness and adapt to fluctuations in demand for products or services, firms have striven increasingly for more flexible relations with employees. In many European countries, including the traditionally more regulated market economies such as Germany, Sweden or France, employment protection legislation constraining individual dismissals, collective redundancies and fixed-term contracts have been relaxed (Grumbell-McCormick 2011). As a result, the number of people in secure, long-term jobs has declined, and – in turn – the number of workers with short- and fixed-term contracts has, on average, grown across Europe. Figure 9.1 shows, however, that there are substantial differences among EU countries with respect to the development of temporary employment.

Similarly, rules concerning temporary agency work have generally been relaxed – including in countries such as Sweden where such work was traditionally bound to strict regulations which sometimes made it practically illegal (Storrie 2002). Hence, there has been an expansion of temporary agency work in most European countries (Grumbell-McCormick 2011), with the number of temporary agency workers in the European Union recently estimated at approximately 4 million

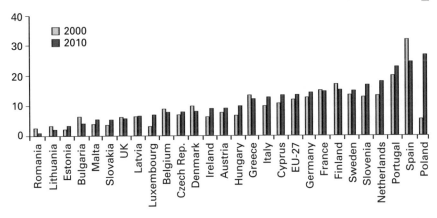

Figure 9.1 Proportion of employees (aged 15–64) with a temporary contract in EU countries in 2000* and 2010.

Source: Eurostat 2013.

*Bulgaria = 2001.

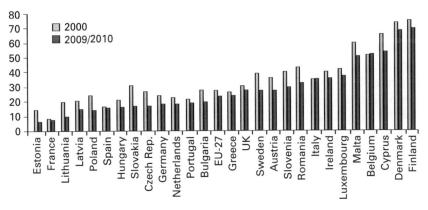

Figure 9.2 Union density in EU countries in 2000* and 2010.**

Source: Visser 2011.

*Lithuania = 2001; Romania = 2002; Latvia, Slovenia = 2003.
**Cyprus, EU-27, France, Greece, Hungary, Latvia, Luxembourg, Romania, Slovakia, Slovenia, Sweden = 2008.

(Arrowsmith 2009). Moreover, besides *numerical* flexibility, increased international competition has also created pressure for flexibility or variation in *wages* (Arrowsmith and Marginson 2009). Although the regulations governing variable and flexible payment systems vary considerably across countries, variable payment schemes have been introduced across the whole of Europe (Van het Kaar and Grünnel 2001).

Figure 9.2 shows the general decline of union density in the European Union. Labour relations literature suggests that increased employment flexibility has undermined the role of trade unions. By communicating and negotiating directly with individual employees over contracts and wages, employers have been able to reduce the unions' influence in collective bargaining (Storey and Bacon 1993). Variable payment, for example, is considered to be an impairment of the union's ability to negotiate wages through collective agreements. In particular, variable payment systems based on individual performance appraisal limit union involvement (Gunnigle *et al.* 1998). Hence, management strategies that focus on individuals instead of collectives, with the aim of increased flexibility, pose a challenge to European trade unions' traditional mission of improving employment security through collective organization (Baglioni and Crouch 1990).

The literature of comparative political economy suggests that the pressures of globalization do not have the same effect on labour markets and employment relations across countries. Based on the influential varieties-of-capitalism approach of Hall and Soskice (2001), Thelen (2001), for example, maintains that employers' search for flexibility has a different effect on labour politics in so-called liberal market economies compared with coordinated market economies. Only in liberal market economies, she argues, is decentralization associated with a general weakening of the labour movement, with the flexibilization of employment intensifying the conflict between employers and labour. In coordinated market economies, labour markets are customarily regulated in a more collectivist fashion, based on non-market relations and cooperation. Therefore, though there is increased flexibility in these settings too, there is less labour conflict and more resilient trade unions than in liberal market economies (Hall and Soskice 2001; Thelen 2001).

In this chapter we integrate the labour relations literature with the varieties-of-capitalism (VoC) approach, investigating the relationship between employment flexibility and the organizational capacity of trade unions in terms of membership and industrial action across in the European Union. We analyse data from the European Company Survey 2009, as this cross-national workplace survey enables us to examine employment flexibility, trade union organization and strikes in over 5000 firms across all 27 EU member states. The research question that we aim to answer is threefold: To what extent is employment flexibilization at the firm level associated with (1) union membership and (2) strike incidence across companies in the European Union? And (3) to what extent is the firm-level relationship between employment flexibility and union membership/strike incidence conditioned by national institutions? Because the analytical design is cross-national and multilevel in nature (that is, firms are clustered in countries), it theoretically connects with the VoC approach in which firms, institutionally embedded in a market system, are the central actors. This chapter, however, provides only very modest evidence of company-level relationships between employment flexibility on the one hand and union membership and/or strike incidence on the other. And, with respect to cross-national variation in these relationships, our findings provide no support for the hypothesis derived from the varieties-of-capitalism approach.

Flexibility, Union Membership and Industrial Action

Many of the expectations in the industrial relations literature seem to rest implicitly or explicitly upon the notion that unions weaken as labour markets liberalize. The decline of workers in fulltime, secure employment will erode the union's traditional membership base. To formulate hypotheses about the relationship between employment flexibility and union organization we therefore start with the popular assumption that with the introduction of personal contracts and individualized working conditions it has become increasingly difficult for unions to represent and organize the workforce. We will use the term 'flexible' employment to denote all types of work other than standard permanent contracts.

Numerical Flexibility and Union Membership

Despite various attempts to adapt to the challenges of a more flexible workforce (Grumbell-McCormick 2011), unions are still focused primarily on the interests of traditional employees with fulltime, long-term contracts with a single employer. Besides the ideological aversion of unions to flexible employment conditions (Grumbell-McCormick 2011), the traditional services of trade unions are aimed at the needs of traditional workers and are less attractive and often less relevant for the atypical worker. Collective bargaining, for instance, is much more complex to provide for flexible workers since it may not even be clear with whom the union should negotiate because employership is not that clear and/or is constantly changing (Croucher and Brewster 1998). In addition, flexible workers increase *interest heterogeneity* among union's membership, which may lead to disputes between members and to higher organization costs for the union since 'mass representation' and collectivism is no longer sufficient (Bacon and Storey 1993; Croucher and Brewster 1998). Therefore, unions consider flexible workers still as a problematic group to represent: they are difficult to reach and serve, their interests are deviant from the traditional member, and their heterogeneous composition makes flexible workers a non-cohesive target. Consequently, because of unions' traditional interest representation and the appeal to cohesiveness and solidarity, flexible workers themselves may feel less represented by the union. Membership in a union may therefore be less attractive for temporary agency workers and workers with fixed-term contracts. Moreover, by nature of their contract, flexible workers change jobs (more) frequently. This would impel them towards making frequent switches between unions, since the traditional unions are occupationally or sector-based. In addition, it is not imaginary that union membership is too expensive for workers who are 'in between' jobs (Croucher and Brewster 1998). Finally, the lower levels of stable and long-lasting professional (social) interactions may affect workers' perceptions of social cohesion (Cooper and Kurland 2002; Kurland and Cooper 2002; Golden *et al.* 2008), which are necessary to identify with colleagues. Identification with colleagues and a sense of collective interest strongly affects union membership (Klandermans and Visser 1995). We therefore expect that union membership is lower in companies with:

H1(a) *a higher proportion of workers with fixed-term contracts;*
H2(b) *a higher proportion of temporary agency workers*

Wage Flexibility and Union Membership

Unions traditionally promote solidarity wages rather than performance-related pay. Gunningle *et al.* argue that performance-related pay schemes undermine the solidarity and the collectivist tradition on which unions are based. Individualism would replace collectivism with respect to pay decisions; decisions about wages are no longer achieved through collective bargaining, and as a result there is no fixed pay scheme which applies equally to all employees (Gunningle *et al.* 1998). Flexible wages may therefore set in processes that reduce membership rates for two reasons. First, individualistic pay systems decrease the rationale for collective bargaining and collective representation interests (Storey and Bacon 1993). Second, performance pay schemes may increase competition between employees and therefore undermine solidarity and the acknowledgement of mutual interests (Wise 1993). We therefore expect lower union membership in companies with:

H1(c) *a higher proportion of workers under performance pay schemes.*

Numerical Flexibility and Industrial Action

The effects of flexible labour relations on union action remain under-analysed in the literature. Because unions generally oppose flexible contracts, the introduction of new legislation allowing firms to hire and fire employees with more ease can stimulate labour conflict. This could lead to more strikes when trade unions campaign against policy proposals that propagate the flexibilization of employment relations. Yet, once such regulations are in operation, strikes might be less likely in companies where employment relations are more flexible and individualized. For one thing, the benefits of strikes are lower for workers whose future career in the organization is only brief, or is unsecured. Industrial action is usually aimed at the improvement of working conditions and employment in the medium or long run. The loss of income during the strike is normally an investment that is only compensated by long-term improvement in wages. Fighting for a wage increase therefore is a low priority for flexible workers. Moreover, temporary agency workers may not even be covered by the gains of the strike, such as a collective agreement. At the same time, the risks associated with participation are higher for temporary workers, for instance when the firm retaliates against participation by withholding tenure, or refusal to rehire temporary workers. Finally, the same applies to strikes as to union membership: unstable jobs and the lack of long-lasting professional (social) interactions affect workers' social cohesion (Cooper and Kurland 2002; Kurland and Cooper 2002; Golden *et al.* 2008), which as previously mentioned is necessary to identify with colleagues. Identification with the union and the resulting solidarity with one's colleagues strongly affect participation in industrial action and union membership (Klandermans and Visser 1995; Akkerman *et al.* 2013). We therefore expect strike frequency to be lower in companies with:

H2(a) *a higher proportion of workers with fixed-term contracts;*
H2(b) *a higher proportion of temporary agency workers.*

Wage Flexibility and Industrial Action

We expect performance pay schemes to reduce participation in strikes for the same reasons as we expect fixed-term contracts and temporary agency workers to. Performance pay schemes increase competition between employees, which decreases workers' senses of collectivism and therefore undermines solidarity and the acknowledgement of mutual interests

(Wise 1993). We therefore expect that strike frequency to be lower in companies with:

H2(c) *a higher proportion of workers under performance pay schemes.*

Varieties of Capitalism

The varieties-of-capitalism approach starts with the firm as the central actor in the economy. According to this approach, firms face coordination problems with respect to employee and industrial relations (Hancké 2009). The main problem is 'how to coordinate bargaining over wages and working conditions with the labour force, the organizations that represent labour, and other employers' (Hall and Soskice 2001:7). According to Hall and Soskice's theory, the mechanisms of coordination differ between national political–economic institutional structures in which firms are embedded. Their theory revolves around 'liberal market economies' and 'coordinated market economies' as two archetypal forms of distinct capitalist systems. In liberal market economies, 'firms coordinate with other actors mainly through competitive markets, arms-length relations and formal contracting', whereas in coordinated market economies 'firms typically engage in more strategic interaction with trade unions, suppliers of finance and other others' (Hall and Gingerich 2009:452).

Using the liberal/coordinated dichotomy, Hall and Soskice claim that firms, and their responses to globalization, are fundamentally different across nations. The firms' call for employment flexibilization, as a reaction to intensified international competition, would not only be stronger in liberal than in coordinated market economies, but would also have different industrial relations outcomes. Hall and Soskice (2001:66) suggest that 'trade unions have been weakened by business initiatives and deregulation in liberal market economies but remain strong in coordinated market economies where cross-class coalitions help to preserve them and some degree of wage coordination' (see also Thelen 2001; Hall and Gingerich 2009; Hall and Thelen 2009).

The varieties-of-capitalism approach therefore seems to predict that hypotheses 1 and 2 do not hold uniformly across countries. The associations between employment flexibility and union membership/strike incidence would depend on the type of market economy; negative association may be expected only, or in particular, in more liberal market economies. Although Hall and Soskice regard the liberal and coordinated categories to represent the ends of a spectrum, scholars commonly use them as a typology, forcing countries into one of the two types (Crouch 2005; Hancké *et al.* 2009). Unfortunately, there were only very few attempts to quantify this spectrum, and available empirical analyses remain ambiguous about the position of many countries, including the new EU member states (see Hall and Gingerich 2009). For a current analysis of EU countries we therefore apply the multi-category typology of the European Commission (2009), which distinguishes two 'mixed', intermediate categories of market economies. In one are clustered Mediterranean countries with 'statist' market economies. In the other we find mostly Eastern and Central European countries with statist-liberal market economies. Assuming that the 'Mediterranean market economies' and 'Eastern European market economies' are somewhere between liberal and coordinated economies, we formulate the hypothesis that the negative effects of flexibility on union membership/strike incidence are:

H3: strongest in liberal, weaker in statist and statist-liberal, and weakest in coordinated market economies.

Data and Methods

To test our hypotheses, we use data from the European Company Survey 2009 (European Foundation for the Improvement of Living and Working Conditions and TNS Infratest Sozialforschung Munich 2010). The ECS-2009 is a large-scale representative survey among private and the public establishments across all 27 EU member states and three acceding and candidate countries (Croatia, Macedonia and Turkey). The survey consists of interviews with both managers and employee representatives of over 27 000 companies with 10 or more employees. The sample includes almost all categories of the statistical classification (revision 1.1) of economic activities in the European Community, abbreviated as NACE (from *Nomenclature statistique des activités économiques dans la Communauté européenne*), except the agricultural sector, private households and extraterritorial organizations. Management interviews, with the most senior person responsible for the personnel in each establishment, were carried out in all surveyed companies ($N - 27\,160$). Interviews with an employee representative, preferably the chairperson of the most important employee representative body in the establishment, were carried out in about 25 per cent of the surveyed companies ($N = 6569$). Information on contractual flexibility and payment schemes is available through the management survey. Questions on strike incidence and union membership are asked in the interview with the employee representative. For this reason we discarded the establishments in which only management interviews were conducted.[2] Furthermore, the analyses presented in this chapter only include companies from the 27 member states – excluding companies from acceding and candidate countries – and cases without information missing on relevant variables. The final sample contains 5616 companies.

We measure *strike incidence* using reports on industrial action by the employee representative. Respondents were asked whether there had been one or more instances of industrial action in their establishment in the past 12 months, and if so, what form of action, that is (1) stoppage of work or strike; (2) strike of one day or more; (3) refusal to do overtime; and (4) other actions. Because the first two response categories are not mutually exclusive, we constructed a binary variable (1/0) distinguishing companies where at least one strike *or* work stoppage occurred in the past 12 months (collapsing category 1 and 2) from companies with no or other forms of industrial action (collapsing categories 3 and 4 with all companies without reported industrial action).

For *union membership rate,* we used the employee representative's estimation of the proportion of employees in their establishment who are union members. If the exact number was unknown, union membership was estimated by means of fixed categories: 'None', 'Less than 20 per cent', '20 to less than 40 per cent', '40 to less than 60 per cent', '60 to less than 80 per cent', '80 to less than 100 per cent', 'All'. These cases were recoded into a proportion by taking the category midpoint: for example '20 to less than 40 per cent' is recoded into 30 per cent.

The indicators for employment flexibility are based on the management representative's estimation of the proportion of staff in their establishment working on *fixed-term contracts* and the proportion *receiving elements of pay on the basis of their individual performance,* using the same procedure as for the union membership rate. With respect to *temporary agency work* the managers were asked to mention the absolute number of temporary agency workers in their establishment (instead of the proportion).[3] If the manager was not aware of this information, he or she was asked to make an estimation (in the following fixed categories: 'None', 'Between 1 and 4', 'Between 5 and 9', 'Between 10 and 19', 'Between 20 and 49' and '50 or more'). In the last case, category midpoints are used as a proxy for the amount of temporary agency workers. Because only 0.5 per cent of the establishments reported 100 or more agency workers, the maximum number is truncated at 100.

To account for differences between individual companies and their likelihood of experiencing incidences of industrial action, we control for

Table 9.1 Descriptive statistics, company-level variables ($N = 5616$)

Variables	Mean	s.d.	Min.	Max.
Strike incidence	0.12	0.32	0	1
Union membership rate	49.42	35.56	0	100
Economic activity[a]				
NACE C–D–E	0.32	0.47	0	1
NACE F	0.06	0.24	0	1
NACE G	0.10	0.29	0	1
NACE H	0.02	0.14	0	1
NACE I	0.04	0.20	0	1
NACE J	0.02	0.15	0	1
NACE K	0.07	0.25	0	1
NACE L	0.11	0.32	0	1
NACE M	0.10	0.30	0	1
NACE N	0.11	0.31	0	1
NACE O	0.05	0.22	0	1
Company size				
10–19 employees	0.11	0.32	0	1
20–49 employees	0.21	0.40	0	1
50–99 employees	0.20	0.40	0	1
100–199 employees	0.14	0.35	0	1
200–399 employees	0.16	0.37	0	1
400–500 employees	0.05	0.21	0	1
500+ employees	0.14	0.35	0	1
Public sector	0.37	0.48	0	1
Company status				
independent	0.62	0.48	0	1
subsidiary site	0.18	0.38	0	1
headquarters	0.18	0.39	0	1
unknown	0.02	0.13	0	1
% Uncovered by collective agreement	18.31	35.81	0	100
% Female	45.34	29.35	0	100
% Part-time	12.29	19.02	0	100
% High-skilled workers	26.56	27.67	0	100
% Fixed-term contracts	7.48	14.10	0	100
Number of temporary agency workers	3.16	11.53	0	100
% Individual performance pay	22.06	35.96	0	100

[a] C–D–E = manufacturing and energy; F = construction; G = wholesale and retail trade; repair of motor vehicles, motorcycles and personal and household goods; H = hotels and restaurants; I = transport, storage and communication; J = financial intermediation; K = real estate, renting and business activities; L = public administration and defense; compulsory social security; M = education; N = health and social work; O = other community, social and personal service activities.

company size measured in seven categories, economic *sector* of activity on the basis of 1-digit NACE categories, *status* (independent, subsidiary site or headquarters), *public ownership* (1/0), and the level on which the *collective agreement* in each company, if any, is negotiated. In this case, the reference category consists of firms in which the collective agreement is negotiated at the company level. We also control for the *proportion of women, part-time workers* and *employees in high-skilled occupations* in a company's workforce, and the proportion of employees who go *uncovered by a collective wage agreement*. Descriptive statistics of all variables are presented in Table 9.1.

On the country level, we account for the *varieties of capitalist systems* in which firms are embedded. Building on the European Commission (2009) typology we distinguish between types of capitalist economy: liberal (Cyprus, Ireland, Malta, UK), coordinated (Austria, Belgium, Denmark, Finland, Germany, Luxembourg, Netherlands, Norway, Slovenia, Sweden), statist or 'Mediterranean' (France, Greece, Italy, Portugal, Spain) and statist-liberal or 'Eastern European' (Bulgaria, Czech Republic, Estonia, Hungary Latvia, Lithuania, Poland, Romania, Slovakia).

Results

We tested hypotheses 1 and 2 by presenting two series of multilevel analyses in which companies (level 1) were clustered in countries (level 2). In the first set of analysis we used union membership rate as the dependent variable. Table 9.2 presents the parameter estimates (b) and their standard errors (s.e.) of these models. Second, we used strike incidence as the dependent variable, and given the dichotomous nature of this variable we estimated a binary logistic model. In this case the parameters (b) are the logit-estimates of strike incidence (see Table 9.3).

Union Membership

In model 1 of Table 9.2 we included only the control variables. The results of this model are largely consistent with earlier findings in the literature. In model 2 of Table 9.2 we added the indicators of numerical and wage flexibility to our model. Adding these variables led to a moderately better model fit, indicated by a chi-squared decrease of 12.77 against 3 degrees of freedom. However, inspection of the AIC value and variance components revealed that adding indicators for employment flexibility and variable pay hardly contributed to explaining union membership.

Table 9.2 Results of the multilevel regression of union membership rate in EU companies

Variable	Model 1		Model 2	
Fixed effects	*b*	(s.e.)	*b*	(s.e.)
Constant	53.158***	(4.14)	53.877***	(4.13)
Economic activity[a] (NACE CDE = ref)				
NACE F	–3.624**	(1.50)	–3.478**	(1.51)
NACE G	–6.457***	(1.27)	–6.261***	(1.28)
NACE H	–9.351***	(2.58)	–9.238***	(2.59)
NACE I	0.255	(1.76)	–0.178	(1.76)
NACE J	–5.219**	(2.30)	–4.740**	(2.32)
NACE K	–8.593***	(1.57)	–8.408***	(1.48)
NACE L	–3.353**	(1.57)	–3.290**	(1.57)
NACE M	4.992***	(1.73)	5.236***	(1.74)
NACE N	–2.556*	(1.54)	–2.607*	(1.55)
NACE O	0.717	(1.73)	0.826	(1.74)
Public sector	9.226***	(1.05)	9.187***	(1.05)
Company size (10–19 employees = ref.)				
20–49	0.496	(1.24)	0.416	(1.25)
50–99	1.917	(1.27)	1.736	(1.27)
100–199	2.495*	(1.37)	2.494*	(1.37)
200–399	4.662***	(1.35)	4.731***	(1.36)
400–500	5.465***	(1.87)	5.489***	(1.87)
500+	7.350***	(1.39)	7.518***	(1.42)
Company status (independent = ref.)				
headquarters	–1.134	(0.94)	–1.105	(0.95)
subsidiary site	3.991***	(0.95)	4.038***	(0.96)
unknown	6.719**	(2.61)	6.840***	(2.62)
% Uncovered by collective agreement	–0.156***	(0.01)	–0.156***	(0.01)
% Female	–0.037***	(0.02)	–0.035**	(0.02)
% Part-time	–0.117***	(0.02)	–0.114***	(0.02)
% High-skilled workers	–0.098***	(0.01)	–0.096***	(0.01)
% Fixed-term contracts			–0.063**	(0.02)
Number of temporary agency workers			–0.006	(0.03)
% Individual performance pay			–0.025**	(0.01)
Random effects				
Variance at country level	414.35	(20.36)	411.40	(20.28)
Variance at company level	612.89	(24.76)	611.85	(24.73)
AIC	52 112		52 123	
–2LL	52 058		52 064	
$\Delta\chi^2$ Model 2 vs. Model 1 (df)			12.77 (3)***	

$N_{level-1}$ = 5616; $N_{level-2}$ = 27; *$p < 0.1$; **$p < 0.05$; ***$p < 0.01$ (two-tailed test).

[a] C–D–E = manufacturing and energy; F = construction; G = wholesale and retail trade; repair of motor vehicles, motorcycles and personal and household goods; H = hotels and restaurants; I = transport, storage and communication; J = financial intermediation; K = real estate, renting and business activities; L = public administration and defense; compulsory social security; M = education; N = health and social work; O = other community, social and personal service activities.

Nevertheless, the results in model 2 largely confirm hypothesis 1: it appears that union membership is lower in companies with more fixed-term workers ($b = -0.063$), and with more workers receiving some form of individual performance pay ($b = -0.025$). The estimates indicate that the difference between a company without fixed-term workers and one with 100-per-cent-fixed-term-contract workforce is respectively 6.3 per cent membership. In the case of performance-related pay this differences is 2.5 per cent (a decrease of 0.025 per cent in union membership with each additional percentage point of workers who receive performance-related pay). Since these effects are rather small, they only provide very modest support for hypotheses 1(a) and 1(c). We do not find any significant effect for the number of temporary agency workers on a company's union membership rate. Hence, hypothesis 1(b) is rejected.

Strike Incidence

After having established to what extent flexible and individual employment relationships in companies are associated with lower levels of union membership, we next proceeded to examine whether these factors account for a lower likelihood of collective action. We therefore estimated two models with strike incidence as the dependent variable. In model 1 of Table 9.3 we include the same variables that we used to explain union membership density in a company. In order to see to what extent the effects of employment flexibility on strikes are accounted for by lower levels of union membership, union membership rate was added as an explanatory variable in the second model.

To test our hypotheses on the effect of employment flexibility on the strike incidence in a company, we looked at the estimates for the indicators of fixed-term employment, temporary agency work and individual performance pay. For our hypotheses to hold, we had to find negative coefficients. However, it appears that the proportion of fixed-term workers in an establishment is uncorrelated to strike incidence. This rejects hypothesis 2(a). For the indicators of temporary agency work and individual performance-related pay we found weak but statistically significant results. Instead of the expected negative effect, we found that the share of employees receiving some form of individual performance-based pay, and the number of temporary agency workers was associated *positively* with strike incidence. Strikes are more likely in companies where more employees receive elements of their pay on the basis of individual performance, and if the amount of agency workers is higher. Again, these effects are only modest in size. For example, in companies where all workers receive

Table 9.3 Results of the multilevel logistic analysis of strike incidence in EU companies

Variable	Model 1		Model 2	
Fixed effects	**b**	**(s.e.)**	**b**	**(s.e.)**
Constant	−3.553***	(0.35)	−4.416***	(0.39)
Economic activity(a)				
(NACE CDE = ref)				
NACE F	−0.868***	(0.32)	−0.813**	(0.32)
NACE G	−0.612***	(0.23)	−0.518**	(0.23)
NACE H	−1.058**	(0.52)	−1.016*	(0.53)
NACE I	−0.102	(0.24)	−0.102	(0.25)
NACE J	−0.997**	(0.44)	−0.936**	(0.44)
NACE K	−0.770***	(0.27)	−0.648**	(0.27)
NACE L	−0.128	(0.21)	−0.036	(0.21)
NACE M	1.050***	(0.23)	1.065***	(0.23)
NACE N	0.319	(0.21)	0.378*	(0.21)
NACE O	−0.406	(0.28)	−0.382	(0.28)
Public sector	0.899***	(0.15)	0.806***	(0.15)
Company size (10–19 employees = ref.)				
20–49	0.363	(0.22)	0.400*	(0.22)
50–99	0.362	(0.22)	0.418*	(0.23)
100–199	0.746***	(0.23)	0.799***	(0.23)
200–399	1.072***	(0.22)	1.089***	(0.23)
400–500	1.294***	(0.27)	1.127***	(0.27)
500+	1.481***	(0.22)	1.462***	(0.23)
Company status (independent = ref.)				
headquarters	0.212	(0.13)	0.219*	(0.13)
subsidiary site	0.566***	(0.13)	0.510***	(0.13)
unknown	0.570**	(0.27)	0.475	(0.27)
% Uncovered by collective agreement	−0.006***	(0.002)	−0.005***	(0.002)
% Female	−0.006**	(0.002)	−0.005**	(0.002)
% Part-time	0.003	(0.003)	0.005	(0.003)
% High-skilled workers	−0.002	(0.002)	−0.001	(0.002)
% Fixed-term contracts	−0.003	(0.003)	−0.002	(0.003)
Number of temporary agency workers	0.007**	(0.003)	0.007**	(0.003)
% Individual performance pay	0.003**	(0.001)	0.003**	(0.001)
% Union membership			0.013***	(0.002)
Random effects				
Random intercept	1.80	(1.34)	2.03	(1.43)
AIC	3 307		3263	
−2LL	3 250		3204	
Δχ² Model 2 vs. Model 1 (df)			46 (1)****	

$N_{level-1}$ = 5616; $N_{level-2}$ = 27; *p < 0.1; **p < 0.05; ***p < 0.01 (two-tailed test).

(a) C–D–E = manufacturing and energy; F = construction; G = wholesale and retail trade; repair of motor vehicles, motorcycles and personal and household goods; H = hotels and restaurants; I = transport, storage and communication; J = financial intermediation; K = real estate, renting and business activities; L = public administration and defense; compulsory social security; M = education; N = health and social work; O = other community, social and personal service activities.

performance pay the odds of a strike are only 1.3 times higher (exp (100 × 0.003)) compared with companies in which none of the workers receive performance pay. Thus we reject hypotheses 2(b) and 2(c).

Finally, we looked at model 2 in Table 9.3. In this model we controlled for a firm's union membership rate. Consistent with earlier findings in the literature, we observed a positive association between union membership and strike incidence. With each percentage point increase in the share of union members in the workforce the odds that an establishment experienced a strike in the last 12 months is 1.013 times higher (exp (0.013)). Including union membership rate in the model leads to a substantially better fit of the model, and generally weakens the effects of other variables in the models, however the effects of employment flexibility on strikes are not affected by controlling for union membership.

Comparing Varieties of Capitalism

So far, we have conducted pooled analyses showing a general picture, namely that employment flexibility has only a modest effect to none at all on the organizational capacity of unions. This general picture, however, might be obscured by differences among countries. The varieties-of-capitalism literature provided some clues for a moderating role of political–economic structures with respect to consequences of flexibility for labour politics. Hypothesis 3 states that the effects of employment flexibility on union membership and strike incidence vary across different capitalist types. The varieties-of-capitalism literature suggests that flexibility is most detrimental to the organizational capacity of unions in liberal economies, but less so in statist and statist-liberal economies, and least of all in coordinated market economies. For hypothesis 3 to hold, we would expect employment flexibility to have a different effect across types of market economies. The most straightforward way to test this hypothesis is to conduct separate analyses for the different types of market economies. Table 9.4 shows the effects of employment flexibility on union membership rate and strike incidence broken down by type of market economy. Because the number of countries is only 4 and 5 in case of the statist and statist-liberal economies, respectively, we include country-dummy variables, and adjust the standard errors for country clustering.

With respect to the relationship between flexibility and union membership rate, model 1(a) suggests that, consistent with the 'overall' results in Table 9.1, in coordinated market economies both the number of agency workers and the proportion of workers receiving performance pay are associated negatively with union membership. However, in other

Table 9.4 Effects of flexibility on union membership and strikes in various capitalist systems

CMEs (N = 2819)	Model 1a Membership rate		Model 1b Strike incidence	
% Fixed-term	-0.03	(0.05)	0.005	(0.006)
N Agency workers	-0.03**	(0.01)	0.012**	(0.006)
% Performance pay	-0.03**	(0.01)	0.001	(0.003)
Country (Austria = ref.)				
Belgium	12.34***	(0.69)	3.81***	(0.18)
Denmark	39.32***	(1.61)	2.69***	(0.25)
Finland	32.44***	(1.11)	2.04***	(0.23)
Germany	-22.35***	(0.97)	4.09***	(0.18)
Netherlands	-7.95***	(1.44)	1.58***	(0.14)
Luxembourg	-19.1***	(1.27)	1.88***	(0.12)
Slovenia	13.38***	(1.94)	2.09***	(0.26)
Sweden	34.70***	(1.05)	0.99 ***	(0.32)

MMEs (N = 1086)	Model 2a Membership rate		Model 2b Strike incidence	
% Fixed-term	0.02	(0.03)	0.003	(0.004)
N Agency workers	-0.002	(0.09)	-0.003	(0.004)
% Performance pay	-0.02	(0.02)	0.005***	(0.000)
Country (France = ref.)				
Greece	60.41***	(0.74)	1.06***	(0.22)
Italy	31.92***	(0.51)	-0.65**	(0.27)
Portugal	27.10***	(1.30)	-0.52***	(0.13)
Spain	12.88***	(1.01)	-1.73***	(0.08)

EMEs (N = 1418)	Model 3a Membership rate		Model 3b Strike incidence	
% Fixed-term	-0.09	(0.05)	-0.005	(0.004)
N Agency workers	0.03	(0.05)	-0.031	(0.019)
% Performance pay	-0.02	(0.02)	0.001	(0.003)
Country (Bulgaria = ref.)				
Czech Rep.	-19.6***	(1.82)	1.61	(0.33)
Estonia	-16.8***	(1.90)		
Hungary	-6.55***	(1.01)	0.36***	(0.17)
Latvia	-9.16***	(1.83)	-0.13	(0.17)
Lithuania	-19.4***	(1.52)	0.99***	(0.22)
Poland	-12.0***	(0.90)	1.23***	(0.21)
Romania	-2.29	(2.10)	0.74***	(0.20)
Slovakia	-10.2***	(0.77)		

LMEs (N = 293)	Model 4a Membership rate		Model 4b Strike incidence	
% Fixed-term	-0.06	(0.08)	-0.037*	(0.022)
N Agency workers	0.11	(0.09)	-0.02***	(0.004)
% Performance pay	-0.06	(0.06)	0.006**	(0.003)
Country (UK = ref.)				
Cyprus	45.85***	(1.63)	-0.51	(1.41)
Ireland	15.69***	(2.07)	-1.76**	(0.89)
Malta	33.94***	(2.12)	-0.32	(0.82)

$*p < 0.1$; $**p < 0.05$; $***p < 0.01$ (two-tailed test).

Coefficients are the *regression estimates* for union membership rate, and the *logit estimates* for strike incidence. Robust standard errors, adjusted for clustering in countries, are reported in parentheses. Models predicting union membership rate are controlled for economic activity, public sector, size, status, % covered by collective agreements, % female, % part-time (see Table 9.2), the strike incidence models are also controlled for % union membership (see Table 9.3).

types of market economies (2(a) to 4(a)), none of the coefficients of employment flexibility reaches significance. These results show that hypothesis 3 should largely be rejected, in other words, there is hardly – in any of the other 'types of capitalism' – any relationship between flexibility and union membership rate, and thus there is no indication that the effects of employment flexibility are stronger in liberal compared with coordinated market economies. The question whether the differences between coordinated market economies and other types of market economies can be interpreted in terms of the varieties-of-capitalism approach should be preceded by the question of whether these differences are substantial and significant. The separate analyses for coordinated, liberal, statist and statist-liberal market economies in Table 9.4 do not formally test whether these effects are significantly different between market economies. This can be tested in a multilevel model which includes cross-level interactions between the flexibility variables and dummies indicating the type of capitalist system. Significant interactions would indicate that the effects of employment flexibility on union membership rate are moderated by the type of capitalist systems. Additional analyses (not shown), however, indicate no sign of cross-level interaction. These checks therefore indicate that the effects of employment flexibility on union membership rate do not vary substantially among capitalist systems in general, nor specifically between coordinated market economies and other types.[4] With respect to differences across national economies, then, the results in Table 9.4 should be interpreted with caution.

The same reservations apply to the cross-national differences with respect to employment flexibility and strike incidence. Models 1(b) to 4(b) report the logit estimates, with strike incidence as the dependent variable. In most types of market economies, we find very little evidence for the impact of employment flexibility on strikes. And if effects are statistically significant, the substantial size is modest. In coordinated market economies for example (Model 1(b)), we find that with each additional agency worker, the chances of a strike are 1.012 times greater (exp (0.012)). Model 4(b) seems to indicate that, in liberal market economies, all flexibility variables are significant: the number of temporary agency workers and the proportion of fixed-term contracts are both associated negatively with strike incidence, whereas performance pay increases the likelihood of strikes. But again these results should be interpreted with caution. Multilevel analyses checking for cross-level interaction do not provide any reason to assume that the effects of employment flexibility on strikes differ among types of market economies.

Conclusion

We started this chapter from the premise that flexible and individual employment relations challenge the role of unions in modern labour relations. In the first, cross-national, part of the analysis we examined all EU-27 countries simultaneously through multilevel analysis. The general picture that emerged is ambiguous. With respect to explaining union density, our results suggest that individual pay and fixed-term contracts weaken union membership at firm level. Although these findings seem to confirm that performance pay can undermine solidarity, and that the union's membership base is still predominantly built on a cohesion and solidarity associated with long-term employment relations, the negative effects of flexibility on union membership rate should not be overestimated. The relationship of fixed-term contracts and individual performance pay is rather weak, and we did not find support for our expectation that an increased number of temporary agency workers in a company reduces union membership rate. With respect to industrial action (that is strikes), we find that contractual flexibility has no effect. This result is surprising, since we did not expect flexible workers to invest in strikes, which are usually aimed at improvements in work conditions and wages in the medium or long run. For the variables for which we do find significant results, as is the case for the amount of temporary agency workers and the proportion of non-managerial staff that receives elements of pay on the basis of individual performance, contrary to our expectations we find positive associations with strike incidence, instead of negative ones.

In the second part of the analyses we therefore broke the analyses down into four types of market economies. These results, however, provide no clear support for the claim that the relationship between employment flexibility and union membership or industrial action is different in the four models of capitalism. Although we find some indication for differences among country clusters, these observations do not convincingly match the prediction that the (negative) effects of flexibility on union membership/strike incidence are strongest in liberal economies, weaker in statist and statist-liberal economies, and weakest in coordinated market ones. While it is tempting to interpret these findings, the observed patterns are relatively small in size, and do not show clear differences across the types of markets economies.

The central conclusion of this chapter is twofold. First, there is only very modest evidence for company-level relationships between employment flexibility on the one hand and union membership and/or strike incidence on the other. Second, with respect to cross-national variation in these relationships our findings do not provide support for the hypothesis derived from the varieties-of-capitalism approach.

A finding in this chapter that needs more attention is that the proportion of workers receiving performance pay is associated positively with strike incidence, instead of negatively. This finding holds specifically for statist and liberal economies, whereas for the statist-liberal and coordinated market economies we find no significant effect at all. We assumed that performance pay schemes tend to increase inter-employee competition and therefore undermine solidarity. We expected that individualistic pay schemes would decrease workers' sense of collectivism, and consequently reduce the capacity of workers to organize a strike. Yet we find that the likelihood of experiencing a strike in a company increases as more workers receive some form of pay on the basis of individual performances. However, it might be the case that unions mobilize employees to oppose individual and variable pay schemes. If this is true, the question arises as to what portion of the workforce is mobilized – those who receive performance-related pay or those who don't. This question taps into another issue we did not address in this chapter: the risks associated with the 'ecological fallacy' (Robinson 1950) – that is, drawing incorrect inferences about individual workers on the basis of aggregate statistics. The ecological fallacy suggests that the correlation between two variables at the company level does not warrant the same conclusion with respect to individual workers in these companies. Individual-level (survey) data would be required to determine whether associations presented here hold for individual workers as well. The negative relationship between temporary contracts and union membership has been established for individual workers (see for example Van den Berg 1995). But the empirical evidence for effects of other aspects of individual and flexible employment relations on union membership and strike participation is largely absent. With the increased flexibility of labour markets across Europe, we would recommend future research into these relationships.

Notes

1 The research for this chapter was supported by Dutch Science Foundation (NWO), grant 432-08-122.
2 The availability of an interview with an employee representative is influenced by country differences and some company-level variables such as size or ownership; see the *Technical Report* (Riedmann *et al.* 2010). But 'the employee representative interviews are not systematically biased towards establishments with a particularly good social

dialogue and they can thus be considered as representative in this regard' (p. 40).

3 We were unable to calculate the proportion of temporary agency workers because sufficiently detailed data are lacking on the total number of employees in each firm, as this information is only available in broad categories.

4 To further account for cross-national differences in the effects of employment flexibility, we allowed a random slope for each the effect of employment flexibility on union membership or strike incidence; thus, we let the proportion of fixed-term contracts, the number of agency workers and the proportion of workers receiving performance pay have a different effect across different countries. Likelihood ratio tests revealed that the random-slope models do not fit the data better than the model with only a fixed coefficient for these variables, respectively. Hence, these results indicate that on average employment flexibility has the same effect over all countries in this study.

REFERENCES

Akkerman, Agnes, Marieke J. Born and René Torenvlied (2013) 'Solidarity, Strikes, and Scabs: How Participation Norms Affect Union Members' Willingness to Strike', *Work and Occupations* 40: 250–280.

Arrowsmith, James (2009) *Temporary Agency Work and Collective Bargaining in the EU*. Dublin: European Foundation for the Improvement of Living and Working Conditions.

Arrowsmith, James and Paul Marginson (2009) *Wage Flexibility*. Dublin: European Foundation for the Improvement of Living and Working Conditions.

Bacon, Nicolas and John Storey (1993) 'Individualization of the Employment Relationship and the Implications for Trade Unions', *Employee Relations* 15:5–17.

Baglioni, Guido and Colin Crouch (1990) *European Industrial Relations: The Challenge of Flexibility.* London: Sage.

Cooper, Cecily D. and Nancy B. Kurland (2002) 'Telecommuting, Professional Isolation, and Employee Development in Public and Private Organizations', *Journal of Organizational Behaviour* 23:511–532.

Crouch, Colin (2005) Models of Capitalism. *New Political Economy* 10:439–56.

Croucher, Richard and Chris Brewster (1998) 'Flexible Working Practices and the Trade Unions', *Employee Relations* 20:443–52.

European Commission (2009) *Industrial Relations in Europe 2008*. Brussels

European Foundation for the Improvement of Living and Working Conditions and TNS Infratest Sozialforschung Munich (2010) *European Company Survey, 2009* [computer file]. Colchester: UK Data Archive [distributor], October. SN: 6568.

Eurostat (2013) *Employment Statistics – Statistics Explained (2013/2/4)*; available at http://epp.eurostat.ec.europa.eu/statistics_explained/index.php/Employment_statistics, accessed: 7 February 2013.

▶

Golden, Timothy D., John F. Veiga and Richard N. Dino (2008) 'The Impact of Professional Isolation on Teleworker Job Performance and Turnover Intentions: Does Time Spent Teleworking, Interacting Face-to-Face, or Having Access to Communication-Enhancing Technology Matter? ', *Journal of Applied Psychology* 93:1412–21.

Gumbrell-McCormick, Rebecca (2011) 'European Trade Unions and "Atypical" Workers', *Industrial Relations Journal* 42:293–10.

Gunnigle, Patrick, Thomas Turner and Daryl D'Art (1998) 'Counterpoising Collectivism: Performance-Related Pay and Industrial Relations in Greenfield Sites', *British Journal of Industrial Relations* 36:565–79.

Hancké, Bob (2009) *Introducing the Debate: Debating the Varieties of Capitalism – A Reader*. Oxford: Oxford University Press.

Hancké, Bob, Martin Rhodes and Mark Thatcher (2008) *Beyond Varieties of Capitalism: Conflict, Contradictions, and Complementarities in the European Economy*. Oxford: Oxford University Press.

Hall, Peter. A. and Daniel W. Gingerich (2009) 'Varieties of Capitalism and Institutional Complementarities in the Political Economy: An Empirical Analysis', *British Journal of Political Science* 39:449–82.

Hall, Peter A. and David W. Soskice (eds) (2001) *Varieties of Capitalism: The Institutional Foundations of Comparative Advantage*. Oxford: Oxford University Press.

Hall, Peter, A. and Kathleen Thelen (2009) 'Institutional Change in Varieties of Capitalism', *Socio-Economic Review* 7:7–4.

Kalleberg, Arne L. (2009) 'Precarious Work, Insecure Workers: Employment Relations in Transition', *American Sociological Review* 74:1–22.

Klandermans, Bert and Jelle Visser (1995) *De Vakbeweging na de Welvaartsstaat*. Assen: Van Gorcum.

Kurland Nancy B. and Cecily D. Cooper (2002) 'Manager Control and Employee Isolation in Telecommuting Environments', *Journal of High Technology Management Research* 13:107–26.

Milner, Susan (2012) 'Towards a European Labour Market. Trade Unions and Flexicurity in France and Britain', *European Journal of Industrial Relations* 18:219–4.

Robinson, William S. (1950) 'Ecological Correlations and the Behavior of Individuals', *American Sociological Review* 15:351–57.

Storrie, Donald (2002) *Temporary Agency Work: Sweden* (National Report). Dublin: European Foundation for the Improvement of Living and Working Conditions.

Storey, John and Nicolas Bacon (1993) 'Individualism and Collectivism: Into the 1990s', *International Journal of Human Resource Management* 4:665–85.

Thelen, Kathleen (2001) 'Varieties of Labor Politics in the Developed Democracies', in *Varieties of Capitalism: The Institutional Foundations of Comparative Advantage*, edited by P.A. Hall and D.W. Soskice. Oxford: Oxford University Press.

Van den Berg, Annette (1995) *Trade Union Growth and Decline in the Netherlands*. Amsterdam: Amsterdam Thesis Publishers.

Van het Kaar, Robbert and Marianne Grünnel, 2001) *Variable Pay in Europe*. Dublin: European Industrial Relations Observatory Online; available at www.eurofound. europa.eu/eiro/2001/04/study/tn0104201s.htm, retrieved 17 October 2012.

▶

Visser, Jelle (2011) *The ICTWSS Database: Database on Institutional Characteristics of Trade Unions, Wage Setting, State Intervention and Social Pacts in 34 Countries Between 1960 and 2007,* Version 3 (computer file). Amsterdam Institute for Advanced Labour Studies, University of Amsterdam, May.

Wise, Lois R. (1993) 'Whither Solidarity? Transitions in Swedish Public Sector Pay Policy', *British Journal of Industrial Relations* 31:75–95.

PART

Within-Country Diversity

Coming to Terms with Firm-Level Diversity: An Investigation of Flexibility and Innovative Capability Profiles in the Transformed 'German Model'

10

Stefan Kirchner and Jürgen Beyer

For many years now, the foundations of the German model have been investigated as one ideal type in comparative political economy (Sorge 1991; Streeck 1991; Lane 1995; Hollingsworth 1997; Hall and Soskice 2001).[1] However, recent empirical findings have highlighted the considerable diversity of firm-level patterns. This questions traditional assumptions about the 'German model'. Drawing on political economy research and labour process theory,[2] this chapter empirically investigates the actual diversity of flexibility and innovative capability profiles in Germany. It contributes to both debates by considering the implications of diversity and dominant firm-level patterns. Based on an empirical analysis of firm-level diversity, a link between the two debates is advanced, highlighting the sectoral embeddedness of firm strategies and labour processes.

The term 'German model' has been related to two main aspects. First, it delineates a specific national institutional framework that enables certain socio-economic activities and constrains others. Second, the model implies the existence of specific firm-level patterns which emerged within the institutional framework. One major firm pattern that has been identified as exemplary for the German economy is diversified quality production (Sorge and Streeck 1988; Streeck 1991). The central argument of the varieties-of-capitalism approach is that the German type of market economy fosters the success of strategies like diversified quality production (Hall and Soskice 2001). Such strategies would thus be expected to be the dominant firm-level pattern within the German model.

Yet, as Jürgens (2004: 412) points out concerning German automotive manufactures, the diversified quality production concept may appear an 'elusive model'. At the same time, diversified quality production applies to a variety of firm-level patterns that are not covered by high-volume standardized production or low-volume craft production strategies (see Sorge and Streeck 1988; Streeck 1991). Furthermore, several authors have provided empirical and conceptual expectations concerning German firm-level patterns that resemble traditional diversified quality production and also extend its basic aspects (cf. Whitley 1999; Hall and Soskice 2001; Amable 2003; Jürgens *et al.* 2006). By linking these different approaches the cornerstones of an underlying 'default' German firm-level pattern can be determined, which represents the attributes that are commonly shared across the different approaches. For the purpose of this chapter, the basic trait of this default pattern can be identified as a manufacturing strategy of large firms with high innovative capability, which builds on a high share of qualified employees (especially so-called *Facharbeiter*). The pattern is also characterized by a focus on internal flexibility – for example the shifting of workers between production lines, or the varying of working time through overtime or short-time work.

Labour process theory has been concerned with considerable diversity as it studies a wide range of workplaces and industries (see Warhurst and Thompson 1998; Sturdy *et al.* 2001; Bolton and Houlihan 2009; Hesmondhalgh and Baker 2011). However, this stream of literature is now facing the challenge of relating these findings of heterogeneity to the general distribution of firm-level patterns. In this respect Thompson and Vincent (2010) stress that labour processes are embedded in a wider institutional framework of national political economy. As labour processes are embedded in organizational structures in firms, an analysis of firm-level patterns provides information on their general distribution in a given industry or national economy. Also for Vidal (2011), the rise in observable diversity poses the essential question of dominant tendencies. There is a need to learn what patterns have emerged and how they relate to their specific contexts.

Although political economy approaches and labour process theory constitute different research traditions, they overlap in their need to address the issue of diversity and dominant firm-level patterns. The aim of this chapter is to bring together both approaches on the basis of an empirical investigation of the actual diversity of flexibility and innovative capability profiles in Germany. Following the implications of the traditional German model perspective, one would expect a dominant profile among large German manufacturing firms that is characterized by a high innovative capability and by skilled workers utilizing internal forms of flexibility. In contrast, non-manufacturing industries and firms of smaller size are expected to display different firm-level patterns. However, the traditional assumptions about the German economy and diversified quality production do not take into account the transformation processes that have taken place within the German economy. In order to reconsider the 'German model', insight into the actual distribution of flexibility and innovation practices is required.

In the next section we start from the current debate in the political economy literature on diversity within national institutional frameworks and develop an approach that reveals different profiles within the German economy. Findings from the labour process literature are reviewed to support the search for sources of diversity at firm level. In the following section, building on the conceptual considerations, we undertake an empirical investigation of flexibility and innovative capability profiles. In the section after this the results are presented. The chapter concludes with a summary of the findings and their implications for political economy research and labour process theory.

Sources of Diversity in National Institutional Frameworks and Labour Processes

In the current discussion about effects of political economy on firms, a counterpoint is posed by a growing number of empirical studies emphasizing the diversity of firm-level strategies. Several authors have provided evidence on firm-level strategies that conflict significantly with the general assumptions of the varieties-of-capitalism approach (for example Herrmann 2008; Crouch, Schröder and Voelzkow 2009; Lange 2009), and thus appear to challenge the approach. It has been acknowledged that the institutional pillars of the German variety of capitalism went through significant transformations in the 1990s (Streeck 1997). From then onwards a liberalization process has been a major underlying trend (Hall and Thelen 2009), altering central institutional pillars of the German model, particularly in labour market regulation. In the debate, the current state of firm-level strategies is largely unexplored, since quantitative investigations are missing and findings mostly rest on case study evidence.

For an empirical investigation the diversified quality production approach and the related research provide a useful set of theoretical assumptions to start with. The research on German firm-level patterns has been predominantly focused on (1) large and (2) manufacturing firms. These two criteria reflect a fundamental size/industry bias in the debate. Therefore it seems beneficial to include the most important excluded categories – small as well as highly innovative non-manufacturing industries.

Diversified quality production and related concepts additionally identify specific firm-level characteristics. This comprises firms using (3) skilled employees, displaying (4) a high innovative capability and relying on (5) internal flexibility. Based on these criteria the existing findings can be summarized to support the search for different profiles as follows:

(1) *Firm size.* Some authors have stressed the importance of smaller firms for employment and economic activity in Germany (see also Streeck 1991; Herrigel 1996; 2010), yet smaller firms have never really been in the centre of the discussion (Berghoff 2006). Berghoff acknowledged that, beside similarities, substantial differences between large and smaller firms can be found. He argued that family-owned and - operated small and medium enterprises (SMEs) with a cooperative orientation towards their workforce and strategies of long-term quality competition comply with the traditional model. In contrast, German SMEs are less well integrated in the wider industrial relations or corporate finance contexts than their larger counterparts.

(2) *Non-manufacturing industries.* Another central source of diversity in the German economy is industry membership. While manufacturing industry is restructuring and remains significant, other sectors of economic activity have gained importance (Hall and Thelen 2009). In respect of different profiles within the German economy, information and communications firms, and firms from the financial and insurance activities industry, are particularly interesting for a study of diversity. Both industries represent so-called 'knowledge-intensive service industries' (see Aschhoff *et al.* 2008).

(3) *Employee skill level.* In many approaches a key defining factor for German firm-level strategies is the employment of skilled workers who have completed vocational training. The shift from an industrial to a so-called 'knowledge economy', a transformation in the education system and in labour markets, has fostered a steady growth of high-skilled employees who hold a university degree (Schmidt 2010). In particular, IT firms rely on high-skilled employees who have completed higher education. This employment pattern departs from traditional German patterns in several ways (Boes and Marrs 2003; Mayer-Ahuja and Wolf 2007). In addition, recent empirical studies show the resilience of unskilled employment. For example, Hirsch-Kreinsen *et al.* (2012) have highlighted the existence of a low-skilled firm-level model in manufacturing industry.

(4) *Innovative capability.* Another basic source of diversity closely linked to the issue of employee skill levels has been identified by the innovation literature. A contrast to the high innovative capability of diversified

quality production firms is posed by firms in so-called 'low-tech industries' (Pavitt 1984; OECD 2003). While the general discussion appears to be focused on high-tech industries and firms, several studies have highlighted the successful survival of 'low-tech' firms (Hirsch-Kreinsen 2008; Heidenreich 2009).

(5) *Forms of flexibility.* The employment system in particular is believed to be subject to a process of liberalization on the institutional level (Hall and Thelen 2009). The result is a growing dualism in the German labour market (Palier and Thelen 2010; Hassel 2012). This dualism, as a consequence of institutional change, has its counterpart at firm level. An increased externalization of flexibility can be observed here (see Davis-Blake and Uzzi 1993; Kalleberg 2001). Two developments at firm level mark this substantial shift away from previous internal flexibility practices. First, Germany has experienced steady growth in temporary agency work, particularly since 2004 (see Bouncken *et al.* 2012). However, absolute numbers for agency workers are still quite low. Second, with the reorganization dynamics of the 1990s, a concentration on core competences has been promoted. The few studies available show that a substantial number of firms have outsourced different functions to subcontractors (Kinkel and Lay 2003). It has also been observed that the outsourcing trend stagnated in 2000 (Görzig *et al.* 2005).

From a labour process theory perspective, several connections to aspects just raised can be shown. The aspects of German firm-level patterns and transformation tendencies as likely sources of diversity connect very well with the observations of key developments (see Thompson and van den Broek 2010; Vidal 2011). In an overview of labour process theory, Thompson and van den Broek (2010) have touched on several potential causes of transformation and significant diversity. These include: firm size (Barrett and Rainnie 2002); differences between manufacturing and service work; and the rise of so-called 'knowledge work' (Warhurst and Thompson 1998; Hampson and Junor 2010). These aspects indicate industry-specific patterns of transformation and a subsequent diversity of labour processes. This list is extended by the more recent transformation of industrial production towards subcontracting and exchange between firms (see Pulignano 2002).

According to Vidal (2011), the increasing vertical disintegration through outsourcing and contingent work marks the transformation from traditional 'fordism' to 'postfordist' organizational forms. Rather than seeing a single postfordist organizational form, he sees a diversity of organizational forms resulting from these transformations. One crucial aspect of this transformation is employee involvement. Here, neotaylorist forms of involvement as a consequence of the diffusing 'lean' model are distinguished from post-taylorist counterparts by the level of actual autonomy granted to workers. In both forms responsibilities are shifted to employees (for example via teamwork), yet neotaylorist forms do so without allowing any 'real autonomy' in the labour process (Harley 2001; Pruijt 2003). Vidal (2011) points to the traditional diversified quality production concept of German manufactures as one form of post-taylorism within the postfordist period . In the light of the transformation in the 1990s and especially the diffusion of neotaylorist practices, it would be particularly interesting to learn whether or not dominant firm-level patterns within the German economy have remained post-taylorist or have become neotaylorist.

As with the issues raised in the political economy literature, differences in firm size and between manufacturing and service sector firms are found in the labour process approaches too. Specific segments within the economy can be expected to be a major reason for diversity. The employee skill level, the respective labour processes and the newly emerging flexibility patterns are also observed as crucial transformations. However, labour process research predominantly relies on case study evidence as well. So far, the diversity found at the workplace level of s appears to be unconnected with the general distributions of different organizational forms within a given economy. As with the studies of diversity in the political economy debate, labour process research needs to be complemented by a quantitative investigation of firm-level patterns. With this empirical step both approaches can advance and relate to each other based on firm-level data.

Data, Measures and Method

In order to identify different profiles within the German economy and to compare their characteristics, two independent analyses were conducted and the results combined. The research builds on separate findings on innovative capability profiles by Kirchner *et al.* (2012) and on research on flexibility profiles by Kirchner (2013). In the latter paper, the respective findings are related and the implications of these integrated results discussed.

The basis of the quantitative analysis was a CATI (computer-assisted telephone interview) that was conducted in the second half of 2010. A random sample of German establishments layered by three size classes and six industries was drawn from federal employment statistics data. The sampling criteria included: establishments[3] with more than 20 insurable employees (*sozialversicherungspflichtige Beschäftigte*) from (1) four subcategories of manufacturing, (2) the information and communication (I&C) industry and (3) the financial and insurance activities (FIA) industry; that were more than 3 years old. The industries are labelled according to the current NACE classification (eurostat 2008). Being in knowledge-intensive service sector industries, German I&C firms and firms from the FIA industry are considered highly innovative (Rammer *et al.* 2010). The response rate was about 21 per cent and the retrieved data set is representative for the sampling criteria.

Table 10.1 Description of the manifest variables from the latent class analysis

	Question in the questionnaire (answer categories)
Variable for innovative capability profiles	
R&D activities	Are research and development activities conducted in your establishment? (Yes/No)
R&D department	Is there a particular organizational unit that conducts research and development in your establishment? (Yes/No)
Specialized personnel	Do you have personnel that are concerned with predevelopment, construction or design of products or services? (Yes/No)
External R&D	Do you make use of research and development output that is provided from other parts of your company or from outside your company? (Yes/No)
Idea management	Does your establishment have a systematic employee suggestion system or ideas management? (Yes/No)
Innovation management	Do you systematically plan and manage innovations in your establishment? (Yes/No)
Skilled employee share[*]	What was the percentage of employees for qualified jobs on 30 June 2010? (Percentage: 0–100)
Variable for flexibility profiles	
Working time flexibility	Importance of the adjustment of individual working hours, for example overtime, short-time work. (1–6) [**]
Shifting of workers between workplaces	Importance of the reallocation of workers to jobs or activities. (1–6) [**]
Flexibility via outsourcing	Importance of the subcontracting of services or functions that have previously been provided onsite. (1–6) [**]
Flexibility via temporary agency work	Importance of temporary agency work. (1–6) [**]

[*] In the survey, interviewers provided the following explanation of the term 'qualified jobs': 'Qualified jobs require accomplished vocational training or a comparable professional training or adequate job experience.'

[**] Wording of question (for example): 'Flexibility via Temporary Agency Work: Please indicate importance between 1: very important and 6: not important.'

Source: Own depiction; own translation from German original.

The analysis of innovative capability profiles included six binary variables as well as one continuous variable (see Table 10.1). This was considered whether or not R&D activities were pursued. The existence of an R&D department was included. To account for innovative capabilities apart from explicit R&D, it was included whether or not firms employed specialized personnel for development, construction or design of products and services. These three measures account for the presence of internal R&D. Also, one binary variable was included, measuring the usage of external R&D. Two variables measured the presence of organizational learning practices. This included the existence of employee suggestion schemes or idea management systems and whether or not a systematic planning and management of innovation processes had been reported. In addition to these binary variables, one continuous variable accounted for the share of skilled employees as a central criterion from the diversified quality production approach.

To analyse flexibility profiles, four categorical variables were included (see Table 10.2). In the CATI questionnaire the respondents were asked to evaluate the importance of several flexibility practices in situations of workload change. This included: flexibility via working time arrangements, flexibility via shifting workers between workplaces, flexibility via outsourcing of previously internally provided functions, and flexibility via temporary agency workers. The answer scale ranged from 1, 'Very important', to 6, 'Not important'.

Latent class analysis (LCA) was performed in order to reveal distinct profiles. Two independent LCA models were computed – one for innovative capability profiles (see Kirchner *et al.* 2012) and another one for flexibility profiles (see Kirchner 2013). The results suggest a four-class solution to be best suited for flexibility profiles and a five-class solution for innovative capability profiles.

Results

In this section the empirical results are reported and discussed. First, the five innovative capability profiles are described and their basic distributions across firm sizes and industries are reported. Second, the link between innovative capability and decentralized work organization (autonomy, responsibility and teamwork) is investigated. Third, the four flexibility profiles are introduced in a similar fashion. In a last step, the results of the two LCA solutions are combined to show the relation between the two separate profile solutions as well as to reveal the general relevance of combinations between flexibility and innovative capability profiles.

Five Innovative Capability Profiles

Table 10.2 displays the underlying firm size and industry distributions of the five innovative capability profiles. The table shows the two service industries and the four major subindustries of manufacturing. To support the interpretation, additional measures for skill levels were employed, including the share of unskilled employees as well as the share of high-skilled employees (holding a university degree).

The five classes are described as the following innovative capability profiles:

Profile A1 – High-skilled employee, high capability profile. The first profile is characterized by a high level of innovative capability in almost all included variables. Overall, 17 per cent of all establishments are grouped into this profile. In comparison with all other classes, the average share of high-skilled employees is the largest while the average share of skilled employees is the smallest. Profile A1 establishments are significantly more frequent in the I&C industry and in larger establishments.

Profile A2 – Skilled employee, high capability profile. The second profile covers 30 per cent of all cases. Like A1 it shows a high level of innovative capability. In contrast to A1 the average share of skilled employees is much higher, whereas the share of high-skilled employees is lower. Compared with other profiles, A2 establishments show a stronger association with manufacturing industry and large establishments.

Profile X – Externally dependent R&D profile. The third profile accounts for 12 per cent of the establishments in the sample. The share of skilled employees is similar to that in A2. In contrast, profile X displays the lowest values for the three variables measuring internal R&D, while the value for external R&D usage exceeds all other profiles. Also, the share of establishments reporting innovation and idea management is very high in this profile. Profile X establishments are most likely to be found in the FIA industry.

Profile B1 – Low capability profile. With a share of 27 per cent of all cases, the fourth innovative capability profile B1 is the second most frequent. The share of skilled employees is similar to profile A2. At the same time, B1 establishments display low values for almost all observed innovative capability variables. This profile displays the lowest share of idea management and innovation management. The B1 profile is most frequent in smaller establishments.

Profile B2 – Low-skilled employee profile. The fifth and final profile accounts for 15 per cent of the establishments in the sample. In several

Table 10.2 Size and industry distributions of innovative capability profiles

| | Innovative capability profiles | | | | |
	Profile A1	Profile A2	Profile X	Profile B1	Profile B2
Description					
Profile name	High-skilled employee, high capability	Skilled employee, high capability	Externally dependent R&D	Low capability	Low-skilled employee
Industry					
M. of food products, beverages, tobacco	14%	25%	7%	29%	24%
M. of textiles, wood, paper	9%	38%	5%	33%	16%
M. of chemicals, pharmaceutics, rubber, basic metal	13%	39%	14%	13%	22%
M. of machinery and equipment	15%	37%	6%	32%	10%
I&C	49%	3%	2%	23%	23%
FIA	0%	15%	56%	24%	5%
Establishment size					
20–49	15%	19%	8%	41%	16%
40–249	17%	39%	16%	14%	15%
250+	24%	49%	17%	3%	7%
Total	17%	30%	12%	27%	15%

Source: CATI Establishment Survey 2010. Own depiction. Row percentages: differences in totals due to rounding. 'M. of' short for 'Manufacturing of'.

respects B2 establishments are similar to B1 establishments since both profiles display an overall low level of innovative capability. The main differences are a higher share of idea management and a lower share of skilled employees. At the same time the average share of low-skilled employees is astoundingly high (53 per cent). Compared with A2 establishments, B2 establishments are more often to be found in the I&C industry. They are also prominent in two subindustries of manufacturing (manufacture of food products, beverages and tobacco as well as manufacture of chemicals, pharmaceuticals, rubber and basic metals).

Table 10.3 summarizes the basic characteristics of the five innovative capability profiles. Overall, the findings reveal a considerable diversity. The differences are due mostly to the employee skill level, which overlaps with a high/low-capability difference.

Table 10.3 Characteristics of innovative capability profiles

	Innovative capability profile				
	Profile A1	Profile A2	Profile X	Profile B1	Profile B2
Description					
Profile names	High-skilled employee, high capability	Skilled employee, high capability	Externally dependent R&D	Low capability	Low-skilled employee
Summarized aspects					
Internal R&D	High	High	Low	Low	Low
External R&D	High	High	High	Low	Low
Organizational learning	High	High	High	Very low	Low
Employee skill level	High-skilled	Skilled	Skilled	Skilled	Low-skilled

Source: CATI Establishment Survey 2010. Simplified depiction based on results reported by Kirchner *et al.* (2012). Interpretation of relative average share of variables by profile.

The analysis reveals two highly innovative profiles: profile A1 reflects the growing importance of high-skilled employees in the labour market and developments in the IT industry. The second highly innovative profile, A2, resembles the diversified quality production pattern in major respects and is the dominant profile in manufacturing industry. Innovative capability profile X establishments share several similarities with A2 but lack in-house R&D. The remaining innovative capability profiles of lower capability are divided by skill levels. While B1 relies on skilled employees, the innovative capability profile B2 reflects the persistence of low-skilled work within the German economy.

Innovative capability and decentralized work organization

Innovative capability resides predominantly at the firm level. However, its characteristics are connected with specific properties of the workplaces within more or less innovative firms (Lam 2005). It is assumed that innovative capability is fostered by decentralized work organization. This reflects the discussion about new organizational structures, which has also been a key issue in labour process approaches. Most important here are the autonomy granted to employees and the responsibility expected of them – especially in various forms of teamwork, as this is a key element of organizational structure (Vidal 2011). Research has shown the coexistence of various workplace types within national economies (Lorenz and

Valeyre 2005). To some extent these findings are aligned with research on the resilience of low-tech industries and low-skilled work in Germany (Hirsch-Kreinsen *et al.* 2012).

In the CATI survey, respondents were asked to indicate their agreement with statements on the autonomy and responsibility of employees as well as on the presence of teamwork. Table 10.4 depicts the average means of autonomy, responsibility and teamwork for each innovative capability profile. The results show that the profiles A1 and A2, of high innovative capability, display higher levels of autonomy, responsibility and teamwork. Inversely, for the two profiles of low innovative capability, B1 and B2, overall lower levels of these three aspects were revealed. Accordingly, a significant difference between high and low innovative capability can be assumed in terms of labour processes, characterized by very different levels of autonomy and responsibility. In this respect, innovative capability profile X cases display a particularly interesting pattern: while teamwork and responsibility show high levels, autonomy levels are closer to those of the low-capability profiles. This finding indicates that in profile X cases teamwork and the shifting of responsibilities do not come with higher levels of autonomy. This resembles the neotaylorist pattern identified in

Table 10.4 Additional information on autonomy, responsibility and teamwork by innovative capability profiles

	Work organization		
	Autonomy 'Employees can try new things at their workplace.'	**Responsibility** 'Employees take on a major share of responsibility in allocation of work and problem-solving.'	**Teamwork** 'Work tasks are coordinated and assessed within workgroups.'
Innovative capability profile			
High-skilled employee, high capability	0.31	0.22	0.19
Skilled employee, high capability	0.16	0.19	0.16
Externally dependent R&D	−0.16	0.06	0.17
Low capability	−0.07	−0.08	−0.41
Low-skilled employee	−0.17	−0.19	−0.29
p-value χ^2-test	0.02	0.01	0.00

Source: CATI Establishment Survey 2010. Own calculation. Legend – agreement with the listed statement: 1 – fully agree, 6 – fully disagree. Standardized means. High value indicates a high average agreement.

the literature. Accordingly, the findings on innovative capabilities can be linked directly with assumptions made in the labour process approach.

Four Flexibility Profiles

The findings on industry and size distributions of the four flexibility profiles are reported in Table 10.5. The average importance of flexibility practices is summarized in Table 10.6.

The characteristics of the profiles can be summarized as follows:

Dual flexibility profile. This flexibility profile is determined by the highest levels of importance for all four items. It thus combines the practices from the internal and external dimension of flexibility. With about 40 per cent of all cases, it is also the most widespread profile. Regarding industry and size, the dual flexibility profile is dominant in larger establishments and in two subindustries of manufacturing (the manufacture of chemicals, pharmaceuticals, rubber and basic metal; and also the manufacture of machinery and equipment).

Table 10.5 Size and industry distributions of flexibility profiles

	Flexibility profile			
	Dual flexibility profile	Internal flexibility profile	Low flexibility profile	External flexibility profile
Industry				
M. of food products, beverages, tobacco	22%	62%	0%	15%
M. of textiles, wood, paper	42%	44%	0%	14%
M. of chemicals, pharmaceutics, rubber, basic metal	53%	30%	0%	16%
M. of machinery and equipment	56%	33%	1%	10%
I&C	9%	36%	46%	9%
FIA	4%	0%	93%	3%
Establishment size				
20–49 employees	29%	48%	15%	9%
50–249 employees	48%	20%	19%	13%
250+ employees	66%	12%	8%	14%
Total	40%	33%	16%	11%

Source: CATI Establishment Survey 2010. Own depiction. Row percentages; differences in totals due to rounding. 'M. of' short for 'Manufacturing of'.

Table 10.6 Average importance of flexibility practices by flexibility profiles

	Flexibility profile			
	Dual flexibility profile	Internal flexibility profile	Low flexibility profile	External flexibility profile
Flexibility practice				
Working time flexibility	High	High	Low	Low
Shifting of workers between workplaces	High	High	Low	Low
Flexibility via outsourcing	High	Low	Low	High
Flexibility via temporary agency work	High	Low	Low	High

Source: CATI Establishment Survey 2010. Simplified depiction based on results reported by Kirchner 2013. Interpretation of relative average importance by profile.

Internal flexibility profile. The second flexibility profile displays a high importance of the two internal practices while both external practices are of lower average importance. A majority, 62 per cent, of the cases in the manufacture of food products, beverages and tobacco are assigned to this profile. The internal flexibility profile is also the most frequent profile for manufacture of textiles, wood and paper. For cases from the I&C industry it is the second most frequent profile, with 36 per cent. It is also the dominant profile for smaller establishments with 20 to 49 employees.

Low flexibility profile. The third flexibility profile is characterized by the lowest average importance levels of all four flexibility practices in question. A major share, 93 per cent, of all cases from the FIA industry belong to this profile. The low flexibility profile also covers the majority of cases in the I&C industry, whereas it is almost completely irrelevant in manufacturing industry. It can often be found in smaller establishments.

External flexibility profile. The fourth and last flexibility profile revealed by the LCA is defined by a high importance of the two external flexibility practices, namely outsourcing and temporary agency workers. The levels of these two variables are similar to those of dual flexibility profile cases. Both internal variables however show considerably lower average values. With an 11 per cent share of all cases, this profile is the least widespread. It is most present in larger manufacturing establishments.

The distribution of flexibility profiles shows a strong sectoral diversity. The FIA industry stands out, with low flexibility as its dominant profile. Low-profile cases challenge the traditional approaches as they indicate a segment of structural inflexibility in terms of the observed items. In contrast, manufacturing industry is characterized by an absence of the low flexibility profile while the dual flexibility and the internal flexibility profiles account for the largest share. The findings show that a single-sided usage of external flexibility is uncommon. However, while many firms still follow internal flexibility practices, a major portion combine them with external flexibility practices. This finding marks a substantial transformation of the German firm-level pattern, which was traditionally believed to be incompatible with external flexibility measures.

Relation of Innovative Capability and Flexibility Profiles

The results presented above reveal a substantial diversity of innovative capabilities as well as of flexibility profiles. In this subsection, the actual relation of innovative capabilities and flexibility profiles can be assessed.

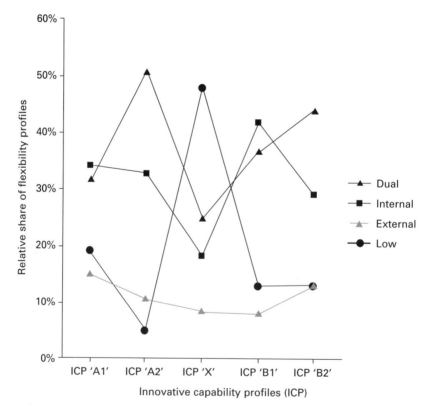

Figure 10.1 Relative shares of flexibility profiles.
Source: CATI survey. Based on 978 cases.

In Figure 10.1, row percentages by innovative capability profile are reported. For each innovative capability profile all shares of flexibility profiles amount to 100 per cent. Accordingly, the relative occurrence of flexibility profiles can be assessed. The external flexibility profile runs on a low level for all innovative capability profiles. A similar pattern can be seen for the low flexibility profile. Only in relation to the X profile, which depends on external R&D, can a high share be found. For this combination the low profile is dominant, with almost 50 per cent of all profile X cases. The results for the remaining innovative capability profiles show a high share of the internal and the dual flexibility profile. The percentages of the two profiles are fairly similar for A1 and B1 cases, with around 30 to 40 per cent. In contrast, for A2 cases the dual profile is dominant, with about 50 per cent, whereas the internal profile only accounts for about 30 per cent. A similar pattern can be found for B2 cases, yet percentages differ since the share of low- and external flexibility profile cases is larger.

Summary and Conclusion

The findings presented on flexibility and innovative capability profiles underline the coexistence of different firm-level patterns within the German economy. The analysis shows substantial differences due to firm size and industry membership. This has implications for political economy research as well as for labour process research. The findings show a fundamental diversity within the German institutional framework. While one profile resembles central characteristics of the traditional German firm-level pattern that can be associated with the diversified quality production pattern, the four remaining profiles each account for diverging economic developments and respective sectors of the German economy. Similarly, the flexibility profiles reveal a coexistence of different approaches which are coupled only loosely with four of the five innovative capability profiles.

The findings presented show the imprints of the major transformations in firms and at the workplaces that have also been observed in the labour process literature. This includes new patterns of flexibility via the externalization of work and employment, as well as differences in autonomy and responsibility in several profiles of innovative capability. The empirically identified diversity also underlines the emergence and coexistence of several organizational forms within the German economy. The results also indicate that each of the profiles found appears to be characterized by specific labour processes.

The dominant innovative capability profile in the manufacturing sector shows a tendency to post-taylorist organizational forms. This profile is also more frequently twinned with the dual flexibility profile which combines external and internal flexibility practices. Considering the underlying distribution of both profiles, the results reveal that large manufacturing firms in Germany still show some basic traits of the diversified quality production concept. However, the same firms appear to have integrated external flexibility practices. Thus in the 'heartland' of the German economy (Crouch 2005) resides a transformed firm-level pattern that in turn indicates a transformed German model on the institutional level. In this heartland basic pillars of the industrial relations systems still prevail, but appear to have co-evolved and to tend to coexist with the transformed dual flexibility pattern (for more detail see Kirchner 2013). Whereas for example collective bargaining has been found to have no influence on temporary agency workers, works councils have been found to increase its usage to protect the core workforce (see Promberger 2006).

Overall the presented findings, the literature on diversity and the literature on transformation all echo the results of an early branch of the political economy debate. Hollingsworth *et al.* (1994) pointed out that sectoral patterns are the key to understanding diversity as well as similarity within and across countries. The coexistence of different profiles appears to be embedded in different sectors within one economy. This analysis implies that it is this very embeddedness that allows for a coexistence of different forms of the labour process. In turn, labour processes express and reflect the specific conditions of sectors that mark the boundaries of industries and thus define the reach of sector-specific institutional conditions.

Notes

1 The authors are grateful to Lutz Bellmann and the whole MINO-team for support and cooperation in the project. They would also like to thank Marc Casper for criticism and advice on earlier versions of this chapter. The research presented in this chapter is based on a joint project of the University of Hamburg and the Institute for Employment Research (IAB) funded by the German Federal Ministry of Education and Research (BMBF) and the European Union's European Social Fund (ESF).

2 The term 'establishment' differs from the notion of a company or firm: A firm can consist of several establishments (plant, subsidiary, headquarters). In many cases the terms 'establishment' and 'firm' coincide

as they are single-establishment firms. For this analysis establishments are treated as the primary organization-level where practices and strategies are realized.

3 In the survey, interviewers provided the following explanation of the term 'qualified jobs': 'Qualified jobs require accomplished vocational training or a comparable professional training or adequate job experience.'

REFERENCES

Amable, B. (2003) *The Diversity of Modern Capitalism.* Oxford: Oxford University Press.

Aschhoff, B. *et al.* (2008) *Innovation in Germany. Results of the German Innovation Survey 2007.* Mannheim: Centre for European Economic Research (ZEW).

Barrett, R. and A. Rainnie (2002) 'What's So Special About Small Firms?: Developing an Integrated Approach to Analysing Small Firm Industrial Relations', *Work, Employment & Society* 16:415–31.

Berghoff, H. (2006) 'The End of Family Business? The Mittelstand and German Capitalism in Transition, 1949–2000', *Business History Review* 80:263–95.

Boes, A. and K. Marrs (2003) 'Arbeitsbeziehungen in der IT-Industrie. Interessenhandeln der Beschäftigten', *Arbeitspapier des Projekts ARB-IT2*, No. 1. München: ISF München.

Bolton, S.C. and M. Houlihan (2009) 'Work, Workplaces and Workers: The Contemporary Experience', in *Work Matters,* edited by S.C. Bolton and M. Houlihan. Basingstoke: Palgrave Macmillan.

Bouncken, R.B., M. Bornewasser and L. Bellmann, (2012) *Die neue Rolle der Zeitarbeit in Deutschland.* München: Hampp.

Crouch, C. (2005) *Capitalist Diversity and Change: Recombinant Governance and Institutional Pioneers.* Oxford: Oxford University Press.

Crouch, C., M. Schröder, and H. Voelzkow (2009) 'Regional and sectoral varieties of capitalism', *Economy and Society* 38:654–78.

Davis-Blake, A. and B. Uzzi (1993) 'Determinants of Employment Externalization: A Study of Temporary Workers and Independent Contractors', *Administrative Science Quarterly* 38:195–223.

Eurostat (2008) 'NACE Rev. 2. Statistical Classification of Economic Activities in the European Community', Methodologies and Working Papers No. KS-RA-07–015-EN-N. Luxembourg: Office for Official Publications of the European Communities.

Görzig, B., A. Kaminiarz and A. Stephan (2005) 'Wie wirkt sich Outsourcing auf den Unternehmenserfolg aus? Neue Evidenz', *Schmollers Jahrbuch (Journal of Applied Social Science Studies / Zeitschrift für Wirtschafts- und Sozialwissenschaften)* 125:489–507.

Hall, P.A. and D. Soskice (2001) 'An Introduction to Varieties of Capitalism', pp. 1–68 in *Varieties of Capitalism: The Institutional Foundations of Comparative Advantage,* edited by P. Hall and D. Soskice. Oxford: Oxford University Press.

Hall, P.A. and K. Thelen (2009) 'Institutional Change in Varieties of Capitalism', *Socio-Economic Review* 7:7–34.

▶

Hampson, I. and A. Junor (2010) 'Putting the Process Back in: Rethinking Service Sector Skill', *Work, Employment & Society* 24:526–45.

Harley, B. (2001) 'Team Membership and the Experience of Work in Britain: An Analysis of the WERS98 Data', *Work, Employment & Society* 15:721–42.

Hassel, Anke 2012) 'The Paradox of Liberalization — Understanding Dualism and the Recovery of the German Political Economy', *British Journal of Industrial Relations*, first published online 20.09.2012).

Heidenreich, M. (2009) 'Innovation Patterns and Location of European Low- and Medium-Technology Industries', *Research Policy* 38:483–94.

Herrigel, G. (1996) *Industrial Constructions: The Sources of German Industrial Power.* Cambridge: Cambridge University Press.

Herrigel, G. (2010) *Manufacturing Possibilities. Creative Action and Industrial Recomposition in the United States, Germany, and Japan.* Oxford: Oxford University Press.

Herrmann, A.M. (2008) 'Rethinking the Link Between Labour Market Flexibility and Corporate Competitiveness: A Critique of the Institutionalist Literature', *Socio-Economic Review* 6:637–69.

Hesmondhalgh, D. and S. Baker (2011) *Creative Labour: Media Work in Three Cultural Industries.* London: Routledge.

Hirsch-Kreinsen, H. (2008) '"Low-Tech" Innovations', *Industry & Innovation* 15:19–43.

Hirsch-Kreinsen, H., P. Ittermann and J. Abel (2012) 'Industrielle Einfacharbeit: Kern eines sektoralen Produktions- und Arbeitssystems', *Industrielle Beziehungen* 19:187–210.

Hollingsworth, J.R. (1997) 'Continuities and Changes in Social Systems of Production', pp. 265–10 in *Contemporary Capitalism. The Embeddedness of Institutions,* edited by J.R. Hollingsworth and R. Boyer. Cambridge: Cambridge University Press.

Hollingsworth, J.R., P.C. Schmitter and W. Streeck (1994) *Governing Capitalist Economies. Governing Capitalist Economies.* New York: Oxford University Press.

Jürgens, U. (2004) 'An Elusive model: Diversified Quality Production and the Transformation of the German Automobile Industry', *Competition & Change* 8:411–23.

Jürgens, U., M. Krzywdzinski and C. Teipen (2006) 'Changing Work and Employment Relations in German Industries – Breaking Away from the German Model?', WZB Discussion Paper SP III 2006–32. Berlin: WZB.

Kalleberg, A.L. (2001) 'Organizing Flexibility: The Flexible Firm in a New Century', *British Journal of Industrial Relations* 39:479–504.

Kinkel, S. and G. Lay (2003) 'Fertigungstiefe – Ballast oder Kapital? Stand und Effekte von Out- und Insourcing im Verarbeitenden Gewerbe Deutschlands', *Mitteilungen aus der Produktionsinnovationserhebung,* No. 30. Karlsruhe: Fraunhofer ISI.

Kirchner, S. (2013) 'Embedded Flexibility Strategies and Diversity Within National Institutional Frameworks: How Many Flexibility Profiles Are in the German Model?', *Management Revue* 24:12–29.

Kirchner, S., Beyer, J. and U. Ludwig (2012) 'Wie viel Heterogenität gibt es im, Modell Deutschland'? Zur Verbindung von betrieblichen Beschäftigungssystemen und Profilen der Innovationsfähigkeit', *Industrielle Beziehungen* 19:211–35.

▶

Lam, A. (2005) 'Organizational Innovation', pp. 115–47 in *The Oxford Handbook of Innovation*, edited by J. Fagerberg, D.C. Mowery and R.R. Nelson. Oxford: Oxford University Press.

Lane, C. (1995) *Industry and Society in Europe. Stability and Change in Britain, Germany and France*. Aldershot: Edward Elgar.

Lorenz, E. and A. Valeyre (2005) 'Organisational Innovation, Human Resource Management and Labour Market Structure: A Comparison of the EU-15', *Journal of Industrial Relations* 47:424–42.

Mayer-Ahuja, N. and H. Wolf (2007) 'Beyond the Hype. Working in the German Internet Industry', *Critical Sociology* 33:73–99.

OECD (2003) *Science, Technology and Industry Scoreboard 2003 – Towards a Knowledge-Based Economy*. Paris.

Palier, B. and K. Thelen (2010) 'Institutionalizing Dualism: Complementarities and Change in France and Germany', *Politics & Society* 38:119–48.

Pavitt, K. (1984) 'Sectoral Patterns of Technical Change: Towards a Taxonomy and a Theory', *Research Policy* 13:343–73.

Promberger, M. (2006) 'Leiharbeit – Flexibilität und Prekarität in der betrieblichen Praxis', *WSI Mitteilungen* 56:263–9.

Pruijt, H. (2003) 'Teams Between Neo-Taylorism and Anti-Taylorism', *Economic and Industrial Democracy* 24:77–101.

Pulignano, V. (2002) 'Dynamic Forms of Control at Work: A Research Note on Integrated Supply Chains in the Motor Industry in Southern Italy', *Work, Employment & Society* 16:185–96.

Rammer, C. *et al.* (2010) *Innovationsverhalten der deutschen Wirtschaft. Indikatorenbericht zur Innovationserhebung 2009*. Mannheim: Zentrum für Europäische Wirtschaftsforschung (ZEW).

Schmidt, N. (2010) 'Auswirkungen des Strukturwandels der Wirtschaft auf den Bildungsstand der Bevölkerung', *Wirtschaft und Statistik* 6:537–51.

Sorge, A. (1991) 'Strategic Fit and the Societal Effect: Interpreting Cross-National Comparisons of Technology, Organization and Human Resources', *Organization Studies* 12:161–90.

Sorge, A. and W. Streeck (1988) 'New Technology and Industrial Relations: The Case for an Extended Perspective', pp. 19–47 in *New Technology and Industrial Relations*, edited by R. Hyman and W. Streeck. Oxford: Basil Blackwell.

Streeck, W. (1991) 'On the Institutional Conditions of Diversified Quality Production', pp. 21–61 in *Beyond Keynesianism: The Socio-Economics of Production and Full Employment*, edited by E. Matzner and W. Streeck. Aldershot: Edward Elgar.

Streeck, W. (1997) 'German Capitalism: Does It Exist? Can It Survive?', pp. 33–54 in *Political Economy of Modern Capitalism. Mapping Convergence and Diversity.* edited by C. Crouch W and Streeck. Thousand Oaks, CA: Sage.

Sturdy, A., I. Grugulis and H. Willmott. (2001) *Customer Service: Empowerment and Entrapment*. Basingstoke: Palgrave Macmillan.

Thompson, P. and D. Van den Broek (2010) 'Managerial Control and Workplace Regimes: An Introduction', *Work, Employment & Society* 24:1–12.

▶

Thompson, P. and S. Vincent (2010) 'Labour Process Theory and Critical Realism', pp. 47–69 in *Working Life: Renewing Labour Process Analysis,* edited by P. Thompson and C. Smith. Basingstoke: Palgrave Macmillan.

Vidal, M. (2011) 'Reworking Postfordism: Labor Process Versus Employment Relations', *Sociology Compass* 5:273–86.

Warhurst, C. and P. Thompson (1998) 'Hands, Hearts and Minds: Changing Work and Workers at the End of the Century', pp. 1–24 in *Workplaces of the Future,* edited by P. Thompson and C. Warhurst. London: Macmillan.

Whitley, R. (1999) *Divergent Capitalisms: The Social Structuring and Change of Business Systems.* Oxford: Oxford University Press.

Coordinated Divergences: Changes in Collective Bargaining Systems and Their Labour Market Implications in Korea

11

Hyunji Kwon and Sanghoon Lim

The decentralization of collective bargaining systems is one of the most significant phenomena in contemporary employment relations. It has drawn scholarly attention as one of the key factors not only of growing divergences in employment practices but also of increasing labour market inequality in most advanced economies (Katz and Darbishire 2000; Western and Rosenfeld 2011). While many Western economies have experienced the decentralization of collective bargaining systems over the last few decades (Katz 1993; Traxler 1996; Wallerstein and Western 2000), Korea, a stronghold of highly fragmented enterprise-level bargaining, has seen a reverse trend towards centralization in some key industry sectors (Jeong 2001; Lee 2011). Prompted by the Asian Financial Crisis in the late 1990s that set extraordinary challenges for labour, fragmented enterprise unions in Korea sought solidarity to enhance their organizational power and protect jobs. Industrial unionism was an answer particularly in some key union sectors including the banking industry, on which our case analysis focuses in this chapter. Our primary objective here is to discuss the implications of this unusual structural change towards increasingly diverging organizational-level employment practices.

The union-led experiment of sectoral bargaining in Korea attracts our attention not simply because of its idiosyncratic diversion from the universal trend of decentralization but for the following two reasons as well. First, while the effects of decentralization on employment relations have been widely documented, we do know less about the implications of centralization under circumstances where the industrial relations system is highly fragmented and the business system is moving quickly towards a liberal market economy (Korczynski 1997). Second, the movement of the unions towards building industrial bargaining in Korea emerged in organizational and institutional conditions very unlikely to favour centralization, and it is worth examining whether a significant level of coordination is likely under such circumstances.

In fact, the transformation of the bargaining structure from enterprise-based to industry-based arose at the end of the twentieth century in Korea when unions' bargaining power, a key factor in determining the centralization of bargaining structure (Katz 1993; Katz *et al.* 2008; Lee 2011), was declining rapidly. Overall union density in Korea had tumbled from 20 per cent to 10 per cent over the previous 10 years (Ministry of Employment and Labor database: www.molab.go.kr) and was in peril of – further decrease as the Asian Financial Crisis led to major corporate restructuring and labour market reforms. Furthermore, the institutional base for sectoral bargaining was weak. Virtually no employers' associations were present at the sectoral level when the industrial unions emerged, which implies a lack of employer-side bargaining partners who would bring their collective interests to the bargaining table. Individual employers at the time preferred to maintain firm-based bargaining, holding unfavourable attitudes toward multi-employer bargaining. Moreover, both unions and collective bargaining had been rooted in the country's firm-based industrial relations system before this time and both union leaders and members, particularly in the large-firm sector, often benefited from the existing firm-based system, enjoying their insider status.

These factors would appear to constrain the movement toward industrial relations and limit unions' ability to standardize employment practices to a large extent. In fact, some commentators have taken a speculative view of this new union initiative and are pessimistic about its prospects (Lee 2004, 2011; Cho 2009). They have claimed that the seemingly new sectoral bargaining systems remain basically the same as the previous fragmented one (Lee 2004; Joo 2006; Cho 2009). This view may seem plausible if one considers that the country has been quickly picking up the characteristics of a liberal market economy over the past decade by deregulating both labour and product markets. Although some students have classified Korea as a 'Northeast Asian coordinated market economy' alongside Japan, as examples of economies with group-based coordination (Crouch 2005), the category hardly seems to fit the country. Apart from its recent move towards a liberal capitalism, the country has never had solid labour market institutions, such as beyond-firm-level collective bargaining or any of its substitutes (like the Japanese Shunto and Keiretsu networks) that would make for coordination by social partners. Rather, since the early 1990s studies have reported firms' increasing levels of flexibility in their choices of employment practices, including human resource management systems, in Korea's liberalized market (Yang 2011). Organizational choices have become increasingly market-oriented and consequently divergent within the national economy, as a stream of political–economic and employment relations theories have suggested (Deakin *et al.* 2000; Katz and Darbishire 2000). In this context, Korea's deep-rooted and predominantly fragmented firm-based industrial relations could be further entrenched, making the long-term success of the changes in the bargaining structure largely uncertain.

However, our view of the centralization of the bargaining structure has a subtle difference from the conventional perspectives. We agree that the new sectoral bargaining system will allow firm-level bargaining partners ample space to complement and modify sectoral agreements, given the aforementioned unfavourable conditions for sectoral bargaining. However, we do not presume that structural changes towards centralization (that is changes from firm-based bargaining to a sectoral bargaining structure) necessarily generate forms traditionally associated with centralized bargaining (that is multi-employer bargaining aiming to standardize wages and working conditions within the bargaining unit).

The new initiative should not be simply assessed by the degree of standardization that sectoral agreements would achieve in centralized bargaining, for standardization might not be set forth as a union's strategic goal. Instead, both central and local leadership may consider centralization of bargaining structure a vehicle for enhancing coordination, seeking a common framework for minimum standards and leaving detailed negotiations to locals. This reasoning is possible because the actors are well aware of the embeddedness of decentralized industrial relations and the internal and external pressures of decentralization. In this vein, we suggest that Korea's emerging pattern of sectoral bargaining be characterized as a 'flexible and coordinated' one. And by making room for coordination, it might also slow down the fast-growing variations in employment practices across firms within the national economy and contain labour market inequality.

We will examine our propositions by using the case of the new sectoral bargaining in the Korean banking industry. The banking industry offers us an ideal case because the industry has made the most stable transformation of the bargaining structures in Korea over the past decade. Moreover, its new coordinated sectoral-level bargaining has had considerable influence on firms' policy choices. A good example is the sectoral-level negotiation for a framework agreement of fixed-term-contract employment that has gradually evolved over several years. The case will show that both local employers and union leaders at the firm level, pressurized by the sectoral bargaining, complied with the coordinated framework agreement on the use of non-standard employment but were still allowed diverse choices of specific practices depending on their particular circumstances. This case will enable us to examine the implications of an unusual re-regulatory institutional change for increasingly diverging organizational choices.

Background: An Unusual Path from Enterprise-Based to Sectoral Industrial Relations Systems in Korea

The traditional industrial relations structure in Korea is extremely decentralized. Enterprise unions are predominant and bargaining activities take place mainly at the firm level. Despite a lack of official statistics, the coverage of collective agreements is known to be very similar to union coverage because there is virtually no firm-level agreement that extends to workers in non-union firms within or beyond the sector the firm belongs to (Kwon 2011). In addition, Korea's fragmented employment system, shaped under a repressive labour regime by an authoritarian government in the stage of industrial development from the 1960s to 1980s, traditionally lacks a societal-level coordination mechanism because of direct state control over union activities. Tripartism began only very recently as one of the socio-political responses to a serious economic crisis in the late 1990s. Under this decentralized and uncoordinated structure, unions and management are more likely to face conflicts at the workplace level.

There are of course some advantages in an enterprise-based industrial relations system. They include a union's better access to business information, its better understanding of workplace issues, and a close relationship between union leadership and members which might facilitate participatory management and potentially more flexible responses to internal and external changes at the firm level.

However, under an enterprise-based system, each individual union, particularly small ones, may have difficulties maintaining the balance of power against its employers. In addition, resources between unions tend to be uneven and large-scale enterprise unions with resources often concentrate on improving the wages and working conditions of their own members rather than engaging in a broader socio-political agenda that would cover the working class as a whole. Inequalities between union and non-union sectors as well as within union sectors could grow in this context, as the rent-seeking behaviour of powerful unions might increase such unions' monopoly effect. Without an effective coordination mechanism, it is much harder for thousands of enterprise unions to unite for a collective voice. In addition, an enterprise-based system does not motivate individual unions to organize workers beyond the firm boundary to include those workers with only a loose relationship with a firm, namely non-standard workers who do not have a permanent or full-time employment contract with their user company; this is particularly problematic when the union sector is small and the vast majority of workforce is not unionized, which is the case in Korea. In fact, Korea belongs to a group with the lowest union density among OECD countries (in 2009 only 10.0 per cent). Though the explosive labour movement in the summer of 1987 increased union density from 15.7 per cent in June 1987 to the peak of 19.8 per cent in 1989, in the 1990s union density started to fall dramatically, down to 12 per cent in 1996 and 11 per cent in 2002.

It is also noteworthy that the composition of union membership in Korea has been biased towards male regular employees. Worker representation through unions is concentrated in male regular employees who are 30 years old and older working in the large-firm sector. Non-standard workers, who now consist of more than 30 per cent of the workforce according to the official statistical source (Economically Active Population Survey 2000–12), have had virtually no chance to be represented by any unions.

These conditions in Korea's labour relations have constrained unions' ability to engage in social movement unionism and have locked many of them in short-term labour pursuits. Discussions and debates that shifted from the extremely decentralized system to centralized types never ceased throughout the 1990s. In particular, many union leaders from the progressive union camp, including some affiliates of the Korean Confederation of Trade Unions (KCTU) who emerged with the growth of the country's socio-political democratic arena in the 1990s, adhered to a strong ideological orientation towards industrial unionism as a tool to achieve socially engaged unionism. However, this objective never actually appeared on union policy agendas until the mid 1990s, mainly because of the significant variations among its affiliated enterprise unions in terms of their resources, interests and bargaining power.

The change that triggered the shift to centralized bargaining came from the outside, with the 1997 Asian Financial Crisis. Fragmented enterprise unions found themselves vulnerable to an unpredicted level of environmental changes, and decentralized bargaining turned out to be inadequate for providing a response to the industrial and corporate restructuring, mass redundancies and deregulation that would directly affect members' job security. Organizing new unions at the enterprise level also became harder as management gained greater power in post-crisis workplaces. In addition, firms held back from new regular hirings, and a significant segment of regular positions were replaced and filled with temporary workers. Transformation to industrial unions was seen as an opportunity to sustain and revitalize the union movement in post-crisis Korea.

In addition, an institutional arena opened up within which unions could engage in the national policy discussion. This was directly linked to industrial and corporate restructuring and motivated the fragmented unions to unite. Faced with the new set of social problems resulting from the fiscal austerity and restructuring programs,[1] the government took an institutional approach to getting social consent. It also started to discuss and implement new social and welfare policies for improving the social safety net as a means to reduce discontent in response to the restructuring programmes. A tripartite committee called the Economic and Social Development Commission (hereafter the Tripartite Commission) was established in 1998 and soon reached an agreement in the form of a 'grand social pact'. Although this commission was viewed critically by some unions, numerous labour market and welfare policy agendas were being tabled and unions simply could not lose the opportunities to minimize the costs of restructuring and improve social security for their workers.

This change required unions to seek better structures in order to be able to get more involved in socio-economic policymaking. For example, the banking industry, viewed as the epicentre of the crisis, had to undertake massive changes including a series of mergers and acquisitions, privatization, industrial deregulation, and the opening of the market to foreign investment (Kwon 2008). The Tripartite Commission created a special subcommittee to deal with these restructuring issues of banking, demanding from the unions a coherent and collective response. This prompted union leaderships to take the centralization option more seriously and quickened their pace towards transformation from a union federation to an industrial union called the Korean Financial Industry Union.

The shift to an industrial union was relatively successful in three sectors: metals, hospital and banking. However, both the pace of development of the new industrial unions and their effectiveness have been varied. The most stable and steady progress has been observed in the banking sector. The new Financial Industry Union, unlike the Metal Workers Union which has a stronger ideological objective to develop industrial unionism, for example, began with a relatively pragmatic approach when it had to deal with restructuring through downsizing, company closure, mergers and acquisitions, and industrial deregulation. The new leadership, being aware of the power relationship between the centre and the locals, did not push ahead with the centralization of resources and negotiations. Rather, it developed a set of new agendas that required legal changes or state-level negotiation and linked these with sectoral bargaining.

The internal composition of this industrial union was much more coherent compared with those of the hospital and metals sector unions: within the commercial banking industry locals, were relatively similar in terms of the size, worker composition and management relations, and they faced similar external challenges. In addition, a long-established, relatively cooperative labour–management relationship and the industrial union's flexible view on sectoral bargaining have facilitated a smoother transition to a sectoral system in the banking sector. This has offered a good example of how a union that shifts from a decentralized to a centralized structure can handle the pressure of decentralization and engage in coordinated bargaining.

The Logic of Coordinated and Flexible Bargaining

According to Katz *et al.* (2008), the degree of centralization of collective bargaining is determined by three factors. First, when a union holds stronger bargaining power it is more likely to have centralized bargaining. Unions that maintain a high level of unionization and hence strong bargaining power have a greater capacity to put pressure on employers to accept centralized bargaining. Second, bargaining structure is affected by public policies. In the US, for example, the National Labor Relations Board (NLRB) has the authority to determine union election units, which creates a range of different bargaining structures. Third, at the firm level, corporate governance structure also matters. When a large corporation maintains a centralized decision-making system, unions' preference is more likely to be for firm-level negotiation than for establishment-level bargaining, which yields a relatively more centralized bargaining structure.

The centralization of bargaining is supposed to present costs and benefits to both sides (Bae 2008, Lee and Jo 2007). Unions are often believed to benefit from centralized bargaining, but employers may also benefit as multi-employer bargaining allows them to avoid union whipsawing tactics. In addition, within the sectoral or national bargaining framework, employers can avoid or at least reduce an unnecessary level of competition. Hence, a structure, as Calmfors (1993) pointed out, is determined not solely by the union side but rather by the interaction between unions and employers. Further, employers continuously iterate their evaluation of the costs and benefits of their current bargaining system within its institutional setting, such as government policies and an extended coverage of collective agreements.

These general factors and conditions for centralized bargaining do not explain entirely why and how the centralized bargaining system emerged in contemporary Korea. For example, when Korean unions experimented with a centralized bargaining structure, they lost bargaining power owing to the economic crisis and many companies facing economic difficulties decentralized their governance structure.

In addition, the actual experiences of developed countries do not provide a plausible explanation in the Korean case. First, industrial bargaining emerged in very different historical contexts. Countries in Europe and North America started to build industrial bargaining structures in the early twentieth century (Bae *et al.* 2008) when the era of industrialization and mass production began. While in some countries such as Sweden a national framework was agreed between the unions and employers to prevent government intervention amid a series of intense industrial disputes, elsewhere governments or institutions initiated sectoral frameworks, as in Germany, France and the US. The most common context was the emergence of semi-skilled and unskilled workers in mass production systems in the manufacturing sector who challenged existing craft unions and became the major proponents of industrial bargaining. Korea did not share this process. Pursuing the state-led industrialization, the state manipulated the bargaining structure, reinforcing fragmented firm-based bargaining under the repressive labour regime(Choi 1993; Koo 2001).

Second, as mentioned previously, the recent changes in bargaining structure in Western countries are the opposite of those in Korea. Industrial agreements between industrial unions and employers' associations used to play a primary role in determining wages and other working conditions in most developed countries, while local agreements between local unions (or works councils) and individual employers were only complementary. However, since the 1980s, under pressure from global competition and marketization, the decentralization of bargaining has become widespread among developed countries (Schulten 2005); this has happened even in Sweden, where national wage bargaining played an important role in the whole national economy (Katzenstein 1985; Lash 1985; Freeman and Gibbons 1995; Whitley 1999). In contrast, Korea has observed the centralization of bargaining as many enterprise unions have become part of an industrial or regional union and industrial bargaining has expanded. As of 2011, according to the KCTU (2011), more than half of its member unions were engaged in industrial-level bargaining. Although the directions of the changes in Western developed countries and in Korea are different, the results of the changes seem similar. The decentralization of the countries with traditionally centralized bargaining is still organized through sectoral-, regional- and national-level framework agreements, while in Korea the centralization leaves space for each firm-level bargaining partner. The coexistence of industrial-level and firm-based (or local) agreements appears in both groups of countries.

The traditional dimension, centralized/decentralized bargaining, is of little use in explaining this dynamic. Instead, the commonality of changes between the two traditionally very different systems can be captured by the concept of 'coordinated bargaining'. Coordination refers to a process of information exchange, consultation, negotiation, decision-making and the exercise of sanctions against those who break joint agreements (Sako 1997:40). As Sisson and Marginson claim (2002), this can be applied to multi-employer collective bargaining at the sectoral level where employer organizations and trade unions negotiate `framework agreements' providing for minimum standards and broad parameters, and leaving detailed negotiations to the company level. As coordinated bargaining takes a range of levels and forms (Sisson and Marginson 2002, Traxler 2003), it is a rather murky concept (Sako 1997), but it needs to be differentiated from the traditional categories of collective bargaining, namely decentralized and centralized bargaining.

The concept of coordinated bargaining gives us meaningful insights to help us understand the recent changes in bargaining structure, especially coordinated decentralization (Traxler 1995). Although it is obvious that coordination is often institutionally reinforced, why unions and employers are involved in coordinated bargaining in a non-supportive institutional context still needs to be explained. Katz (1993) has argued insightfully that globalization calls for coordinated bargaining. Globalization increasingly demands flexibility and decentralization, which accordingly weakens union power and exacerbates societal inequality. Coordinated bargaining can be a response to globalization and its negative impact on organized labour and society in general. Following his logic, unions supposedly initiate coordinated bargaining in the interests of improved moral economy and solidarity among workers (Western *et al.* 2012). However, a bargaining structure is not constructed solely by unions but is a result of the interactions between unions and employers. In particular, unions hardly pursue coordinated bargaining when they are losing bargaining power. Thus, it is important to understand the advantages that coordinated bargaining offers to employers.

We pay particular attention to the interdependency between unions and employers as a motivation to generate coordinated bargaining. The concept of interdependency is defined as the extent to which participants in bargaining are aware of their partners when they make decisions and put them into action (Thomas 1957). Interdependency leads participants in bargaining to produce collective goods – the more interdependent participants are, the more likely they are to produce collective goods.

However, factors that affect interdependency have not been widely uncovered. Katzenstein's work on small states and their economic success (Katzenstein 1985) can provide some insights. The openness of the national economy can be regarded as one of the key factors of interdependency. Greater openness means that a national economy is more dependent on the world economy. This dependency leads employers and unions to seek mutual interest, achieving national competitiveness and collaborating with each other based on their understanding that industrial conflicts present uncertainty to their national economy. Thus, they become more aware of their partnership in bargaining. This reasoning enables us to formulate the proposition that globalization, challenging as it does both employers and unions, some of which are particularly vulnerable to environmental changes, tends to raise interdependency between the two parties by minimizing uncertainties and increasing mutual interests. Therefore, coordinated bargaining is an attempt to produce collective goods resulting from the interdependency between unions and employers as collective actors.

In post-crisis Korea, industrial unions and employers, particularly those in the banking sector, faced the external demand of corporate and industrial restructuring that neither of the parties had expected to happen. They shared the objective of undertaking relatively smooth restructuring by reducing organizational shock. For negotiations with the state agents, coordination between management and labour was inevitable. In the meantime, the proliferation of direct-hire temporary workers, the result of massive job cuts and the need to maintain a lean and cost-effective organization, was not carefully planned in most banks. It caused serious unintended internal problems (for example discrimination against temps, inequality and tensions between regular and temporary workers, and so on) and prompted criticism within society at large. However, neither individual employers nor local unions were able to improve this situation.

For employers, the priority was survival against market competition that became increasingly intensified with the changing industrial environment, with the movement towards megabanks (which cancelled out the market niches of individual banks), privatization, and the deregulation towards universal banking (which tore down the regulatory wall between commercial banks and investment banks) (Kwon 2008).

Meanwhile, each union (and later each local), organizing only regular workers, focused on the job security and short-term economic interests of its own members, who had the constant fear of redundancy, and this, whether intentionally or unintentionally, exacerbated typical insider–outsider problems (Kwon and Kwon 2006; Kwon 2008). Thus, neither individual employers nor unions were capable of dealing with the urgent problem of the growing use of temps. Coordination via an industrial framework agreement could provide an escape from this dilemma for both employers and unions because it could reduce the employers' economic burden of competing with one another on costs while it helped the local union leadership transfer the political burden to the industrial union.

Flexible bargaining is certainly associated with the decentralization of bargaining, but it needs to be conceptually differentiated from decentralization. This is important because the centralization movement seen in recent Korean industrial relations does not necessarily run counter to the increasing pressure of flexible bargaining. Researchers equate decentralized company/workplace bargaining with bargaining for flexibility (Iversen 1996; Howell 2009). In the same vein, they regard centralized bargaining at the national/sectoral level as creating rigidity because central agreements are inclined to standardize wages and working conditions regardless of differing situations among companies and workplaces. This tendency appeared after the 1980s when there were ongoing debates as to whether or not industrial relations had been transformed in the US (Kochan *et al.* 1986; Eaton and Voos 1992; Dunlop 1993; Cutcher-Gershenfeld and Kochan 2004). The same applied to the discussions on whether or not European industrial relations systems have changed (Katz 1993; Locke *et al.* 1995; Bamber *et al.* 2004). Decentralization of bargaining structures in Europe was viewed as having reduced rigidity and increased flexibility. However, decentralization appeared in diverse ways with distinct outcomes. In some countries, decentralization has been recorded as the dissolution of national bargaining but the strengthening of industrial bargaining. In others, decentralization has meant the collapse of industrial bargaining and its substitution by local bargaining.

We question the conventional assumption that decentralized bargaining results in greater flexibility while centralized bargaining curbs flexibility. The bargaining process needs to be differentiated from bargaining's results. The decentralized bargaining process is usually more flexible than a centralized bargaining process in that the former has less-rigid terms and conditions, needs less steps to be negotiated and amended, and responds more quickly to the environment the firm faces.

However, this does not necessarily mean that decentralized bargaining produces more-flexible working rules and conditions than does centralized bargaining. For example, individual employers involved in decentralized bargaining often do not obtain as much flexibility in wages or employment as they intend to, facing considerable resistance to the changes from their employees and the union, particularly when the union has strong bargaining power. Centralized bargaining sometimes makes room for flexibility in the labour market. In many European countries, central unions, peak employers' associations and government negotiate over social welfare and employment restructuring to increase labour market flexibility. When central bargaining allows the costs of employment restructuring to be paid at the social level, individual employers often enjoy high flexibility in the labour market (Ebbinghaus and Kittel 2005).

Thus, we do not accept the assumption that the decentralization of bargaining structure means higher flexibility. In other words, flexibility is not assured by the decentralization of bargaining structure per se but can be combined with coordinated bargaining. Rather as Ebbinghous and Kittel (2005) found, the combination is largely dependent on the actors' choice, which is shaped mainly by the interaction between external environment and internal politics (that is, how control is distributed between the central organizations and their member organizations).

The Korean case supports this view. If we apply the aforementioned assumption – that decentralization facilitates flexibility – to the Korean case, we should expect an increase of rigidity and a decrease of flexibility to have taken place in the recent transformation to industrial bargaining. However, such an outcome has hardly been realized here. Instead, while Korean unions and employers have been engaged in centralized bargaining, they have taken account of the diverse organizational and financial situations of individual companies in that bargaining. This coordinated and flexible bargaining may accommodate the similar results of 'organized decentralization' (Marginson *et al.* 2004), 'regulated flexibility' (Lehndorff 2007) and 'negotiated flexibilization' (Supiot 1999).

In the next section, we show briefly how this coordinated flexible bargaining has come about, using the example of Korea's banking industry. There, the employers' association and the industrial union came up with a series of framework agreements on the use of temps and their working conditions but still left room for flexible adaptation at the local level within the framework agreement. The result, we will suggest, is coordinated divergence or coordinated flexibility.

Divergent Employment Relations and the New Bargaining System: The Case of the Banking Industry

As a result of decentralization, diverse choices of employment patterns are more likely in contemporary labour markets. Katz and Darbishire (2000) have identified four different patterns as ideal types, namely low-wage, human resource management, Japanese-oriented, and joint-team-based strategies, and argue that the variation in employment patterns is increasing within countries (Katz and Darbishire 2000). The divergence of employment patterns across firms within the country have also been taking place in Korea as a longitudinal process.

Traditionally, firms in Korea had a highly homogeneous employment relations system. From the beginning of industrialization in the 1960s until socio-political democratization in the late 1980s, union organization was extremely limited and the state-controlled low-wage system was pervasive for production workers (Koo 2001). White-collar workers on a managerial track at large firms and in the public sector were better off in terms of wages and working conditions. Firms copied Japanese-style internal labour markets, offering seniority wages attached to life-time employment as well as various company welfare schemes to white-collar workers who were care-fully selected at the entrance level in order to attract and retain relatively rare well-educated employees. Although wage levels for the white-collar workers were still controlled by the authoritarian government, firms intro-duced various allowances like family allowances and financial support for children's education to meet employee expectations (Kwon 2008).

Socio-political democratization followed by the great labour move-ment aiming for independent and democratic unionism in the late 1980s brought layers to the previously simple employment relations systems in Korea. Internal labour markets were extended to include some production workers in the manufacturing sector and semi-skilled personnel in the service sector. The extension occurred mainly in the large-firm and unionized sectors. Union threat effects were reported in the large-firm non-union sector as well (Jung 1992; Lee et al. 1995). The low-wage and Japanese-style employment relations were the two dominant patterns throughout the 1990s. Firm size and the presence of unions at the firm level were the key factors that divided the two systems (Lee et al. 1995; Hwang et al. 2005). In banking, a tightly state-regulated sector, employ-ment relations across the banks were also highly standardized until the late 1990s. The previous internal labour markets, segmented by gender (that is, male employees on the upper managerial tier versus female employees on the lower tier of ILMs, concentrating on service work)

(Kwon 2008), were relaxed and the homogeneity of employment relations was enhanced within the sector for about 10 years between the democratization in the late 1980s and the Asian Financial Crisis in the late 1990s.

The traditional system faced a sea change at the turn of the century, brought on by the Asian Financial Crisis in 1997. While the size of the regular workforce who enjoyed lifetime employment and wage premiums was significantly reduced in the large-firm sector (Jung 2006; Kim and Han 2008), non-standard employment has become the norm. A large part of the workforce is now involved with outsourcing and subcontracting firms, and market-oriented employment practices have added significant weight to the casualization of employment. Human resource management focusing on direct relationships between individual employees and management, individual differentiation, and performance-oriented practices have also increased (Rowley and Bae 2002; Bae 2012). The rapidly spreading human resource management pattern began replacing or modifying the Japanese employment pattern to a significant extent. These changes together have resulted in divergences in employment relations and increased labour market inequality.

The banking sector, which had had homogeneous and solid internal labour markets until the late 1990s, was hit hardest by the crisis and was unable to ward off the changes. Massive downsizing then the replacement of a large number of regular employees by relatively cheap temps, with an emphasis on performance-oriented human resource practices, were put in place (Kwon 2008). Employers in some banks with an enterprise union that was weak in comparison with others enjoyed a greater degree of freedom to instigate a human resource management pattern. Despite some variation across the firms, labour unions in the banking sectors remained relatively strong, by getting engaged in the restructuring and policymaking process based on their having a practical approach compared with those in other sectors. One of the union's strategic decisions, in order to enhance its influence on restructuring, and thus maintain unreduced its organizational power within the sector, was to transform its own organizational and bargaining structure (that is centralization).

Although post-crisis restructuring by and large empowered management to enhance performance-related human resource practices and lean organization, the transformation of the union and bargaining structure has enabled the unions in this sector to maintain their bargaining power and to be relatively successful in protecting their members both from the direct imposition of individual performance practices and from further mass redundancies.

Coordinated Flexibility in the Korean Banking Industry

The banking industry in Korea offers several notable examples that show bargaining partners engaging in coordinated and flexible bargaining. Local leaderships of both employers' associations and unions are officially engaged in the key process of central bargaining, and the central bargaining integrates local-level supplementary bargaining into the official process. This shows that the bargaining structure ensures that the local voice is officially heard and incorporated throughout the bargaining process, and that local leaderships hold significant power.

In the previous section, we developed the argument that coordinated bargaining is a process of creating collective goods. The collective goods in many cases are hard to achieve because of between- and within-class competition. The most notable example is the framework agreement on the use of non-standard work arrangements. As stated earlier, the most destructive labour market outcome of the crisis was the proliferation of non-standard workers, particularly temps. Staffing levels (that is the numbers of regular permanent staff) were strictly controlled by the financial authority for a few years after the crisis, and in the meantime the temps reached 20 to 40 per cent of the total workforce in most banks (KFWU 2003). The increase continued even after the crisis, as Table 11.1 shows.

Most temps were employed as tellers working side by side with regular workers but were paid much less, often less than 50 per cent of what comparable regular workers earned. While employers enjoyed the cost reduction and increased workforce flexibility, the local unions did not increase their activity on behalf of those tellers with temporary employment contracts, since almost no temps were unionized and they could provide a buffer against redundancies (interviews by Kwon).

However, tensions increased internally alongside broader social censure of firms abusing temps as public awareness grew of the temps' precarious conditions (Kwon 2008). Banks often became a target of opprobrium, as their practices were easily exposed to the public and

Table 11.1 Share of nonstandard workers in the banking industry (percentage, December each year)

1999	2000	2001	2002	2003	2004	2005	2006
18.5	22.9	22.9	25.6	29	28.8	28.6	31

Source: Financial Supervisory Service, Statistical Information System.

there was great disparity between their regular workers and temps. Internal tensions originated from managerial discriminatory treatment against temps and the temps' increasing frustration at not being integrated into the internal labour market, remaining on the periphery as so-called perma-temps, their contracts simply renewed repeatedly (interviews).

Although cost containment was the employers' key motivation in using temps, banks also needed to retain temps and internalize them to a certain extent, as temps had strategic importance as frontline service providers in the retail sector because Korean banks were not highly globalized but instead competed for a narrow margin in the domestic market. In addition, the increasingly diversified products of service and sales required skilled tellers. Banks had to reconcile the advantages of using relatively cheap and flexible labour with the increasing demand for skills and commitment. This dilemma intensified with public pressure to improve the temps' working conditions. However, given the increasing market competition and the lack of laws to regulate firms' use of temps, individual banks were not highly motivated to single themselves out by improving their employment practices. While unions often become more vulnerable than employers to criticism from the public since they promoted the idea of a moral economy to justify their existence, individual union locals had it as their prior objective to protect their members' immediate interests, with a tendency to consider as secondary the improvement of workplace equality. This delayed local unions' intervention against managerial misconduct in the use of temps.

The industrial-level union, however, relatively free from local union dilemmas and more keen on pursuing the moral economy, intervened in the situation. Despite employers' reluctance to negotiate the issue of non-standard workers with the union because such employees were not covered by the union, the union pushed forward, and in 2003 achieved the small victory of having the two parties sign a somewhat declaratory agreement, stating: 'We agree to make collective efforts to contain the abuse of non-standard employment and improve working conditions for non-standard employees.' This agreement took an open-clause approach as seen in the working hours agreement by having each local decide the details, including the limit of both the number and the share of temps, the job categories that were allowed to use temps and the union's right to consultation prior to any changes in temp use.

Based on their publication of a white paper on non-standard workers in the banking sector, the industrial union reinforced its intervention and reached a special agreement with rather concrete guidelines in 2004. This agreement was composed of eight clauses, including pay increases for temps at twice the rate of regular workers' pay rises, the reduction of the share of temps to an agreed level at each local, and more importantly the introduction of the practice of temp-to-perm conversion. Again, the details were left for the locals' negotiation and supplementary agreement. This effort led to some changes. According to a 2004 report by the Tripartite Commission, the majority of banks surveyed had implemented temp-to-perm conversion plans (Jung 2004). The framework agreement was no threat to a bank's discretion to bargain flexibility with its local union but rather provided it with a chance to gain social legitimacy as a decent employer. Some employers saw this agreement of temp-to-perm conversion as their strategic tool because limited use of temp-to-perm conversion could enhance internal competition and thus yield better performance among temps who were anxious to become permanent regular employees. (interviews with HR managers 2005). Temp-to-perm conversion remained fairly limited at most banks however until a new law, the Act on the Protection, etc. of Fixed-Term and Part-time Employees, was passed in late 2006. The law, which strictly limits the duration of temp use to 2 years and orders equal treatment, complemented and stimulated the unions' collective bargaining effort in the sector.

Although the law opened a range of choices for a firm – after two years employing a temp, it could terminate the existing contract or hire the temp by offering a new open-ended contract – the firm's decision was largely dependent on the unions' bargaining power as well as the individual temp's market power. Unlike other sectors where a significant number of firms chose to terminate existing contracts or use third-party temp agencies to avoid legal obligations (Kwon 2009), the banks in the bargaining unit made significant numbers of temp-to-perm conversions. Ongoing bargaining in the previous few years had contributed to the adaptability of the union and employers to institutional changes and enabled them to be ready to negotiate further details. The 2006 industrial agreement took the framework approach that had each firm determine the details of temp-to-perm conversion, including the numbers of the converted, their contract type for the next few years and the working conditions that applied. Each local union ended up with a different conversion policy and related temp-use policies, depending on their current scale of temp use, the local union's bargaining power, the ways in which the bank used temps, and the bank's main objectives in the use of non-standard employment. The divergent patterns are summarized in Table 11.2.

As shown in the table, the banks commonly implemented an internalization programme for their temps that complied with the framework

Table 11.2 Conversion patterns in the financial sector, with examples

Pattern	Bank; size of temp-to-perm conversion; details of changed policies
1	Bank A: 3,100 – *Internalization by creating a second tier of the internal labour market with a separate set of HRM practices.* All temps converted. Employment guaranteed until retirement, equal benefits, quota to nonstandard workers when recruiting for standard positions, job position system integrated from deputy-director onward.
2	Bank B: 606 – *Internalization by creating a lowest grade of the existing internal labour market system.* 79% of temps (768) converted, the lowest Job grade 7 newly installed and integrated into the existing wage/position system for regular employees.
3	Bank O: 1,000 – *Enhancement of job security by having the current set of HRM for temps remain the same but by offering an open-ended contract to those selected.* 1/3 of temps converted. Applied an open-ended contracts, then conversion to regular jobs through open-competition based selection
4	Bank D: 2,300 – *Creation of a separate system for the converted but having two tiers within the new system* Specialized tellers given regular status through evaluation and exams, others to be converted to general tellers who have limited tasks with simple transaction

Source: Interviews by Kwon, summer 2007.

agreement, but their chosen policies showed wide variations in detail. As a result, the extent of the use of temps and the gap between temporary and regular workers still vary considerably across the banks (statistics from the Financial Supervisory Service 2012).

This example from the Korean banking sector demonstrates how the structural transformation of collective bargaining towards centralization adapts the internal and external pressures of decentralization and produces coordinated divergences across organizations within the sector.

Conclusion

This chapter has discussed an unusual case of the transformation of collective bargaining in Korea, from an extremely fragmented system to a centralized one. Although the direction of the changes has diverged from what other advanced countries have experienced over the last few decades (that is the decentralization of centralized systems), we have demonstrated how the processes and outcomes of contemporary bargaining have converged somewhat towards coordinated decentralization. We have suggested that the centralization experiment in Korea cannot be properly understood in terms of the traditional contrast between the centralization and the decentralization of bargaining structure. Rather, we argue that the centralization was chosen strategically, mainly by the unions, as a vehicle of coordinated and flexible bargaining to remedy the extremely decentralized and fragmented former bargaining system. To deal with the strong embeddedness of decentralized systems, the internal politics of strong local and emerging central union leadership, and the employers' pressure to enhance flexible and performance-oriented human resource management systems, the new industrial union could hardly have chosen centralized bargaining. Rather, the focus of the strategic objective of centralization has been on coordination to achieve a degree of union control over increasingly and extremely fragmented employment relations. We have also shown that the social partners' interdependence has enabled this new initiative to remain sustainable.

Our case study of Korean banking clearly illustrates the union's deliberate and practical approach to coordinated bargaining at the sectoral level, giving local partners room to enjoy a significant level of flexibility. The consequences are the divergent outcomes across the firms within the boundary of broadly set framework agreements. This coordinated divergence might be converging somewhat towards what other formerly centralized bargaining systems have experienced under the pressure of decentralization. It might be interesting to observe whether this ongoing experiment in Korean banking can survive in the current landscape of Korea's employment relations, which is still predominantly decentralized.

Note

1 When the crisis occurred unexpectedly in 1997, the government made a decisive step to carry out tough, neoliberal restructuring measures demanded by the International Monetary Fund in exchange for the bailout. These measures significantly altered the landscape of the Korean economy to the direction of a liberal and open economy (Kang 2010). In addition, both fiscal austerity and restructuring programmes brought about a sharp rise in unemployment and, as a result, a dramatic increase in poverty.

REFERENCES

Bae, K. (2008) 'The Conditions of Forming The Industry Level Bargaining Structure: Lessons from European Experiences', in *Collective Bargaining Structures in Europe* (in Korean), edited by K. Bae *et al.* Seoul: Korea Labor Institute.

Bae, K. (ed.) (2012) *Changing Employment Relations in Korea*. Korea Labor Institute.

Bae. K. *et al.* (2008) *Collective Bargaining Structures in Europe* (in Korean). Seoul: Korea Labor Institute.

Bamber, G.J., R.D. Lansbury and N. Wailes (2004) *International and Comparative Employment Relations: Globalisation and the Developed Market Economies*. Sydney: Allen & Unwin.

Calmfors, L. (1993) 'Lessons from the Macroeconomic Experience of Sweden', *European Journal of Political Economy* 9, 1:25–72.

Cho, S. (2009) Industry Level Collective Bargaining in the Metal Industry. in *The Theories and Practices of Industry-Level Collective Bargaining* (in Korean), edited by S. Cho *et al.* Seoul: Korea Labor Institute.

Choi, J.J. (1993) 'Political Cleavages in South Korea', pp. 13–50 in *State and Society in Contemporary Korea*, edited by K. Hagen. Ithaca, NY: Cornell University Press.

Crouch, C. (2005) *Capitalist Diversity and Change: Recombinant Governance and Institutional Entrepreneurs: Recombinant Governance and Institutional Entrepreneurs*. Oxford: Oxford University Press.

Cutcher-Gershenfeld, J. and T. Kochan (2004) 'Taking Stock: Collective Bargaining at the Turn of the Century', *Industrial & Labbor Relations Revivew* 58, 3:3–26.

Deakin, S., C. Lane, and F. Wilkinson (2000) 'Performance Standards in Supplier Relations: Relational Contracts, Organisational Processes and the Institutional Environment in a Cross-National Perspective', pp. 53–78 in *National Capitalisms, Global Competition, and Economic Performance*, edited by S. Quack, G. Morgan and R. Whitley. Amsterdam: John Benjamins.

Eaton, A. and P. Voos (1992) 'Unions and Contemporary Innovations in Work Organization, Compensation and Employee Participation', pp. 173–215 in *Unions and Economic Competitiveness*, edited by L. Mishel and P. Voos. New York: Sharpe.

Ebbinghaus, B. and B. Kittel (2005) 'European Rigidity Versus American Flexibility?', *Work and Occupations* 32, 2:163–95.

Freeman, R.B. and R.S. Gibbons(1995) 'Getting Together and Breaking Apart: The Decline of Centralized Collective Bargaining', pp 345–70 in *Differences and Changes in Wage Structures*, edited by Richard B. Freeman and Lawrence F. Katz. Chicago: University of Chicago Press.

Howell, C. (2009) 'The Transformation of French Industrial Relations: Labor Representation and the State in a Post-Dirigiste Era', *Politics & Society* **37**, 2:229–56.

Hwang, S. Jeong, J. Kim, S. and Nam, J. (2005) *Wages and Labor Markets in Korea*. Seoul: Korea Labor Institute. (in Korean)

Iversen, T. (1996) 'Power, Flexibility, and the Breakdown of Centralized Wage Bargaining: Denmark and Sweden in Comparative Perspective', *Comparative Politics* 28, 4:399–436.

▶

▶

Jeong, J. (2001) 'Pursuing Centralised Bargaining in an Era of Decentralisation? A Progressive Union Goal in Korea from a Comparative Perspective', *Industrial Relations Journal* **32**, 1:55–70.

Joo, M. (2006) *Unions' Organizational and Leadership Characteristics: The Case of the Korean Metalworkers Union* (in Korean). Seoul: Hanul

Jung, E. (1992) 'Internal Labor Market Changes and Industrial Relations in the Korean Manufacturing Sector' (in Korean), PhD thesis, Seoul National University.

Jung, E. (2004) 'Report on the Survey of Nonstandard Employment in the Banking Industry', Economic and Social Development Commission (in Korean). Seoul.

Jung, E. (2006) *Political Sociology of Contemporary Labor Markets* (in Korean). Seoul: Humanitas.

Kang, N. (2010) 'Globalisation and Institutional Change in the State-led Model: The Case of Corporate Governance in South Korea', *New Political Economy*, 15, 4:519–42.

Katz, H.C. (1993) 'The Decentralization of Collective Bargaining: A Literature Review and Comparative Analysis', *Industrial and Labor Relations Review* 14, 1:3–22.

Katz, H.C. and O.R. Darbishire (2000) *Converging Divergences: Worldwide Changes in Employment Systems*. Ithaca, NY: Cornell University Press.

Katz, H.C. et al. (2008) *An Introduction to Collective Bargaining and Industrial Relations*. Boston: McGraw-Hill/Irwin.

Katzenstein, P.J. (1985) *Small States in World Markets: Industrial Policy in Europe*, Ithaca, NY: Cornell University Press.

Kim, Y. and Han. J. (2008) 'The Dual Process of Korean Labor Market Transformation; Decomposing the Size-Wage Gap, 1982–2004', *Korean Journal of Sociology* 42, 7:111–45.

Kochan, T. A., H.C. Katz and R.B. McKersie (1986) *The Transformation of American Industrial Relations*. Ithaca, NY: Cornell University Press.

Koo, H. (2001) *Korean Workers: The Culture and Politics of Class Formation*. Ithaca, NY: Cornell University Press.

Korczynski, M. (1997) 'Centralisation of Collective Bargaining in a Decade of Decentralisation: The Case of the Engineering Construction Industry', *Industrial Relations Journal* **28**, 1:14–26.

Korea Financial Workers Union (KFWU) (2003) *2003 Annual Report* (in Korean). Seoul.

Korean Confederation of Trade Unions (KCTU) (2011) *KCTU 2011 Annual Report* (in Korean). Seoul.

Kwon, H. (2008) *The Search for Flexibility: Internal Labor Markets, Non-Standard Work and Gender Segregation in Korean Banking*. Ithaca, NY: Cornell University, Jan.

Kwon, H. (2009) 'Temp-to-Perm Transition: Recent Legislation on Fixed-Term Employment and Firm's Choice', *Labour Issues in Korea*, 2009/7:100–41.

Kwon, H. and H. Kwon (2006) 'The Growth of Nonstandard Employment, Changing Labor Market Structure and Industrial Relations', pp. 209–55 in *The Transformation of Industrial Relations in Large-Size Enterprises in Korea: Appraisals of Korean Enterprise Unionism*, edited by C. Lee. and S. Kuruvilla. Seoul: Korea Labor Institute.

▶

Kwon, H. (2011) 'A Korean Country Report for the European Commission's Project on Socially Responsible Restructuring: Comparative Overview Analysis of the Ways in which the Restructuring Phenomenon Is Dealt with Worldwide', unpublished manuscript for a workshop, European Commission, Brussels.

Lash, S. (1985) 'The End of Neo-Corporatism? The Breakdown of Centralised Bargaining in Sweden', *British Journal of Industrial Relations* 23, 2:215–39.

Lee, B.H., and H.J. Jo (2007) The mutation of the Toyota production system: adapting the TPS at Hyundai Motor Company. *International Journal of Production Research, 45* (16), 3665–3679.

Lee, J., H. Song and H. Kwon (1995) 'The Structure of Product Markets and Large Firms' Wage Policy' (in Korean), *Korean Journal of Sociology* 29, 1: 69–104.

Lee, J. (2004) *Collective Bargaining Systems in Korea and Their Policy Implications* (in Korean). Seoul: Korea Labor Research Institute.

Lee, J. (2011) 'Between Fragmentation and Centralization: South Korean Industrial Relations in Transition', *British Journal of Industrial Relations* 49, 4:767–91.

Lehndorff, S. (2007) 'Flexibility and Control: New Challenges for Working-Time Policy in the European Union', *Labour and Industry* 17, 3:9–28.

Locke, R., T. Kochan and M. Piore (1995) 'Reconceptualizing Comparative Industrial Relations: Lessons from International Research', *International Labor Review* 134, 2:139–61.

Marginson, P., K. Sisson and J. Arrowsmith (2004) *European Integration and Industrial Relations: Multi-Level Governance in the Making*. Basingstoke: Palgrave Macmillan.

Rowley, C. and J. Bae (2002) 'Globalization and Transformation of Human Resource Management in South Korea', *International Journal of Human Resource Management* 13, 3:522–49.

Sako, M. (1997) *Wage Bargaining in Japan: Why Employers and Unions Value Industry-Level Co-ordination* (No. dp0334) Centre for Economic Performance, LSE.

Schulten, T. (2005) 'Changes in National Collective Bargaining Systems Since 1990', *European Industrial Relations Observatory On-Line*.

Sisson, K. and P. Marginson (2002) 'Co-Ordinated Bargaining: A Process for Our Times?', *British Journal of Industrial Relations* 40, 2:197–220.

Supiot, A. (1999) 'The Transformation of Work and the Future of Labour Law in Europe: A Multidisciplinary Perspective', *International Labour Review* 138, 1:31–46.

Thomas, E. J. (1957) 'Effects of Facilitative Role Interdependence on Group Functioning', *Human Relations* 10, 4: 347–66.

Traxler, F. (1995) 'Farewell to Labour Market Associations? Organized Versus Disorganized Decentralization as a Map for Industrial Relations', pp. 3–19 in *Organized Industrial Relations in Europe: What Future?*, edited by C. Crouch and F. Traxler. Aldershot: Avebury.

Traxler, F. (1996) 'Collective Bargaining and Industrial Change: A Case of Disorganization? A Comparative Analysis of Eighteen OECD Countries', *European Sociological Review* 12, 3:271–287.

Traxler, F. (2003) 'Coordinated Bargaining: A Stocktaking of Its Preconditions, Practices and Performance', *Industrial Relations Journal* 34, 3:194–209.

▶

Wallerstein, M. and B. Western (2000) 'Unions in Decline? What Has Changed and Why', *Annual Review of Political Science* **3**, 1:355–77.

Western, B. and J. Rosenfeld (2011) 'Unions, Norms, and the Rise in US Wage Inequality', *American Sociological Review* **76**, 4:513–37.

Western, B., D. Bloome, B. Sosnaud and L. Tach (2012) 'Economic Insecurity and Social Stratification', *Annual Review of Sociology* **38**, 1:341–59.

Whitley, R. (1999) *Divergent Capitalisms: The Social Structuring and Change of Business Systems*, Oxford University Press on Demand.

Yang, H. (2011) The Trend of and Challenges facing HRM Systems in Korean Firms. *Korean Journal of Management*, 19 2: 31–49.

The State and Employment in Liberal Market Economies: Industrial Policy in the UK Pharmaceutical and Food Manufacturing Sectors

12

Enda Hannon

Over the last two decades social scientists from various fields have shown great interest in issues of comparative political economy, in particular in examining the adjustment of national economies to processes of globalization and intensifying international competition (Whitley 1999; Hall and Soskice 2001; Amable 2003). A key contribution of this research has been how it has demonstrated that economic activity continues to be largely influenced and shaped by the particular institutions, regulatory frameworks and cultures within both individual countries and groups of countries.

The most high-profile recent example in this vein is the literature adopting a varieties-of-capitalism framework. A central feature of this approach is the distinction it draws between two basic but contrasting types of economy, namely liberal market economies and coordinated market economies. It is argued that economic activity in liberal market economies such as the US and UK is predominantly characterized by market transactions undertaken by atomistic firms. In contrast, varieties-of-capitalism authors highlight how in coordinated market economies such as Germany and Japan individual firms tend to be embedded into local, regional or sectoral networks, with non-market forms of economic regulation more prevalent (Hall and Soskice 2001).

The varieties-of-capitalism approach has both deepened understanding and generated critical debates and perspectives regarding the analysis of models of capitalism. Important perceived weaknesses of prevailing frameworks include the insufficient attention given to the role of the state in shaping economic and regulatory trajectories, and a failure to recognize the extent of heterogeneity existing within national economies (Crouch 2005; Howell 2007; Weiss 2010; Lane and Wood 2011).

The varieties-of-capitalism literature has been extensively referenced by employment scholars, with research from a varieties-of-capitalism perspective examining the impact of different institutional frameworks and governance regimes on employment outcomes, wage levels and skills (Estévez-Abe *et al.* 2001; Doellgast *et al.* 2009; Batt *et al.* 2010).

The focus of this chapter is on addressing one of the key gaps in the varieties-of-capitalism literature, namely the inadequate attention given to the role of the state. We explore the impact of the state on employment in liberal market economies, with a particular focus on state industrial policy. Specifically, we examine the employment implications of state industrial policy in the UK pharmaceutical and food manufacturing sectors. In this way the chapter responds to calls for the connection of labour process research to 'a broader political economy' (Thompson 2003; Thompson and Vincent 2010).

We draw on secondary sources, including previous academic research; official statistics; government, state agency and industry body reports; periodicals and other news sources. This is supplemented with primary data consisting of interviews with policymakers, industry officials, senior managers and operational employees within the UK dairy processing and pharmaceutical sectors, undertaken in 2003–04 and 2008–10 respectively.

Our research identified substantial differences in state industrial policy towards the two sectors, which in turn underpinned divergent outcomes relating to employment, working conditions and skills. In pharmaceuticals a strategic and resource-intensive industrial policy on the part of government has enabled the UK sector to perform strongly and led to the creation of high-quality jobs. In contrast, in food manufacturing the predominant reliance on market mechanisms has negatively impacted industry performance and resulted in poor job quality and deteriorating working conditions.

These findings illustrate the problematic nature of dominant paradigms and policy prescriptions regarding the role of the state in liberal market economies within the literature on comparative capitalism. In contrast, the positive potential impact of active state industrial policies on employment is emphasized. The chapter highlights the various ways governments in liberal market economies intervene in the economy and the important employment consequences of this, again challenging prevailing analytical frameworks.

The chapter first considers existing theory and research on the role of the state in liberal market economies. Next the definition and nature of state industrial policy is considered. The main findings regarding UK government industrial policy and its impact on employment in the pharmaceutical and food processing sectors are then presented. Finally, an analysis and conclusion is provided.

The Role of the State in Liberal Market Economies

Dominant Conceptions

In the varieties-of-capitalism framework, the primary function of the state in liberal market economies is seen to be to ensure the free operation of market forces, as this it is argued is the most effective method of coordinating firms and economic activity and hence enhancing economic welfare in such countries (Hall and Soskice 2001).

In his elaboration of national business systems, Whitley (1999, 2005) presents the 'arm's-length state' as a distinctive type of state approach to economic management and regulation, and notes how most so-called liberal market economies tend to be characterized by such an approach. He notes how arm's-length states tend to concentrate on establishing and enforcing the framework and rules within which market transactions take place, while leaving the nature of economic activity and organization within these frameworks to be largely freely determined by relevant economic and social actors.

Schmidt (2002) identifies 'market capitalism' as one of three main types of capitalism in Europe, while Amable's (2003) more wide-ranging study identifies 'market-based' systems as a distinct model. For these and the above authors, countries such as the US and UK, conventionally described as liberal market economies, are distinctive because of their emphasis on competitive markets as the central drivers of growth and the predominantly hands-off role of the state in economic management.

Theoretical and Empirical Critique

Although typically presented as ideal types, these dominant conceptions of the role of the state in so-called liberal market economies are properly subject to both theoretical and empirical critique. In this regard, authors adopting a 'regulation approach' highlight the pervasive influence of the state on the economic sphere (Boyer 1990; Jessop 2002). For Boyer (1990:42), the state 'plays a definite role in the establishment, rise, and crisis of every regime of accumulation'.

Following Polanyi, Block (1994) notes how even in market-dominated systems, the state strongly shapes economic activity. Rueschemeyer and Evans (1985:45) observe how, in idealized market models, 'collective goods' will be inadequately provided and 'negative externalities' not controlled, which calls for state action to address these problems. Moreover where markets are not operating perfectly, state intervention is needed to stimulate and discipline entrepreneurial behaviour.

While noting the dominance of 'liberal market capitalism', Clift and Woll (2012) highlight the inadequate consideration of the role of the state in the comparative literature. In developing theory on economic patriotism, they flag up the great expansion in state economic intervention since the 2008 financial crisis aimed at promoting economic growth and welfare at national, subnational and sectoral levels. This has been evident in liberal market economies such as the US and UK as well as others countries, with renewed interest in particular in industrial policy (ibid.). Previous empirical work by both economic sociologists and political scientists demonstrates the validity of these observations regarding the role of the state in liberal market economies (O'Riain 2004; Weiss 2010).

From an employment relations and labour process perspective, the policy prescriptions for states in liberal market economies contained in the models of capitalism literature are highly problematic. The analysis of Hall and Soskice (2001) and colleagues leads to the conclusion that in liberal market economies the free operation of market forces should be accentuated as far as possible. In addition, governments in liberal market economies are seen to be advised to concentrate industry support measures on sectors characterized by 'radical innovation' (for example biotechnology) that are best supported by flexible institutional frameworks (Casper 2007).

However, numerous researchers have identified how deregulated, market-based systems create undesirable employment outcomes, including high levels of wage inequality, work intensification and job insecurity, and often provide limited opportunities for career progression and skills development for many workers (for example Finegold and Soskice 1988; Burchell et al. 2002; Beynon et al. 2002; Green 2006).

Employment researchers are therefore interested in the scope for alternative approaches to economic management in liberal market economies to underpin more desirable employment outcomes, across a range of sectors. Following the discussion above, the potential of an active state industrial policy is currently of particular relevance (Hannon et al. 2011). We next consider the definition and forms of industrial policy.

Defining and Identifying State Industrial Policy

Following Johnson (1984:8), we define industrial policy as concerned with 'the initiation and coordination of governmental initiatives to leverage upward the productivity and competitiveness of the whole economy and of particular industries in it'. The question of which policy mechanisms come within the realm of industrial policy is much debated (Coates 1996). We can nevertheless draw on the work of Block (2008) and others in identifying key state activities in this regard.

Block (2008) outlines four key ways in which states endeavour to pursue technology policy objectives. States engage in *targeted resourcing*, which involves identifying particular technological problems or areas of potential economic importance, and providing financial resources to support firms and other institutions in working on these. Second, states can engage in *opening windows*, which, Block (2008:172–3) explains, involves governments supporting more bottom-up, less-targeted innovation by providing funding and other support to many different projects and institutions.

Third, states engage in technological and business *brokering*. The former involves connecting different actors or groups so that they can take advantage of each other's knowledge. Business brokering includes helping technologists attempting to commercialize a product obtain the required funding, make necessary business connections and identify potential customers. Finally, *facilitation* encompasses a wide range of activities such as creating appropriate regulatory frameworks for new products or ensuring suitable physical infrastructure is in place.

Other key industrial policy activities identified in the literature include the creation of *financial incentives*, for example in the form of taxation rates or R&D tax credits; *attraction of foreign direct investment*; *developing capabilities* (for example general research capabilities or workforce education and training); and *public procurement* (Porter 1990; Huggins and Izushi 2007; Weiss 2010). These various concepts can be used to evaluate state industrial policy in specific sectors. We now consider the role of state industrial policy in the UK pharmaceutical sector.

Industrial Policy and the UK Pharmaceutical Sector

Pharmaceuticals is a sector in which the role and importance of industrial policy is very apparent. In developing new products, pharmaceutical firms need to draw on research conducted by universities and research institutes, and they also rely on these actors to supply them with an educated workforce (Van Egeraat and Barry 2008). Similarly, they require close relationships with health sector organizations in order to test the clinical utility of new products as well as find buyers for them. In addition, given the extremely expensive nature of new product development in the sector, any financial incentives that governments or other actors can provide are much sought after (ibid.; Thomas 1994).

Various aspects of the industrial policy context historically promoted the development of the UK pharmaceutical sector, including demanding product safety requirements imposed by national regulatory agencies; the development and expansion of the National Health Service; the favourable rules of the UK's pricing system for pharmaceutical products; the very strong public science base; and the government's strategic attraction of foreign direct investment of an innovative nature (Thomas 1994; Lane and Probert 2003; Slinn 2005). Although not without its critics (Froud et al. 1998), pharmaceuticals is frequently highlighted as one of the success stories of the British economy, while a strong biotech/biopharma industry has also been developed (Lawton-Smith and Bagchi-Sen 2006).

Over the last 10 to 12 years industrial policy towards the sector has become progressively more active. The Labour government established the Pharmaceutical Industry Competitive Taskforce in 2000 to examine the competitive position of the industry (PICTF 2001). This led to the establishment of the Ministerial Industry Strategy Group, which has since met twice a year, bringing together industry and government representatives to discuss key issues affecting the sector.

The Office for Life Sciences was set up in January 2009 as a cross-departmental body with the task of promoting the competitiveness of the UK life sciences sector. Various working groups comprising representatives from government, industry and academia were formed, which led to the development of an overarching 'blueprint' document in 2009 and a subsequent progress report in early 2010 (OLS 2009, 2010).

The policies of the Conservative–Liberal government have built closely on those of its predecessor. Pharmaceuticals and biopharmaceuticals are seen, within the context of the wider life sciences sector, as being industries of great strategic importance, and they benefit from very substantial and hands-on support. The government presented its *Strategy for UK Life Sciences* in December 2011 (BIS/OLS 2011). This outlined thirty-one specific actions to be implemented, with progress and additional initiatives outlined in a report published in December 2012 (HM Government 2012a).

The various actions and initiatives include examples of each of the ways in which states may act in the industrial policy sphere outlined above. A high-profile example of Block's (2008) 'targeted resourcing' and 'opening windows' categories is the Biomedical Catalyst Programme. Funded to a total of £180 million over three years and managed by the Medical Research Council and the Technology Strategy Board, this involves the provision of grants to small and medium enterprises and universities to develop innovative solutions to particular biomedical challenges. Support is provided for feasibility, early- and late-stage projects. By the end of 2012, £49 million had been committed to 64 projects, with an additional £25 million of private sector funds leveraged from this (HM Government 2012a:9).

An important government objective announced in 2012 is to enable UK institutions and businesses to tap into the enormous therapeutic and commercial potential of genomic research. The government has outlined measures aimed at combining the UK's existing strengths in genome research with the National Health Service's status as a world-leading and data-rich healthcare system, to create a framework from which innovative genome-related products, technologies and services may be developed (HM Government 2012a). The Department of Health is to invest £100 million to fund the sequencing of 100 000 whole genomes, support the linking of data and treatment options, and aid the development of related skills. Additional funding will be provided by the Medical Research Council and the Technology Strategy Board (ibid.:45–7).

In addition to opening windows, this is arguably an example of 'facilitation' (Block 2008). In this example as well as throughout the life sciences strategy as a whole, there is a strong emphasis on harnessing the National Health Service's role as procurer and user of medicines and treatments to the advantage of both industry and patients. The initiatives listed also involve the government and its related agencies in 'brokering' activities (Block 2008). A notable feature is the support for collaborative projects between firms, universities and National Health Service institutions.

The creation of financial incentives is also clearly evident. In direct response to lobbying and policy critique on the part of the life science sector, the Conservative–Liberal government introduced a 'patent box' system from April 2013. This applies a lower tax rate (10 per cent) to profits from patents developed and commercialized in the UK, with the expectation that this will create incentives for firms to develop and commercialize products in the country. This measure sits alongside the progressive reduction of corporation tax from 26 per cent to 20 per cent and ongoing refinements to the R&D tax credit scheme.

The attraction of foreign direct investment is an important focus, with the government agency UK Trade & Investment having developed a specially tailored life sciences marketing and promotion campaign. From August 2012 this has been the responsibility of a dedicated unit within UK Trade & Investment, the Life Sciences Investment Organisation.

A number of the measures outlined above can be said to 'develop capabilities'. Other initiatives in this regard relate to skills and training. The *Strategy for UK Life Sciences* outlined the objective of increasing the number of apprenticeships and industry placements being taken up in the life sciences sector. Cogent, the state-funded Sector Skills Council for process industries, introduced a Higher Level Apprenticeships in Life Sciences in 2012, as well as a Technical Apprenticeship Service that supports employers in the recruitment, selection and training of apprentices (HM Government 2012a:53).

Performance and Employment Outcomes

As outlined above, the industrial policy context historically promoted the development of the UK pharmaceutical sector. Alongside increasing demand for pharmaceutical products underpinned by rising levels of economic welfare and the expansion of national health systems, this supported sustained levels of high growth in the UK sector from the 1950s to the 1980s (Froud *et al.* 1998; Slinn 2005). The number of R&D professionals employed expanded significantly during the 1950s, while total employment in the sector increased from 60 000 in 1963 to 80 000 in 1992 (Froud *et al.* 1998:562; Slinn 2005:182).

Over the last two decades the world pharmaceutical sector has been characterized by enormous turbulence. In the 1980s incumbent firms came under increasing pressure due to a decline in the rate of successful new drug development; shorter effective patent life due to lengthier development and approval processes; downward pressure on margins exerted by cost-conscious national governments; and increased competition from manufacturers of generic drugs (Froud *et al.* 1998; Van Egeraat and Barry 2008). These pressures prompted very significant rationalization within the UK industry from the early 1990s, involving various acquisitions and mergers between firms as well as cost-cutting within individual businesses (Froud *et al.* 1998).

This process of change and rationalization is ongoing. Outsourcing activities such as the conduct of molecule screening or later-stage clinical research has become commonplace, while there is a move among the leading firms to target investments in fundamental research to emerging countries such as China and India (Ernst and Young 2010). In addition, the progressive development of the medical biotechnology sector has challenged existing firms and operating models. This has led to a shift in innovation to small firms and greater collaboration between them and the larger incumbents (ibid).

The employment consequences of these processes have been evident in the UK in recent years. The US multinational Pfizer closed its flagship R&D facility at Sandwich in Kent in 2011 with the loss of 1800 jobs, although this was partially offset by an expansion of the company's Cambridge research centre. AstraZeneca, a leading Anglo-Swedish firm, announced the closure of its principal UK R&D site in Cheshire in March 2013 with the loss of 550 jobs, having previously undertaken substantial job cuts in 2010 and 2012. AstraZeneca's R&D activity is now to be located in Cambridge, with a new facility employing 1600 scientists. The extent of the reduction in R&D jobs at these and other larger firms is reflected by the fact that the Royal Society of Chemistry estimated there to have been a 20 per cent drop in the number of its members doing pharmaceutical research since 2008 (RSC 2011).

Recent trends, and those in R&D in particular, are seen by industry officials and company managers to be due primarily to competitive trends in the pharmaceutical sector as opposed to deficiencies in the UK policy context (House of Commons Science and Technology Select Committee 2011; HM Government 2012a). Some critics disagree, arguing that despite the various initiatives the UK government does not invest sufficiently in science and technology, with MNCs preferring to invest in countries such as the US and China where government expenditure is far greater (Mazzucato 2011). In manufacturing the UK has lost jobs to countries such as Singapore and Ireland that offered more attractive financial incentives for investment. Jobs have similarly been lost in clinical-trial-related activities owing to perceived weaknesses in relevant policies and processes (Whitehead 2013). A major perceived weakness is the persistently low frequency of adoption by the NHS of new medicines, with the Association of the British Pharmaceutical Industry highlighting this as a serious impediment to innovation and investment (ABPI 2013).

While the latter constitute perceived weaknesses and negative effects of the UK policy context, other recent announcements reflect efforts to improve the policy framework for the sector. In March 2012, in direct response to the government's decision to introduce the patent box system and reduce corporation tax, the British company GlaxoSmithKline announced a £500 million investment in UK manufacturing, which is expected to lead to the creation of 1000 jobs. Notably this includes the opening of a new biopharmaceutical manufacturing facility. In partnership with the government, other public agencies and the Wellcome Trust, GSK has also invested in an open innovation bioscience campus with potential to house 1500 scientists.

Other positive developments in the last few years include the US multinational Lilly opening a new neuroscience R&D facility supporting the work of 130 scientists, and the establishment by three other pharma MNCs – Astellas, Eisai and Quintiles – of European headquarters in the UK. Lilly's management expressly highlighted the UK's world-class reputation in neuroscience as central to that firm's new development, with representatives from the other firms also mentioning the advantages of UK government policy and the broader environmental context. As noted above, Pfizer has expanded its existing R&D centre at Cambridge, while AstraZeneca is to open a new facility there. AstraZeneca's CEO identified the UK government's support for life sciences and the very strong biomedical cluster in Cambridge as key reasons behind the latter decision.

Officials from the Bioindustry Association, which represents biomedical firms, note that the government's Biomedical Catalyst, patent box and corporation tax initiatives have significantly strengthened investment and business confidence in that sector (BIA 2013). They nevertheless continue to call for additional investment support (ibid.).

Despite fluctuations, overall pharmaceutical employment remained largely stable between 1995 and 2010 (ABPI 2011). A recent government report outlines that there are approximately 96 000 people working in pharmaceuticals and medical biotechnology in the UK (HM Government 2012b). Employment in the former decreased by 10 per cent between 2011 and 2012, reflecting the ongoing rationalization at the larger firms outlined above. In contrast, numbers in medical biotechnology increased slightly, by 0.3 per cent.

Turnover in UK pharmaceuticals and medical biotechnology in 2012 was approximately £30 billion and £4 billion respectively (ONS 2012a). The pharmaceutical sector invested £5 billion in business R&D in 2011, which represented 28 per cent of total UK investment, and has a positive trade balance of almost £7 billion (ONS 2012b; BIS 2012:47). Provisional data from the Annual Survey of Hours and Earnings show that in 2012 the median gross hourly wage in pharmaceuticals was £16.20, compared with £12.15 for manufacturing as a whole and £11.26 for all UK employees. Cogent (2010:11) estimates that 58 per cent of the pharmaceuticals workforce are educated to National Vocational Qualification level 4 or above (that is degree level or above), compared with under 32 per cent for the labour force as a whole.

Industrial Policy and the UK Food Processing Industry

Historically, the UK food manufacturing industry for the most part developed incrementally and autonomously. Small, family-owned businesses that supplied local or regional markets were commonplace, in particular in traditional food sectors such as bread, meat and dairy (Burns 1983; Smith *et al.* 1990). In contrast, newer products and activities such as chocolate manufacture that were marketed and advertised nationally lent themselves more readily to increased scale and the use of mass production technologies (Smith *et al.* 1990).

While state industrial policy was not central, government action and policies were nevertheless important in facilitating the development of the sector, for example by regulating the marketing and safety of food products (Burns 1983; Burden 1996; French and Phillips 2000). As with pharmaceuticals, the ability of food manufacturers to draw on the research capabilities of UK universities has historically aided innovation in the sector (Armstrong 2003). The government's limited regulation of monopolies and mergers within the industry as well as market share in food retailing was seen to underpin the dramatic concentration that took place from the 1960s (Burns 1983; Smith *et al.* 1990).

One area of the food industry in which government action was historically more prominent is dairy processing. From the 1930s until 1994, Milk Marketing Boards established by government operated as monopoly purchasers of raw milk across the UK, setting the farm gate price of milk for both the liquid and manufacturing sectors using a system of 'end-use pricing' (Banks 2000). The system also provided dairy processors with fixed and typically high margins for the production of specified products.

Central objectives of this regulatory framework were to secure a high milk price for farmers and to promote the development of dairy processing. Important public-good structures were established, notably a collaborative research and development programme and shared-use pilot plant facilities (Armstrong 2003). However the Conservative government deregulated the dairy industry in 1994, which led to the breakup of this system and related institutions (ibid.).

Since the 1990s, UK government policy relating to dairy and other subsectors of the food industry has placed a strong emphasis on promoting competition and efficiency, with progressively more attention also devoted to achieving environmentally friendly, sustainable production that underpins healthy consumption patterns (DEFRA 2002a and b; Cabinet Office 2008; HM Government 2010).

The New Labour governments did not see food manufacturing as a strategic industry from an industrial policy perspective. The Conservative–Liberal government is developing a strategy for the 'agri-tech' sector aimed at harnessing the UK's strengths in agricultural science and technology to develop products and technologies promoting efficient and sustainable production (BIS 2012). The focus here appears predominantly on agriculture, which food industry representatives have challenged (All-Party Parliamentary Food and Drink Manufacturing Group 2012).

The government and related agencies have nevertheless adopted a range of measures relevant to food manufacturing in recent years. The Technology Strategy Board opened a Food Processing and Manufacturing Efficiency competition, funded by the Technology Strategy Board, the Department for the Environment, Food and Rural Affairs, and two research councils. This focused on encouraging more efficient processing, packaging and distribution, and the recycling of by-products and waste, with successful projects granted up to 50 per cent public funding (from £100k to £2.5m). In December 2012, £11 million was awarded for 32 collaborative research projects involving businesses and academic or research institutions.

The Technology Strategy Board also operates a Nutrition for Life competition, which supports new product development aimed at developing healthier, safer and more nutritious food. In 2011, £6.5 million was awarded for 27 major collaborative projects focused on the development of innovative technologies or processes. In addition, 24 small and medium enterprises were supported in carrying out small-scale technical feasibility studies (obtaining up to £25 000 each). Food-manufacturing firms can also apply for funding under the TSB's High Value Manufacturing competition.

While total public expenditure on agriculture and food research is substantial (for example totalling £415 million in 2008–09), the emphasis tends to be on agricultural or more fundamental food research as opposed to 'near market' research that would be of potential application by processing firms.

In January 2012 Defra published a Plan of Action on *Driving Export Growth in the Farming, Food and Drink Sector* (Defra 2012a). This was drawn up together with UK Trade & Investment and representatives from four trade associations. The development of specific action points was overseen by the Agri-food and Drink Exports Forum, comprising top exporting companies and co-chaired by the Minister of State for Farming and Food and the CEO of Nestlé UK.

The Action Plan identified the potential of food and drink exports to drive growth in the agri-food sector and in that way contribute to the wider development of the UK economy. Relevant activities and initiatives announced included the holding of regional events to encourage companies to export; making export paperwork simpler and easier for companies to access; and financially supporting inexperienced companies to showcase their products at international trade shows (ibid.). Government ministers have committed to promoting British produce abroad.

The Conservative–Liberal government is also taking action intended to better regulate processor–retailer relationships. The Groceries Code Adjudicator Bill 2012–13 is currently going through Parliament and when implemented will establish an adjudicator to monitor and enforce the Groceries Supply Code of Practice, which applies to large retailers. The intention is to better protect farmers and food processors in their dealings with the latter.

Finally, food manufacturing firms are drawing on the government's funding of apprenticeship training, which amounted to £1.5 billion for 2012–13. The Food and Drink Federation announced a target of doubling the number of apprentices in the sector between August 2011 and December 2012. This was more than achieved, with the number of apprentices increasing from 1700 to 4700 (FDF 2012a). The industry was assisted in this process by two publicly funded organizations, the National Apprenticeship Service and the National Skills Academy for Food and Drink (ibid.).

Performance and Employment Outcomes

Historically food and drink manufacturing has been an area of strength for the UK economy. While US multinationals assumed powerful positions in the industry, British-owned firms remained dominant into the 1980s (Smith *et al.* 1990). As outlined earlier, the sector witnessed very substantial concentration from the 1960s, with industry structures becoming rather oligopolistic. Food retailers became more powerful during the 1970s, prompting further rationalization within the industry (ibid.).

The position of retailers has become even stronger over recent decades and combined with a relative decline in consumer expenditure on food and an increase in imports this has placed substantial downward pressure on turnover levels within the UK industry (James and Lloyd 2008:212). As a consequence the UK fell behind Germany and France to become the third-largest food manufacturer in Europe (ibid.).

In the dairy sector, deregulation by the Conservative government in 1994 led to enormous turbulence. Combined with a short-term financial orientation characteristic of many larger British firms, the difficult competitive conditions prompted a number of indigenous companies to curtail investment in new product development and exit the industry. A consequence of this was a significantly reduced presence on the part of indigenous firms in higher-value activities such as the manufacture of yoghurt and desserts, which instead became dominated by foreign MNCs (Hannon 2005). While working conditions at the latter are potentially highly desirable, in the lower-value, commodity-type markets for milk and cheese, low pay, work intensification and a lack of training and development are commonplace (Hannon 2005, 2010).

Case study research on other food sectors has similarly identified a notable deterioration of working conditions in recent years, with wages in relative decline, benefits being cut back and work intensified (James and Lloyd 2008; Newsome et al. 2009; Hopkins 2012). In addition, food processing employers are making greater use of flexible labour practices and many are reliant on migrant workers to fill positions. The flexible and light-touch regulatory framework, and the emphasis on the free operation of market forces on the part of the UK government, are seen to underpin these outcomes (James and Lloyd 2008; Newsome et al. 2009). While job quality has in general therefore deteriorated, there is significant heterogeneity within the industry. Working conditions at large branded manufacturers and some foreign-owned MNCs operating in commodity-type sectors can be comparatively good (FDF 2012b; Hannon 2005, 2010).

The food manufacturing sector has nevertheless performed quite strongly over the last few years, with a 9 per cent increase in industry turnover between 2008 and 2011 (ONS 2012a). Notably, food and drink continues to be the UK's largest manufacturing sector by both turnover and employment, with turnover of £72 billion in 2011 (ibid.). Exports of agri-food products have also grown rapidly since 2005 (Defra 2012b; FDF 2012b). The UK however still has a very large trade deficit in food, feed and drink of £18.6 billion (Defra 2012:37). The food manufacturing sector invested £350 million in business R&D in 2011, which accounted for 2 per cent of total UK expenditure (ONS 2012b).

Industry officials have acknowledged the recent support provided to the sector by the UK government and state agencies (FDF 2012). At the same time, they identify various areas for improvement and express the view that in comparison with other sectors, food manufacturing has received relatively little industrial policy assistance (*The Engineer*, 9 May 2011).

It is argued that UK food manufacturing has not received the support needed to undertake the radical innovation required to stay ahead of international competition, with a lack of funding for applied research highlighted. The Director General of the Food and Drink Federation has called for a strategy to be developed for the sector and for government to work with the industry to assess objectives for R&D and innovation and allocate funding to these (All-Party Parliamentary Food and Drink Manufacturing Group 2012).

Total employment in UK food manufacturing fell from 510 000 in 1998 to 381 000 in 2010, reflecting continual rationalization in the sector. Provisional data from the Annual Survey of Hours and Earnings show that in 2012 the median gross hourly wage for the manufacture of food products was £9.17. This compares unfavourably with the figures for the wider manufacturing sector outlined earlier. James and Lloyd (2008:217) note how one-third of process operatives in the sector are paid below the low-pay threshold, with the dominance of low-skill jobs reflected by the fact that over half of the sector workforce does not possess the equivalent of a school-leaving qualification.

Analysis and Conclusion

The research undertaken identified important differences in employment outcomes between the pharmaceutical and food manufacturing sectors. In pharmaceuticals there has and continues to be substantial change in the composition of employment, with high-profile recent job losses at larger firms. However total numbers across the sector as a whole remain comparatively stable, with jobs being highly skilled and paid. In contrast, numbers employed in food manufacturing have fallen substantially, with a notable deterioration in working conditions and job quality in evidence in recent years.

While wider sectoral characteristics and trends are key, the research findings highlight the importance of state economic policy in influencing processes and outcomes within both sectors. The government has historically played a central role in shaping the development of the UK pharmaceutical sector, with a plethora of measures and initiatives involving very sizeable financial resources in evidence in recent years. Although subject to criticism, these measures have helped UK pharmaceutical companies maintain a strong competitive position as well as enter new markets and activities. This in turn has supported employment and job quality in the sector.

In contrast, food manufacturing in the UK historically developed more autonomously and government policy towards that sector has prioritized the free operation of market forces, albeit with some recent signs of a more active approach. While relevant indicators reflect promising performance over the last few years, UK food manufacturers continue to lag behind their foreign counterparts in terms of innovation and presence in higher-value market segments. The intense competitive environment and flexible regulatory framework has led to extensive rationalization of employment and causes many of the remaining jobs in the sector to be characterized by low wage and skill levels and work intensification.

These findings highlight the problematic nature of dominant paradigms and policy prescriptions regarding the role of the state in liberal market economies within the literature on comparative capitalism. The evidence from food manufacturing demonstrates the negative consequences for employment and working conditions of the predominant reliance on market forces to regulate and promote economic activity in liberal market economies, as envisaged by Hall and Soskice (2001) and colleagues. The findings from food also challenge the suggestion that governments in liberal market economies should focus economic support on certain sectors to the exclusion of others (Casper 2007).

In contrast, the evidence from pharmaceuticals points to the potential for and positive employment effects of an active state industrial policy, even in liberal market economy contexts (Hannon *et al.* 2011). The identification of state industrial policy as a key determinant of competitive and employment outcomes is particularly pertinent at the current time, as the credit crunch and recession have prompted an increase in state intervention in the economic sphere (ibid.; Clift and Woll 2012). In this regard, the chapter responds to Thompson and Vincent's (2010) call for more research on the 'connective tissue' between the labour process and the broader political economy.

Our findings and analysis support the work of authors who have criticized prevailing conceptions of the role of the state in liberal market economies (Block 2008; Weiss 2010; Clift and Woll 2012). While the UK is commonly identified as a country in which the state focuses primarily on ensuring the free operation of market forces, the reality is more nuanced. The evidence from pharmaceuticals in particular provided detailed examples of the various general ways in which governments can intervene from an industrial policy perspective, contrary to dominant conceptions regarding the role of the state in liberal market economies (Hall and Soskice 2001; Block 2008; Weiss 2010).

Acknowledgements

The primary research for this chapter was supported by two research awards from the Economic and Social Research Council (R42200034459 and RES-062-23-1183). Thanks to the editors for very helpful comments on earlier drafts.

REFERENCES

All-Party Parliamentary Food and Drink Manufacturing Group (2012) Meeting Notes from Innovation Round Table, 22 October. London: Food and Drink Federation, www.appgfooddrink.org.uk.

Amable, B. (2003) *The Diversity of Modern Capitalism*. Oxford University Press.

Armstrong, D. (ed.) (2003) *The History of the Society of Dairy Technology*. Bicester: Society of Dairy Technology.

Association of the British Pharmaceutical Industry (ABPI) (2011) Knowledge Hub web pages. London www.abpi.org.uk.

Association of the British Pharmaceutical Industry (ABPI) (2013) 'ABPI Response to FT Article on Health of UK Pharmaceutical Industry', ABPI statement, 26 April. London www.abpi.org.uk.

Banks, J. (2000) 'Reorganisation of Milk Marketing Arrangements in the United Kingdom, 1994–2000', pp. 379–405 in *Dairy Industry Restructuring*, edited by H. Schwarzweller and A. Davidson. Oxford: Elsevier.

Batt, R., H. Nohara and H. Kwon (2010) 'Employer Strategies and Wages in New Service Activities: A Comparison of Co-ordinated and Liberal Market Economies', *British Journal of Industrial Relation*, 48, 2:400–35.

Beynon, H., D. Grimshaw, J. Rubery and K. Ward (2002) *Managing Employment Change: The New Realities of Work*. Oxford: Oxford University Press.

Bioindustry Association (BIA) (2013) 'Growing UK Biotech Sector Discusses Growth and Jobs in Westminster; BIA Taking the Bioscience Sector to Parliament', press release, 31 January. London, www.bia.org.uk.

Bioscience Innovation and Growth Team (BIGT) (2009) *The Review and Refresh of Bioscience 2015: A Report to Government by the Bioscience Innovation and Growth Team*. London: Department for Business, Enterprise & Regulatory Reform.

Block, F. (1994) 'The Roles of the State in the Economy', pp. 691–710 in *The Handbook of Economic Sociology*, edited by N. Smelser and R. Swedberg. Princeton, NJ: Princeton University Press.

Block, F. (2008) 'Swimming Against the Current: The Rise of a Hidden Developmental State in the United States', *Politics & Society* 36, 2:169–206.

Boyer, R. (1990) *The Regulation School: A Critical Introduction*. New York: Columbia University Press.

Burchell, B., D. Lapido and F. Wilkinson (2002) *Job Insecurity and Work Intensification*, London: Routledge.

Burden, T. (1996) 'Agriculture', pp. 112–34 in *Industrial Policy in Britain*, edited by D. Coates. London: Macmillan.

Burns, J. (1983) 'A Synoptic View of the Food Industry', pp. 1–17 in *The Food Industry*, edited by J. Burns, J. McInerney and A. Swinbank. London: Heinemann.

Business, Innovation & Skills, Department for (BIS) (2012) 'Industrial Strategy: UK Sector Analysis', BIS Economics Paper No. 18. London.

Business, Innovation & Skills, Department for, and Office for Life Sciences (BIS/OLS) (2011) *Strategy for UK Life Sciences*. London.

▶

Business, Innovation and Skills, Department for (BIS) (2010) *A Strategy for Sustainable Growth*. London.

Cabinet Office (2008) *Food Matters: Towards a Strategy for the 21st Century*. London: Cabinet Office Strategy Unit.

Casper, S. (2007) *Creating Silicon Valley in Europe: Public Policy Towards New Technology Industries*. Oxford: Oxford University Press.

Clift, B. and C. Woll (2012) 'Economic Patriotism: Reinventing Control Over Open Markets', *European Journal of European Public Policy* 19, 3:307–23.

Coates, D. (1996) 'Industrial Policy: Introduction', pp. 3–30 in *Industrial Policy in Britain*, edited by D. Coates. London: Macmillan.

Cogent (2010) *UK Sector Skills Assessment 2011*. Warrington: Cogent, www.cogent-ssc.com.

Crouch, C. (2005) *Capitalist Diversity and Change: Recombinant Governance and Institutional Entrepreneurs*. Oxford: Oxford University Press.

Defra (2002a) *Strategy for Sustainable Farming and Food – Facing the Future*. London: Department for Environment, Food and Rural Affairs.

Defra (2002b) *Response to the Report of the Policy Commission on the Future of Farming and Food by HM Government*, Cm 5709. London: Department for Environment, Food and Rural Affairs.

Defra (2012a) *Driving Export Growth in the Farming, Food and Drink Sector: A PLAN of Action*. London: Department for Environment, Food and Rural Affairs.

Defra (2012b) *Food Statistics Pocketbook 2012*. London: Department for Environment, Food and Rural Affairs.

Dench, S., J. Hillage, P. Reilly and J. Kodz (2000) 'Employers Skill Survey: Case Study – Food Manufacturing Sector', Skills Task Force Research Paper No. 34. Sheffield: Department for Education and Employment.

Doellgast, V., U. Holtgrewe and S. Deery (2009) 'The Effects of National Institutions and Collective Bargaining Arrangements on Job Quality in Front-Line Service Workplaces', *Industrial & Labor Relations Review* 62, 4:489–509.

Egeraat, C. van and F. Barry (2008) 'The Irish Pharmaceutical Industry Over the Boom Period and Beyond', National Institute for Regional and Spatial Analysis Working Paper No. 39. Maynooth: National University of Ireland.

Ernst and Young (2010) *Beyond Borders: Global Biotechnology Report 2010*. Ernst & Young, www.ey.com.

Estévez-Abe, M, T. Iversen and D. Soskice (2001) 'Social Protection and the Formation of Skills: A Reinterpretation of the Welfare State', pp. 145–83 in *Varieties of Capitalism: The Institutional Foundations of Comparative Advantage*, edited by P. Hall and D. Soskice. Oxford: Oxford University Press.

Finegold, D. and D. Soskice (1988) 'The Failure of Training in Britain: Analysis and Prescription', *Oxford Review of Economic Policy* 4, 3:21–53.

Food and Drink Federation (FDF) (2012a) *Delivering Growth Through Apprenticeships*. London.

Food and Drink Federation (FDF) (2012b) *20/20 Vision for Growth Achievements 2012*.

French, M. and J. Phillips (2000) *Cheated Not Poisoned? Food Regulation in the United Kingdom 1875–1938*. Manchester: Manchester University Press.

▶

Froud, J. *et al.* (1998) 'British Pharmaceuticals: A Cautionary Tale', *Economy and Society* 27, 4:554–84.

Green, F. (2006) *Demanding Work: The Paradox of Job Quality in the Affluent Economy.* Princeton, NJ: Princeton University Press.

Hall, P. and D. Soskice (eds) (2001) *Varieties of Capitalism: The Institutional Foundations of Comparative Advantage.* Oxford: Oxford University Press.

Hannon, E. (2005) 'Prospects for the Upskilling of General Workers in Britain: A Case Study Comparison of the English and Irish Dairy Processing Industries', unpublished PhD thesis, University of Warwick.

Hannon, E. (2010) 'Employee-Focused Research in HRM: The Case of Dairy Processing', *International Journal of Human Resource Management* 21, 6:818–35.

Hannon, E. *et al.* (2011) 'The State and Industrial Policy in Ireland: A Case Study of the Irish Pharmaceutical Sector', *International Journal of Human Resource Management* 22, 18:3692–710.

HM Government (2010) *Food 2030.* London: Department for Environment, Food and Rural Affairs.

HM Government (2012a) *Strategy for UK Life Sciences: One Year On.* London: Department for Business, Innovation and Skills.

HM Government (2012b) *Strength and Opportunity 2012: The Landscape of the Medical Technology, Medical Biotechnology, Industrial Biotechnology and Pharmaceutical Sectors in the UK.* London: Department for Business, Innovation and Skills.

Hopkins, B. (2012) 'Explaining Variations in Absence Rates: Temporary and Agency Workers in the Food Manufacturing Sector', *Human Resource Management Journal*, first published online 26 October.

House of Commons Science and Technology Select Committee (2011) *Oral and Written Evidence: Pfizer's Decision to Close its Research and Development Facility at Sandwich*, www.publications.parliament.uk.

Howell, C. (2007) 'The British Variety of Capitalism: Institutional Change, Industrial Relations and British Politics', *British Politics* 2, 2:239–63.

Huggins, R. and H. Izushi (2007) *Competing for Knowledge: Creating, Connecting and Growing.* London: Routledge.

James, S. and C. Lloyd (2008) 'Supply Chain Pressures and Migrant Workers: Deteriorating Job Quality in the United Kingdom Food-Processing Industry', pp. 211–46 in *Low-Wage Work in the United Kingdom*, edited by C. Lloyd, G. Mason and K. Mayhew. New York: Russell Sage Foundation.

Jessop, B. (2002) *The Future of the Capitalist State.* Cambridge: Polity Press.

Johnson, C. (ed.) (1984) *The Industrial Policy Debate.* San Francisco: ICS Press.

Lane, C. and J. Probert (2003) 'Globalisation and Its Impact on Competitiveness: The Case of the British And German Pharmaceutical Industry', ESRC Centre for Business Research, Working Paper No. 262. University of Cambridge.

Lane, C. and Wood, G. (eds) (2011) *Capitalist Diversity and Diversity Within Capitalism.* London: Routledge.

Lawton-Smith, H. and S. Bagchi-Sen (2006) 'University–Industry Interactions: The Case of the UK Biotech Industry', *Industry and Innovation* 13, 4:371–92.

Mazzucato, M. (2011) *The Entrepreneurial State.* London: Demos.

Newsome, K., P. Thompson and J. Commander (2009) 'The Forgotten Factories: Supermarket Suppliers and Dignity at Work in the Contemporary Economy',

▶

▶

pp. 145–61 in *Work Matters: Critical Reflections on Contemporary Work,* edited by S. Bolton and M. Houlihan. Basingstoke: Palgrave Macmillan.

Office for Life Sciences (OLS) (2009) *Life Sciences Blueprint.* London.

Office for Life Sciences (OLS) (2010) *Life Sciences 2010: Delivering the Blueprint.* London.

Office for National Statistics (ONS) (2012a) *Annual Business Survey 2011 (Provisional Results).* London.

Office for National Statistics (ONS) (2012b) *Statistical Bulletin: Business Enterprise Research and Development, 2011.* London.

O'Riain, S. (2004) *The Politics of High-Tech Growth: Developmental Network States in the Global Economy.* Cambridge: Cambridge University Press.

PICTF (2001) *Pharmaceutical Industry Competitive Task Force Final Report.* London: Department of Health/Association of the British Pharmaceutical Industry, March.

Porter, M. (1990) *The Competitive Advantage of Nations.* London: Macmillan.

Royal Society of Chemistry (RSC) (2011) 'Government at Half Way House in Its Life Sciences Plan, Says Chemistry Chief', press release. London, www.rsc.org.

Rueschemeyer, D. and P. Evans (1985) 'The State and Economic Transformation: Towards an Analysis of the Conditions Underlying Effective Intervention', pp. 44–77 in *Bringing the State Back In,* edited by P. Evans, D. Rueschmeyer and T. Skocpol. Cambridge: Cambridge University Press.

Schmidt, V. (2002) *The Futures of European Capitalism.* Oxford: Oxford University Press.

Slinn, J. (1995) 'Research and Development in the UK Pharmaceutical Industry from the Nineteenth Century to the 1960s', pp. 168–86 in *Drugs and Narcotics in History,* edited by R. Porter and M. Tiech. Cambridge: Cambridge University Press.

Smith, C., J. Child and M. Rowlinson (1990) *Reshaping Work: The Cadbury Experience.* Cambridge: Cambridge University Press.

Thomas, L. (1994) 'Implicit Industrial Policy: The Triumph of Britain and the Failure of France in Global Pharmaceuticals', *Industrial and Corporate Change* 3, 2:451–89.

Thompson, P. (2003) 'Disconnected Capitalism: Or Why Employers Can't Keep Their Side of the Bargain', *Work, Employment and Society* 17, 2: 359–78.

Thompson, P. and S. Vincent (2010) 'Labour Process Theory and Critical Realism', pp. 47–69 in *Working Life: Renewing Labour Process Analysis,* edited by P. Thompson and C. Smith. Basingstoke: Palgrave Macmillan.

Weiss, L. (2010) 'The State in the Economy: Neoliberal or Neoactivist?', pp. 183–209 in *The Oxford Handbook of Comparative Institutional Analysis,* edited by G. Morgan *et al.* Oxford: Oxford University Press.

Whitehead, S. (2013) 'Championing a UK Success Story – Making Growth Sustainable', On-line Opinion Piece, London: ABPI, 13 February, www.abpi.org.uk.

Whitley, R. (1999) *Divergent Capitalisms: The Social Structuring and Change of Business Systems.* Oxford: Oxford University Press.

Whitley, R. (2005) 'How National are Business Systems? The Role of States and Complementary Institutions in Standardising Systems of Economic Co-ordination and Control at the National Level', pp. 190–231 in G. Morgan, R. Whitley and G. Moen (eds), *Changing Capitalisms? Internationalization, Institutional Change and Systems of Economic Organisation.* Oxford: Oxford University Press.

Does Political Congruence Help Us Understand Trade Union Renewal?

13

Martin Upchurch, Richard Croucher and Matt Flynn

In this chapter case study areas for future research and analysis are identified where the concept of political congruence may prove of value to the study of trade union renewal. It is suggested that strategic change in trade unions is more likely to succeed when political congruence exists between the values, expectations and intended outcomes of the three subsets of leaders, activists and ordinary members in a union. We argue that political congruence is dependent on, and sometimes a pre-condition for, 'effectiveness'. By effectiveness, we mean both organizational effectiveness (the internal 'health' of a union) and its 'ability to deliver' (Bryson 2003:5–6).

For political congruence to occur we need a chemistry of factors to coalesce. Borrowing primarily from social movement theory we identify these independent factors as: shared political frames of reference and collective identity (expressed as an outcome of frames and values); participation and socialization encouraged through innovative practice, networking and education; and rank-and-file mobilization. Shared political frames, collectively constructed values and the identity of a movement are time-specific, often in response to external threats from employers and/or states (see McAdam *et al.* 2001:14–16). Collective identity, participation and socialization are all internal motor agents which act to bind the union and develop repertoires of collective action, and are most likely to occur when a distinct political identity is developing.

Periods of exceptional UK union growth have occurred 'with the stream', when membership of unions was generally increasing, or 'against the stream', when individual unions grew even though general union membership was in decline or growing only slowly. A historical example of 'with the stream' was the 'Great Unrest' in Britain between 1910 and 1914, characterized by the development of rank-and-file militancy which clashed with union leaderships recently tied into national agreements. Such episodes of exceptional union growth within labour history, especially those which occur against the stream, need to be further studied and understood, in order to make sense of problems surrounding contemporary debates on union 'renewal'. Two examples which the authors are currently examining in the UK are those of the Amalgamated Engineering Union (AEU) from 1935 to 1945, and the Public and Commercial Services Union (PCS) in the period since 2000. We present a 'contextualized comparison' in which we are afforded the opportunity to understand how similarities of experience can occur within different time periods and under different institutional arrangements (see Locke and Thelen 1995). Both unions exhibited growth which appeared exceptional in the historical moment.

The AEU grew from 190 695 members in 1933 (Jefferys 1970:228) to over 900 000 in 1945 (Croucher 1982). Membership of all unions in the UK doubled during this period, but growth in the AEU exceeded the national trend by some margin. The union changed its orientation and identity from one based on craft to one which eventually embraced the apprentices' revolt of the late 1930s and the entry of women into the trade as full participants during the years of wartime production.

The second case, the PCS, has shown growth against the stream in the less favourable climate of Britain under neoliberalism. Its source of membership – the civil service and related agencies – has experienced job cuts and significant political hostility, but against this background of job cuts the union has managed to increase its density of membership.

Our proposition is that the achievement of political congruence within a union increases the likelihood of success in recruitment, retention and renewal. We therefore explore past studies within the social psychology of union activism to supplement the insights gained from social movement theory in addressing the political congruence concept. Before defining the concept in more detail we briefly review and contextualize the 'state of the debate' on union renewal.

Trade Union Renewal: The Need for 'Politicization'?

Contemporary literature on trade union renewal is framed by the retreat of trade unionism in the face of globalizing neoliberal restructuring. The retreat is partly for structural reasons, linked to the withdrawal of institutional support for collective bargaining, the relative decline of industrial sectors where unions have traditionally been strong, and also trends towards increased flexibilization, such as outsourcing and informal working in a context of higher unemployment. It may also be the result of an ideological retreat or confusion, as unions have struggled to dissuade their members from believing the inevitability of marketization, commodification and the 'threat' of wage competition from abroad. In effect many of the certainties of trade union legitimacy within Western European liberal democracies have been undermined in this period, through processes of union marginalization and 'de-institutionalization' of pluralist processes such as collective bargaining. In consequence trade union leaderships have struggled to maintain their position as recognized mediators between capital and labour as the hitherto neo-corporatist consensus has begun to fade and crumble. Academic literature, however, has tended to focus on the emerging responses from unions constructed within the *technical* contrast between the servicing and organizing models, and between a partnership approach as opposed to an organizing approach. It essentially objectifies unions within a vanished status quo, failing to fully appreciate the *political* crisis of industrial relations pluralism (Upchurch and Mathers 2012). Simms and Holgate (2010:159) have also observed in the UK, with respect to the organizing approach, that 'it appears to us that UK scholars have largely accepted organizing as a set of practices and tactics rather than as a wider political initiative'. If this faithfully reflects the current state of research, questions arise as to what might be the 'wider political initiative'.

There are exceptions to de-politicization. Munck (2010), in reviewing union movements, states that 'the old national-statist-corporatist model is no longer hegemonic but what will emerge from the current period of global turmoil is not entirely settled either' (2010:225). He argues the need to rediscover the 'original characteristics of combination, a common moral economy and an instinctive internationalism' (2010:229). Sentiments of a common moral economy echo Edward Thompson's (1971) description of the norms and values of the common people when contrasted to those of liberalism and the market economy. Thompson's approach found parallels in the work of other British Marxist historians whereby 'history from below' emphasized class consciousness as a predeterminant of labour as a movement (Kaye 1995). Radical movements of the dispossessed, in these writings, expressed not only economic concerns but also broader categories of the human condition embracing social and political justice. Protest movement theorists such as Charles Tilly and Sydney Tarrow continued the tradition, and developed theoretical constructs to analyse the ingredients of successful movements.

Political framing, political opportunity structures, repertoires of action and cycles of contention are now well understood tools of analysis. Each new cycle of contention may be determined by an exogenous shock to the status quo, whereby the union finds itself at a critical juncture where strategic reorientation is necessary for survival. The Great Unrest of 1910 to 1914, for example, was framed within a cycle of contention sparked by engineering and other employers in Britain attempting to reduce real wages to compete with Germany and other industrial nations. Factory occupations, work-ins and worker cooperatives against redundancies in the 1970s in the UK also represented a particularized and time-specific repertoire of action as rank-and-file members responded with forms of direct action to an extended period of forced industrial restructuring (Darlington and Lyddon 2001; Tuckman 2010).

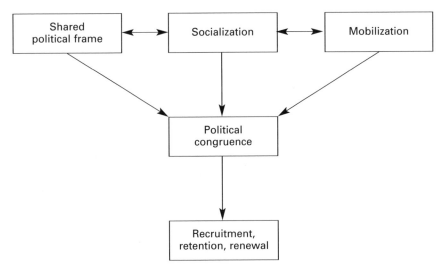

Figure 13.1 Sources of political congruence.

What Is Political Congruence?

We suggest that the creation of political congruence (Figure 13.1) within a union is an explanatory factor for relative union success both in periods when unions may be growing with the stream and when a union may be growing, or simply 'holding its own', in periods against the stream. So how can we define political congruence in more detail? The concept of political congruence combines a political dimension with theories of congruence rooted in social psychology. Almond and Verba (1963), in *The*

Civic Culture, hypothesized that active participation within political systems is more likely when there is high frequency of awareness and positive feelings between activists and the associated political structures and institutions. Feelings could be measured by cognitive, affective and evaluative orientations. The degree of positive feelings and hence participation within the political structure (or political organization) influences the likelihood of success in goal achievement. High positive feeling within all three orientations is identified as congruence, while high negative feeling is identified as incongruence. The concept is frequently applied to political parties, but has resonance in the study of religious and single-issue organizations, as well as the construction of shared values between parents and their children in the family home. Congruence/ incongruence might also be viewed as a binary condition, a 'geometric abstraction' that 'either exists or not, never as something more or less' (Eckstein 1998:10). Eckstein relates congruence, inter alia, to norms and expectations of patterns of authority relations within organizations, whereby congruence (and hence the likelihood of high performance) exists if the authority patterns of 'social units' are similar (1998:12). For trade unions this presents a dilemma, given the bureaucratic cleavage that may be apparent between paid fulltime officials, rank-and-file activists and ordinary members (see Darlington and Upchurch 2012, for a review of this debate). Increased rank-and-file activity, while increasing membership participation and socialization, may threaten leaders' control. High membership mobilization, when driven from below by the rank-and-file, might be viewed with caution by trade union leaders.

Child *et al.* (1973) alluded to this dilemma, and include a model of congruence within the framework of a union's administrative and representative rationality, ostensibly as a countervailing force to Michels's predictive iron law of oligarchy (also see Anderson 1978). The key to understanding the potential for congruence, they argue, comes through an alignment of expectations of both administrative and representative rationality, assessed through member participation and attachment to the union as a social unit. In constructing their analysis Child *et al.* bemoaned that 'the general lack of appreciation of member orientations, of the processes leading to their emergence and the way they are acted out through behaviour in the union, have been serious omissions (in studies of trade unions)' (1973:75). In examining the debates stirred by Child *et al.* and others in the 1960s and 1970s, Dufty (1976) expressed such coalescence of administrative and representative expectations in terms of the simple concept of solidarity. Union solidarity had two basic roots: 'one lies in the congruence of membership goals and perceived union goals...The other lies in the social relations between members, a matter strongly influenced by the technology of the industry as well as purely social factors' (1976:207). As defined by Sayles and Strauss (1967:132), goal congruity refers to 'intellectual' acceptance of the union, while 'emotional' acceptance is a function of social factors. For our purposes, intellectual acceptance may focus on agreement with political goals, while emotional acceptance is constructed through socialization and mobilization.

We recognize that the need to encourage activism as a route to union renewal is subject to political constraint. As such, the development of shared political frames in unions, defined as ways of understanding and acting upon a given situation, is likely to be spurred by external shocks, which threaten or challenge union or class solidarity. Most importantly, borrowing from social movement theory, to be a *successful* movement unions need to supplement their 'conventional' contentious participative action (strikes, demonstrations and so on), and construct alliances, adopt strategies and expand their repertoires by using innovative practice that has utilized 'skill and creativity to produce protest performances that gained followers, attracted attention from third parties, and challenged opponents' (Tarrow 1998:104). But unions' traditional commitment to 'social-democratic' institutionalization will constrain their ability to be disruptive in both conventional *and* innovative forms. Leaders tied to traditional social-democratic repertoires may be reluctant to adopt more radical strategies, and unions may lack capacity to alter ways of working. In particular, as Gamson *et al.* (1982:15) suggest, successful social movements must challenge the dominant set of beliefs that represent the status quo 'with an alternative mobilizing belief system that supports collective action for change'. As such, contention is more often than not 'framed' by alternative ideology or sets of beliefs; it is necessarily politicized in vision and oppositional in character. Of course, political congruence as a conceptual framework can be used as an explanatory factor of success in movements of the right as well as of the left. However, in order to develop political congruence in unions, which are agents of class-based interest, we suggest that the ideological framework will be left oppositionist, and often in contradiction to prevailing normative union behaviour.

From theories of social psychology we are aware that the degree to which activists are willing to participate is also dependent on the degree of socialization. We may define socialization as a process of imbibing shared norms of behaviour and attitudes within the union. As such, socialization processes provide the vehicle for adopting shared political frames. Aryee and Debrah (1997) have drawn on insights from the 1970s studies to develop a hierarchical regression analysis on felt attitudes of Singapore-based union members. They confirmed the prime significance of union socialization in developing satisfaction with, commitment to, and participation in a union. Such dialectics have been integrated into theories of social capital formation, whereby participation increases as degrees of reciprocity and trust are formed through networking activity and collective learning and education (Hooghe 2001). Networks act as 'envelopes of meaning', aiding identity formation and the creation of opportunities to participate (Passy 2003:41), and networks also act as conduits for high-risk social activism (McAdam 1986). Self-organized rank-and-file groups are recognized as vehicles for the development of shared values, sometimes as a result of organizational and political neglect by the union leaderships (McBride 2001; Humphrey 2002). Even when such groups are established they may remain marginalized from the mainstream, whether by the leadership, the activists or the general membership, making the dynamic a complex one. For example, the relationship between political discourse on race and gender and actual political practice may be a lagged one, from which trade unions are not immune (see, for example the graphic description of the process in Sivanandan 1981, and also Wrench 1986). On the other hand, Kirton and Healy (2004) have shown that the establishment of women's networks can heighten union identification, acting as a countervailing current to conservatism. Johnson and Jarley (2005) found similar processes at work with young workers, framing their findings in the 'raising social capital' setting. Shared values, it would seem, need to be developed on a political dimension if congruence is an intended outcome. Union education programmes may play a vital role in enhancing and encouraging democracy and participation, as evidenced in case studies conducted by Bridgford and Stirling (2000) and Croucher (2004). Active learning methods are utilized which focus on a tutor as a *facilitator* of a collective problem-solving process rather than on traditional didactic approaches of a tutor as a *director*. Concomitantly the democratic nature of such an education process within unions has been shown to raise participation and enable activists to influence the policy and political direction of the union, further increasing possibilities for political congruence.

One barrier to innovation is reliance on routine ways of working (Argyris and Schön 1978), often prevalent in ossified union structures. Indeed, much custom and practice within the 'social-democratic' model of trade unionism developed under the relatively protective umbrella of the Keynesian welfare state whereby, as Offe (1985) argued, the cost of integration into the mechanisms of the Keynesian welfare state for unions was that they had jettisoned their old transformative agenda in return for piecemeal gains. As Choi (2008) suggests, this makes the case for organizational learning more urgent. We also make a distinction between *participation in* a union and *democracy within* a union. Carol Pateman's (1970) analysis of democracy suggests that union decision-making structures can be more *or* less democratic, but *more* democratic structures are *more likely* to allow greater participation in union affairs, and also more likely to challenge bureaucratic control by union leaderships. Greater participation should be measured not just by attendance at meetings, voting and so on but also by tests of inclusivity, including the existence of formal and informal structures within the union that seek to organize and progress the concerns of 'non-traditional' members such as women and ethnic minorities.

We might note the development of a virtuous circle, whereby socialization increases cognitive, affective and evaluative orientations that are then reinforced by the act of mobilization. For Kelly and Kelly (1994), in reaching out to the links between participation, mobilization and attachment, the most significant correlate of participation was the strength of group identification, followed by collectivist orientation and the degree to which the out-group (management) were perceived in a stereotypical fashion. They refer to 'belief congruence theory' (Rokeach 1968) whereby 'perception of out-group members as dissimilar in their attitudes and values paves the way for their dehumanization which in turn facilitates aggressive action' (Kelly and Kelly 1994:67). In other words, strong feelings of 'them and us' will be likely to increase attachment to the union and participation. While John Kelly (1998) later utilizes mobilization theory as a method of understanding struggles over distributive concerns, mobilization also creates a qualitative culture of solidarity within the union (Fantasia 1998). As Kelly (1998) further outlined, the role of union leaderships and activists may be crucial in mobilizing feelings of them and us, through identification and articulation of grievance, creation of a sense of collective identity, and attribution of blame to management. Modelling of political congruence thus implies a crucial role for leadership within a union in order to 'frame' what the union should be fighting against, and/or what it should be fighting for. Most importantly, congruence theory would suggest that there should be similar values, norms and expectations of this vision between leaders, activists and members (or at least a critical mass of members) as a precondition of high performance and successful outcomes. Our two case studies both exhibit periods of substantial if not exceptional mobilization which may relate to developing collective identity established through grievance and attribution of blame.

The Amalgamated Engineering Union 1935–45

In our AEU case, a left oppositionist leadership came from the Communist Party of Great Britain which enabled rank-and-file participation and mobilization through the creation of networks and through prominent left leaders such as Jack Tanner and Wal (or Wally) Hannington. The union suffered substantial membership losses following the disastrous 1922 Engineering Lockout, from its involvement in the 1926 General Strike and from the ravages of the Great Depression so that by August 1933 it had just 190 695 members, before rising to over 900 000 in 1945. Levels of member involvement in the union's affairs were low by comparison with the period 1914–22, while elected shop stewards were very unusual (the rules allowed district committees to appoint them) and had almost disappeared from the industrial landscape (Hinton 1994). In political terms, the union's leadership was middle-of-the-road Labour, although hostile to 'National Labour'.

Framing

From 1935, an upturn occurred in the AEU's fortunes led by the shop stewards with members of the Communist Party among them providing a national network and leadership. A degree of political framing was evident, as the union leadership turned towards a policy which directly confronted employers through the dogged perusal of shopfloor grievances, in which the industrial cadre of the Communist Party could play a leading role at rank-and-file level. On a much broader canvas, and beyond the purity of workplace grievances, the union had been suffused with industrial-democratic ideas hotly debated on the shop floor by the 'shop floor citizens' created by intensely politicized dialogues in workplaces. Communist 'Popular Front' politics were far more conducive to constructing an alliance with Left Labour activists than previous policies which had been more hostile to the rest of the labour movement; while Left Labour had some separate existence in the AEU during our period, this grouping was closely allied to the Communist Party until the onset of the Cold War (Schneer 1988). This was already a dramatic political change from just three years previously, when the Communist-Party-led Minority Movement had been dissolved, after several of its leading members had been disciplined by the union's leaders (Jefferys 1970). The Communist Party was compromised by its support for the war effort after the collapse of the Stalin–Hitler pact in 1941, but despite significant issues, political congruence was nevertheless apparent in major organizational changes as well as the (more general) high levels of support for the Labour Party in 1945.

(New) Socialization and Mobilization

The burgeoning new aircraft factories created a specific set of employment issues which the Communist Party stewards initially used to demand a separate national agreement with the powerful aircraft employers. Thus, their initial policy was to capitalize on their real sectoral strength, and to begin to socialize the membership in key sectors through an agitational perspective. This process was undoubtedly driven by the Communist Party activists, who played a central role in forming an Aircraft Shop Stewards' National Council, led a series of successful disputes and founded a national aircraft workers' newspaper, *Propellor*, soon renamed *New Propellor*. The union was also 'shocked' into action by the apprentices' revolt involving strikes by young workers over a period of two decades in both the pre- and wartime years. The apprentices conducted strikes all over Britain displaying many of the characteristics of social movements, with dramatic symbolic public actions in a prolonged 'cycle of contention' (Hinton 1994). Again, the Young Communist League and to a lesser extent the Communist Party played a significant role within them although in a less structured way than in the aircraft industry (Croucher 1982). The apprentices demanded decent pay and training as well as union representation, and in the strikes it was not unusual for them to picket out their grandfathers, fathers, uncles and brothers. The 'rate for the job' was also given major political and practical significance as women poured into the workshops; they had historically been given separate women's rates rather than the far higher rates paid to the male workers whom they replaced (Croucher 1982; Bruley 2001). The formal admission and mass recruitment of women began in 1943, after a special Rules Revision Conference. By the end of that year, 138 717 women had joined, many of them paying the political levy. This led to a massive influx of women into the manual unions in more general terms, and indirectly created conditions for the many women's strikes, such as the Hillington women's strike for equal pay in 1944, which have been overlooked or downplayed in much literature (Wightman 1995; Bruley 2001).

Tensions over women in the union remained and many mobilizations were opposed by the union's leadership (and of course the communists), but the AEU insistence on the rate for the job was adopted as a slogan by the strikers. It is significant that they had expropriated the union's rhetoric. The disagreement was therefore about means rather than ends. This was an important point of political congruence: a key union industrial policy could no longer be considered simply a traditional craft demand: it coincided with women's interests.

Congruence

The political congruence theory places considerable emphasis on leadership. In our case, Tanner, with his syndicalist background and his feminist associations and sympathies, played a vital role. But the other indispensable element was the constellation of left shop stewards with the Communist Party at their core, a network which provided the national president with a vital link to the members to influence opinion and implement his policies. The networked alliance framed and articulated certain worker grievances, stressing inequality of sacrifice, excess profits, and management reluctance to cede control over production even in the interests of the war effort. A collective identity was created by this key group in the union through the *New Propellor*. This was consolidated by the links that stewards forged with members through shop stewards' papers, workplace meetings and micro-interactions between themselves and workers on the wide range of existential issues experienced by employees in wartime. Cultural change in the union was also forced endogenously on the previously craft and elitist union culture by participation of both women (in wartime production) and young apprentices.

PCS from 2000

Despite job cutbacks, between 2003 and 2006 PCS membership grew from 293 063 to 313 432, before falling back to 301 000 in July 2010 as further cutbacks of tens of thousands of civil service and related agency jobs transpired (PCS 2007, 2010). Further major cuts in civil service jobs took place in 2010/2011; in total 35 000 posts were cut, but PCS increased membership density during this period by 1.8 per cent to 69.4 per cent as membership losses were far less than job losses (PCS 2012:7). The union identifies 'activists' for the purposes of recruitment and organizing; significantly, their number increased from 10 142 in 2006 to 11 173 in 2009 (PCS 2010), while the percentage of workplaces with an identified 'face-to-face' distributor of union material increased from 63 to 68 per cent in the year 2010 to 2011 (PCS 2012:4). How might we explain this against-the-stream growth?

Framing

In the case of the PCS we observe a consolidation of left leadership throughout the union after Mark Serwotka's election from the shop floor to be general secretary in 2000, followed by re-election in 2005 and again in 2009. This consolidation manifested itself in an elected leadership at national and key sectional levels dominated by left and far-left individuals and groupings. In his re-election message to members in 2005 Serwotka began a process of political framing and outlined a 'vision' of commitment to abolishing inequality and campaigning unionism, which also clearly identified the union as to the left of the dominant 'New Labour' camp within union politics:

> It is not surprising that people are rejecting the notion that New Labour is as good as politics can get. Our task is, first, to map out a strategy to defend ourselves from the immediate attacks and, secondly, to articulate something better which is politically achievable. (Serwotka 2008)

The union, not affiliated to the Labour Party, has since adopted a policy position of defence of the public service and jobs, and remains a left oppositionist pole within the TUC. Most crucially, the union has shifted away from a partnership orientation and has been prone to dispute in terms of both national actions and localized disputes. As importantly, the union's left leadership has exhibited a propensity to conduct political campaigns and engage with organizations outside the trade union in progressing those campaigns. For example, PCS launched a 'Coalition for Better Civil and Public Services' in March 2006 attracting support from 'London Citizens', the Citizens' Advice Bureaux, and the Howard League for Penal Reform. The union then established a 'Protect Public Services' campaign unit within its HQ and has linked with other unions to establish a 'Public Services Not Private Profit' public campaign. The union followed this up with a 'Make Your Vote Count' initiative for the May 2007 local elections, the 2010 general election and subsequent local elections whereby candidates were questioned by activists.

Socialization

The socialization process undertaken within the union has not been straightforward. The establishment of the PCS in 1998 marked the last stage in the amalgamation process of civil service lower and middle occupational grades that had begun a century earlier. During the course of that century more than 40 unions had merged within the civil service (see www.unionancestors.co.uk for a full account). The core unions forming the final merger had each established a distinct identity and way of working which for many years had militated against amalgamation. The Civil and Public Services Association, for example, had represented the lower administrative grades and had been subject to left–right factional battles leading to unstable leadership coalitions. The National Union of Civil and Public Servants (the middle and executive grades union) and its forerunners, in contrast, were politically influenced in the 1970s and 1980s at leadership level by the Communist Party. The union membership, however, was more conservative in its political outlook, and consequently the leadership tended to suppress democratic decision-making in the union in order to ensure its structural authority. The Inland Revenue Staff Federation was a cross-occupational sectoral union in the Inland Revenue, and had developed its own distinct identity over the years. Amalgamation in 1998 was made possible by changing and shifting political allegiances at the top of the unions together with the exigencies of the perceived need for merger as a defensive strategy (for a more detailed account see Fairbrother 2000:34–51). The abolition of pay comparability machinery and its associated strict grading boundaries also released the unions from much sectoral and occupational competition in their own pay negotiations. The 1998 amalgamation thus upset the balance of forces that fed divisions within the unions, but at the same time allowed for a common sense of unity across the majority of civil service grades and a critical mass of members in the majority of workplaces with a common occupational identity. While this common sense of unity was created, it nevertheless continues to sit side-by-side with the historical legacy of the different sectional and grade differences, thus restricting the potential for political congruence to emerge. The Department for Work and Pensions section of the union, for example, is likely to have a more 'militant' culture than the Revenue section, which was formed from the old Inland Revenue Staff Federation union. Despite these difficulties socialization has been encouraged in the PCS through the establishment of a variety of representative subgroups. Our 2007 survey of PCS activists, for example, found that 45 per cent of branches now have a women's subcommittee or group, 37 per cent a black/Asian group, and 26 per cent an LGBT group (Upchurch 2007). PCS has also created a Young Members' Network to encourage processes of socialization and integration. In addition, the chosen vehicle for the Make Your Vote Count campaign has been newly established PCS town committees, bringing activists together, including retired members, from across traditional sectional boundaries within the union.

Mobilization

For the PCS as a whole, the fractured nature of pay bargaining has been met with a series of sectional disputes. National disputes with one-day strike action of all members occurred in 2004 and again in 2007 over job cuts and changes to sick pay, and in March 2010 against proposed changes to the redundancy provision. Recent national/sectional strike action has also occurred in the Scottish courts, Hewlett Packard Enterprise Services (2009), and the National Gallery (2010). Within the Department for Work and Pensions, PCS led 21 separate one-day strikes in the 4 years to 2009, with a high degree of mobilization closely associated with membership growth (McCarthy 2009). Over a quarter of all union members are in the DWP group, which has also shown the greatest rate of membership increase (authors' interview notes). This experience contrasts, for example, with the more passive experience of the HMRC (tax and revenue) section of the union (see Carter *et al.* 2012). Most recently, during 2011 and 2012, the PCS has participated alongside other unions in four national strikes over pensions, and has developed its own 'Alternative to the Cuts' agenda; early in 2013 it successfully conducted a national ballot for action over pay and conditions throughout the civil service, including a 'long weekend' of strikes followed by targeted action within a rolling programme of strikes and action short of a strike.

Congruence

We discern in the PCS a coalescence, at least in important sections on the union, of processes of political framing, socialization and mobilization which has led to the development of political congruence. The political framing appears inspired by a combination of anti-marketization and a campaign of 'defence' of the public service, which has united the left union leadership with a critical mass (in terms of numbers) of activists and members. This has been combined with a limited de-bureaucratization of the union structure, initiated by a decentralization of decision-making from national to regional officers and a focus on organizing both existing and minority-group members.

Towards Political Congruence

Political congruence may lead to more effective outcomes and act as a precursor to union renewal. Political congruence is strongly linked to collectivist identity and attribution of blame to the 'other' and is obtained through membership participation, inclusivity and the development of common political vision between leaders, activists and ordinary members of a union. Such common vision is necessarily 'emancipatory' and framed within opposition to prevailing practice. Oppositionist tenets may prove a challenge to traditional social-democratic models of representative democracy in unions, and may require a break with bureaucratic practice, a renewal of rank-and-file networks independent of the leadership, and a consequent 'opening-up' of unions to alternative, more radical identity and practice. These processes are difficult to launch during periods when unions have been forced to adopt highly defensive stances. Unions are neither single-issue organizations nor political parties. It is difficult to establish common norms and expectations, as unions will embrace different layers of consciousness among members and members will be of different political persuasions. What might be nurtured or occur, however, is a critical mass of (left/radical) leaders, activists and members who are able to work within the union in 'common cause', overlaying factional difference to a degree sufficient for commonality of cause to outweigh difference.

The achievement of political congruence within a union is a process which has dialectical features, whereby participation, activism, leadership, education, socialization and mobilization feed from each other in a virtuous path towards the state of congruence. We may certainly measure congruence, its existence or not at a single point in time, in a psychological sense by establishing the presence or not of cognitive, affective and evaluative orientations. However, we assume that *political* congruence might be more difficult to measure quantitatively as it is dependent on the socio-political relationships developed over time between the union leadership and an unquantifiable critical mass of activists and members. It is also likely to occur in time-specific political economy, conditioned by changing relationships between state, labour and capital. This assumes a dynamic process, in which phenomenological study would be a more appropriate ontological tool. Thus our two case studies must be viewed within their own institutional context, the AEU during a period of relatively closed economy and wartime production, and PCS under neoliberal conditions of marketization. However, in both cases we can unpick a strong match between the political inclinations of the union leadership and a critical mass of activists, which enabled a process of (re)framing political opposition. This was combined with a turn towards mobilization measured by disputes at local, sectional and national level. Socialization of the membership was also engendered. In the AEU case this occurred as a result not only of initiative from above in the guise of newssheets and political discourse, but also from below, enacted by women and apprentices. In PCS the turn towards organizing less traditional groups and the deepening of democratic structures enabled socialization in a different fashion.

It is possible to construct a picture of events, opinions, and actions which enable us to confirm the *direction* of the process either towards or away from congruence. Progress towards might be measured by voting figures for candidates of radical persuasions in union elections, by positive or negative attitudes of members towards information and communication, by the incidence (high or low) of networking and other socialization vehicles, by evidence of de-bureaucratization, by incidence of activity both in and beyond the workplace, and by degrees of member mobilization in industrial disputes. As such our research agenda, as outlined here, requires an exploratory process in which we must first identify those unions that have experienced an 'exceptional' period of growth either *against* the stream, in a period of declining employment opportunity and retreating union power, or *with* the stream during periods of union expansion. Our chosen case studies can be placed within this framework, and so testing of the salience of the concept of political congruence can be undertaken.

REFERENCES

Almond, G. and S. Verba (1963) *The Civic Culture: Political Attitudes and Democracy in Five Nations*. Princeton, NJ: Princeton University Press.

Anderson, J. (1978) 'A Comparative Analysis of Local Union Democracy', *Industrial Relations* 17:278–95.

Argyris, C. and D. Schön (1978) Organizational Learning: A Theory of Action Perspective. Reading, MA: Addison-Wesley.

Aryee, S. and Y. Debrah (1997) 'Members' Participation in the Union: An Investigation of Some Determinants in Singapore', *Human Relations* 50, 2:129–47.

Bridgford, J. and J. Stirling (2000) 'European Systems of Trade Union Education', pp. 7–28 in *Trade Union Education in Europe*, edited by J. Bridgford and J. Stirling. Brussels: European Trade Union College.

Bruley, S. (2001) *Working for History: A Diary of Life in a Second World War Factory*. London: Sutton.

Bryson, A. (2003) 'Working with Dinosaurs? Union Effectiveness in Delivering for Employees', Research Discussion Paper No. 11. London: Policy Studies Institute.

Carter, R. *et al.* (2012) '"Nothing Gets Done and No One Knows Why": PCS and Workplace Control of Lean in HM Revenue and Customs', *Industrial Relations Journal* 43, 5:416–32.

Child, J., R. Loveridge and M. Warner (1973) 'Towards an Organizational Study of Trade Unions', *Sociology* 7, 1:71–91.

Choi, C. (2008) 'Why and How are Some Strikes More Effective than Others? Evidence from the Korean Banking Sector', *Economic and Industrial Democracy* 29, 4: 467–91

Croucher, R. (1982) *Engineers at War*. London: Merlin.

Croucher, R. (2004) 'The Impact of Trade Union Education: A Study in Three Countries in Eastern Europe', *European Journal of Industrial Relations* 10, 1:90–104. ▶

Darlington, R. and Lyddon, D. (2001) *Glorious Summer: Class Struggle in Britain, 1972*. London: Bookmarks.

Darlington, R. and Upchurch, M. (2012) 'A Re-Appraisal of the Rank-and-File Versus Bureaucracy Debate', *Capital & Class* 36, 1:77–96.

Dufty, N. (1976) 'Trade Unions and Their Operations', *Journal of Industrial Relations*, 18:203–19.

Eckstein, H. (1998) 'Congruence Theory Explained', pp. 3–34 in *Can Democracy Take Root in Post-Soviet Russia?*, edited by H. Eckstein, F. Fleron, E. Hoffman and W. Reisinger. Lanham, MD: Rowman & Littlefield,

Fantasia, R. (1998) *Cultures of Solidarity: Consciousness, Action and Contemporary American Workers*. Berkeley, CA: University of California Press.

Fairbrother, P. (2000) *Trades Unions at the Crossroads*. London: Mansell.

Gamson W.A., B. Firema and S. Rytin (1982) *Encounters with Unjust Authority*. Homewood, IL: Dorsey.

Hinton, J. (1994) *Shop Floor Citizens: Engineering Democracy in 1940s Britain*. Aldershot: Edward Elgar.

Hooghe, M. (2001) 'Value Congruence Within Voluntary Associations: A Social Psychological Extension of Social Capital theory', unpublished paper, Department of Sociology, Free University of Brussels.

Humphrey, J. (2002) *Towards a Politics of the Rainbow*. London: Ashgate.

Jefferys, J.B. (1970) *The Story of the Engineers*. New York: Johnson Reprint Corp.

Johnson, N. and Jarley, P. (2005) 'Unions as Social Capital: The Impact of Trade Union Youth Programmes on Young Workers' Political and Community Engagement', *Transfer* 11, 4:605–16.

Kaye, H. (1995) *The British Marxist Historians*. London: Macmillan.

Kelly, C. and J. Kelly (1994) 'Who Gets Involved in Collective Action? Social Psychological Determinants of Individual Participation in Trade Unions', *Human Relations* 47, 1:63–88.

Kelly, J. (1998) *Rethinking Industrial Relations: Mobilization, Collectivism and Long Waves*. London: LSE/Routledge.

Kirton, G. and G. Healy (2004) 'Shaping Union and Gender Identities: A Case Study of Women-Only Trade Union Courses.' *British Journal of Industrial Relations* 42, 2:303–23.

Locke, R. and K. Thelen (1995) 'Apples and Oranges Revisited: Contextualised Comparisons and the Study of Comparative Labor Politics', *Politics and Society* 23, 3:337–67.

McAdam, D. (1986) 'Recruitment to High Risk Activism: The Case of Freedom Summer', *American Journal of Sociology* 92, 1:64–90.

McAdam, D., S. Tarrow and C. Tilly (2001) *Dynamics of Contention*. Cambridge: Cambridge University Press.

McBride, A. (2001) *Gender Democracy in Trade Unions*. Aldershot: Ashgate.

McCarthy, N. (2009) 'Union Organising in a Recognised Environment – A Case Study of Mobilisation', pp. 107–30 in *Union Revitalisation in Advanced Economies: Assessing the Contribution of Union Organising*, edited by G. Gall. Basingstoke: Palgrave Macmillan.

▶

Munck, R. (2010) 'Globalisation and the Labour Movement: Challenges and Responses', *Global Labour Journal* 1, 2:217–32.

Offe, C. (1985) 'New Social Movements: Challenging the Boundaries Of Institutional Politics', *Social Research* 52, 4:817–69.

Passy, F. (2003) 'Social Networks Matter: But How?', pp. 21–48 in *Social Movements and Networks: Relational Approaches to Collective Action*, edited by M. Diani and D. McAdam. Oxford: Oxford University Press.

Pateman, C. (1970) *Participation and Democratic Theory*. Cambridge: Cambridge University Press.

PCS (2007) *Commix Statistics 2007*. London: PCS.

PCS (2010, 2012) *National Organising Strategy Report*. London: PCS.

Rockeach, M. (1968) *Beliefs, Attitudes and Values*. San Francisco: Jossey-Bass.

Sayles, L. and G. Strauss (1967) *The Local Union*. New York: Harcourt Brace.

Schneer, J. (1988) *Labour's Conscience: The Labour Left 1945–1951*. London: Unwin Hyman.

Serwotka, M. (2008) 'Building an Alternative to New Labour'. *Socialist Review* January, issue 321.

Simms, M. and Holgate, J. (2010) 'Organising for What? Where Is the Debate on the Politics of Organising?', *Work, Employment and Society* 24, 1:157–68.

Sivanandan, A. (1981) 'From Resistance to Rebellion: Asian and Afro-Caribbean Struggles in Britain', *Race and Class* 23, 2:111–52.

Tarrow, S. (1998) *Power in Movement: Social Movements, Collective Action and Politics*, 2nd edn. Cambridge: Cambridge University Press.

Thompson, E.P. ([1971] 1993) 'The Moral Economy of the English Crowd in the Eighteenth Century', repr. 1993 from *Past and Present*, pp. 185–258 in *Customs in Common*. New York: The New Press,

Tuckman, A. (2010) 'Occupation, Worker Co-Operatives and the Struggle for Power: Britain in the 1970s', paper presented to the 28th International Labour Process Conference, Rutgers, New Jersey, 15–17 March.

Upchurch, M. (2007) *PCS Survey of Activists*. London: Middlesex University.

Upchurch, M. and Mathers, A. (2012) ' Neo-Liberal Globalization and Trade Unionism: Towards Radical Political Unionism, *Critical Sociology* 38, 2:265–80.

Wightman, C. (1995) *More than Munitions: Women, Work and the Engineering Industries 1900–1950*. London: Longman.

Wrench, J. (1986) 'Unequal Comrades: Trade Unions, Equal Opportunity and Racism', Policy Papers in Ethnic Relations No. 5, Centre for Research in Ethnic Relations, Warwick University.

Quality of Work in the Cleaning Industry: A Complex Picture Based on Sectoral Regulation and Customer-Driven Conditions

14

Vassil Kirov and Monique Ramioul

The cleaning sector in Europe is experiencing job growth because of the continuous trend of outsourcing and at present accounts for almost 4 million jobs in the European Union (EU). Working in the cleaning industry involves high risks due to precarious employment conditions, poor job quality and limited opportunities for adequate representation at company level. A combination of factors shaping the employment relationship lie at the root of this high-risk configuration, such as the fragmentation of the workforce over different client sites, the impact of cost reduction strategies of clients on wages and job content, and the growing rationalization of work.

Yet it appears that in several EU countries, as well as at European level, sectoral social dialogue structures and practices succeed in mitigating some of the negative effects for employees. Guaranteed employment conditions in case a client's site is transferred to another service provider, joint actions promoting socially acceptable working times, attempts to influence public procurement and agreements on new work methods reducing health and safety risks are marked examples of such sectoral collective bargaining outcomes. This demonstrates how working conditions and employment relations in service sectors where workers are particularly vulnerable may be improved through sectoral agreements. Such relatively consensual sectoral social dialogue, which is observed in a number of EU countries, is rooted in joint interests among the social partners to combat unfair competition, on the one hand, and to negotiate profitable contracts with clients that are beneficial to both the service provider and the workers, on the other. Cross-country sectoral convergences in employment regulation have previously been observed in other sectors by Katz and Darbishire (1999). Combined with the general observation that working conditions between sectors increasingly diverge within countries, among other things as a result of outsourcing strategies (Flecker 2010), this cross-country convergence endorses previous critics of varieties-of-capitalism arguments that assume coherent national systems of work and employment relations.

Nevertheless, it comes to the fore that sectoral regulation does not prevent persistent variations in employment conditions within companies in the different countries, even in subsidiaries of the same transnational firms. This suggests first that, even in a context of globalized corporate strategies and sectoral regulation, national systems still have an influence. Second, as we will argue in this chapter, the triangular relationship 'employer–client–worker', which is characteristic for this type of externalized service, provides a key explanation of the organizational varieties. This effect may not have been sufficiently examined in previous institutional comparative research on employment regulation. In the triangular relationship in service work, the employment relationship and job quality are shaped not only by the service provider, as the formal employer, but also by the local client, at whose site the work is actually carried out. Both the limitations for sectoral unions to effectively influence employment conditions at the client's site and the powerful sectoral social dialogue rooted in the alliance between the service providers and the trade unions can be explained by this triangular relationship.

In this chapter, we combine different theoretical perspectives to gain a deeper understanding of this complex configuration of employment regulation and its impact on the job quality of office cleaners. This is done on the basis of a combination of investigations into sectoral social dialogue in three European countries as well as case studies in a number of large multinational service providers. We first summarize the theoretical debates to which we turn to understand the observations. In a second section, the empirical research is described. The data used in this chapter are based on the cleaning industries in three countries: Austria, Belgium and Norway. In the third section, we describe the office cleaning sector in the three countries and some recent corporate strategies while in the fourth section we analyse the similarities and differences in employment regulation. In the conclusion, we summarize key findings and discuss how the chapter contributes to the theoretical literature.

Convergence and Divergence in Employment Regulation and the Triangular Relationship in Service Work

The varieties-of-capitalism (VoC) approach has been developed on the basis of previous theories such as the social-systems-of-production approach (Hollingsworth and Boyer 1997) and national business systems (Whitley 1992). The social-systems-of-production approach argues that market and other coordination mechanisms of a country or a region are integrated in a social configuration that includes the industrial relations system, the training structure, the firm's governance structure and so on (Hollingsworth and Boyer 1997:2). The authors argue that countries vary in types of coordination mechanisms and social systems of production (ibid. p. 36). The national business systems are 'particular arrangements of hierarchy-market relations which become institutionalized and relatively successful in particular contexts' (Whitley 1992:6). According to Whitley (1992:37) such variations in the national homogeneity and distinctiveness of business systems and dominant institutions emphasize the contingent nature of national hierarchy–market configurations.

The VoC approach has become a key institutional framework for the study of comparative capitalism following the publication of Hall and Soskice's work (Hall and Soskice 2001). They suggest that 'also there are variations within each group, a pronounced clustering is evident' (Hall and Soskice 2001:19). Other literature on employment regulation, however, has observed increasing *within*-country variation. Katz and Darbishire (1999) examine changes in employment practices in seven industrialized countries (with a focus on the automotive and telecommunications industries) since the 1980s and find a trend of growing divergences within national employment systems combined with striking commonalities (convergence) across countries that are very different historically and economically. In all countries, they observe trade union decline and a decentralization of collective bargaining as well as important changes in work organization, such as the introduction of teamwork and of modern HRM practices. As a result of declining union power, the seven countries studied all faced growing income inequality and employment insecurity. In addition, the authors also observed growing divergences within unionized sectors, which they explain by the spread of specific practices at workplace level. The outcomes for workers and the extent of the within-country divergences, however, still appeared to be influenced by national institutions (ibid.).

Other authors who have discussed internal heterogeneity include Herrigel (1996), Quack and Morgan (2000), Dörrenbächer (2002), and Herrigel and Zeitlin (2010). Already in 1996 Herrigel developed the argument that the focus on large companies renders the image of the development of the German industrial economy incomplete (Herrigel 1996:19) for not taking into account regional systems of small and medium enterprises, their interrelations with large firms, and so on. In his recent book *Manufacturing Possibilities: Creative Action and Industrial Recomposition in the United States, Germany, and Japan* (2010) Herrigel develops this argument further, criticizing the VoC approach. Based on qualitative research in ten German MNCs that have invested in Hungary during the 1990s, Dörrenbächer (2002) criticizes some central arguments of the national business system approach towards corporate internationalization, especially the notion of a rather strong and uniform country-of-origin effect. Herrigel and Zeitlin (2010) accentuate their critique of VoC by pointing out dynamic governance processes whereby actors at the sectoral or regional level jointly develop strategies and practices to tackle more effectively the problems they are confronted with. Such creative problem-solving efforts lead to recompositions of social relations within the economy and contribute to 'differences in industrial practice across various national (and regional) political economies over time' (Herrigel and Zeitlin 2010:7). Rather than emphasizing the path dependency of institutional arrangements as is done in VoC, such a dynamic approach accounts for variety and change in political-economic practice.

Based on a comparative analysis of employment regulation in a number of industries, Flecker (2006, 2010) finds that work and employment conditions are becoming increasingly diverse, not only at the global level but also within countries, within sectors and even within organizations. These growing divergences are related to processes of contractual outsourcing and spatial relocation, which are defined as types of value chain restructuring: 'Here, fragmentation means that different employment relations and conditions apply to workers carrying out tasks that were previously, or partially still are, performed within the client organization' (Flecker 2010:16). In general, the argument is that outsourcing contributes to divergences because the receiving sectors mostly have less-institutionalized industrial relation systems and are consequently less likely to be covered by sectoral collective agreements (Flecker 2010). However, Flecker finds that the within-country divergences are also influenced by national employment systems. These can mitigate differences in employment conditions when they provide relatively homogeneous and comprehensive labour regulations at the national level. But even in employment systems with a relatively high degree of centralization, marked differences between collective agreements may exist and boost externalization of work (Flecker 2010:17).

Flecker further emphasizes that employment systems, especially when they provide comprehensive regulation of work at the national and sectoral levels, may be able to cover the externalized workforce, contribute to the stabilization of industrial relations in new and growing sectors and lead eventually to the 'normalization' of working conditions. These sectoral collective agreements, however, contain serious concessions and offer lower levels of protection (lower wages and more flexibility) as compared with previous standards. This leads to an increase of within-country differentiations in employment conditions.

In sum, it becomes increasingly difficult to support the argument of coherent and unified national systems of work and employment. There seem on the contrary to be indications of diverging employment conditions within countries – due to, among other things, continuous processes of externalization leading to new sectoral regulations. These may diverge from existing national standards or from those prevailing in the sectors of origin, but may also lead to a better outcome as compared with what would be achievable solely at the company level. To the extent that such collective bargaining at the sectoral level can be observed in countries with differing national employment systems, this suggests a convergence of sectoral employment regulation across countries. Yet, it appears that this sectoral regulation does not prevent persistent variations in working conditions *within* companies across the different countries. Here, the specific characteristics of service work industries, more precisely the triangular relationship, can provide an additional explanation as to how working conditions are shaped. This structural feature of a wide range of services, involving the fact that some dimensions of the job are determined by the client, may not have been sufficiently addressed in institutional approaches. Taking account of the scale and scope of the externalization of services as a key element in the tertiarization of post-fordist economies (Vidal 2013), it is useful to consult the literature that attempts to specify the employment regulation from this triangular perspective.

There is an understanding that service work was marginalized and neglected in sociology up until the 1990s. Recently, however, sociologists of work, especially those in the labour process tradition, have increasingly made it their key focus and during the last decade there has been a growing corpus of literature focused on service work. As Korczynski (2009) concludes, 'Studies of service work have now become the empirical mainstream in the sociology of work' (2009:952). Among the dominant topics that have come to rectify this 'historical neglect of service work' is the triangular relationship between managers, workers and clients. According to Vosko (1997), the triangular employment relationship creates serious tension within prevailing regulatory regimes associated with the standard employment relationship. Already in 2000, Korczynski *et al.* considered the nature of control and the role of consumers in service work (for example in call centre services) (Korczynski *et al.* 2000). Bolton and Houlihan (2010) point out that it is widely recognized that the growth of service work has introduced the customer as a third and, in many accounts, powerful party to conceptions of the employment relationship. According to Lopez (2010), the triangular power relations between workers, managers and clients or customers dominate the experience of work more than ever. Leidner's (1996) notion of three-way interest alliances made a key contribution by reframing the client or customer as not simply an antagonist but also potentially as an ally of workers and of managers (Leidner 1996). In this chapter, we argue that the triangular relationship is also a relevant framework for a whole range of on-site services and that it is reflected in strong, compensating alliances at sectoral level.

The triangular relationship puts the organization where the service work activities are taking place at the centre of the analysis. This may contribute to understanding variations in outcomes for workers between countries and companies. Cleaning is typically one of those jobs where a worker is employed at a site which is not the place where his or her employer resides and consequently the control of work is distributed between the employer and the local manager of the client company. The employee has a contract with the cleaning company that settles the wages and contractual conditions, but most of the operational aspects of the job, including working hours, work environment, health-and-safety risks and so on are determined at the client's site. Hence, this triangular relationship strongly impacts on job quality. The triangular relationship is also a key determinant for the establishment of collectives and for generating opportunities for shopfloor collective action (Denis 2008). The fragmentation and distribution of the workforce over different sites, the temporary dimension of the allocation of workers to those sites, with regular shifting to new sites, the widespread use of part-time work and the absence of local employee representatives (who mostly have no access to clients' sites) are the main reasons why collective action at company or site level is limited and difficult to organize.

The question is now as follows: At what levels and by what mechanisms are job quality and employment regulated in the different countries under study and why?

Table 14.1 Interviews with stakeholders from the cleaning industry in WALQING

	Trade unions	Employers' associations	Public authorities	Other stake-holders	Total number of interviews per country
Austria	1	2	3	–	6
Belgium	3	2	-	1	6
Norway	2	2	-	1	5
EU level	1	1	-	1	3
Total	9	8	3	3	23

Research Method

The chapter is based on the research carried out in the framework of a large comparative European project investigating work and life quality in new and growing jobs.[1] Based on a quantitative analysis of employment trends in the EU (Vandekerckhove et al. 2010), a number of sectors, including office cleaning, were selected to be studied in depth. In the analysis of office cleaning in Austria, Belgium and Norway, the data come from sectoral reports on stakeholder strategies based on interviews carried out at European and country level with employers' representatives and trade union organizations. As depicted in Table 14.1, a total of 23 interviews were carried out.

In addition, 10 company case studies were carried out in the cleaning industry (Holtgrewe and Sardadvar 2012) and 105 cleaners in the three countries were interviewed (Hohnen 2012).

The Cleaning Sector in Europe

Setting the Scene

Overall, the cleaning industry is growing in Europe. According to the European Federation of Cleaning Industries (EFCI), commercial cleaning represents one of the most dynamic areas of corporate services, with more than 158 000 cleaning contractors employing 3.75 million employees across Europe (about 1.8 per cent of total employment in the European Union) in 2010 and generating turnover of nearly €62 billion (EFCI 2010). Market penetration (defined as the share of cleaning services

Table 14.2 Cleaning industry in examined countries

	Austria	Belgium	Norway
Number of employees	51,003 (2008)	46,237	56,000 (2008)
% of women	65.3%	n.a.	80%
% of part-time work	16.4% men	About 70%	10% men
	66% women		40% women

Source: National Reports (WALQING Social Partnership Series, http://www.walqing.eu/index.php?id=64).

contracted out to specialized cleaning companies) by cleaning companies is still growing and is now at a level of about 63.8 per cent in general and over 80 per cent in countries such as Austria or the Netherlands. This means that this process of outsourcing is reaching its limits and the market is becoming saturated.

In terms of employment, the sector is dominated by a number of large, mostly multinational firms. A few large companies, representing about 1.4 per cent of the total number of enterprises, contribute to almost half of the total turnover in the industry. Next to this formal segment of big and mostly well-regulated companies there are very many, very volatile small and micro businesses. Market entry is relatively easy and 74 per cent of companies employ less than 10 people. Micro companies have a bad reputation because they often operate on the edge of illegality, offer undeclared work and precarious contracts, apply practices of unpaid overtime, provide no training and resist any form of formal social dialogue structures (EFCI 2010). Table 14.2 highlights some basic characteristics of the sector for the countries involved.

The two main vulnerable groups in the sector are migrants and mothers of young children. In Austria, nearly two-thirds of the workers were women and in Norway this climbed to 80 per cent. Almost half of the workforce in Austria was non-Austrian, with a sizeable majority of immigrants coming from countries outside the EU. In Norway as well the sector employs a high percentage of immigrant workers. In Belgium, the great majority of workers were working part-time.

Job Quality in Office Cleaning

Across the cases in the three countries, similar risks and vulnerabilities were reported. The stakeholders interviewed described the work in cleaning as physically demanding, mostly unskilled low-wage work that is made worse by the prevalence of socially difficult working hours. As one Austrian trade union respondent defined it, motivation in cleaning is at the lower end and workers are mostly 'in it for the money' (Holtgrewe and Saradvar 2011). Cleaning offices in administrative sectors (such as in banks) is generally preferred over cleaning offices in manufacturing companies, where the work is harder and cleaners report that they get less respect from the client's employees. Another common issue is that the most vulnerable groups of cleaners are those working for 'junk enterprises' (Torvatn 2011). These companies employ migrant workers of different legal statuses and vulnerable people who for various reasons have trouble entering the workforce and have somehow been excluded from the regular job market (returning from long-term sickness, alcohol and/or drug problems, and so on).

Some specific characteristics of office cleaning contribute negatively to the quality of the work. The first concerns the specific working hours, resulting from the need to adapt to the operating hours of the client, while the second relates to the widespread use of part-time work. With some exceptions, cleaning services are predominantly performed outside the usual periods of occupation of the premises. This is particularly true for office cleaning, but also applies to technical cleaning and to commercial premises or buildings with public access. According to UNI-Europa,[2] the average working day distribution consists of 26 per cent of work in the early morning and 43 per cent of work in the late afternoon. There are, however, significant differences between EU countries. According to the European Federation of Cleaning Services (EFCI), in Norway daytime cleaning has become the rule and represents 80 per cent of total cleaning time (EFCI 2010), followed by Belgium, where about half of cleaning is done during daytime. In other countries, daytime cleaning remains extremely limited despite the fact that sector representatives see it as a desirable improvement in working conditions. They are, however, confronted by the reluctance of clients to have cleaners around during office hours.

Part-time work remains the most frequent form of employment in this sector and covers 70 per cent of the workforce in Europe (EFCI 2010:19). In theory, part-time work may be a mechanism for facilitating work–life balance, but in practice many of the jobs in office cleaning have working times that adapt poorly to the needs of family life. Working time arrangements in fact depend greatly on the sites workers are sent to and on their relationship with the front-line managers who make the work schedules (Holtgrewe and Sardadvar 2011). In addition, part-time work leads to jobs that hardly secure a viable income, despite the fact that collectively agreed hourly wages are not necessarily low for the type of workforce in this industry (mostly low-skilled groups) as compared with other low-wage sectors.

A key trend that holds a high risk of deteriorating job quality is that contracts with clients are increasingly getting shorter and are being concluded for smaller volumes, which has a direct impact on the working conditions of cleaners. Being a highly labour-intensive sector, salaries are the most important cost and represent about 75 per cent to 80 per cent of total employer outlays (EFCI 2010). Consequently, this is where competition is the toughest. Cost reductions related to the awarding of contracts directly affect the economic margins of the cleaning contractors and this puts employment contracts, wages, working times and benefits under high pressure. Obviously, clients procuring cleaning services aim for costs to be reduced. This has been all the more true since cost reduction to increase competitiveness has become an increasingly important part of business strategies in both the private and public sectors (Lehndorff and Jaehrling 2012). Public procurement is growing all over Europe as a result of liberalization and privatization of public services, leading to more outsourcing, and nowadays this is combined with the increased budget restrictions and austerity programmes of public authorities (OECD 2011). There is some evidence that the fixation on price only, rather than on the quality of the services or on a combination of both, is intensified because of the economic and financial crisis (Petersen *et al.* 2011). According to Martinez (2010) and as confirmed in the WALQING research (for example Antentas 2011), a trend of constantly increasing rationalization is observed as a result. Despite the fairly comprehensive collective agreements overall, competition on wages mainly revolves around getting people to do the same type of job in fewer hours, which leads to a spiral of lower incomes and increasing work intensity. In addition, this rationalization affects not only employment conditions and collective bargaining margins, but also job quality itself.

A last development is indeed that in all countries cleaning activities have gradually undergone a process of what service providers themselves call 'professionalization', which in fact concerns a number of interventions to increase productivity: systematic implementation of sophisticated techniques and equipment (such as dry cleaning or ergonomic carts), increased use of standardized calculations and work method prescriptions based on detailed work analyses (for instance, the number of square metres that can be cleaned in different types of spaces) and specific training for cleaners. As a result, office cleaning is in no way comparable to cleaning at home. On the one hand, these new workplace practices may reduce specific health and safety risks such as back problems. On the other hand, however, they also lead to work intensification because they are directly related to productivity increases in a context of tougher contract negotiations and strong competition. The question now is at what levels and by what mechanisms job quality is regulated in the different countries under study.

Regulating Job Quality in Office Cleaning

Employment Regulation at the Sectoral Level: The Cross-Country Convergence

The cleaning sector has a well-structured social partnership at European level. Over the past few years, both EFCI and UNI-Europa have developed a number of initiatives such as the promotion of daytime work and the battle against undeclared work. In most of the old member states, including the three countries under study, social dialogue in cleaning is similarly well developed (Adam 2012), as described in Table 14.3. The relative strength of sectoral collective bargaining structures, practices and outcomes is quite remarkable for the type of activities (low-skilled and standardized work, mostly part-time) and type of workforce (vulnerable groups) involved. This also contrasts highly with the mostly very weak representation structures and trade union power at client sites. Here, the fragmentation and spatial distribution of the workforce considerably complicates any form of trade union influence and collective action.

Further to the interviews with the social partners represented, two explanations stood out to explain the generally well-functioning sectoral social dialogue. A first explanation is the joint interest in combatting unfair competition, in particular by small and micro enterprises. These so-called junk enterprises (Torvatn 2011) operate at social dumping conditions and practice undeclared work, unpaid overtime, highly flexible contracts and working hours, low wages, and so on. As a result, competition on the cleaning services market is not on equal terms, and this harms the competitive position of the larger, well-regulated service providers. The very high turnover of these micro companies combined with the extremely low barriers to market entry (a number of buckets and brooms are sufficient to set up a cleaning company) make the battle against this type of competitor a never-ending story.

The second and increasingly pertinent explanation is the alliance between unions and cleaning sector employers' federations to negotiate better contracts with clients. Here, the common goal is to base the awarding of contracts not only on price but also on the quality of the service

Table 14.3 Social partners and social dialogue in examined countries

Country	Employer federations	Unions	Collective labour agreements
Austria	Economic Chamber/Guild of Commercial Cleaning.	VIDA (representing 12,000 employees in the cleaning sector).	Developed social partnership/sectoral agreement covering all blue-collar workers.
Belgium	ABSU, the Federation of Cleaning Companies, represents 71.7% of all employed workers in 183 companies.	ACV and ABVV; 18 136 employees.	Constructive sectoral social dialogue/detailed collective agreements covering all workers.
Norway	Business Confederation of Service in private sector and Kommunenes Sentralforbund (KS), organizing all municipalities.	Union of General Workers (private sector) and Norwegian Union of Municipal and General Employees (public sector), both in the Trade Union Council.	Strong social partnership. Collective agreements covering part of the private sector (38% of cleaners working within NHO Services) and roughly all public sector workers.
EU level	EFCI.	Uni-Europe.	Good social partnership. Several initiatives for daytime cleaning, OHS, image of the sector.

Source: WALQING National Reports, interviews at EU level.

and to negotiate longer contracts (or to limit contract termination conditions). Increasingly, clients, including those from the public sector, seem to emphasize cost rather than quality of service and have an interest in the deregulation of contract conditions in order to more easily shift service contracts to a cheaper provider. Cheaper prices result in lower wages, minimal contractual obligations and flexible working times for the service provider's employees. The service providers, in contrast, realize they benefit from more regulation on these issues. Better contracts generate greater profits and contract regulations applicable to the entire sector stop the downward spiral of competition within the sector. Better contracts are obviously also to the benefit of the workers because they make it possible to limit work intensification and offer enhanced employment security, higher wages and better working time arrangements, and they justify investments in training. As one employer put it: 'The larger the pie, the bigger the pieces for everybody' (Pauwels and Ramioul 2011). Based on this common interest, the social partners for the cleaning sector lobby jointly to develop European regulations for public procurement. Further, at EU level and in different countries, they take part in several initiatives to better regulate the terms and conditions of contracts, for instance on new work methods reducing health and safety risks, on uniform standards for the time needed to clean similar square metres and on working times, as illustrated below. It came quite generally to the fore during the interviews in the three countries under study and at EU level that the crisis and austerity programmes to which the public authorities (which are very important clients) are subjected put even more pressure on contract negotiations. This reinforces the importance of building strong alliances between the sectoral social partners in response. Finally, the convergence observed across countries as regards this sectoral employment regulation can be explained by the fact that the employers' federations are dominated by large companies, which increasingly operate at international level (owing to continuous processes of capital concentrations and mergers and acquisitions).

In conclusion, as expressed by the sectoral social partners, strong alliances between trade unions and employer organizations are needed to provide a counter-tendency to the downward spiral of employment deregulation and fiercer competition, which are reinforced by the economic crisis. The social dialogue established as a response to this development has resulted in a number of sectoral regulations that mitigate some of the intrinsic risks for cleaning workers.

A first outcome commonly observed in different countries is the generalization of sectoral collective agreements to all companies belonging to the industry. Making collective agreements generally applicable is a system for establishing a uniform minimum level of wages and rights within a sector. In Norway, the respondents emphasized that this system makes it possible to prevent social dumping on wages in enterprises without collective agreements (Torvatn 2011). In Belgium too, generally applicable collective agreements have been concluded for the cleaning sector. A prime example of when such a generalization is beneficial both for the service provider and for the workers is in the case of a transfer of a service contract. When a client awards the service contract to another service provider, the cleaners are often transferred to the new service provider as well. When the new service contract is based on cheaper prices, this may worsen the employment conditions of the transferred workers. The generalized collective agreement secures the employment conditions for the workers involved because it regulates the transfer of acquired rights: the 'existing' employees can stay at the same site and for at least 6 months their working time schedules have to remain unchanged. This system is also beneficial for the service providers since it discourages clients from constantly renegotiating contractual conditions and shifting service contracts. In Austria, collective agreements ensure some job protection during contract renewals, but here it is reported that if contractors and their clients want to save on accrued claims for holiday pay or bonuses, they may use the change of contracts as an opportunity to replace employees (Holtgrewe and Sardadvar 2011).

A second example of convergence across the different countries is the joint promotion of daytime cleaning. Here, the social partners' initiatives at national level are strongly encouraged and supported by a joint declaration on daytime cleaning by the EU-level social partners of the cleaning sector (Uni Europa n.d.). In many countries, the debate about working time schedules is quite heated. While companies in Belgium and Austria face similar situations with regard to split shifts, which imply that cleaners have to work both in the morning and in the evening at the same site, and work at socially difficult hours in office cleaning, Norway has already successfully rendered daytime cleaning commonplace (Holtgrewe and Sardadvar 2012). The table of the WALQING case studies (Table 14.4) shows that in all cases daytime and fulltime work is the norm in Norway.

In Austria, the social partners have expressed a common interest in banning the practice of split shifts, albeit for different reasons. While the trade union wants to improve working conditions and work–life balance, the employers' association wants to improve recruitment and get rid of the additional labour costs linked to night shifts. Hence, an expansion of daytime cleaning would improve the quality of work considerably, albeit at the expense of some stagnation in the number of jobs. In this respect,

Table 14.4 Contracts and working time arrangements in office cleaning

Case/ country	Contracts	Amount of working time	Working hours
CLEANCOMP AT	Open-ended contracts with short period	Usually part-time; contracted notice hours regularly adapted of to hours actually worked	Peaks 6–9 a.m. and 4–8 p.m.; often split shifts
LARGECLEAN AT	Permanent contracts with short period of notice	23% fulltime (= 40 hours), part-time on average 20 hours	Often split shifts, mornings, evenings
CENTIPEDE BE	Blue-collar workers on permanent contracts	Standard time 37 hours; majority works part-time	Often split shifts
MUNICLEAN NO	Majority on open-ended contracts	Majority full-time; part-time on worker's demand	Daytime
REGIOCLEAN NO	All on permanent contracts (after a 6-month probation period)	Most cleaners work 80%–100% (37.5 hours/week)	Daytime
BIGCLEAN NO	80% permanent employees	6 hours/day on average	Daytime

Source: Based on Holtgrewe (2012).

Austrian sectoral stakeholders ask for more policy support for their joint desire to promote daytime cleaning, especially since the public sector represents a large share of the customer base (Holtgrewe and Sardadvar 2011). In Belgium, trade unions have initiated the promotion of daytime cleaning in collaboration with the employers' association ABSU. Both the sector's employers' organization and the trade unions admit that it will always be difficult to prevent some clients from requiring that cleaning staff remain 'invisible' to their employees (Pauwels and Ramioul 2011). Nevertheless, ABSU acknowledges that splitting working hours can be hard for workers and costly to employers. The joint action included raising awareness about the benefits of daytime cleaning among the broader public, for instance by posting a related message on public transport (buses in all large cities) and public places and by distributing leaflets. With this joint action, the social partners wanted to convince clients and their employees of the advantages of working during the day: companies are more accessible by public transport, less energy is wasted for heating when cleaning during the day, fewer security personnel are required, and the safety of cleaning staff improves.

Persistent Differences in Job Quality Across Companies

Next to these similarities, and to the growing convergence of sector-level collective bargaining, both at the EU level and across the three countries studied, the case studies also exposed considerable differences in working conditions between countries and companies. As regards the generalized working times in Norway as illustrated above, this was most strikingly illustrated when we compared the work organization and skill formation strategies between different subsidiaries, a Belgian and a Norwegian one, of a large transnational service provider. In Belgium, one the largest employers of facilities services, nicknamed 'Centipede', was in the middle of a so-called 'cleaning professionalization programme' at the moment of the investigation. This involved the generalized use of new ergonomic equipment aimed at alleviating certain ergonomic risks, such as lifting heavy buckets full of water. But the programme involved most of all a comprehensive analysis of all operations leading to detailed and standardized prescriptions and a far-reaching fragmentation of cleaning tasks. This was accompanied by the calculation of strict timeframes for each of the short-cycled operations. In this process the cleaning procedures were completely redesigned, leading to less interesting work: rather than letting a small team jointly do all the cleaning tasks for each office, the work was distributed differently. One cleaner was responsible for emptying the waste bins of all offices, the other for doing (only) all writing desks, a third did nothing but dust, and so on. Furthermore, the role of 'team leader' was now reduced from that of a frontline manager responsible for organizing and distributing the work among the different teams to that of a simple supervisor watching the correct execution of the prescribed tasks.

Since the company investigated in Norway belonged to the same transnational service provider, we were able compare the new workplace practices promoted in the two countries. The Norwegian subsidiary used the same new cleaning technology and equally changed their cleaning methods and work organization. However, the latter contrasted greatly with the Belgian practices. In Norway, the company adopted advanced forms of teamwork and employee involvement schemes. Here, tasks were deliberately broadened and organized in teams. The team leader had a far-reaching autonomy to distribute the work among the team members and only the aggregate time schedules had to be respected. Every morning, the team leaders discussed the daily distribution of work with all the cleaners at the site. This enabled much more variation in tasks and assignments, leading to more interesting work and learning opportunities. As a consequence, it was also recognized that cleaning requires a specific set of skills and that, consequently, investments in training are justified. This also led to increased wage levels and a higher status.

This case shows a stark contrast between the low-road strategy based on taylorism in the Belgian subsidiary and the high-road strategy based on teamwork in the Norwegian one. This on the one hand confirms the point made by Vidal (2011, 2013) that postfordist regulation regimes, to which all the three countries involved in the study belong, continue to generate a structural demand for low-autonomy work as a result of the profit-driven social division of labour. Not only does the job quality deteriorate in terms of wages and contracts because of externalization; these new jobs are also characterized by high work intensity, low skills levels and poor training investments. On the other hand, it appears that in individual organizations jobs are still configured in a variety of ways. Vidal refers to these variations as resulting from the 'cultural framing of the situation' by managers when they adopt a logic of substantive empowerment (Vidal 2013). In the study at hand, these differences between subsidiaries across countries can be related to the fact that the Norwegian corporate strategy is fully in line with the Scandinavian tradition of high-involvement workplaces and the historical endorsement of the importance of good job quality to competitiveness at the national level by both employer organizations and trade unions. In Norway, the awareness of the importance of good job quality is embedded in the social dialogue and is an essential element in industrial relations practices (Finnestrand and Ravn 2011). Such a 'national compromise on job quality' is absent in the institutionalized employment regulation in Belgium. Here, social partners at different levels have historically limited the quantitative redistribution of productivity increases to the improvement of employment conditions (wages and working times) and purchasing power, and have seen this as the cornerstone of the fordist compromise, while the design of the labour process remains almost entirely the competence of the employer (POLEKAR 1985; De Volder 2003).

Conclusion

The cleaning industry provides a strong example of an increasingly complex interplay between national, sectoral and organizational employment regulation. As a service industry, it is clear that the growth of the sector can to an important extent be explained by the tendency of organizations to reduce their costs by externalizing non-core business activities to companies that operate more cheaply by offering lower job security, less fulltime work, more flexible working times and lower wages. Since this trend can be observed all over Europe and in different employment regimes, such externalization contributes to a growing divergence in working conditions within countries. At the same time, the sectoral regulation in the cleaning industry shows remarkable similarities across countries. The aim of combating unfair competition by small companies operating at the edge of legality is an important driver for alliances between trade unions and employer federations. The growing globalization and concentration among large service providers persistently faced with the social dumping practices of a constantly renewing number of often ephemeral micro companies is a first explanation of this convergence across countries. A second explanation is found in the fact that in the triangular relationship (between workers, service providers and clients) trade unions and service provider employer federations have common interests as well. The difficulty involved in setting up a proper social dialogue for cleaners at the client's site plays a key role in this respect. At the local sites, it is extremely difficult to set up a powerful employee representation and develop strategies that effectively improve working conditions. The local site manager, as the client, has an overwhelming say in how and under what conditions work is actually done. The coexistence of weak workplace representation and similarly weak on-site bargaining positions on the one hand, and a powerful and effective sectoral social dialogue on the other, is not a contradiction but is precisely induced, and can be explained, by the triangular relationship (Denis 2008). The common interest between the trade unions and employer federations of service providers is rooted in the fact that better contracts, and contract-awarding procedures, are to the benefit of both parties. Their alliance is reflected in a range of collective agreements that regulate employment conditions for all operating companies. Various such initiatives explicitly address job quality issues, such as the promotion of daytime work. Others have indirect impacts on job quality, such as the common position against the principle of the most advantageous economic offer in contract awarding (public procurement) or the transferring of acquired rights. It has also come to the fore that these alliances are reinforced as a response to increasing pressure on service contracts due to the economic crisis.

Two important qualifications have to be made with respect to this observed cross-country convergence. First, sectoral regulation does not fully prevent a deterioration of working conditions for externalized jobs, as the persistent use of part-time work, difficult working times and low wages in cleaning demonstrate. Hence, the employees of service providers are likely to end up with worse working conditions than the employees of their clients to whom their jobs originally belonged. This supports the argument of a growing within-country divergence that accompanies the growing cross-country sectoral convergence. On the other hand, the cases also demonstrate that the national employment system, institutions and practices still play their role in setting standards for all workers. In other words, the national systems still can make the difference in the outcome for the workers when job quality is compared cross-nationally. This became quite clear from looking at the standards in Norway concerning fulltime work, daytime cleaning, work organization design and training investments. Second, sectoral regulations do not completely prevent differences existing between companies in any given sector within a country. The key role of the client in determining when and under what conditions the work is done appears to be an obstinate factor working against attempts to achieve homogeneous and generally applicable regulations through sectoral bargaining. The seemingly ineradicable presence of deregulated micro companies in the market of service provision obviously plays a role here. Generally speaking, clients still emphasize price rather than quality of service, they shorten contract durations in order to be able to easily renegotiate contractual conditions, and, where possible, they prefer not to have cleaners around during office hours. These observations indicate that competitiveness between companies may still triumph over the power of sectoral social dialogue.

Notes

1 Work and Life Quality in New and Growing Jobs (WALQING), financed under the EC 7FP RTD (SSH-CT-2009-244597), carried out by a consortium of 12 research institutions from 11 EU member states between December 2009 and November 2012.
2 UNI-Europa is a European trade union federation. It unites trade unions organizing in services and skills sectors in 50 different countries. With over 320 affiliated trade union organizations, UNI-Europa represents 7 million workers, including from the cleaning sector.

REFERENCES

Adam, Georg (2012) *Representativeness of the European Social Partner Organisations: Cleaning Activities Industry.* Dublin: European Foundation for the Improvement of Living and Working Conditions.
Antentas, Josep M. (2011) 'INTERCLEAN: A Cleaning Case Study from Spain', Internal Report for WP6 of the Walqing project, SSH-CT-2009-244597. Barcelona.

▶

▶

Bolton, Sharon C. and Maeve Houlihan (2010) 'Bermuda Revisited? Management Power and Powerlessness in the Worker–Manager–Customer Triangle', *Work and Occupations* 37, 3:378– 40.

Denis, Jean-Michel (2008) *Les Relations professionnelles dans le secteur du nettoyage. Du syndicalisme en milieu précaire* (The Professional Relations in the Cleaning Sector. Trade Unionism in a Precarious Environment), Document de travail. Paris: IRES.

De Volder, Conny (2003) 'Een Belgische "Sonderweg" De sociopolitieke agenda van het ondernemingssyndicalisme (1937–1959)' (A Belgian 'Sonderweg'? The Sociopolitical Agenda of Corporate Trade Unionism (1937–1959), *Belgisch Tijdschrift voor Nieuwste Geschiedenis/Revue Belge d'Histoire Contemporaine* XXXIII, vol. 3–4, pp. 577–641. Gent: Jan Dhondtstichting.

Dörrenbächer, Christoph (2002) *National Business Systems and the International Transfer of Industrial Models in Multinational Corporations: Some Remarks on Heterogeneity.* Discussion paper, Wissenschaftszentrum Berlin für Sozialforschung, Forschungsschwerpunkt Arbeitsmarkt und Beschäftigung, Abteilung Organisation und Beschäftigung, No. FS I 02–102.

EFCI. (2010) *The Cleaning Industry in Europe: An EFCI Survey.* Brussels.

Finnestrand, Hanne O. and Johan E. Ravn (2011) 'The Duality Between Generous and Demanding Work: BIGCLEAN – a Cleaning Case Study from Norway', Internal Report for WP6 of the WALQING project, SSH-CT-2009-244597. Trondheim.

Flecker, Jörg (2010) 'Fragmenting Labour: Organisations Restructuring, Employment Relations and the Dynamics of National Regulatory Frameworks', *Work Organisation Labour and Globalisation* 4, 1:8–23.

Flecker, Jörg. *et al.* (2006) *Restructuring Across Value Chains and Changes in Work and Employment.* Leuven: HIVA.

Hall, Peter A. and David Soskice (2001) 'An Introduction to Varieties of Capitalism', pp. 1–70 in *Varieties of Capitalism: The Institutional Foundations of Comparative Advantage*, edited by Peter A. Hall and David Soskice. Oxford: Oxford University Press.

Herrigel, Gary (1996) 'Industrial Constructions: The Sources of German Industrial Power. Structural Analysis', Structural Analysis in the Social Sciences Series, Book 9. Cambridge: Cambridge University Press.

Herrigel, Gary and Jonathan Zeitlin (2010) 'Alternatives to Varieties of Capitalism', *Business History Review* 84, 4:667–74.

Hohnen, Pernille (2012) 'Capacities and Vulnerabilities in Precarious Work. The Perspective of Employees in European Low Wage Jobs', Synthesis Report on Employees' Experience And Work Trajectories for Work Package 7 of the WALQING Project, SSH-CT-2009–244597. Roskilde University, Copenhagen

Hollingsworth, J. and R. Boyer (eds) (1997) *Contemporary Capitalism: The Embeddedness of Institutions.* Cambridge: Cambridge University Press.

Holtgrewe, Ursula and Karen Sardadvar (2011) 'The Commercial Cleaning Sector in Austria: Social Partnership in Unlikely Places,' Walqing Social Partnership Series 2011.1, WALQING project, SSH-CT-2009-244

Holtgrewe, Ursula and Karen Sardadvar (2012) 'Hard Work. Job Quality and Organisation in European Low-Wage Sectors', Synthesis Report on Company

▶

▶

Case Studies for Work Package 6 of the WALQING Project, SSH-CT-2009-244597. Vienna.

Katz, Harry C. and Owen Darbishire (1999) *Converging Divergences: Worldwide Changes in Employment Systems,* Ithaca, NY: ILR Press/Cornell University Press.

Kirov, Vassil (2011) 'How Many Does It Take to Tango? Stakeholders' Strategies to Improve Work in Europe', WALQING Project, SSH-CT-2009-244597. Sofia.

Korczynski, Marek (2009) 'The Mystery Customer: Continuing Absences in the Sociology of Service Work', *Sociology* 43, 5:952–67.

Korczynski, M., K. Shire, S.J. Frenkel and M. Tam (2000) 'Service Work in Consumer Capitalism: Customers, Control and Contradictions', *Work, Employment and Society* 14, 4:669–87.

Lehndorff, Steffen and Karen Jaehrling (2012) 'Anchors for Job Quality: Policy Gaps and Potentials', Final Report of Work Package 8 and Deliverable 8.9 ('Report on Possibilities and Gaps of (Stakeholder and State) Policies') of the WALQING Project, SSH-CT-2009-244597. University of Duisburg-Essen.

Leidner, Robin (1996) 'Rethinking Questions of Control: Lessons From Mcdonald's', pp. 29–49 in *Working in the Service Society,* edited by C.L. Macdonald and C. Sirianni. Philadelphia, PA: Temple University Press.

Lopez, Steven (2010) 'Workers, Managers, and Customers: Triangles of Power in Work Communities', *Work and Occupations* 37, 3:251–71.

Martinez, Esteban (2010) *Les Salariés à l'épreuve de la flexibilité.* Editions de l'Université de Bruxelles.

OECD (2011) *Government at a Glance 2011.* Geneva: OECD.

O'Riain, Sean (2010) 'The Missing Customer and the Ever-Present Market Software Developers and the Service Economy', *Work and Occupations* 37, 3:320–48.

Pauwels, Fernando and Monique Ramioul (2011) 'Quality of Work in Belgium's Cleaning Industry: Intrinsic Risks and Sectoral Regulation', Walqing Social Partnership Series 2011.3, WALQING Project, SSH-CT-2009-24

Petersen, Ole Helby, Ulf Hjelmar, Karsten Vrangbæk and Lisa la Cour (2011) *Effects of Contracting Out Public Sector Tasks: A Research-Based Review of Danish and International Studies from 2000–2011,* AKF:128. Copenhagen: Danish Institute of Governmental Research.

POLEKAR (1985) *Het laboratorium van de crisis: debat over een nieuwe maatschappelijke ordening* (The Laboratorium of the Crisis: Debate About a New Societal Order). Leuven: Acco.

Quack, Sigrid and Glenn Morgan (2000) 'National Capitalisms, Global Competition and Economic Performance: An Introduction', pp. 3–25 in *National Capitalisms, Global Competition and Economic Performance,* edited by Sigrid Quack, Glenn Morgan and Richard Whitley. Amsterdam: John Benjamins.

Torvatn, Hans (2011) 'Cleaning in Norway – Between Professionalisation and Junk Enterprises', Walqing Social Partnership Series, WALQING Project, SSH-CT-2009-244597. Trondheim.

UNI Europa (s.d.) *Joint Declaration on Daytime Cleaning,* available at http://ec.europa.eu/employment_social/dsw/public/actRetrieveText.do?id=113 64, accessed 13 June 2013.

▶

▶

Vandekerckhove, Sem, Bart Capéau and Monique Ramioul (2010) 'Structural Growth of Employment in Europe: Balancing Absolute and Relative Trends', WALQING Working Paper, WALQING Project, SSH-CT-2009-244597. Leuven.

Vidal, Matt (2011) Reworking Postfordism: Labor Process Versus Employment Relations, *Sociology Compass* 5, 4:273–86.

Vidal Matt (2013) 'Low-Autonomy Work and Bad Jobs in Postfordist Capitalism', *Human Relations* 66, 4:587–612.

Vosko, Leah F. (1997) 'Legitimizing the Triangular Employment Relationship: Emerging International Labour Standards from a Comparative Perspective', *Comparative Labor Law and Policy Journal* 19:43–77.

Whitley, Richard (1992) *Divergent Capitalisms: The Social Structuring and Change of Business Systems*. Oxford: Oxford University Press.

International Organizations and Liberalization

Posted Migration, Spaces of Exception, and the Politics of Labour Relations in the European Construction Industry

15

Nathan Lillie, Ines Wagner and Lisa Berntsen

European integration restructures relationships between states in ways which challenge traditional notions of sovereignty. These changes are not class-neutral, but rather enable restructuring of labour processes in ways which favour capital over labour (Lillie 2011). All over Europe worker 'posting' has becoming a standard way for employers in the construction industry to access cheap unregulated labour (Menz 2005; Fellini *et al.* 2007; Lillie and Greer 2007). 'Posted workers' are a specific kind of work migrant sent by their employer to work in another country. In practice, these workers are largely employed via work agencies and subcontractors, and now form a significant portion of the construction labour market throughout Europe. This pan-European segmented labour market is made possible by the deliberate market-opening political agenda of European Union (EU) institutions, most importantly the European Commission and European Court of Justice, who have used alleged incompatibilities between national labour regulation and EU free movement rights to deconstruct national industrial relations systems (Lillie 2011). This is accomplished via deregulatory 'spaces of exception', which are physical or social spaces in which a state of exception applies, and in which unregulated activities can occur (Palan 2003), allowing firms to opt out of national industrial relations systems via transnational subcontracting.

Spaces of exception have been seized on by firms as a way of restructuring the labour process outside national industrial relations institutions. The opportunity for them to do this was generated by the dynamics of Europeanization and a shift in the structure of the inter-state system. In the past, in the ostensibly insular contexts of national industrial relations systems, employers could not escape from national laws, regulations and informal norms, because these comprehensively regulated the entire space in which they operated. Employers had to comply with rules or face the consequences, but this backstop of enforcement also created a space inside which the employers structured their interests to take advantage of national industrial relations rules. In the current environment, spaces of exception provide employers with a flexible exit option (Wagner and Lillie 2013), with which regulatory arbitrage becomes an element of management strategy on the micro-level of the individual worksite. This exit option introduces elements of other (national) rule systems, making the application of host country norms unclear. Furthermore, this legal uncertainty blurs the distinction between informal norms and formal rules, because firms can access alternative *formal* institutional frameworks from other EU member states, as well as informal norms and practices. Thus, it is possible for employers to avoid following host country rules. Furthermore, the developing practice of not following host country rules builds a grey economic infrastructure, which reconfigures employers' instances in ways which ensure they no longer perceive an interest in following the rules.

Labour process theory has traditionally been concerned with the way management introduces new structures and systems as means of increasing its control over the workforce. A central tenant of labour process theory has been that capital's changes in work processes and workplace technologies are not simply technically based, and neutral in respect of class relations (Marglin 1974). This has been examined in terms of work organization, managerial control system, and labour effort in workplace contexts (see Thompson and Smith 2010; Bolton and Houlihan 2009). We show how these changes are connected to changes in the national institutional superstructure, and the international system. The growth of spaces of exception follows a path laid by the gradual unfolding of tensions between the international system and national industrial relations institutions, representing a particular form of what Bruff (2010) calls an 'articulation between the national and the international'. Geographies of sovereignty and state boundaries are socially reconstructed so that regulatory regimes and firm practices reference alternative sovereignties and hence alternative regulatory regimes. By 'decoupling of sovereignty from geography', we refer to the declining territorial exclusivity of social regulation – that is when actors geographically external to a given territory regulate aspects of social life. The decoupling of sovereignty from geography makes possible regime competition between national industrial relations systems in localized industries (Lillie 2010). Often, this is in fact not regulation at all, but a way to conceal the emergence of deregulated social spaces. These spaces of exception are protected from (local) regulation by reference to alternative sovereignties; that is to say they are regulated extraterritorially. In practice, we are talking about the kind of situation where a Polish construction worker on a German construction site working for a Polish subcontractor does not, either in practice or in law, have the same rights as a German or Polish worker working for a German subcontractor because the employment relationship in the first instance is in many respects regulated from Poland. Sovereignty has been reconfigured, through EU law and firm practice, so that it is no longer entirely dependent on territory, but also on other contingencies.

Cases and Evidence

We have conducted fieldwork in three institutionally dense national systems, Finland, Germany and the Netherlands – countries whose political economies and national production systems are highly dependent on institutional coordinating mechanisms and shared normative frameworks (Kettunen 1999; Hall and Soskice 2001; van Dyk 2006). This is because in contexts where strong actors , such as unions and the state, attempt to monitor workplace relations and maintain common standards across workplaces, employers are more likely to see a need to segment the labour market using regulatory spaces of exception, isolating migrant workers from native ones in terms of expectations in wages and working standards. As Bonanich (1972) observes, there needs to be a strong social basis for enforcing segmentation if different prices of labour are to be maintained between different groups of workers. That firms in institutionally dense contexts are more likely than firms in market-based contexts to use spaces of exception is, admittedly, only a hypothesis which we do not attempt to prove here, as it would require further evidence from other contexts; we leave this to further research.

From the data we have collected at various interview sites around Europe a common narrative emerges in all cases; employer behaviours are more similar than they are different, and this similarity is made possible by the state of regulatory exception surrounding posted workers and their work environments. While employer transnational subcontracting *practices* are the same everywhere, there are differences in posted worker market penetration. Our own impression and that of trade unionists we interviewed is that posted workers have overwhelmed the construction labour market in Germany, are a significant presence in the Netherlands, and in Finland make up an important minority.

Overall posting data based on A1 forms (until recently called E101 forms) tell a different story. Employers are supposed to file A1 forms with national authorities when they post a worker, in order to exempt that worker from host country social security payments. According to the A1 forms, Finland saw 16 930 postings in 2009, which makes for 3.2 posted workers per thousand population, Germany 221 220, or 2.7 posted workers per thousand, and the Netherlands 81 850, or 4.9 per thousand. This data set, however, has serious limitations; it does not specify the sector, many employers do not fill out A1 forms, and management expatriates are included, although their situation is conceptually different (Eurofound 2009). However, it is enough here to note that existing research shows that posted workers are a significant labour market presence in all three countries, but enough native workers remain to fuel continuing union concerns about protecting the market. Although we found (relatively minor) differences in the scale of the phenomena across countries, what was striking was actually the commonalities in the way spaces of exception are constructed and used as tools of management control, facilitating and interacting with higher levels of hierarchy and control on the shop floor, with a corrosive effect on national industrial relations systems.

Data Collection

This research took place in the context of the larger project, Transnational Work and the Evolution of Sovereignty (ERC Staring Grant #263782), which looks at posted work in a variety of contexts around Europe. This chapter focuses on the construction industry. This is not the only industry with a pan-European labour market; labour markets in shipbuilding, warehouse distribution, and trucking, to name just three examples, have all been transformed by low-wage labour migration in recent years. However, in construction the transnational labour supply system is at its most developed. We interviewed migrant workers about their job market strategies, and labour relations at the sites where they have worked, unionists about employer practices and migrant worker conditions, and employers about how they locate, recruit and manage staff in an international job market.

Institutions and the Double Game

Firms are subverting institutions by playing a double game: accessing the international job market for their peripheral employees, and referencing alternative sovereignties as a way of segmenting the labour market by isolating these employees from host country institutions. While the institutionalist literature predicts the continuing resilience of national varieties of capitalism because of the self-reinforcing nature of interlocking national institutional subsystems (Hall and Soskice 2001), this perspective has been increasingly criticized for its inability to explain institutional change (see Streeck and Thelen 2005, for example). We find useful the terminology of Greif and Laitin (2004) in explaining how national systems are circumvented and undermined by European free mobility, despite the stability-inducing advantages which accrue to capital from national varieties of capitalism. Europeanization has shifted the construction industrial relations systems in European countries from self-reinforcing systems – that is institutional systems whose reproduction tends to reinforce the self-enforcing aspects so that they apply to an ever growing range of situations – to self-undermining systems, which are systems whose reproduction tends to reduce the range of circumstances under which self-enforcement can be relied upon. Self-enforcing institutional systems rely on actors' belief that participation in the system is in their rational self-interest; they become self-reinforcing when the behaviour encouraged by self-enforcement tends to shore up the system, making it applicable in a wider variety of situations and creating path dependency. Greif and Laitin (2004) use this to explain how institutions evolve over time, even when there are no sudden shocks or breaking points.

Institutional systems tend to create path-dependent logics, because the institutions interact with each other, because they reduce transactions costs, and because they tend to interact with other institutional subsystems following stability-reinforcing logics, supported by the tendency to shift towards an efficiency-promoting equilibrium (Hall and Soskice 2001). This implies that the institutional foundations of a society are likely to remain stable and change only slowly; this can either happen through a buildup of internal contradictions, as in Greif and Laitin's (2004) explanation of self-undermining systems, or from shifts in outside parameters. Either way, actor interests come out of alignment with the expectation and reward structures of the subsystem in which they take part. For Streeck and Thelen (2005) external and 'legitimate' enforcement of rules is crucial to their definition of institutions. This becomes problematic when enforcement exists, but is contested, insufficient or inconsistent, or when alternative legitimate frameworks present themselves, which actors can access to protect themselves from enforcement. In the EU construction industry, this creates an overwhelming temptation to cheat, as employers' interests come out of alignment with institutional-self-enforcing behaviour.

In cheating, actors risk sacrificing some of the benefits they derive from their institutional subsystem, but perceive the benefits of cheating as higher than punishments, or believe they will not be caught, and can free-ride. Another way to state this is that weak rule enforcement is presenting employers with an exit option – the norms and rules they are accustomed to following, and are politically embedded in, point to one behaviour, but their immediate material interests point to another. Some employers continue to comply with host country industrial relations norms and rules, but others cheat, and save on labour costs. This creates a competitive game in which the norm followers eventually lose. Even if norm followers gain something from the continued existence of the institutions they support, those collective goods may also be available to the cheaters. In any case, at some point defections will cause the institutions to lose viability. In the next section, we will show how this can occur through regulatory arbitrage in the EU framework.

EU Multilevel Game and Institutional Change

EU regulation gives new options to national (capital) actors without directly affecting national industrial relations systems – that is, national industrial relations institutions remain as they are, but function over only a reduced range of circumstances. This means it is still possible to argue, as some have, that the EU regime for labour mobility is mediated by national industrial relations systems; this argument follows a varieties-of-capitalism logic which predicts that employers will support and enforce the maintenance of national industrial relations systems. Menz (2005), for example, maintains that national varieties of capitalism filter the impact of European regulations, with this resulting in different regulatory outcomes to EU-wide policies for regulating industrial relations and labour mobility in the construction industry. We find, however, that construction main contractors are not supporting national industrial relations systems in practice, although they do so rhetorically. In construction, main contractors are construction firms which manage and coordinate projects; they normally engage subcontractors for specific jobs on the projects, and coordinate the activities of these subcontractors. Main contractors benefit from the national systems in which they are embedded for the reproduction of their highly skilled core workforces. Collectively, main contractors have an interest in maintaining the norms, because these norms help to support the smooth functioning of national labour markets. However, the material interests of main contractor firms in specific instances conflict with this consensus. They deal with this by separating their workforces into a core of permanent workers, who are products of the national system of skill formation, and a periphery of temporary workers, engaged via transnational subcontracting (Lillie 2012).

Cross-national uniformity of interest suggests there is a material basis for a continued strengthening of the political influence of transnational capital at the EU level. Neo-Gramscians explain EU normative agendas in terms of alternative 'projects', which represent class and industrial-structural formations of material interest, linked to ideological/normative structures. Each project therefore has a different strategic orientation towards Europeanization, based ultimately on its material interest (van Appeldorn 2002; Bieler 2006). Van Appeldorn identifies supranational social democracy, neomercantilism and neoliberalism as the main projects of EU integration. Neoliberalism and neomercantilism focus on capitalist interests, while social democracy is a cross-class strategy (van Appeldorn 2002:80-81). Bieler adds a transnational-versus-nontransnational-capital dimension, reflecting the degree to which capital is dependent on national systems (Bieler 2006) – this is also heavily reflected in our empirical data, where certain elements of the construction industry seek to retain national frameworks, which other elements circumvent or reject. In particular, smaller domestic firms – subcontractors who compete directly with Eastern European subcontractors – have sometimes been supportive of stronger labour market regulation (Alfonso 2012). There are fractions, both of labour and capital, which resist the undermining of national institutions for regulating labour conditions in construction, but by and large the EU institutions' project of transnationalization is giving firms an exit option, which shifts the balance of capital's interest away from national systems, as well as providing capital with an alternative normative framework permissive of regulatory evasion and arbitrage as ways to further free market goals.

Regulatory Evasion, Arbitrage and the EU Framework

In our country cases, we find widespread use by construction firms of techniques of regulatory evasion and arbitrage in their employment relations, enabled and encouraged by European institutions such as the European Court of Justice and the EU Commission. Regulatory arbitrage is 'the manipulation of the structure of a deal to take advantage of a gap between the economic substance of a transaction and its regulatory treatment' (Fleischner 2010:4). It occurs when a firm strategizes about the regulatory treatment of a transaction; for example when it can select between two (or more) alternative regulatory regimes, perhaps from different sovereign territories. When a firm does business in Germany but chooses to be incorporated in Poland because it can pay its employees less regardless of where they work, it is exercising regulatory arbitrage. Regulatory evasion (or avoidance) is direct noncompliance with the rules, without the excuse of complying with a different regulatory regime. The two are connected, as often construction firms will claim they are complying with the rules of another country and the Posted Workers Directive, but these claims are difficult to check, and they may be violating their home country's regulations as well.

Organizationally, firms have developed techniques for accessing cheap labour: intra-corporate transfers, transnational subcontracting, transnational agency recruitment, and false self-employment are all means by which firms bring in foreign labour. It is also common to hire foreign workers locally, but claim that they were posted so as to access cheaper regulatory regimes (Union officials, European Federation of Building and Woodworkers; Meeting, Brussels, Belgium, 2011). Different recruitment techniques use different organizational mechanisms, and are treated differently under national and EU law, but all take advantage of accessing different sovereign territorial regulatory regimes. Regulatory arbitrage and evasion have become a way to segment the European construction labour market.

In the situation of the construction industry, firms (main contractors, subcontractors, and work agencies) strategically decide between several strategies. They can:

1. Conform to and support existing consensus national industrial relations systems.
2. Selectively move between systems depending on context, violating host country norms but not formal regulations – *regulatory arbitrage*.
3. Violate existing consensus rules and norms and attempt to conceal the violations – *regulatory evasion*.

Regulatory arbitrage is encouraged by the EU 'Free Movement' regulatory framework, which allows firms to base themselves in other countries with low regulatory requirements, but do business in countries with high ones, with only a limited set of requirements for compliance with host country employment regulations. The Posted Workers Directive, passed in 1996, establishes that posted construction workers are entitled to the statutory minimum conditions of either their host state or sending state, whichever is better from the worker's perspective, thus allowing national regulation of employment at transnational subcontractors. However, the

Posted Workers Directive *only* allows enforcement of statutory minimums and of these *only* in the areas specifically enumerated in the directive; four landmark rulings of the European Court of Justice clarify that the directive not only empowers national regulators (governments and trade unions) to enforce home country standards in the areas mentioned above – this list also comprises a comprehensive limit to what national regulators are allowed to regulate.[1] European Court of Justice jurisprudence makes clear that governments and unions cannot seek to enforce any standards for posted workers which are not both explicitly mentioned in the directive and set down in national law. The full range of benefits accorded to native workers and individual migrants cannot be mandated for posted workers – only the more limited set in the directive. Furthermore, minimum-wage laws (or legal extension of collective agreements) and not collective bargaining per se must be the mechanism to enforce wage levels. Therefore, even when the law and collective agreements are fully applied, it is possible that posted workers end up being cheaper than domestically recruited workers.

Regulatory evasion is possible because migrants' expectations are focused on what is normal in their home country, and because it is difficult for regulators to monitor and enforce working conditions. Because of an implicit or explicit bargain between posted workers and their sending firms not to seek to access host country rights, and because of high levels of intimidation, it is difficult for regulators in host countries to gain the cooperation of posted workers to enforce the wages and benefits to which posted workers are legally entitled.

Workers in many Eastern European countries have become accustomed to illegal work arrangements. While they do not exactly accept them on a moral level (Woolfson 2007), and in fact occasionally express considerable anger about them, they also usually feel powerless to challenge them. This, plus the fact that national governments and private actors are legally constrained via the free movement rights of firms, makes it easier for firms to get away with regulatory evasion as well. Alternative sovereignty is used as a shield, to allow capital to operate without regulatory constraints in reconfiguring the terms of the employment relationship. One of our interpreters, after a discussion with some Polish workers, wrote:

> Their experiences with Polish job-market were very bad – but also quite scarce as both of them spent the vast majority of their time working abroad. Both pointed to mobbing, poor wages and extensive cheating as flaws of the Polish job market. They also connected these features with Polish contractors offering work abroad. (Polish workers, group interview, Netherlands, 2011)

Some argue there has been an increasingly specific division of labour between the large contractor companies, and smaller and medium subcontracting firms, thus fragmenting further an already fragmented construction industry (Fellini *et al.* 2007). Contracting chains permit main contractors to benefit from cheaper labour employed under norm-violating standards, while claiming no knowledge of or responsibility for violations. As one Finnish union official stated:

> Subcontracting allows the main contractor to take a cheap offer, knowing that the subcontractor can't be following the rules to have such a low offer. The main contractor doesn't have to know about the details though. We try to hold the main contractor responsible, if he really is, and sometimes we can succeed in pressuring him. It can be hard to keep up with fluid subcontracting arrangements, so the problem is keeping track of it all. Companies are always changing names. (Finnish union official, interview, Helsinki, Finland, 2005)

While it is commonly recognized that the main contractor is the main beneficiary and powerholder, and any strategy to control the labour market must ultimately hold them responsible, unions cannot help but be caught up in the shell game of tracking subcontractors, as the specifics of the cases they deal with inevitably revolve around which contractor did what to whom. In addition to the fluidity, foreign contract documents in foreign languages, and unclear and unfamiliar legal constraints interfere with the ability of unions to monitor the construction labour market.

Another cost-saving strategy is the deliberate misqualification of workers' professional skills. Employers label highly qualified workers as 'unskilled', and place them in the lowest pay category, while still appearing to comply with the collective agreement. This means that to prove that a contractor is in violation of the collective agreement, the union or worker must prove not only that they worked a certain number of hours, but also that the work done matched that of a high-skill grade on the legally extended collective bargaining agreement. A works councillor from a Dutch firm on a Dutch construction site noted of a group of posted workers:

> They do the same work. Only my company tries to put these people in other wage scales saying that they are not doing the same. They are qualified as helpers, but that is not true... These people are all very experienced. (Works councillor, interview, Netherlands, 2011)

Many firms build their strategies around circumventing regulations and collective labour agreements. Trade unions and regulatory authorities have noticed that temporary employment agencies increasingly use Cyprus, but also Luxembourg and Slovakia, as places to incorporate. This 'Cyprus route' allows firms to pay (lower) social fees in Cyprus instead of in the Netherlands (*het Financieele Dagblad*, 22 December 2011).

> What they [agency firms] do, is look for the countries with the lowest social contributions, in this case Portugal... and pay social fees in Portugal instead of in the Netherlands or Poland. And if you compare these rates, there is an easy difference of 25 per cent. (Dutch union official, interview, Netherlands, 2011)

The growth of the market for posted agency workers has resulted in the appearance of numerous 'fly-by-night' work agencies supplying cheap labour at substandard conditions (Finnish union official, interview, Helsinki, Finland, 2005). These are shell firms, which disappear if regulatory authorities take too close an interest; they often just change their names and move elsewhere. One Finnish shop steward referred to them as 'the guys with lots of chains, a cell phone and an SUV' (Finnish shop steward, interview, Turku, Finland, 2009).

However, there are also professional agencies which engage in a hardcore strategy of regulatory evasion. One such is Atlanco Rimec, a company of Irish origins which uses shell companies based in Cyprus to employ workers, and which divulges almost no information about itself publicly (Norberg 2012). Rimec presents a respectable public face, advertising itself as an 'expert in the mobilization and management of teams of workers within the borders of Europe to meet the needs of our clients' (Atlanco Rimec website, 22.10.2012). Atlanco Rimec has offices around Europe and appears to be a firm of substantial size and resources (although the firm is not forthcoming with information, our own encounters with them as well as their website suggest that this is the case). However, Rimec appears to be following a systematic and professionalized version of the fly-by-night operator strategy. Workers who have worked for them, and unions which have dealt with them, accuse them of not paying regularly, of dismissing workers who complain, of using double contracts and of paying wages both less than the collective agreement and less than what was originally agreed. Rimec has been involved in two industrial and legal disputes we are aware of, one at Eemshaven in the Netherlands, and another at Olkiluoto 3 in Finland, as well as other legal disputes in various countries (Norberg 2012).

Creation of a Segmented Labour Market

As Meardi *et al.* (2012) show, the underlying goal of transnational labour sourcing is labour market segmentation, in order to lower wage costs and achieve higher degrees of flexibility. The social and/or regulatory landscape serves to segment the labour market, by offering certain workers access to full citizenship rights and protections while others are denied them; employers strategize around these cleavages (Ong 2006; Lillie 2010). The shifting locus of regulation within firms and production processes becomes a mechanism for increasing competition between workers, in order to take advantage of new opportunities afforded by the macro environment – in this case new labour markets opening up in Eastern Europe and the development of an EU regulatory framework for mobility. Tiered labour markets are developing, with native workers usually only occupying highly skilled and/or managerial positions. Migrants occupy a wide variety of positions, but dominate in lower-pay categories. Furthermore, the presence of migrants, and of the firms which bring them, shape working methods, undermining structures of worker representation.

Labour markets are segmented, based on the position of the employing firm in the value chain, and on citizenship. Menz (2001) for example finds a three-tier segmentation of the labour market in the German construction industry. Where the first tier consists of workers directly employed by domestic companies, the second segment is made up by transnationally posted workers and the third layer comprises illegally employed EU nationals and illegal third-country nationals. This is consistent with what we have found, although sometimes the status of legally present third-country nationals is better than that of posted workers because their situation must be clarified for purposes of their work permits (Kontula 2010). Workers are put, based on their nationality, under different regimes regulating their work, which endows them with a different set of rights and different employment conditions. In all of the contexts we have looked at, construction employers use spaces of exception, more or less clearly defined, to engage in wide-scale social arbitrage and to systematically interfere with the enforcement of national industrial relations norms and regulations on migrant employment.

The existence on worksites of groups of posted workers outside the normal 'web of rules' governing industrial relations creates a cost-based competitive dynamic with native workers, as well as with individual migrants. This fuels an interest by trade unions in controlling, monitoring and limiting the use of posted workers. It also creates a functional and ideologically based pressure to organize and represent them, which from the perspective of organizational strategy contradicts the impulse to limit their use (Penninx and Roosblad 2000). In general, unions have taken the position that posted workers have a right to work in their host countries, but their pay must be in line with local standards. This is, for example, the stance of the European Trade Union Confederation, which supports worker mobility as long as it does not undermine the principles of equal wages for equal work within the same territory, national collective bargaining, or the enforcement of labour laws (ETUC 2009).The European Trade Union Confederation's position is broadly consistent with the official positions of most important trade unions (interviews 2005–12; Lillie and Greer 2007; Gajewska 2009).

The appeal of migrant labour for employers is explained in Michael Piorc's *Birds of Passage* (1979). Foreign labour is often recruited to cover labour shortages, but the real appeal is that they accept jobs at the bottom of the labour market, which native workers refuse to accept because their jobs abroad are merely to earn money to be used back home. While there is clearly an implicit bargain involved in paying posted migrants less, this is not because posted workers accept this as a just and fair state of affairs. For example, one Polish pipefitter working for a Cypriot work agency at the Eemshaven construction site in the northern Netherlands, who was earning less than what he was entitled to according to Dutch labour provisions, told us: 'For us it is funny, humiliating and racist' (Polish worker, interview, Eemshaven, Netherlands, 2011). These workers often feel, and are in fact, treated differently according to their nationality. References to racism as an aspect of the differential treatment of nationalities are frequent; one Finnish shop steward, angered by the radicalization of Polish workers and their poor treatment, noted that 'The Poles have become the new white niggers' (Finnish shop steward, interview, Olkiluoto, Finland, 2009).

Difference in treatment is also felt to be related to which firm a worker works for. Another Polish pipefitter, employed by a German agency in the Netherlands, noted: 'The big companies, the contractors, they have their own employees and they are treated differently than employees of an agency firm' (Polish worker, interview, Netherlands, 2011). Firm centrality in production chains interacts with nationality in ways which reinforce segmentation by nationality.

The Politics of Posted Work Regulation

EU policies on posted work follow a two-track discourse: a market-opening discourse designed to shape the ground-level reality, and a social protection discourse which is designed to be talked about but not enforced.

Because policymaking in the EU is a 'multi-level game' (Hooghe and Marks 2001), policy arenas of the EU, and of EU member states, and ground-level policy implementation are intertwined, and must be understood together. EU-level policy arenas are not simply implemented identically throughout the EU space, but operate through a filter of national institutions and policies (Menz 2005). Our research, however, shows that the actual impact of regulation is limited by regulatory arbitrage and evasion. However, this does not mean there is no multi-level game occurring. Instead of change pressures occurring within formal institutions, pushing national cases down their various paths, change is occurring via corrosion: that is, ever larger numbers of peripherals are employed inside their contained bubbles, while a shrinking core of workers within national systems remains. Firms' competitive advantage depends in part on their ability to manage this demarcation effectively, and on their ability to circumvent and evade regulation. This then affects the political agendas they support – that is, it creates a political impetus for regulation which is unenforceable by design.

Since the 1990s, visions of a Social Europe have faded into the background in favour of the neoliberal vision of market integration, which regards national regulation, by industrial relations systems for instance, as impediments to free movement. While some continue to see Social Europe developing in terms of EU initiatives for opening access to social welfare regimes, for example (Caparaso and Tarrow 2009), others point out that the dominant trend of mutual recognition actually serves to undermine national social welfare regimes because of the way social funding is constructed (Höpner and Schäfer 2012). Social Europe has been not explicitly rejected, but rather circumvented and undermined (Bieler 2006:13–14) via weak regulatory constructions which permit and promote avoidance.

The neoliberal discourse of market-making, and the sanctioning of regulatory avoidance and arbitrage, is evident in many of the texts the EU bureaucracies create for public consumption. For example, the EU Commission's website explains the EU's role in safeguarding the free provision of services in the EU. The Commission explains that free access of 'companies' to the 'internal market' is one of the 'central principles' of the EU. Despite this, the Commission finds, 'the overall Internal Market for services is not yet working as well as it should'. The diagnosis is that certain 'cross-border' barriers, found to include 'red-tape' and 'administrative complexities', are preventing small and medium companies in particular from achieving full mobility (quotes taken from EU Commission 2003), but it should be noted that an identical discourse is prevalent throughout Commission documents discussing free movement and the internal market. Absent is a discussion of what public policy goals administrative complexities and red-tape might be intended to achieve, and whether it is necessary to consider both the positive and negative effects of the removal of specific provisions deemed to inhibit movement in order to come to a balanced assessment of costs and benefits. In this discourse, people are conceived entirely in market terms, companies become entities whose 'rights' must be protected, and access to markets becomes a right which is violated by red-tape. Because these policies inhibiting free movement have administrative and political rationales in their domestic context, they cannot be directly challenged; instead, the regulatory framework circumvents them.

There is also explicit and outcome-focused reasoning in the European Court of Justice's decisions on the relationship between national industrial relations and EU free movement rights, which justifies the setting aside of national relations rules in order to create regime competition. While the Posted Workers Directive was originally intended to justify national regulation of labour standards for posted workers (Dutch former union official, interview, Amsterdam, Netherlands, 2012), the European Court of Justice reinterpreted it in the context of EU constitutional law as a framework for limiting the rights of national actors to regulate posted migrant work. For example, in the Laval (Case C-341/05) decision, the European Court of Justice concludes that:

> The right of trade unions of a Member State to take...collective action [designed to raise the pay and conditions of posted workers above legal minimums] is liable to make it less attractive, or more difficult, for undertakings to provide services in the territory of the host Member State, and therefore constitutes a restriction on the freedom to provide services within the meaning of Article 49 EC.

Since within the construction industry in our country cases, and throughout most of the EU-15, collective bargaining has traditionally been the way in which wages and conditions were determined, this sentence amounts to a rejection of non-market labour regulation for posted workers. Nonetheless, none of this amounts to a direct attempt to turn back workers' rights in the contexts where these are established; rather it puts a ring around the contexts in which industrial relations rules can be enforced.

Spaces of Exception and Institutional Change

Institutionalist accounts involve constructing ideal types, which focus on formal practices, rules and norms. While institutionalists recognize that noncompliance can be a systemic problem, and ideal types do not represent the entire reality of a system (Streeck and Thelen 2005:14), in the contemporary construction industry, calculated noncompliance with national industrial relations norms, achieved through references to alternative regulatory regimes, *is becoming* the system, rather than merely a problem which threatens to undermine it. The result is the growth of a class of:

> unruly capitalists [who are] always dissatisfied with their current state of affairs, insatiable and unendingly greedy regardless of past achievements in accumulation, which makes them invent ever new ways of converting social arrangements into profit, undermining them when this proves impossible. (Streeck 2009:241)

The EU's encouragement and enabling of regulatory spaces of exception has made national institutional enforcement ineffective, and increasing competition with low-cost, rule-evading firms means national-actor interests no longer self-enforce national institutional arrangements. The ability to reduce labour cost and increase flexibility by engaging in regulatory avoidance is a key aspect of firm competitive advantage; subcontracting and agency labour allow firms to maintain plausible deniability for violations. With the help of EU Commission and the European Court of Justice, who are motivated to remove barriers to the free functioning of markets, institutions are being redesigned to encourage and facilitate regulatory evasion, while for appearances' sake maintaining a formal regulatory structure in compliance with popular norms of industrial democracy. Thus, formal institutions of social partnership in Europe's coordinated market economies continue to uphold the appearance of socially oriented labour market regulation, but the effects of this consensus and the ineffectual rules it produces have declining relevance to the practices of firms and the working lives of individuals. Thus, national systems are not mediating the application of EU rules, as asserted by Menz (2005). Rather, the institutional rules of national industrial relations systems are being applied to an increasingly narrow set of circumstances, fitting Greif and Laitin's (2004) description of self-undermining institutions.

Conclusion

We have collected data from three coordinated market economies in the EU. In each case, employers are presented with an exit option – a decision whether to disregard national industrial relations norms and rules in order to access a cheaper labour supply, and whether to support or oppose vigorous enforcement activities. Although in each case we see employers' vocal support for compliance, their actual behaviour is overwhelmingly one of regulatory avoidance, in opposing the introduction or continuation of effective enforcement mechanisms which would close out the noncompliance option. One could argue that the impossibility of norm enforcement means individual main contractors have a dilemma. In a given situation they can either demand compliance by subcontractors with the law or not. However, they have no control over whether other main contractors do the same. Selecting only subcontractors who will obey industrial relations norms and rules and monitoring them is expensive, both because monitoring costs money, and because labour costs will be higher. Main contractors who insist on maintaining national industrial relations norms lose competitiveness, and will have less success in winning contracts, because their costs are higher.

The tendency of firms to practice avoidance of national industrial relations norms, rather than comply with them or actively support them, goes well beyond passive and reluctant acceptance of the situation. Enforcement difficulties did not simply fall down from outer space, but came about as a result of the systematic development of regulatory avoidance capabilities, with the active support of EU regulatory actors such as the Commission and the European Court of Justice. Construction firms actively engage in creating the conditions which make regulatory evasion a viable option, and go to great effort to conceal the norm-violating activities, both legal and illegal, which regulatory evasion involves. While we do not take issue with the varieties-of-capitalism view on the self-reinforcing nature of national systems, and their potential to explain the diversity of response to changes in EU regulation (for example Menz 2005), our evidence underlines the fragility of capitals support for national varieties of capitalism, and how it depends on a degree of national insularity which no longer exists. Critiques of the varieties of capitalism's emphasis on stability, such as Streeck and Thelen (2005), suggest that evolutionary institutional change comes from internal dynamics as well as external shocks. Our evidence shows these are not necessarily different things; in the EU, regulatory systems originating from different countries compete side-by-side in production systems, and even in the same physical spaces. Institutional research, even as it accommodates the idea of change, still implicitly assumes the fundamental building blocks of the system – modern nation states – as stable in terms of territorial coherence, which they are not.

Note

1 Viking Line vs. the Finnish Seamen's Union and the International Transport Workers' Federation; Laval un Partneri vs. the Swedish Construction Workers Union and Swedish Electrical Workers Unions; Dirk Rüffert vs. Land Niedersachsen and The Commission of the European Communities vs. Luxembourg.

REFERENCES

Alfonso, Alexandre (2012) Employer Strategies, Cross-Class Coalitions and the Free Movement of Labour in the Enlarged European Union, *Socio-Economic Review* 10, 4:705–30.

Bieler, Andreas (2006) *The Struggle for a Social Europe: Trade Unions and EMU in Times of Global Restructuring.* Manchester: Manchester University Press.

Bolton, Sharon and Maeve Houlihan (eds) (2009) *Work Matters: Critical Reflections on Contemporary Work.* Basingstoke: Palgrave Macmillan.

Bonacich, Edna (1972) 'A Theory of Ethnic Antagonism: The Split Labor Market'. *American Sociological Review* 37, 5:547–59.

Bruff, Ian (2010) 'European Varieties of Capitalism and the International', *European Journal of International Relations* 16:4, 615–38.

Caparaso, James and Sidney Tarrow (2009) 'Polanyi in Brussels: Supranational Institutions and the Transnational Embedding of Markets', *International Organization* 63, 4:593–620.

Commission (of the European Union) (2003) 'Communication from the Commission to the Council, the European Parliament, the European Economic and Social Committee and the Committee of the Regions – Internal Market Strategy – Priorities' 2003–2006' /* COM/2003/0238 final */.

European Trade Union Confederation (ETUC) (2009) 'ETUC Resolution on Conditions for Free Movement: More Protection of Workers and Fair Competition', http://www.etuc.org/a/6212, accessed 27 October 2009.

Fellini, Ivana, Anna Ferro and Giovanna Fullin (2007) 'Recruitment Processes and Labour Mobility: The Construction Industry in Europe', *Work, Employment & Society* 21, 2:276–98.

Financieele Dagblad, het, 22 December 2011.

Fleischner, Victor (2010) 'Regulatory Arbitrage', Colorado Law Legal Studies Research Working Paper No. 10–11. University of Colorado Law School.

Gajewska, Katarzyna (2009) *Transnational Labour Solidarity: Mechanisms of Commitment to Cooperation Within the European Trade Union Movement.* London: Routledge.

Greif, Avner and David Laitin (2004) 'A Theory of Endogenous Institutional Change', *American Political Science Review* 98, 4:633–52.

Hall, Peter and David Soskice (2001) *Varieties of Capitalism: The Institutional Foundations of Comparative Advantage.* Oxford: Oxford University Press.

▶

Höpner, Michael and Armin Schäfer (2012) 'Embeddedness in Regional Integration: Waiting for Polanyi in a Hayekian Setting', *International Organization* 66, 3:429–55.

Hooghe, Lisbet and Gary Marks (2001) *Multi-Level Governance and European Integration*. Lanham, MD: Rowman & Littlefield.

Kettunen, Pauli (1999) 'The Nordic Model and the Making of the Competitive "Us"', pp. 111–37 in *The Global Economy, National States and the Regulation of Labour*, edited by Paul Edwards and Tony Elger. London: Mansell.

Kontula, Anna (2010) *Näkymätön kylä*. Helsinki: Into Kustannus.

Lillie, Nathan and Ian Greer (2007) 'Industrial Relations, Migration, and Neoliberal Politics: The Case of the European Construction Sector', *Politics & Society* 35, 4:551–81.

Lillie, Nathan (2010) 'Bringing the Offshore Ashore: Transnational Production, Industrial Relations and the Reconfiguration of Sovereignty'. *International Studies Quarterly* 54, 3:685–706.

Lillie, Nathan (2011) 'European Integration and Transnational Labor Markets, pp. 112–28 in *Transnational Europe: Promise, Paradox, Limits*, edited by A. Hurrelman and J. DeBardeleben. Basingstoke: Palgrave Macmillan.

Lillie, Nathan (2012) 'Subcontracting, Posted Migrants and Labour Market Segmentation in Finland', *British Journal of Industrial Relations* 50, 1:148–67.

Marglin, Stephen (1974) 'What Do Bosses Do?'. *Review of Radical Political Economy* 6, 2:60–112.

Menz, Georg (2001) 'The Domestic Determinants of National Response Strategies to EU-Induced Liberalization: Examining the Regulation of Wages for Posted Workers in Austria And Germany', *Politique européenne* 3, 2:137–65.

Meardi, Guglielmo, Antonio Martin Artiles and Mariona Lozano Riera (2012) 'Constructing Uncertainty: Unions and Migrant Labour in Construction in Spain and the UK', *Journal of Industrial Relations* 54, 5:5–21.

Menz, Georg (2005) *Varieties of Capitalism and Europeanization*. Oxford: Oxford University Press.

Norberg, Ann-Lena (2012) 'NCC, Atlanco and the Lies' url: http://www.stoppafusket.se/2012/07/02/ncc-atlanco-and-the-lies/.

Ong, Aihwa (2006) Neoliberalism as Exception: Mutations in Citizenship and Sovereignty. Durham, NC: Duke University Press.

Palan, Ronen (2003) *The Offshore World: Sovereign Markets, Virtual Places and Nomad Millionaires*. Ithaca, NY: Cornell University Press.

Penninx, Rinuth and Roosblad, Judith (2000). *Trade Unions, Immigration and Immigrants in Europe, 1960–1993*. New York: Berghahn.

Piore, Michael (1979) *Birds of Passage: Migrant Labor and Industrial Societies*. Cambridge: Cambridge University Press.

Streeck, Wolfgang and Kathleen Thelen (2005) 'Introduction: Institutional Change in Advanced Political Economies', in W. Streeck and K. Thelen *Beyond Continuity: Institutional Change in Advanced Political Economies*. Oxford: Oxford University Press.

Streeck, Wolfgang (2009) *Re-Forming Capitalism: Institutional Change in the German Political Economy*. Oxford: Oxford University Press.

▶

Thompson, Paul and Chris Smith (eds) (2010) *Working Life: Renewing Labour Process Analysis*. Basingstoke: Palgrave Macmillan.

van Appeldorn, Bastiaan (2002) *Transnational Capital and European Integration*. London, Routledge.

van Dyk, Silke (2006) 'The Poldermodel and Its Order of Consensus: A Foucauldian Perspective on Power and Discourse Within the Process of Consensus Creation', *Acta Politica* 41, 4:408–29.

Wagner, Ines and Nathan Lillie (2013) 'Institutionalismus und territoriale (Dis-) Integrität in der Vergleichenden Kapitalismusforschung: Arbeitsbeziehungen auf der Baustelle der Europäischen Zentralbank', in *Kapitalismusvergleich, Kapitalismusanalyse, Kapitalismuskritik,* edited by I. Bruff, M. Ebenau, C. May and A. Nölke. Münster: Westfälisches Dampfboot.

Woolfson, Charles (2007) 'Pushing the Envelope: The Informalization of Labour in Post-Communist New Member States', *Work, Employment and Society* 21, 3:551–64.

Employment Relations Under External Pressure: Italian and Spanish Reforms during the Great Recession

16

Guglielmo Meardi

Despite pervasive debates around globalization, the impact of international organizations on labour relations has received little attention in industrial relations and in labour process theory: the former has long focused on national institutions, while the latter has focused on the company level or on capitalism in general. The drastic reforms passed in Southern Europe since 2010 under direct pressure from the European Commission, the European Central Bank and the International Monetary Fund, and indirect pressure from the German government, raise therefore interesting questions regarding the interdependence between national and supranational actors.

This chapter discusses the cases of Spain and Italy, which at the time of writing have not needed state rescue by the International Monetary Fund and have not been under direct supervision (although Spain needed a bank bailout in June 2012), but have been forced by the sovereign debt crisis to comply with unprecedented requirements laid down by the European Commission and the European Central Bank. The chapter will reconstruct the reform paths of these two countries, in connection with both changing European Union (EU) policy tools (before and after the crisis) and the state of the so-called Mediterranean model of capitalism and of labour relations. The analysis, based on documents, secondary literature, press and interviews with social partners and European Commission representatives, points to a form of institutional change through displacement by foreign patterns that is faster than generally assumed by institutional theories (Streeck and Thelen 2005). Being promoted by foreign agents more than by internal ones, it preconfigures the emergence of disembedded or disconnected forms of capitalism that are particularly unstable, unless a Polanyian counter-movement emerges, whether in a conservative or a progressive direction.

International Organizations and Changes in Labour Relations

Despite multiplying debates around globalization, employment relations and the labour process have been long analysed as an essentially closed system, between employers, employees and possibly other local institutions such as the state; in particular, institutional approaches to industrial relations have kept stressing the path dependency of national industrial relations in the face of global and international pressures (see for example Traxler *et al.* 2001). In the case of the varieties-of-capitalism approach, economic internationalization is seen as even reinforcing national specialization and therefore differences through the institutional arbitrage of international investors (Hall and Soskice 2001). This approach has gained a dominant status in industrial relations, despite criticism being raised against the idea of uniform and continuous national models of capitalism, especially in the context of financial globalization (Streeck 2009).

The labour process perspective, with its focus on managerial strategies, has paid less attention to national institutions. Its reference to the political economy context tends to limit itself to the broader concept of capitalism: 'national models... spend too much time on the variety and not enough on the capitalism' (Thompson 2010:12). While the capitalist labour process has been effectively contrasted with non-capitalist ones (Burawoy 1985; Smith and Thompson 1992), labour process theory is more sensitive to micro-variations among workplaces than to national variations within capitalism. Globalization is mostly criticized as instrumental managerial and neoliberal propaganda, but it is also mentioned, in line with neo-Marxist theory (Wright 2000), as a contributing factor to the fragility of institutional compromises between labour and capital (Thompson and McHugh 2009). The analytical tool elaborated by labour process theory to deal with the international level, namely the system, society and dominance model (Smith and Meiksins 1995), gives priority to system-level capitalism, and second place to those national models that reach a 'dominant' position such as the United States or Japan.

Interest in supranational actors has focused on more peripheral, economically dependent countries, such as postcommunist ones (for example Upchurch and Weltman 2008), but rarely on Western capitalist countries. The most prominent example is the frequent dismissal of the EU's role in the social sphere as window dressing (Streeck 1995). Typically for institutionalist approaches, Crouch had dismissed in the early 1990s the hypothesis that the European Economic Community could enforce international convergence in industrial relations: 'to date there is little sign that systematic differences of approach to the occupancy of political space are even perceived by policy-makers, let alone have become an object of harmonization' (Crouch 1993:350). But while 'positive' integration through the development of a European Social Model is very weak, for instance in the new member states (Meardi 2012), 'negative' integration through 'market-making' and the replacement of national democratic governance through an international technocratic one is more visible (Höpner and Schäfer 2007).

The economic crisis that started in 2007 makes the issue of international economic influences more topical. It has been argued that crises and shocks offer the opportunity for international actors to restructure national economies (Stiglitz 2002; Klein 2008). The financial crisis may have revamped, rather than undermined, neoliberalism (Crouch 2011). By transferring debt from private to public hands, financial rescues have made national states more vulnerable financially. Germany has seemed to emerge as a model of reference thanks to its stronger economic and especially employment resilience, but in a way that differs from the traditional idea of the German social market economy: the emphasis is now on budgetary discipline, wage restraint and labour flexibility.

While traditional EU policies in the area of employment (whether 'hard' in the form of directives, or 'soft' in terms of coordination) have had little impact to date, the sovereign debt crisis has increased the interference of supranational institutions over national industrial relations in the countries that needed either bailouts or European Central Bank intervention on the sovereign bond market. The impact was most visible in Southern Europe. In only a few months, Southern European countries passed deeper reforms than over the previous 20 years, with very little debate and social negotiation. If successfully enforced, by decentralizing collective bargaining, liberalizing employment protection and raising the retirement age, the reforms would produce a systemic change in the so-called Mediterranean employment and social model.

Following the sovereign debt crisis, the EU and, more specifically, the Eurozone, have introduced stronger economic governance tools since the beginning of the crisis: a 'European semester' of scrutiny over national budgets, the so-called 'Six-Pack' regulations on preventing macroeconomic imbalances, which include a reference to unit labour costs, and a European Fiscal Pact enforcing tougher budget discipline (Erne 2012). Both the structural reforms and the Six-Pack imply a triple departure from EU traditions: first, from EU treaties, which explicitly excluded wage-setting and collective bargaining from the realm of EU policies (Article 153 of the Lisbon Treaty); second, from the idea of Social Europe as a concern with a minimum floor of rights – the new wave of reforms implies the subordination of social rights to competitiveness priorities; finally, from soft regulations in the employment area to a very hard one – a strict 'multilateral surveillance procedure' including fines has been laid down, and the proposed structural reforms, even if not legally binding, offer no alternatives except state bankruptcy.

Two policy proposals have been particularly important for the European Commission and the European Central Bank since 2010 within the Europe 2020 Agenda. First, new wage-setting frameworks have been promoted in Spain and Italy in order to contribute to the alignment of wages and productivity growth at sector/company level (European Commission 2012) – that is, the decentralization of collective bargaining. Second, the liberalization of employment protection has been promoted through a flexible 'single open-ended contract' that would overcome labour market segmentation, which was proposed in the *Agenda for New Skills and Jobs* (European Commission 2010b). However, there is very little evidence that such proposals may help the economy or the labour market (Esping-Andersen and Regini 2000; Traxler *et al.* 2001). Moreover, they contradict many of the previous Commission's Directorate-General Employment and Social Affairs's own elaboration, expressed in particular in 2006 in both the *Employment in Europe* and the *Industrial Relations in Europe* reports, which acknowledged some advantages both of employment protection legislation for human capital investment and of coordinated collective bargaining to increase productivity and stabilize wage developments. The shift of power, within the European Commission and the European Council, from the Employment and Social Affairs divisions to the Finance ones, and the increased influence of the European Central Bank have coincided with the abandonment of expertise on the social side of the labour market, and the adoption of simplistic targets of flexibility and decentralization.

From a labour process perspective, the puzzling issue is that the content of the reforms has been dictated by supranational institutions, and does not directly coincide with the demands of employers at the national level. Even if the enacted reforms can be defined as pro-employer, radical decentralization of collective bargaining and liberalization of employment protection were not on the agenda of local employers' associations. These associations actually prefer some degree of coordinated wage-setting (in order to avoid company-level bargaining and related transaction costs) and labour market dualism between core and peripheral workforce as indispensable tools to keep control of the workplace. External pressure also outmanoeuvred the trade unions, which found their traditional industrial action weapons ineffective and tried to achieve national political compromises, but found these increasingly precarious.

Mediterranean Labour Relations and EU Reforms

Italy and Spain are relatively little explored in comparative studies and are often combined in a so-called Mediterranean model. According to the varieties-of-capitalism theory, they are hybrid cases that can rely neither on coordination nor on liberal markets and they should be condemned to underperformance. Yet for much of the 1990s (Italy) and 2000s (Spain), their economic performance was impressive, attracting considerable international attention, especially on the model of Italian industrial districts of small and medium enterprises (SMEs), and on Spain's successful attraction of foreign labour and foreign investment.

The more multidimensional typology of capitalisms elaborated by Amable (2003) provides a description of Mediterranean capitalism as a combination of regulated product markets, regulated (or 'rigid') labour markets, bank-based finance, and weak education systems. According to Amable, labour market regulations in Mediterranean capitalism are made of 'limits to temporary work' and 'conflictual manager–employee relations'. This is not precise, though. Spain holds the Western European record for temporary work, which was liberalized in 1984 and has since oscillated between 25 per cent and 35 per cent of the workforce, more than twice the European average. 'Conflictual' management–employee relations are measured by Amable on the basis of the *World Competitiveness Forum Yearbooks*, but this unduly generalizes what are more specifically, according to industrial action statistics, conflictual union–management and union–government relations. The conflictual definition does not correspond to the more paternalistic relations that exist in SMEs, exemplified by the fact that in parts of Italy it is common for workers to call union officials by surname, but the employer by first name.

Molina and Rhodes (2007) have paid more specific attention to Spain and Italy as mixed market economies, underlining the role of the state, employer fragmentation, union political divisions and class conflicts. In terms of labour relations, they identify the problem of Mediterranean countries in fragmentation rather than conflict: in fact, both countries have engaged in social dialogue, notably through tripartite social pacts in the 1990s. Analytically, they focus on an important distinction between micro and macro levels and forms of coordination. Regini (1995) had already underlined how in Italy the local and national levels of industrial relations were not mutually consistent, but rather counterweighed one another: during the 1970s and 1980s, when conflict prevailed nationally, cooperation took place locally, and vice versa; one level allowed for democratic expression while the other safeguarded the system's stability and performance. Moreover, Molina and Rhodes identify a number of important differences between the two Mediterranean countries: in Italy, the power balance between unions and employers' associations is more advantageous for labour, and the more proportional parliamentary system involves more veto players and therefore more resistance to reforms. As a result, marketization since the 1980s is deemed to have been stronger in Spain, pushing it towards a liberal market economy (Banyuls *et al.* 2009).

A further specificity of Mediterranean capitalism, especially in Italy, is regional differentiation (Trigilia and Burroni 2009). Even if no performing institutional complementarities are apparent at the national level, there may well be some, both formal and informal, at the local level. In particular, local relations among SMEs reduce transaction costs and allow businesses to achieve some economies of scale while maintaining flexibility and direct control of the labour process. These largely informal relations would explain the enduring performance of some industrial districts which operate as local production systems in defiance of increased global competition (Simonazzi 2012).

Despite a similar GDP contraction in 2009 (–3.7 per cent in Spain, –5.2 in Italy), labour market developments have been different. Spain witnessed the most spectacular explosion of unemployment across the EU (from 7 per cent to 20 per cent between 2007 and 2009), while Italy engaged in labour hoarding, reducing working time rather than employment (unemployment rose from 6 per cent to 7.5 per cent in the same period). During 2010 and especially 2011, both countries were affected by the sovereign debt crisis, although for different reasons. Italy has a low deficit and even a primary surplus, but a very high accumulated debt (118 per cent of GDP in 2010). Spain has a relatively low public debt (61 per cent of GDP in 2010), but started running very high deficits (11.2 per cent in 2009). In both cases, the weak financial situation led to government change in 2011 and very strong pressure from European institutions to enact both public finance and labour market reforms.

The Italian Case

According to the European Commission's Employment in Europe Report of 2006 (European Commission 2006), Italy no longer belongs to its traditional Mediterranean group of countries with low flexibility and medium-low security, but to an Eastern European one of high flexibility and low security: a situation which has been defined as 'flex-insecurity' (Berton *et al.* 2012).

This was largely the result of labour market reforms passed in 1997 and 2003, which had become law following negotiations with employers' associations and all or some of the trade unions. Radical reform measures had been avoided: the largest Italian union, the CGIL (Confederazione Generale Italiana del Lavoro), through a 3-million-strong demonstration in Rome in 2002 and a general strike in 2003, forced the government to abandon the proposed partial liberalization of dismissals (the reform of Article 18 of the 1970 Statuto dei Lavoratori).

With the crisis, Italy initially avoided a rise in unemployment thanks largely to the state-subsidized working time reduction (the Cassa Integrazione wage guarantee fund and the *contratti di solidarietà* on working time reduction). Italian collective bargaining and unions had been more resilient than those in most European countries, with coverage and density essentially stable since the 1980s. However, Italy did not recover after 2009 and the high public debt inherited from the 1980s made it very vulnerable.

In January 2009, employers and the unions, CISL (Confederazione Italiana Sindacati Lavoratori), and UIL (Unione Italiana del Lavoro) agreed a reform of collective bargaining, limiting the amount of wage indexation. The largest union, the CGIL, did not sign the agreement, thereby restricting its implementation. More drastic changes were introduced in 2010–11 by the largest Italian industrial company, Fiat, now controlling Chrysler and managed by an Italo-American CEO, Sergio Marchionne. By threatening relocation to Poland, Marchionne obtained the consent of the CISL and the UIL, and of a majority of employees in referenda, to new plant agreements outside the sectoral metalworking agreement. These plant agreements introduced more working time flexibility and a social peace clause, and were subsequently extended to the whole of the Fiat group at the end of 2011.

The Fiat agreements were of historic relevance because Italy had lived since 1948 under the illusion of an *erga omnes* system of sectoral agreements. While technically not legally binding, sectoral agreements were routinely used by the courts as references for setting the constitutional rights to a fair wage and fair working time. The totality of employers, therefore, tended to comply with them. Moreover, by abandoning multi-employer agreements, Fiat also withdrew from the one of 1993 on work-place union representation, which had established the hybrid works-council system of *Rappresentanze Sindacali Unitarie*. Fiat was now bound solely by the law, that is the Statuto dei Lavoratori (Law 300 of 1970), which only protects the unions that are signatories of collective agreements. The FIOM (Federazione Italiana Operai Metallurgici, the CGIL's metalworker federation), by refusing to sign the new Fiat company agreement, found itself expelled from the factories despite being by far the largest trade union in the Italian Fiat plants and in the metalworking sector. By exiting the Italian collective bargaining system, Fiat also clashed with the employers' federation Confindustria, which defends sectoral agreements while asking for more flexibility.

On 28 June 2011 a new tripartite agreement was signed to reform sectoral collective agreements. This time, it was also signed by the CGIL, while still being opposed by the FIOM. The agreement designed a form of organized decentralization, which saved sectoral agreements and met the need of SMEs to avoid company-level negotiations (due to transaction costs and to the paternalistic attitude of most small and medium employers). However, the agreement was unsatisfactory for Fiat, as it was not retroactive. On 18 July, the first court ruling on the first Fiat plant agreement (in Pomigliano) stipulated that the agreement was legal but that the resulting exclusion of FIOM was not. Fiat started to call for a law to legalize its position, but collective bargaining in Italy had never been subject to legal intervention except under the generic principles in the Constitution of 1948. (The only law ever passed to regulate collective bargaining, in 1961, was actually ruled unconstitutional for interfering with trade union freedom.)

In August 2011 the situation came to a head because of financial turmoil in the Eurozone. The Italian 10-year bond spread over the German ones went over 5 per cent, a level close to the one that had forced Greece, Ireland and Portugal to ask for financial rescue. Confindustria and the three main unions called for a six-point plan, including, crucially, vague references to labour market liberalization and collective bargaining reform. On 5 August, the European Central Bank's incumbent president and president-elect, Jean-Claude Trichet and Mario Draghi, wrote letters to the Italian and Spanish governments, asking for austerity budget measures and for structural and constitutional reforms as implicit conditions for intervening, from the following week, on the secondary markets and purchasing Italian (and Spanish) bonds. The letters were not made public but the content of the one to Italy was revealed at the end of September by the Italian daily *Corriere della Sera* (Trichet and Draghi 2011). The letter included important labour market 'essential measures', adding that they had to be passed as decree-laws as soon as possible, with parliamentary ratification by the end of September. The two crucial requests were 'to further reform the collective wage bargaining system allowing firm-level agreements to tailor wages and working conditions to firms' specific needs and increasing their relevance with respect to other layers of negotiations' and 'a thorough review of the rules regulating the hiring and dismissal of employees' (Trichet and Draghi 2011). The European Central Bank also advised the amendment of the constitution to introduce, following the recent German example, a commitment to balanced budgets.

In response to this letter, then still unpublished, the Berlusconi government prepared an austerity budget and a draft reform bill on Saturday 13 August. The following Monday the European Central Bank started to buy Italian and Spanish bonds. In Italy 15 August is a bank holiday and for most of the month workplaces are closed for summer holidays, so no union protest was possible. On 18 August, Berlusconi presented emergency measures, implemented by government decree and bypassing parliamentary debate, which met all the European Central Bank's requirements: a new austerity budget, labour market reforms and a draft constitutional reform.

The austerity budget then went through political negotiations within the ruling coalitions and its final version did not include a cut in state pensions, apart from the raising of the retirement age for women. By contrast, the labour market reforms were retained in the final bill, and were more drastic than any previous ones. They included collective bargaining reform, which was made explicitly retroactive in order to satisfy Fiat. The new law allowed company agreements to deviate not simply from sectoral agreements but also from employee protection legislation, including that on dismissals. Thus Article 18 of the Statuto dei Lavoratori, which had survived since 1970 and had been successfully defended by the CGIL in 2002–03, was now potentially emptied of content. Trade unions reacted angrily and pledged themselves publicly never to sign company agreements deviating from Article 18. On 21 September, a new bipartite agreement was signed with Confindustria, committing the parties to negotiate at company level matters previously agreed by the confederations at national level. This measure meant, in substance, a union veto on negotiations on Article 18. As protest, Fiat quit Confindustria completely, causing political and financial problems for the association. The bipartite agreement of 21 September 2011 appeared to hold, however: no case was registered in 2011–12 of negotiations on company-level derogation from employment protection legislation.

The sovereign debt crisis was not over, and in November 2011 Italy was faced with new urgent requests for further reforms from the European Commission and the European Central Bank, and with strong distrust on the financial markets, with the spread of Italian bonds reaching new highs. Berlusconi resigned and was swiftly replaced by Mario Monti, the former European commissioner for the Internal Market, who formed a technocratic government with a very broad parliamentary majority. Monti immediately passed a drastic austerity budget for €30 billion, including the postponement of retirement age, against which the trade unions called a 3-hour general strike on 12 December, with little response and to no effect.

On 12 March 2012 the government announced its labour market reform, affecting Article 18 directly for the first time. The social partners were consulted but, unlike in the concertation process of the 1990s, there were no real negotiations and no agreement was signed. The CGIL called a 16-hour general strike and obtained some minor concessions, but the reforms were approved by parliament in July 2012.

Labour Minister Elsa Fornero's statement that the measures 'had not been dictated by the EU' was widely seen as an unrequested excuse that proved the opposite. The employers' associations themselves had shown little enthusiasm for a reform, notably with the bipartite agreement of 21 September. Small employers are not preoccupied with Article 18, as it covers only companies above 15 employees. In our interviews, representatives of both Assolombarda (Milan's region employers' association, the strongest component of Confindustria) and the American Chamber of Commerce relegated Article 18 to what was a side issue compared with the complex variety of employment contracts and with the notorious slowness of labour court cases (up to 8 years for a dismissal case). Assolombarda representatives denied that Article 18 was a barrier to SME growth, identifying the real obstacle as their personalized, family-based management culture that could not cope with larger organizations and more formal relations. The day after the reform announcement, Confindustria elected the moderate Squinzi as its new president in preference to the more radical candidate supported by Fiat. In addition, strong criticism of the reform was expressed by the Catholic Church.

The Fornero reform plan focused on both flexibility and security and was explicitly inspired by the Danish model, although the single-contract proposal was dropped. On the security side, a new and comprehensive unemployment insurance scheme (ASPI) was introduced, eliminating or downsizing the previous schemes that privileged larger companies and therefore the core union constituency. On the flexibility side, the law replaced, in the case of dismissal for economic reasons, the previous right to be reinstated into the job with financial compensation of up to 27 months' salary. Under pressure from the unions and the left, a degree of court scrutiny was reintroduced on whether dismissals are really on economic grounds, rather than discriminatory ones. Confindustria expressed moderate satisfaction, but also some concerns regarding costs.

The Spanish Case

Labour market liberalization in Spain started soon after the end of the authoritarian Francoist system, and proceeded largely under socialist governments (Rand Smith 1998). Temporary contracts were liberalized in 1984, and multiplied from half a million in 1984 to over 8 million in 1996. More reforms were introduced in 1988, 1992, 1994, 1997 and 2003.

The effects of the economic crisis have been particularly sharp in Spain. While GDP fall in 2009 was slightly less than in Germany and Italy, unemployment quickly more than doubled, reaching 25 per cent in 2012. With a fast-rising budget deficit, the country soon had to face financial market pressures. During the first Greek crisis in May 2010, the socialist prime minister Zapatero made a U-turn in economic and social policies to introduce an austerity budget that, for the first time since democracy, involved wage cuts for public sector employees.

Employer and trade union representatives in the Economic and Social Council reported that the Bank of Spain, in association with the European Central Bank, had started to exert strong pressure for liberalization (our interviews). Certain changes, including reforms of collective bargaining and the labour market, were demanded as signs of recovery. In particular, the Bank of Spain promoted the introduction of a flexible unique employment contract to overcome the dualization between permanent and temporary contracts, and the decentralization of collective bargaining, which was also explicitly recommended by European Commissioner Laszó Andór (*El Economista*, 26 April 2011). Actually, the drastic fall in employment suggests that the Spanish labour market is, if anything, excessively flexible numerically. Also, deviation from multi-employer collective agreements' pay rates (the *discuelgue salarial*) had been possible since 1994, and collective bargaining has been responsive to the crisis, at least since 2009 (Martín 2010). These requests for radical deregulation from European institutions do not even correspond to the interests of Spanish employers. Despite some support from business schools such as the ESADE (Escuela Superior de Administración y Dirección de Empresas) the single contract is rejected by the leadership of the employers' federation the CEOE (Confederación Española de

Organizaciones Empresariales) and, in the Barómetro de Empresas surveys, by nearly half of the employers. The status of permanent employee is a very important tool for the management of human resources in the structurally segmented Spanish labour market and Spanish companies, as proven by the lack of success, despite financial and legal incentives, of any intermediate contractual form such as the 'special contracts for the promotion of permanent employment' (*contratos de fomento de la contratación indefinida*), which tend to be rejected by employees as second-class contracts. With regard to collective bargaining, Spanish SMEs, like their Italian counterparts, are not ready for company-level negotiations and therefore need the external reference of a multi-employer agreement, even if preferably a flexible one.

The Spanish government responded to the crisis and to the guidelines of the European Commission of April 2010 by launching a series of labour market reforms. The first major reform, announced in June 2010, significantly eased the preconditions and costs of layoffs and for the *discuelgue salarial*, added incentives to the *contratos de fomento de la contratación indefinida* and liberalized temporary work agencies in sectors where they were banned, like construction. Trade unions opposed the reform but could do no more than call a largely ritual general strike on 29 September; unlike all previous general strikes in Spanish history, it had no impact on government decisions. In February 2011, a tripartite agreement was reached to reduce pensions and to start negotiations on a collective bargaining reform. Negotiations on that reform started well but collapsed at the end of May, after the most hard-line component of the CEOE, the Madrid region's employer federation, CEIM (Confederación Empresarial de Madrid), withdrew its support from the earlier deal. The immediate reasons for the negotiations' failure were political: a triumph of the right at the local elections of 22 May, and radicalization of the left under pressure from the spontaneous movements of the *indignados*, a precursor of the Occupy movement across Western countries.

In the absence of agreement, the government legislated unilaterally, although it amended some details after pressure from employers and unions. The final bill downgraded provincial agreements (which are important in some sectors without national agreements, for example construction) and limited the automatic prorogation of agreements, opening up the possibility for worsening employment conditions over time. In order to obtain the crucial vote of the autonomist parties of Cataluña and the País Vasco, the government introduced the principle of the superiority of regional collective agreements (autonómicos), against the wishes of both unions and employers.

It was a far from definitive reform. As already noted, in August the yields of government bonds increased, and the Spanish government received from the European Central Bank a letter similar to that sent to the Italians. It complied by immediately amending the constitution to introduce the balanced-budget principle, which is particularly striking given that the Spanish Constitution of 1978 had only been amended once, in 1992, and was considered to be close to untouchable. On 26 August the government announced a further labour market reform to facilitate temporary agreements, resulting in a U-turn from a reform of 2008 and the 'flexicurity' principles of reducing labour market dualization.

Facing increased unpopularity, the socialist government announced snap elections in November 2011, which were won by the conservative Partido Popular. As in Italy, the new government moved swiftly to new austerity measures and then, in February 2012, labour market and collective bargaining reforms. At the end of January, unions and employers' associations signed a new national agreement on wages, confirming the responsiveness of Spanish collective bargaining to worsening economic conditions. But the agreement did not slow down the reforming impetus of the government. The reform of February 2012 introduced a variety of measures:

1. An employer's unilateral prerogative to introduce 'internal flexibility' (changes in job tasks, locations and timetables) without the need for union or works council consent.
2. A new employment contract, 'the contract of support to entrepreneurs' (*contrato de apoyo a los empredadores*), with one year's probation without employment security (similar to the *contrat nouvelles embauches* proposed by the French government in 2005, and later condemned by the International Labour Organization).
3. The reduction of compensation for dismissals (including unexplained ones) from 45 to 20 days per year worked, the end of 'bridge pay' for dismissed employees waiting for a court ruling, and the removal of any need for administrative permission for collective dismissals.
4. The absolute priority of company-level agreements over multi-employer ones, and employer prerogatives to reduce wages without union consent, subject to arbitration.
5. The reduction of the time extension (*ultraactividad*) of collective agreements, hitherto indefinite, to a maximum of 2 years, after which all established rights from previous agreements terminate until a new agreement is signed (in Spain, some agreements have been extended for up to 10 years).

The overall effect of the reform, against which the trade unions called two general strikes during 2012, was a major increase of employer power. As in Italy, it is difficult to understand the economic urgency of these measures. In the first 3 months the result was not only the destruction of 179 400 permanent jobs (previously largely protected from redundancies), but, contrary to the optimism of the reformers, also a 10 per cent fall in job creation. In an implicit recognition of fault, in November the labour minister Fátima Báñez asked employers to show 'sensitivity' in the application of the new rules (*El País*, 9 November 2012). The reform, by reducing administrative and collective procedures for establishing working conditions and setting disputes, is likely to lead to a significant increase in legal disputes at the company level. The decentralization of collective bargaining would also make company-level industrial relations more 'distributive' than 'integrative', removing the embryonic codetermination potential of the Spanish dual channel of employee representation (trade unions and works councils). In the construction sector, even the employers feared the disruptive effects of the new rules and hurriedly signed a collective agreement under the old system, causing a legal dispute with the government as to whether the text was covered by the reform or not. By the spring of 2013, the CEOE president, Joan Rosell, conceded that it was advisable to extend the *ultraactividad* to prevent regulatory voids (*El País*, 17 April 2013).

Conclusion

The recent changes in Southern European countries envisage a shift from locally embedded to more disconnected forms of capitalism and labour process, with high risks of unintended consequences. It is too early to say whether change will actually be systemic: it remains to be seen if the actors will actually implement the reforms, either at the sector or the company leve. These countries have a tradition of inconsistencies between higher formal levels and lower informal ones, with lower levels often providing the flexibility that the higher ones seemed to preclude (Regini 1995). Several liberalization reforms of the last few years (many parts of the 2003 and 2011 Italian reforms and the *contrato de fomento del empleo* in Spain) have remained very little used. Yet the changes enabled by recent reforms affect the core of Italian and Spanish labour market regulations: coordinated collective bargaining and employment security.

The developments in Spain and Italy have been more radical than their institutional path would have predicted, and have been actively promoted from the outside by the European Commission, the European

Central Bank and the German government. As a principal promoter of reform lamented (Ichino 2011:98), in Italy both rightwing parties and employers' associations had no appetite, in the late 2000s, for any legislative reform of labour market regulations, following the defeat by the CGIL of the previous attempt in 2002–03, and thanks to well-developed informal adaptation to the existing legal constraints. Similarly, in Spain the general strike of 2002 had succeeded in amending the labour market reform by the conservative Aznar government.

In other words, in a few months, the European Commission and the European Central Bank achieved what Spanish and Italian employers and rightwing governments had not even dared to ask. Labour resistance, which had previously had some success, was futile against a more elusive opponent, uninterested in local political exchange and unaffected by general strikes. The new preaching by the European Central Bank, in particular, is not necessarily in line with the needs of employers in the real economy, and departs from previous European goals of 'more and better jobs' (European Council 2000). In fact, the combination of austerity measures and labour market deregulation (such as has occurred for temporary contracts in Spain) results in the promotion of 'fewer and worse jobs'.

The two main lines of reform promoted by EU institutions have been decentralization of collective bargaining and the liberalization of employee dismissals. Both pose risks for large parts of the Italian and Spanish production systems. The former, which many industrial relations studies (for example Traxler *et al.* 2001) have shown to be not economically rational, runs the risk of increasing transaction costs in SMEs, where currently employers are very hostile to collective bargaining and prefer combining reference to sectoral wage agreements with internal unilateral, paternalistic management. The latter, while undermining the typical segmentation of the labour markets, has been opposed by large sections of the employers, as it disrupts an established way of managing human resources, through cultural loyalty for the core workforce and by means of despotic threats for the flexible layer. The reduction of dualism means that employers will have to find more expensive ways to motivate their core workforce. The reforms do not tackle the more serious economic problems of Southern Europe, such as low investment in research and development and misguided industrial and fiscal policies. Instead, they undermine those institutional arrangements which, while suboptimal and in some regards dysfunctional, were crucial for the coordination of the economy. It is not surprising that the result of liberalization is increased unemployment and a further fall in investment (Rangone and Solari 2012).

A discrepancy between a disembedded (Polanyi 1944), externally induced legislative level and an embedded, diversified labour process is emerging. The emergence of something similar to the idea of disconnected capitalism (Thompson 2003), in the sense of governance detached from local economic organizations and associations, calls for the combination of two analytical tools, all too often treated separately: industrial relations institutional analysis, and labour process analysis. In this disconnected form, the strategies of capital appear as particularly contradictory (Hyman 1987).

The reforms contrast not only with trade unions' preferences and established employee rights. They also affect core features of production in many Spanish and Italian firms, and raise three problems for their labour processes:

1. The decentralization of collective bargaining increases transaction costs for SMEs, and hampers their collaboration in industrial districts by introducing competition on wages, while promoting collective bargaining within the enterprises – something employers in these countries have long disliked, preferring to bargain 'at arm's-length'.
2. Changes in employment protection laws, as well as giving priority to company bargaining, challenge traditional paternalistic forms of managerial controls, which implied a dualism between core loyal employees to be motivated through symbolic-cultural means, and marginal, flexible employees who could be managed in a despotic manner. The reforms risk jeopardizing core employees' loyalty and limiting managerial control over temporary employees, and therefore may involve higher costs where employees have to be motivated through higher pay.
3. The new regulations undermine the core informal resources and trust relations of local production systems such as the industrial districts, which require a stable and predictable environment.

Some have interpreted the new trends in Southern Europe as a new form of dependency: richer European countries forcing austerity and labour market reforms on peripheral ones (in the East and in the South), despite their apparent economic uselessness and even harmfulness, in order to poach skilled labour and to reduce potential competitors to the subordinate role of low-skill, low-added-value producers (Neguerela 2012). For others, this is the last stage of a process of monetary union that was from the beginning in the sole interest of the German economy (Bagnai 2012). This interpretation finds support in the fact that the Italian companies most negatively affected by the crisis are those of the previously most successful and internationally competitive industrial districts. However, the availability of alternative pools of cheap labour in Central and Eastern Europe, and the variety of employers and of employment patterns in each country, call for more sophisticated analysis than the merely geopolitical one of 'Germany against Southern Europe'. If one considers the diversity of managerial approaches and labour processes within each country (Vidal 2011), the reforms correspond more precisely to the interests of some industries in Germany, of financial capital and of some new or larger employers in the countries concerned, which rely less on traditional informal relations and paternalistic management (for example Fiat and Vodafone) and hope to proceed to collective dismissals at a lower cost.

What emerges is a pattern of reform that may suit some less-embedded employers but destabilizes many others. While weakening traditional forms of resistance and compromise, this change is likely to cause widespread conflicts on many aspects of the labour process that will need to be renegotiated, or reimposed, company by company. Change appears to be towards a Central and Eastern European scenario involving weaker social partners, a decentralized labour market, high levels of emigration, but ongoing state interference and large areas of informality. But despite similar trends in Italy and Spain, there are also differences between the two countries, which depart from stereotyped visions of an undifferentiated Mediterranean model: associational governance is still much stronger in Italy, while state influence and government power are more powerful in Spain, which explains why in Spain unemployment has risen faster, and reforms have been more radical and unilateral than in Italy.

There are two alternative scenarios that could stop this process of change. Local institutional resistance to change could emerge, not so much against the reforms, but against their implementation: trade unions, sections of employers' associations, local authorities and the Church may combine in slowing down change, making sure that practice on the ground will not be disrupted excessively by change on paper, possibly with some benign neglect from the governments. Alternatively, radical opposition could grow, whether through unions, new social movements like the *indignados*, populist parties or informal organizational misbehaviour such as a fall in organizational commitment and increased turnover. Mass protests in Portugal and Spain in the autumn of 2012 forced governments to yield some concessions; however, overall, given the differences between the two countries, resistance to change is more likely to succeed in Italy than in Spain.

REFERENCES

Amable, B. (2003) *The Diversity of Modern Capitalism.* Oxford: Oxford University Press.

Bagnai, A. (2012) *Il tramonto dell'euro.* Reggio Emilia: Imprimatur.

Banyuls, J. *et al.* (2009) 'The Transformation of the Employment System in Spain: Towards a Mediterranean Neoliberalism?', pp. 247–79 in *European Employment Models in Flux,* edited by G. Bosch, S. Lehndorff and J. Rubery. Basingstoke: Palgrave Macmillan.

Berton, F., M. Richiardi and S. Sacchi (2012) *The Political Economy of Work Security and Flexibility.* Bristol: The Policy Press.

Burawoy, M. (1985) *The Politics of Production. Factory Regimes Under Capitalism and Socialism.* London: Verso, .

Crouch, C. (1993) *Industrial Relations and European State Traditions.* Oxford: Oxford University Press.

Crouch, C. (2011) *The Strange Non-Death of Neoliberalism.* Oxford: Polity.

Erne, R. (2012) 'European Industrial Relations after the Crisis. A Postscript', pp. 225–35 in *The European Union and Industrial Relations – New Procedures, New Contex,* edited by S. Sismans. Manchester: Manchester University Press.

Esping-Andersen, G. and M. Regini (eds) (2000) *Why Deregulate Labour Markets?* Oxford: Oxford University Press.

European Commission (2006) *Employment in Europe 2006.* Luxembourg: Office for Official Publications of the European Communities.

European Commission (2010) *An Agenda for New Skills and Jobs.* Strasbourg: Communication of the European Commission.

European Commission (2012) *Wage Setting Systems and Wage Developments.* Brussels, http://ec.europa.eu/europe2020/pdf/themes/wage_settings.pdf.

European Council (2000) *Presidency Conclusions.* Lisbon European Council, 23 and 24 March 2000).

Hall, P.A. and D. Soskice (eds) (2001) *Varieties of Capitalism: The Institutional Foundation of Comparative Advantage.* Oxford: Oxford University Press.

Höpner, M. and A. Schäfer (2007) 'A New Phase of EU Integration? Organized Capitalism in Post-Ricardian Europe', MPIfG Discussion Paper No. 07/4. Cologne: Max Planck Institute for the Study of Societies.

Hyman, R. (1987) 'Strategy or Structure? Capital, Labour and Control', *Work, Employment & Society* 1, 1:25–55.

Ichino, P. (2011) *Inchiesta sul lavoro.* Milan: Mondadori.

Klein, N. (2008) *The Shock Doctrine.* New York: Metropolitan Books.

Martín, R.B. (2010) 'La incidencia de la crisis económica en la negociación coletiva', pp. 9–34 in *La negociación colectiva ante la crisis económica,* edited by R.B. Martín. Albacete: Bomarzo.

Meardi, G. (2012) *Social Failures of EU Enlargement. A Case of Workers Voting with Their Feet.* London: Routledge.

Molina, Ó. and M. Rhodes (2007) 'The Political Economy of Adjustment in Mixed Market Economies: A Study of Spain and Italy', pp. 223–52 in *Beyond Varieties of Capitalism,* edited by B. Hanché, M. Rhodes and M. Thatcher. Oxford: Oxford University Press.

Neguerla, E. (2012) 'Un nuevo papel en Europa para los países del sur', *Informes de la Fondación,* 47. Madrid: Fondación 1º de Mayo.

▶

▶

Polanyi, K. (1944) *The Great Transformation*. New York: Rinehart.

Rand Smith, W. (1998) *The Left's Dirty Job: The Politics of Industrial Restructuring in France and Spain*. Toronto: Toronto University Press.

Rangone, M. and S. Solari (2012) 'From the Southern-European Model to Nowhere: The Evolution of Italian Capitalism, 1976–2011', *Journal of Economic Public Policy* 19, 8:1188–206).

Regini, M. (1995) *Uncertain Boundaries: The Social and Political Construction of European Economies,* Cambridge: Cambridge University Press.

Simonazzi, A. (2012) 'Italy: Chronicle of a Crisis Foretold', pp. 183–98 in *A Triumph of Failed Ideas: European Models of Capitalism in the Crisis,* edited by S. Lehndorff. Brussels: ETUI.

Smith, C. and P. Meiksins (1995) 'System, Society and Dominance in Cross-National Organizational Analysis', *Work, Employment and Society* 9, 2:241–67.

Smith, C. and P. Thompson (1992) *Labour in Transition: The Labour Process in Eastern Europe and China*. London: Routledge.

Stiglitz, J. (2002) *Globalization and Its Discontents*. New York: Norton.

Streeck, W. (1995) 'Neo-Voluntarism: A New European Policy Regime', *European Law Journal* 1, 1:31–59.

Streeck, W. (2009) *Re-Forming Capitalism: Institutional Change in the German Polisical Economy*. Oxford: Oxford University Press.

Streeck, W. and K. Thelen (2005) 'Introduction: Institutional Change in Advanced Political Economies', pp. 3–39 in *Beyond Continuity: Institutional Change in Advanced Political Economies,* edited by W. Streeck and K. Thelen. Oxford: Oxford University Press.

Upchurch, P. and D. Weltman (2008) 'International Financial Institutions and Post Communist Labour Reform: A Case of Utopian Liberalism?', *Debatte* 16, 3:309–30.

Thompson, P. (2003) 'Disconnected Capitalism: Or Why Employers Can't Keep Their Side of the Bargain', *Work, Employment and Society* 17, 2:359–78.

Thompson, P. (2010) 'The Capitalist Labour Process: Concepts and Connections', *Capital & Class* 34, 1:7–14.

Traxler, F., S. Blaschke and B. Kittel (2001) *National Labour Relations in International Markets*. Oxford: Oxford University Press.

Trichet, J-C. and M. Draghi (2011) 'Un'azione pressante per ristabilire la fiducia degli investitori', *Corriere della Sera*, 29 September 2011; http://www.corriere.it/economia/11_settembre_29/trichet_draghi_inglese_304a5f1e-ea59-11e0-ae06-4da866778017)shtml?fr=correlati.

Trigilia, C. and L. Burroni (2009) 'Italy: Rise, Decline and Restructuring of a Regionalized Capitalism', *Economy and Society* 38, 4:630–59.

Vidal, M. (2011) 'Reworking Postfordism: Labor Process Versus Employment Relations', *Sociology Compass* 5, 4:273–86.

Wright, E.O. (2000) 'Working-Class Power, Capitalist-Class Interests, and Class Compromise', *American Journal of Sociology* 105, 4:957–1002.

Index